Cyber Rights

Cyber Rights

Defending Free Speech in the Digital Age

Revised and updated edition

Mike Godwin

The MIT Press
Cambridge, Massachusetts
London, England

© 2003 Massachusetts Institute of Technology

This book was set in Sabon by Achorn Graphic Services, Inc.
Printed and bound in the United States of America.
Library of Congress Cataloging-in-Publication Data

Godwin, Mike, 1956–
   Cyber rights : defending free speech in the digital age / Mike Godwin.—Rev. and updated ed.
      p.   cm.
   Includes bibliographical references and index.
   ISBN 0-262-57168-4 (pbk. : alk. paper)
   1. Freedom of speech—United States. 2. Internet—Law and legislation—United States. I. Title.
KF4772.G63   2003
342.73′0853—dc21
                                                      2002044493

10   9   8   7   6   5   4   3   2   1

For my daughter, Ariel

Contents

Preface to the Revised Edition

It is a bit traumatic to come back to a book that was produced in a particular historical period, and in a particular period of one's own life, with an eye to improving the text and making it relevant to a new audience. The worst aspect of this task is the discovery of how many sentences and passages one could have, and should have, written better. Almost as bad is to come across the occasional generalization or argument that seems dated and perhaps even naive from the perspective of only a few years' more experience.

Overall, however, I have not found it necessary to revise this book too much for this reissue. True, in many chapters, I added appropriate notes to make the material more relevant or immediate in 2002 and wording changes to correct for some of the more obvious and painful infelicities of style. In some, I've added a "2002 Update" to explore how the issue has progressed since this book was initially published. Finally, I've made a point, in the months after the terrorist attacks of September 11, 2001, to underscore issues and arguments that remain relevant even as the United States has labored to recover from terrorism, to prepare for and conduct a war, and to guard itself against future attacks.

At its heart, however, this book is essentially a mid-1990s book, and most of its remaining faults are a function of that temporal context and of my own limits and biases both then and now. I've refrained from trying to revise this book into something more than what it first was—a kind of snapshot of the early history of free speech and civil liberties advocacy concerning computers and the Internet. When I've provided some kind of substantive update, the goal is less to say something wholly new than it is to provide a second perspective, a kind of parallax, with regard to the topic being discussed.

Revising the text for a new edition has been a relatively straightforward task; the principles and values I advocated in the first edition do not themselves require any revision, even when the actual text of advocacy could use a rewrite. These principles and values—which include the need for constitutional constraints on even well-meaning government power, the refusal to make decisions about the Internet based on reflex or fear, and the insistence on our obligation to trust fellow citizens with the power of computers and the Internet—remain as sound in the post–September 11 era as they ever were. And I count myself fortunate to have seen the values that we early Internet civil libertarians advocated so fervently in the twentieth century continue to bear fruit in the twenty-first.

Washington, D.C.
May 2002

Acknowledgments

I owe the greatest debt for this book to Charisse Castagnoli, whose experience at managing software projects turned out to be just what I needed when I found myself stalled; it was her management skills and motivational support that enabled me to complete this very different kind of software project.

My friend and agent, Gerard Van der Leun, and my editor at Times Books, Tracy Smith, also deserve my thanks for continuing to have faith in me and in this project, even when I put that faith to the test.

Tracy Quan's detailed and often skeptical editorial comments were valuable at several stages in the development of this book, and she saved me from one or two cultural blunders as well.

My long-term employer, the Electronic Frontier Foundation, gave me the freedom I needed to balance the writing of this book on the one hand with my advocacy for EFF on the other. The Freedom Forum's Media Studies Center's unqualified support during the final stages of preparing this book was also invaluable.

My friends Clifford Stoll and Bruce Sterling have been, in many different ways, helpful inspirations to this first-time author. My former legal interns (now colleagues) Deborah Pierce, Tess Koleczek, Lisa Sanger, and Beth Noveck each gave me significant assistance at various critical points in the development of this manuscript. My legal intern in the summer of 2002, Glenda Sino-Cruz, was invaluable in helping me to prepare the new edition for publication by the MIT Press. While many others have helped me in reading this manuscript, I must take special note of Julie Cohen, who read early versions of chapter 7 for me and provided helpful insight on copyright issues generally.

I also must thank John Perry Barlow, John Gilmore, and, most important, Mitchell Kapor—the founders of EFF—for giving me my shot at the great adventure of defending individual freedom in cyberspace. Mitch in particular deserves credit not only for patiently funding my on-the-job post-law-school education, but also for reinforcing (through his own example) my best impulses toward public service. It was Mitch's leap of faith in me that directly led to my being hired as EFF's first full-time employee back in 1990. I would like to think that in the years since then, I have justified at least some of that faith.

Introduction: Two Mornings in Cyberspace

November 1994

One fine Maryland morning, I wake up and go first to the computer, as I always do. I dial up the Electronic Frontier Foundation's (EFF) Unix system and check for mail. There's always new mail. Some of it is routine and not directed toward me at all. I'm a member of a few mailing lists, and everyone who participates in those lists gets the same mail. But there are always letters meant just for me, and today is no exception. Of the dozens of new letters, a few stand out. Some kid is in legal trouble in Ohio: the Secret Service has searched his house and seized his computer bulletin board system (BBS). A friend, a sharp pop culture maven who hosts a conference on the WELL (a computer system like a BBS, only much larger and connected to the Internet) wants to know if I'll be available for brunch when I'm in San Francisco next week. A philosophy professor asks me to read his article about a crackdown on software pirates in Italy. A legal scholar argues for (what seems to me to be) a particularly goofy interpretation of the First Amendment as it applies to the Internet. A woman in Texas who writes for an alternative newspaper sends me a flirtatious note—just the thing I need to brighten up my morning. Other friends, many of whom I see only a few times a year, if that, keep me up-to-date about their lives. I push my chair away from the computer desk and contemplate my answers to some of these letters while I begin the morning breakfast-shower-shave ritual. My cat head-bumps against my ankles ("Why are you paying attention to that humming box rather than to me?"), and I reach down and tug her ears.

I start to work on a few replies, disposing of the ones that require only short answers or that I can answer by e-mailing one of my articles to the correspondent. I tell the kid in Ohio to call me at the office; I need to discuss his case with him more before I can make any recommendations. I forgo answering the woman in Texas. To send something properly flirtatious back takes time, and I'd better put it off until the lunch hour. The scholar's comments irritate me, though, and I start composing a reply, listing citations for my point of view and attempting, on the fly, to analyze his position logically for flaws.

Then I look at the clock. In the fury of composition I've lost track of time, and I see that I should have left for work twenty minutes ago. (I take the Metro from my neighborhood in Maryland into the District of Columbia, where EFF maintains its offices.) It's a muggy day. Twenty minutes later, I'm panting and sweating, but I'm at the Metro station. And in a minute or two, I'm dashing into the air-conditioned interior of the train, which at this point on the line is running on an elevated track. With a little luck, the blots of sweat on my shirt will have evaporated by the time I get into work.

I often think about my good luck when I take the Metro into the District. My life is nothing like that of the countless lawyers who graduated from law school the same year I did. I don't wear a suit much, and I'm never in a courtroom, yet my practice ranges from criminal law to copyright law to constitutional law. It's a lawyer job that couldn't have existed a decade ago.

It's also a job that I defined myself, shortly after EFF's cofounder Mitchell Kapor discovered my postings on Usenet and decided that maybe I was someone for the fledgling civil liberties organization to hire. If the electronic frontier is truly to be civilized, we both concluded early on, people need to know how the legal system applies to this new domain of human interaction. My job is, in part, to explain (and sometimes to guess) how a centuries-old system of law will shape discourse, relationships, and commerce in the newest mass medium, cyberspace.

It's a medium that raises countless First Amendment issues, many of them new to the legal system, and more of them every day. I feel an unbounded allegiance to the First Amendment (before I was a lawyer, I was a journalist), but it's becoming increasingly clear to me that freedom of speech in the digital age is going to create a lot of controversy before society and the legal system become comfortable with it.

My work is cut out for me. Indeed, it seems that the work I do (especially the part about explaining legal issues for on-line communities) has a tendency to expand to fill my available waking hours. Even after I go home tonight, I'll be online again, answering mail, providing pointers, and arguing legal principles. My typing speed has improved dramatically.

But all that time online never seems to wear me down. Instead I find that even apart from work, my online life makes me feel connected to other minds in a way that I never feel at a party, or watching a TV show, or seeing a play. It's as if there were a grand online society, a meritocracy of writers and thinkers and observers—but one that anyone can be a part of just by showing up and writing well. For the most part, the time I spend online is time I used to spend watching TV. That trade-off was a no-brainer.

The rewards of this online world had been a revelation when I first discovered them for myself in 1984, as an ex–graduate student, unsuccessful freelance journalist in Austin, Texas. I'd been thrashing about that year, looking for the next current in my life. In the previous three years, I'd dropped out of two different graduate programs in succession and had gone through two mainstream jobs almost as fast. I couldn't make enough money as a freelance writer. Worse, I was hungry for something meaningful to do with my life but couldn't put my finger on what that something was.

One day, not long after I'd taken a computer sales job to make ends meet, it hit me: what I missed, after years of undergraduate and graduate education, was the life of the mind. In school, there was always someone, maybe a student and maybe a professor, with whom to discuss the way the world works, the implications of a particular philosophy, the quality of a novel or a poem.

For many people, college is the last time in their lives where they're routinely surrounded by people who are excited about ideas. Where can we go to find a similar environment once we've realized that we can't go to school forever? Here in the late twentieth century, we don't live in a world of literary salons anymore (and even when salons were more commonplace, only a minority of the population ever had access to one).

And not everyone in our secular society is comfortable seeking a social outlet in church. What *do* people normally do to find society these days? I didn't have an answer. Late twentieth-century America, I suspected, had fragmented so many social institutions that few people knew how to make friends anymore, except at work.

I found myself spending increasing amounts of time online on local BBSs, searching for the ones where thoughtful, articulate people congregated. I found several—they had quirky names like "the Diner," "Flight," and "SMOF-BBS." And on one of them, I encountered the woman with whom I spent the next eight years of my life. Kathy is very smart—smarter than I am, it seems to me. Still, she laughed at the one-liners I'd post in BBS discussion topics, and I'd admire her frankly assertive online manner. In our online exchanges, we discovered how much we had in common and how spiced that commonality was by our differences. We quickly advanced to what onliners call "f2f" (face-to-face) meetings, began dating, and soon were inseparable. In the ensuing years, Kathy and I cohabited, then married, then produced a beautiful little girl before, finally, we discovered that we'd grown apart and so decided amicably to divorce. For each of us, our relationship marked a turning point—our respective passages from twenty-something postadolescence to adulthood. I'd helped Kathy get back into school; she'd inspired me to go to law school.

Yet had there been no BBSs, no e-mail, we'd never have met. I might still be a slacker in Austin, Texas, and she might still be working for a pittance at some service bureau there. And our beloved daughter would never have been born.

As the Metro plunges underground just before arriving at Union Station, I think of my own plunge into the world of the Internet. My postings on BBSs reached dozens of readers at a time; my postings on Usenet, the Internet's distributed conferencing system, certainly would reach thousands of readers, and a few of them might well be read by millions. It was as if I had suddenly acquired my own TV or radio station.

And not only was the Internet itself a "place" to be, but it also served as a conduit to other digital places, like the WELL (the Whole Earth 'Lectronic Link in Sausalito, California) or ECHO (the East Coast Hang Out in New York City).

The Metro pulls in at Metro Center, near the offices of EFF. When I get into the office, the rest of my e-mail will be waiting for me. I'll spend much of today answering questions, discussing legal and other issues, and advising those who are groping their way into new social realities online.

Increasingly, there are people who, like me, spend most of their workday online—and then go home and spend a significant amount of their social life online too. We're not computer hermits. We still get outdoors and we still enjoy meeting people face-to-face. Yet online life has acted as a catalyst in thousands of ways in the other spheres of our lives, from business to recreation to romance, and it's impossible to avoid the sense that this kind of catalyzing electronic experience will transform the lives of more and more Americans and more and more people around the world.

In the spring of 1993, I had a personal lesson in just how real a "virtual" community could be. I was relocating from Arlington, Massachusetts, to Washington, D.C., as part of my job and had contracted with Mayflower to have my household goods moved. In what turned out to be a freak electrical accident, the moving van carrying my household goods caught fire. When I heard this news, I was stunned, then distraught. I had lost most of my library, which I'd been building since I was twelve or thirteen years old. I was crushed.

Later that day, I posted about the incident on the WELL, mainly to vent my distress:

news.1262.0: Mike Godwin (mnemonic) Thu 20 May 93 11:32
I have just relocated from EFF's now-closed Cambridge office to its headquarters in DC. The move has turned out to be more costly than I ever imagined.

I was called by Mayflower this morning. They told me that there had been a fire on the truck that was moving my household and the remaining EFF-Cambridge materials to DC. They estimate that 90 percent of the property was destroyed by fire or water damage.

They are going to pay my way to the Delaware site where the remaining property is being shipped, so that I can recover, if possible, any remaining property. My property was insured, but probably not adequately (who ever anticipates a total loss of everything?), and of course there was much that is irreplaceable: particularly books and papers.

I'm devastated. It is almost impossible to grasp how much is gone.

WELL users were quick to post sympathetic messages. Within a few hours, dozens of people had contributed to the discussion, including one

Bay Area lawyer and longtime WELL user named Elliott Fabric, who wrote the following:

news.1262.13: Elliot Fabric (elliot) Thu 20 May 93 13:11
I bet if you post a list of the irreplaceable books, some of us just might mail you our copies. Good luck.

Other users chimed in:

news.1262.20: Roger Karraker (roger) Thu 20 May 93 15:23
My beams to you, Mike; this is indeed terrible. I really like Elliott's idea about a Mike Godwin book-a-thon. Please let me know if I can help.

news. 1262.21: Is the plural of fax, faxen? (booter) Thu 20 May 93 16:05
Yes, I have some nerd books I never use that I could send you. I too am puzzled as to how a truck could go up like that. I have art stuff and I can see that as being flammable, but sofas just don't go up on their own, y'know?

What a kind suggestion, I thought. Maybe a few of my books will be replaced. So after visiting the warehouse and compiling a list of all the books that had been lost, I posted the list to the WELL, not expecting to have more than a few people send me their extra copies of a few of the books on the list.

To my surprise, the list started generating responses within a week or two. Dozens of books started arriving in the mail, more often than not from people I had never met face-to-face. For the next six months, not a week went by in which someone, somewhere, did not send me a book to replace one of the volumes I'd lost. And when I went downstairs to get my mail, I'd be overwhelmed by each new package—still another WELL user who'd taken the time to help someone he'd never met in, uh, "realspace."

I've begun to share this story with other people when I speak about the meaning and value of cyberspace and of the importance of protecting freedom of speech there. I cannot yet tell this story without feeling my throat tighten, without my voice breaking, without my eyes blinking back tears of wonder and gratitude.

March 1996

The alarm clock whistles, and I start out of a dream, then lean over and turn it off. But before I pull myself off my futon and go to my computer, I listen to the new sounds and smell the new air of my new surroundings.

I live in Berkeley, California, now. I moved across the country from Maryland half a year ago, and I haven't yet learned to take the character of my new geographic situation for granted.

Berkeley, like so much of the Bay Area, is beautiful and peaceful this morning. Which makes it the opposite of the Net this year.

Not that the Net was ever peaceful, really. Like any other bastion of real democracy, it has always been a tumultuous, unsettling place, full of countless voices striving to be heard—some full of information and even wisdom, others splenetic or confused. But over the past year, the Net as a whole has been under attack to an unprecedented and frightening degree, and the communities of the Net are anything but calm and complacent in the wake of that onslaught. The First Amendment–related controversies that I'd reflected on that morning in Maryland a year and a half ago have taken distressing forms that even at my gloomiest I had never anticipated.

Back in 1994, I had thought there were only two causes of antagonism and fear toward the Net: (1) backlash against the original (over)hype of the Internet and (2) simple ignorance about what makes the Net the same as the First Amendment's "speech or . . . the press" and what makes the Net different or better. What I discovered in the course of 1995, however, was that there were forces in our society who actively cultivated fear of the new medium for their own purposes. It was a summer in which my every paranoid speculation about what might be going on turned out to be true—quite a traumatic experience for a determined antiparanoid like me.

The phone rings. It's seven A.M., but the East Coast media often assume that the rest of us are on the same timetable they are. I get up and take the call. It's a producer from a radio show who wonders if I'm available to debate my friend Cliff Stoll, whose book, *Silicon Snake Oil,* is just out in paperback. The producer is looking for someone "pro-Internet" to face off against Cliff, whom he takes to be "anti-Internet." I demur. Cliff and his book aren't any more "anti-Internet" than I am, I tell the guy, and I don't much like this whole notion of dividing up the world into "pro-Internet" and "anti-Internet" contingents.

So I tell the producer that while I won't debate Cliff, I'd be happy to participate in a show about the people who helped generate what I keep thinking of as the Great Cyberporn Panic of 1995, generated partly by the efforts of political extremists on the right and by the gullibility of a major newsweekly, *Time*.

Once the producer's off the line, I head to the bathroom and start a shower. I reflect on how much I'd discovered about the religious right organizations and their (ultimately successful) efforts to persuade Congress to pass broad new censorship regulation of the Net. Almost everything I learned about those efforts came from an Internet-wide detective story I "staged" (one is always questioning one's choice of verbs in cyberspace) during the summer and fall of 1995: the investigation of a thirty-year-old undergraduate named Martin Rimm. Not only did I organize the successful online effort to discredit Rimm's largely fabricated "study" of so-called cyberporn, but our efforts ultimately forced *Time,* the nation's most prominent newsweekly, to publicly admit its mistake in hyping Rimm and his "study." As far as I know, this was the first instance in which anyone had used this new, hyperdemocratic communications medium, the Net, to hold a traditional media powerhouse accountable for its mistakes.

Although this initial success didn't prevent Congress from passing a bad law, it did lay some of the groundwork for the eventual court challenges of that law. The first of those challenges, an American Civil Liberties Union (ACLU) lawsuit in which EFF is a party and for which I'm one of the lawyers, was filed within minutes of President Clinton's signing of the Telecommunications Reform Act of 1996, which contained the Internet censorship provisions.

Still in my terrycloth bathrobe, I walk to my home office to call Chris Hansen of the ACLU. "There's a good chance," I tell him, "that the government is going to get some direct assistance from our friends on the right." They won't be satisfied merely to file amicus briefs, I say. They'll offer to help the government write *its* briefs. And after several months of reading legal materials from groups like the National Law Center for Children and Families and the Family Research Council, I'm pretty sure I can recognize the writing styles of some of the religious right lawyers if in fact they do lend a hand. Chris and I then discuss how to prepare witnesses for our preliminary injunction hearing in the Philadelphia federal court where we've filed our case.

After talking with Chris, I make a few more phone calls. Then, and only then, can I begin to look at my e-mail. The character of my correspondence has changed a bit over the past year. It's now much less social and much more anxious. Lots of users and system administrators are quizzing me about how the new censorship law might affect them. A few are responding to the articles I've written and speeches I've given over the past few months regarding the Net backlash in general and the new censorship laws in particular. The volume of speech requests and writing opportunities has now gotten so great that I have to turn most of them down. I sit in my living room, still damp, still dressed in my bathrobe, with my PowerBook in my lap, and I sigh.

In my heart of hearts, you see, I've never lost my own vision of the Net's unleashing the full democratic potential of a society where democracy has all too often been a dream rather than a reality. The fearmongering about the Net, aided and abetted by sensationalistic media, and the ignorant lawmaking by less-than-courageous and less-than-informed representatives and senators have only reinforced my resolve to make sure that the democratic ideals of the founders of the Republic are rediscovered and honored in the online world.

But this isn't the kind of thing a guy can do on his own, and it isn't the kind of thing that can be left to the lobbyists or the lawyers or the technicians or the police. What it takes, I think, is a social consensus that the benefits of this medium outweigh the risks, that the legal and social institutions we've relied on for so long are strong enough and flexible enough to handle the changes this new medium will bring.

What it needs, I find myself thinking, is a book. The stories in this book would be designed to do four things:

1. Explain what the online world is and why it is valuable

2. Show how the law and the Constitution apply, or should apply, in cyberspace

3. Answer the fears about new technology, or of new social consequences, brought about by the Net

4. Defend the Net against those who would do damage to it for their own purposes

In the course of exploring the legal and social issues that face us in the online world, the stories would detail a number of events and phenomena that have shaped our understanding of our "cyber rights." These range from the early antihacker panics that colored law enforcement activities in the early 1990s, to the struggle between the Church of Scientology and its critics on the Net, to the ever-growing disputes about protecting copyrighted works on the Internet, to the Great Cyberporn Panic. That panic, which humbled a national magazine (if only for a moment), also laid bare the plans of those who hoped to use the parts of our lives that we value most—our children—to impose a new censorship regime on what otherwise would be the most liberating communications medium the world has ever seen.

But most important, readers could see how anyone—not just lawyers, or journalists, or policymakers, or the rich and well connected—can use the Net to level the playing field, to hold media and political institutions accountable, and to ensure that the truth is known.

These are the kinds of things I'm already telling people in e-mail and in public online forums, even as I'm sitting on my couch in my bathrobe, preparing myself for the rest of the day. But then I stop, look up from my computer screen, and take a breath. I need to finish getting dressed, go outside, and feel the sunshine for a minute. So I put down my laptop, stand up and walk to my bedroom, and pull on my working outfit, which, in today's heat, will be jeans and a T-shirt. (I still don't dress up to prac- tice law these days.) I slip on my beat-up old wing-tips. Then I walk again into my living room, where I come across a picture of my little girl, Ariel, in the lap of her mother. The picture is sitting in a plastic mounting on one of my bookshelves. Behind it I can see several books that my commu- nity on the WELL sent to me after the moving van fire back in 1993.

Then I walk to the front door and open it, taking care not to let my cat, Francie, escape into the yard. I step outside into the Northern California sunshine. I walk to the sidewalk and look up and down my peaceful street, and I think of my daughter.

The people who've been fighting to censor the Net say that they're the ones who care about families and children. They say that those of us who oppose them—who insist that the real danger lies in *not* giving the Net the same freedoms we give to magazines and newspapers, to libraries and bookstores—don't care about our children.

They can't be talking about me. Not a day goes by when I don't worry about my little girl, when I don't worry that I haven't provided properly for her future. And part of the future I want to give her is the freedom of the Net. Somehow I have to help find the right answer to the Net backlash—to take the law and society of cyberspace and begin to explain them to those who have never been there, as well as to those who will someday live there. For increasing numbers of us, cyberspace will be where we build our lives and our communities in the future and where we must transplant the freedoms that we have come to require in the material world. It will be a place where my daughter does a large part of her growing up. "This is for you, sweetheart," I say out loud, standing there on the sidewalk in the sunshine. "I'm doing this for you."

I stand on the sidewalk for another minute or so and think about the future. Then I turn around and go back to my front door, open it, and walk inside, pick up the laptop, and sit down. Once again, I log on.

November 1994–November 1997

1

A New Frontier for Free Speech and Society

Your first experience in free speech in cyberspace may not seem like speaking at all. Or much like writing, for that matter. Your mouse click or key press enters a command at a computer console, and (if you use a telephone modem rather than a cable modem or digital subscriber line (DSL) or some other newfangled broadband connection) you may hear a dial tone and a rapid series of tones. One or two rings later and the modem on the other end responds with a high-pitched squeal. Your modem answers back with a similar squeal. The login message prompts you for your name and password, and soon you're connected.

But connected to what? Not too long ago, it most likely would have been a hobbyist's computer bulletin board system or maybe a university's mainframe computer. Nowadays you're likelier to be logging into an Internet service provider or a commercial information service, perhaps to read your e-mail or to do research on the World Wide Web. But no matter what you're connected to or why you're there, you're once again another explorer, and perhaps even a settler, of what is now widely recognized as the newest frontier for the exercise of the freedom of expression: "the freedom of speech, or of the press" guaranteed to Americans by the First Amendment of the U.S. Constitution. Coming to grips with the immense expressive power given to us by the Net—and with the legal and social issues that power generates—will be one of the central challenges of our generation. And it won't be just the politicians, or the lawyers, or the activists, or the technicians who take up the challenge. Every one of us must explore this new frontier, which is in some sense a medium and in another sense a territory.

The first step toward mapping this territory—which I normally refer to as "cyberspace" or "the Net"—is to understand how dependent it is on freedom of expression. Many nations provide protections for freedom of expression, but I'm an American lawyer, and I'm most familiar with the cases, the laws, and the social issues in my own country. That's why this book focuses on the First Amendment and on how it defines and protects our cyber rights. But even if you're not an American, I hope that you'll find something of worth in this book's treatment of free speech on the Net.

The term *free speech,* which appears in this book's subtitle as well as in its text, is used more or less interchangeably with *freedom of the press, freedom of speech,* and *freedom of expression* to refer to all the expressive rights guaranteed by the forty-five words of the First Amendment, as interpreted by U.S. courts. The First Amendment reads in its entirety as follows: "Congress shall make no law respecting an establishment of religion, or prohibiting the free exercise thereof; or abridging the freedom of speech, or of the press; or the right of the people peaceably to assemble, and to petition the government for a redress of grievances."[1]

Back to the Future

Pluralism is central to the design of our Constitution, and especially to the antimajoritarian guarantees of the Bill of Rights, including the First Amendment.[2] It's no accident that the Constitution includes so many roadblocks to the will of the majority. James Madison, whom most regard as the primary architect of the Constitution and the Bill of Rights, designed the Constitution to function that way. Like other Enlightenment intellectuals, Madison had been educated to regard simple majority rule with a certain measure of fear. Arguments dating back at least as far as Plato's *Republic* had shaped Madison's thinking about unlimited democracy. He understood that "pure" democracies often led paradoxically to dictatorships, since majorities can easily be swayed by a crisis or a social problem to put all the power into the hands of those few who claim to be able to solve the problem.

The problems and issues I discuss here will, I believe, be relevant to citizens of every country touched by the Net.

I've written this book to do three things:

First, I want to teach you how the First Amendment protects (or, at least, should protect) freedom of speech on the Net. By dealing with individual stories and cases, some of which I've been involved with, I want to show you how the framework of free speech set up by the First Amendment is not one in which your individual rights must necessarily stand in opposition to the rights of other individuals, or to the values of communities, or to the needs of the nation. I hope to convince you instead that the individual rights protected by the First Amendment function overall to *strengthen* the rights of others, as well as to give rise to communities and to enhance the public life of the nation.

Second, I'll identify problems raised by freedom of expression on the Net, such as libel, sexual harassment, copyright issues, and cyberporn. The immense degree to which this new medium empowers individuals to exercise their First Amendment rights is, for some people, a scary development. I want to show you how the First Amendment, when properly understood, resolves most of these problems. At the same time, I'll discuss some situations when the First Amendment *doesn't* protect your speech on the Net—ideally you'll learn how to avoid those situations that overstep your First Amendment bounds. In addition, I want to answer the fears some people have expressed about the new technology, or of the new social consequences, brought about by the Net. Since fear of a new medium is often used to justify treating it more restrictively, and less rationally, than older forms of communication, I want you to learn to see past the fears, which are usually overblown.

Finally, I want to show you some of the ways in which you can be active yourself in defending free speech on the Net. Armed with the power of the Net and a measure of mass media savvy, you have immense power to improve the environments both within and outside our new virtual communities and to level the playing field between individuals and traditional mass media, as well as that between individuals and other large corporate or government institutions. We are each obligated to use freedom of speech on the Net to defend that same freedom from those who would damage or destroy it.

A Cyberspace Roadmap

Maybe you don't think the world of computer communications, often called cyberspace, is anything new. If you're a journalist, for example, you've known for years that computer technology and freedom of expression are intimately linked. In the United States, all urban newspapers and most rural ones rely on computers for word processing and typesetting. Computers also mediate the transmission of wire service stories to subscribing newspapers. Broadcast journalism has long relied on computers for gathering news, presenting it graphically, and transmitting it by satellite. These trends have accelerated in the past twenty-five years as the personal computer industry has made this technology more and more affordable.

But only in the past ten years has the true *social* significance of the spread of computer technology and the Net begun to register among journalists and nonjournalists alike. Remember the first time you heard the word *Internet*? For most Americans, that wasn't too long ago.

You'd think that American journalists, who've been coping longer than the rest of us with the increasing connection between computer technology and everyday life, would be quickest to grasp the First Amendment significance of this technology. Strangely, however, for all the influence of automation in the newsroom, many members of the press (even broadcast journalists) still think primarily of words printed on paper when they hear the term *freedom of the press.*

We have often seen this lead to a couple of outcomes. We've seen the professional press, who should know better, seize on a particular story—maybe a computer crime story or a story about "cyberporn"—and conclude (or at least imply) that all the new freedom the Net gives us is as much a threat as it is a boon.[3] Second, we see various members of the press, preaching from their editorial pulpits, condemning the Net's diversity as chaos, its often fractious public dialogues as divisive, its lack of editorial control as a guarantee that only a fraction of its content has any value.

Neither conclusion is correct. Sure, some people use computers or the Net to do bad things (just as people have used telephones or the printing press to do bad things), but that doesn't invariably mean there's a crisis to be handled or a new law that needs to be passed. And sure, "flames" (insulting or otherwise provocative messages) and political rants may seem to be of little value when you're looking for the answer to a question or just a little good company. But one of the things you learn as you spend more time on the Net is that it's big enough to carry everything—whether you're looking for a "flame war" or a friend.

Increasingly, citizens of the world will be getting their news from computer-based communications—electronic bulletin boards, conferencing services, and networks—which differ institutionally from traditional print media and broadcast journalism. And as we rely more and more on the Net as a third source of information (along with print and broadcasting), we have still another reason to ensure that this medium is afforded First Amendment protections at least as strong as those we insist on for more traditional media.

The first step toward understanding how the First Amendment applies to the Net is to understand how the various online free speech forums are structured. The model that's easiest to understand is the computer bulletin board system (BBS). The operator of a BBS typically dedicates a computer and one or more phone lines (or an Internet connection) at his home or business for the use of a virtual community of users. Each user, working with a computer and modem, logs into the BBS and leaves public messages that can be read by all other users. Each user may also be able to send mail to another individual user that remains private, inaccessible to the rest of the system. BBSs become forums—digital public houses, salons, and Hyde Park corners—for their users, and users with similar interests can associate with one another, publicly and privately, without being hindered by the accidents of geography.[4]

A step up from the BBS in complexity is the conferencing system or information service. Functionally similar to BBSs, only much larger, these systems are typically based on a single computer or set of computers located in a particular geographic area. They differ from BBSs primarily in their capacity: they are able to serve multitudes of users at the same time. America Online (AOL) and the WELL (Whole Earth 'Lectronic Link, based in Sausalito, California) are two better-known examples of such conferencing systems. Each is home to a lively set of communities of users located all across the country. CompuServe, AOL, and the WELL were at one time reachable primarily through proprietary computer networks that enabled users to dial in without racking up immense long-distance charges, although they were still expensive. (The WELL and a few other systems piggybacked on CompuServe's privately owned network, while some other services, such as America Online, maintained proprietary networks.) Nowadays these systems are all reachable through the Internet, which I'll describe in greater detail as we progress.

Still further up the scale in complexity is the distributed network, which is not located in a particular geographic area but is maintained and supported on a large number of computers located all over the country (or all over the world). The best-known example of a distributed network is the Internet, which directly connects thousands of computers at universities, government entities, and commercial and noncommercial organizations around the world. The Internet is a key conduit for Usenet, a distributed worldwide conferencing system whose "newsgroups" (discussion forums) touch on just about every topic human beings can think of. The Internet is also the foundation for the World Wide Web, a relatively recent form of graphically oriented publication on the Net that has grown dramatically over the past decade Thousands of other computers gain access to Internet-connected systems by dialing up providers through local telephone lines.

Together, this range of increasingly interconnected computer forums is often called *cyberspace,* and its public and private conferencing systems (from Usenet to America Online to the WELL), its new modes of publication (such as the World Wide Web), and even its simplest e-mail services have spawned hundreds of virtual communities of like-minded individuals. The immediacy of such Net communications has already led to their supplanting scientific journals as the major communicators of scientific discovery and research—and in some sense, the virtual community is itself a scientific discovery. (I hear you thinking: What's a virtual community? I'll be talking about this in greater detail later, but for now, think of it as you would any other community, except that *this* community's members are connected to one another primarily through computer communications rather than through neighborhoods, cars, mass transit, the phone, or the television.)

The Age of Reason: Finding True Democracy on the Net

Increasingly, computer networks have transcended the limits of geography for those who use them. In the coming decades, expect to see an acceleration of the growth and interconnection of national and international public network systems—the infrastructure on which everyone, whether a large private company, a government, or a single individual, will be able to build a range of information services and forums for expression and association.

All these systems, from the smallest single-phone-line BBS to the Internet, have one thing in common today: their reliance primarily on text. This is an especially interesting development, since it has been argued that the power of visual media will continue to undermine the influence of the printed word. It's useful to note, however, that the year 2001 marked both the twentieth anniversary of MTV and the twentieth anniversary of the IBM personal computer. For all that legislators tend to view the Internet as just another form of television, the Net has flowered in a very different way. Even as cable television watchers have grown increasingly accustomed to fast, slick, and thrilling visual images, the burgeoning population of computer users has grown more adept at *writing* effectively to each other. To some degree, this has made the world of the networks a true democracy: your influence is measured not by wealth or position, but by how well you write and reason. It's true that over time, the Net will increasingly support other kinds of communication—audio, video, and so on—but as I explain later, the efficiency and power of text mean that written expression will always play a central role on the Net.

This reliance on the printed word is, of course, something that the computer-based services share with traditional print media. But they differ from print and broadcast media in two very important ways. First, the means of communication are approaching the point where they're cheap enough for almost everyone in the industrialized world to gain access: a desktop computer and a modem can be purchased now for a few hundred dollars, which renders this form of communication far more democratic than the publishing and broadcast media, whose production costs are prohibitive for all but a few. The economic costs of participation on the

Net are minuscule compared to the cost of access to any other mass medium, and those costs are continuing to shrink.

The second difference follows from the first: While traditional print and broadcast media rely on a one-to-many model, computer-based communications of the new sort can function as many-to-many. A newspaper is a typical one-to-many system: information gathering and reporting is supervised by a hierarchy of editors and other management personnel, who control the flow of copy and make numerous editorial judgments about what information to include or discard. Information tends to go in one direction only: from the editors to the readers.

Computer forums, in contrast, can function as many-to-many systems—in general, they rely on little or no hierarchical editing. Instead these networks are a colloquy of different voices with different styles, with information flowing in multiple directions at once. The filtering function performed by newspaper editors is left to the readers, who also may be contributors and correspondents. The very distinction between reader and reporter is blurred. Compare computer forums to the World Wide Web, which is arguably an adaptation of the one-to-many model: information on a Web page is disseminated outward from a single source. The Web is democratic too, but its democratic impact derives less from the interplay of voices and opinions within a page than from the low economic barriers to entry for Web publishers, which result in lots of Web pages overall. (And increasingly these pages link to one another.)

This may sound like anarchy, but in practice it's more like a town hall meeting, albeit one in which everyone has a chance to speak, no one is shouted down, and everyone has time to develop and explain his or her ideas. Some systems, like America Online, rely on moderators to keep conferences on track, but their role is less that of the editor, who may make line-by-line changes of a writer's copy, than that of a discussion leader. At their best, these online conferences manifest a give-and-take that surpasses even that of face-to-face discussions. When we're face-to-face, the intimacy of physical proximity tends to be offset by inevitable starts, stops, and hesitations of oral conversation and by the distractions of physical presence. Online, each of us has the chance to write paragraphs rather than sentences—to develop arguments rather than interject comments.

In a nutshell, the structure, the dynamic, and the sheer cheapness of access to the Net mean that this is the first mass medium ever with the potential to give each of us a voice with the reach of a newspaper or TV station, but with the intimacy and responsiveness of the telephone.

The Unlonely Pamphleteer: How Freedom of the Press Applies to the Net

We've had some success at getting our legal system to recognize the First Amendment dimensions of the Net. Still, even in the United States, which gives a lot of lip-service to the ideal of free speech, our fight to ensure that the First Amendment protects online communications has often been an uphill battle. First Amendment arguments are not as popular as they used to be. One reason the hill has been steep is that freedom of the press is routinely identified with professional journalism these days, and journalists aren't as popular as they once were. Sure, journalists were held in high regard after the reporting of the Watergate scandal, but it's clear that this high-water mark has yet to be reached again. When I worked as a journalist in the 1980s, I was constantly reminded by sources of the common assumption that a newspaper or magazine article wouldn't get things right or would distort the facts to reflect a particular bias. More recently, in 1991, opinion polls showed the public to be unsympathetic to media complaints about how the military limited their ability to do on-the-scene, unsupervised reporting during the Gulf War. The major newspapers, magazines, and television networks, which are typically, if not always, components of larger corporate organizations, are increasingly regarded by Americans as just another special interest. Invoking the First Amendment looks like special pleading.

Compare the American media today with the printers and publishers in eighteenth-century America. In the most famous freedom-of-expression case in the American colonial era, printer-publisher John Peter Zenger put his own freedom on the line for what he published. In 1732, Zenger, who published the *New-York Weekly Journal,* was tried for "seditious libel" after he published criticisms of the colonial governor in the *Journal.* The law of seditious libel made it a crime to publish political criticisms that undermined the respect given to government officials, to government generally, or to the law. Although it was not a defense under colonial law to show that one's statements were true, Zenger chose to defend himself by arguing to the jury that citizens should have the right to speak the truth about public officials. Zenger was acquitted. His plight—that of an individual printer-publisher whose commitment to freedom of speech might mean his own imprisonment—was one his fellow Americans in the jury box could identify with.

But do the heads of AOL Time Warner or CBS or Gannett have the same concerns as Zenger? Face the same risks? Clearly they do not. And does the average American today have the same opportunity to be a publisher—to be heard—that Zenger had? Until recently, the answer to this second question also was no.

But freedom of the press has undergone a sea change, thanks to computers and the Net. Many of us are familiar with *New Yorker* writer A. J. Liebling's famous observation: "Freedom of the press belongs to those who own one." It was because those who "owned one" were increasingly large, inaccessible corporations that legal scholar Jerome Barron began arguing in the late 1960s that there was—or ought to be—an "emerging First Amendment right": the right of the public to have access to media to disseminate their own voices and views. The problem then was that most people didn't, and couldn't, own a newspaper or radio station. To contribute to public debate, they could write a letter to the editor, take part in a demonstration, or solicit signatures on a petition drive. But the chances of their being heard were minuscule compared with those of NBC's Tom Brokaw or the *Times*'s Frank Rich or Michael Kinsley (the former CNN *Crossfire* moderator, former editor of the *New Republic,* and recent editor of *Slate,* the online opinion journal). That the Net may have turned this balance around is underscored, perhaps, by Kinsley's decision to put aside both TV and the print media and serve instead as editor *of Slate,* the Web-based publication supported by Microsoft.[5]

The world of computer communications, however, has turned out to be the great equalizer. Suddenly anyone can become a publisher, reporter, or editorialist. What's more, each of us has as good a chance of being heard as anyone else in the electronic community. The new computer-based forums for debate and information exchange are witnessing perhaps the greatest exercise of freedom of expression that the United States, and the rest of the world, has ever seen.

But does this new medium have the same First Amendment protection in the United States that is afforded to the traditional press? Even before the U.S. Supreme Court addressed the issue in 1997, there were a number of Court precedents suggesting that it does. In one early case (*Lovell* v. *City of Griffin,* 1938), for example, the Court gave a fairly broad definition of "the press" for the purposes of interpreting the First Amendment's press clause: "The liberty of the press is not confined to newspapers and periodicals. It necessarily embraces pamphlets and leaflets. . . . The press in its historic connotation comprehends every sort of publication which affords a vehicle of information and opinion." Freedom of the press, said the Court, includes "the right of the lonely pamphleteer who uses carbon paper or a mimeograph as much as of the large metropolitan publisher who utilizes the latest photocomposition methods."

Surely online communications, including e-mail and the Web, are numbered among "every sort of publication which affords a vehicle of information and opinion." And the main difference between computer users and "the lonely pamphleteer" is that technology has made the former a lot less lonely.

But if you're not a lawyer, you may not care much that some fussy attorney like me can cite old cases that support constitutional protections for new media like the Net. What does it matter, you may ask, that the First Amendment protects this medium? Even if that's true, our policy-makers and our opinion leaders question whether the Net *deserves* the same degree of protection that traditional publications have enjoyed.

Many Americans, like many citizens of other countries, passionately believe that although full First Amendment protections are appropriate for traditional written and spoken expression, it's equally appropriate to impose more restrictive rules on radio and TV content. It has been argued that broadcast media are special in a number of ways that justify a special governmental role in controlling their content. I hope to show in this book why the assumptions behind the regulation of TV and radio don't apply to cyberspace.

Even if you're convinced that the Net isn't the same as broadcasting, you could still come up with one kind of argument—based on certain fundamental (but untestable) assumptions about human nature—that is particularly hard for me to answer. Turning my own argument against me, you could ask if the Net is special because of the new scope and power it gives our First Amendment rights, doesn't this in itself make the case that the Net also deserves special restrictions? After all, won't too much freedom of speech damage our society's stability and undermine the very values that bind our communities together?

I've written this book to challenge the assumptions behind these questions. Our society still rests on the foundations that Madison and the other framers of the Constitution laid down more than two centuries ago. These foundations include the social premise that the unchecked power of government is far more of a threat to what we care about than is the empowerment of the individual. From our society's very beginnings, we have insisted that individuals can be trusted with liberty. And I believe that anyone who looks at the Net today with a clear eye and an unbiased heart will see that this trust has borne fruit—that protecting so much individual freedom has been worth the risk. This book aims to show that striking the balance in favor of individual rights has always been the right decision for us and that it remains so even when technology gives us new ways to exercise those rights. Individual liberty has never weakened us; freedom of speech, enhanced by the Net, will only make us stronger.

This book argues that our technologically expanded freedom of expression on the Net is not merely something to be tolerated; it's something to be treasured and celebrated. Only when each of us has a voice will we be able to draw upon the full strength of an open society as we face the new problems of a new century. Whether the Net will remain as free in the future as it is today will depend in large part on how well the case is made to Congress, the courts, and the general public that free speech on the Net—even with the problems it occasionally creates—deserves the full protection of the First Amendment.

I Hear America Typing: Pluralism on the Net

Computers and the Net are already giving us far more than they can take away. And I'm not talking just about greater industrial efficiency or greater consumer comforts. The Internet—or, to put it more precisely, the technology symbolized by the Internet—marks a permanent change in American and world culture. Call it *radical pluralism.*

What is radical pluralism? It's the kind of public participation that will characterize public life in the next century; we saw the first wave of it in the 1990s. But don't confuse it with the first vision of "electronic democracy"—the one we saw bandied about by Ross Perot during the 1992 presidential campaign. That vision was a pretty sterile one that had something to do with online voting: one day, we were told, we'd listen to pundits and politicians debate the issues, and then we'd vote, maybe by pointing our remotes at our TV or computer monitors.

Radical pluralism is something different. It's what happens when you put the power of a mass medium—computer communications—into the hands of individual citizens who could never have afforded creative access to other mass media like TV or newspapers. Everyone is now a "content producer."

Suddenly, to paraphrase Mr. Whitman, I hear America typing. And, sure, not everything they say is well thought out or even well intended, but suddenly there are a lot more voices being heard and a lot more people listening, and you discover that the whole liberal versus conservative, Republican versus Democrat dichotomies don't mean much anymore and that they were never terribly valid in any case. Spend enough time on the Net, and you discover that the pictures we've been given by traditional mass media of the range of political opinion have been vastly oversimplified. (If you find this a particularly difficult claim to swallow, you haven't spent enough time online.)

What's more, you see Net-based voices causing action to take place in the nonvirtual (that is, the "real") world. This action ranges from the now legendary campaign to get ABC to show the final episodes of *Twin Peaks* to the nuking of Lotus's privacy-threatening Marketplace product. (Then Lotus chief Jim Manzi woke up one morning to find thousands of letters in his digital mailbox, protesting this CD-ROM product, which contained detailed financial profiles of families all across the country.)

To bring together all the threads of this book, we'll explore the political intrigue, the legal issues, the media tactics, and the detective work that frame the exposure of a phony cyberporn study that snookered, then shook, *Time* magazine.

Will this Net-assisted radical pluralism be comfortable? Hardly. Sometimes the old mass media and the political establishment will wish for us
just to shut up. But I have a message for those folks: The rules have
changed. Fasten your seat belts—it's going to be a bumpy century.

Our Town: Virtual Communities on the Net

The ability of individuals to be heard is not the only benefit wrought by
the Net. Give people freedom, and they find new things to do with it—
things that spring from the First Amendment even though no drafters of
the Bill of Rights ever anticipated them. It's no accident that conferencing
systems and Web-based forums like the WELL and ECHO function as
stable virtual communities; these forums have built in a strong tolerance
for freedom of speech. Freedom of speech for individuals turns out to be
the key element in building stability and connectedness for communities—so important, in fact, that I've explored the connection between
these two values at some length in this book.

I believe virtual communities promise to give to Americans at the beginning of the twenty-first century what many of us feel was lost in the decades at the beginning of the twentieth: a stable sense of community, of
place. Ask those who've been members of such a virtual community, and
they'll tell you that what happens there is more than an exchange of electronic impulses in the wires. It's not just virtual barn raising of the sort
I experienced when, after my library was damaged in a moving van fire,
my "neighbors" on the WELL sent me hundreds of volumes to replace
the ones I'd lost. It's also the comfort from others that a man like Phil
Catalfo of the WELL can experience when he's up late at night caring
for a child suffering from leukemia, and he logs on to the WELL and
pours out his anguish and fears. People really do care for each other and
fall in love over the Net, just as they do in geographic communities. And
that virtual connectedness is a real sign of hope in a nation that's increasingly anxious about the fragmentation of public life and the polarization
of interest groups and the alienation of urban existence.

Empowering people to speak freely on the Net in all the ways that we
allow them to speak freely in other media, and with all the privacy that
we've allowed them in other media, is a necessary condition for the myriad benefits that the online world has to offer us.

Increasingly we hear stories about regular folks (as distinct from dedicated computer hobbyists) who use online communications as an integral part of what can only be called communal activities. Citizens' groups rely on electronic forums to organize events, develop policies, and conduct meetings. Stepmothers and foster parents share the difficulties of, and the wisdom about, caring for children who are not biologically related, but who now are part of the family unit. Lonely individuals find new ways to connect with the rest of humanity.

This is a benefit worth working for. Consider this: one of the chief changes in American public life in the twentieth century was the transition from a primarily rural to a primarily urban culture. And one of the common tragedies of urban life, for some of us, at least, is our sense that we have lost community—that feeling of being part of a larger whole, of having neighbors we can talk to, neighbors who'll step in to help us in a tough time. Is it any surprise that the notion of virtual community has such resonance? Many of us know that community is what we've been missing all this time, which is why we treasure it when we find it in the online world.

There are, of course, millions of individuals around the world who are already beginning the hard work of settling these online communities, investing tens of hours in learning arcane computer commands and telecommunications tricks, installing their Ethernet cards and cable or DSL modems, perhaps, followed by hundreds of hours online. These people are our trailblazers—our first resources when we explore what kinds of online communities succeed and what kinds of laws and institutions we need to accommodate the successful ones. As journalists, communications theorists, and policymakers begin to recognize the significance of events on the electronic frontier, these early explorers will be our guides to the new territory, pointing the way to the new social forms of the twenty-first century.

A Brave New World: The Struggle between Freedom and Fear

The central political and social struggle in the next few decades will be over whether we can tolerate a technological framework that puts the full promise of freedom of the press (and, not incidentally, a much greater power to ensure communications privacy) into each individual's hands.

The dominant threat will be whether governments and other large, established institutions, acting out of fear of both social instability and their own loss of control, institute repressive measures that limit or destroy the full democratic potential of this new medium.

Although the freedoms guaranteed by the First Amendment may benefit society generally, or communities in particular, we don't condition those freedoms on whether how we use them benefits anyone. There is no legal or constitutional requirement that each individual use these freedoms wisely. That is part of what it means to live in an open society: you get to make your own choice about whether to acquire wisdom. We don't let government choose for us.

In the past, this kind of trust in the individual doesn't seem to have done us any great harm. Among the principles in place that have seemed to work for us are individual freedom of expression (especially for those whose expression offends us) and a strong individual guarantee of privacy in our First Amendment–protected communications. We allow each other a great degree of privacy, even though the instruments of privacy—which range from tools like encryption software and so-called anonymous remailers to the Fourth Amendment's prohibition against unreasonable search and seizure and the Fifth Amendment's prohibition of compelled self-incrimination—may make it a little harder for police to investigate and prosecute crimes. Society hasn't yet crumbled just because we assume that most individual citizens can be trusted with freedom and privacy. Indeed, that assumption seems implicit in the kind of government we've chosen for ourselves—we trust individuals with freedom for the same reason we trust them with the right to vote or the right to contribute to the laws and policies of our country as they are made. We have chosen to believe that most people are rational and capable of deciding for themselves how to promote the greater good and that if we give them all the facts, we can trust them in general to make the right decisions. In fact, we make the leap of faith that if we trust each other with this kind of freedom, which includes the freedom to act antisocially and foolishly and to be heedless of what would benefit society, society is still likely to benefit.

Justice Louis Brandeis, who served on the Supreme Court from 1916 to 1939, tackled this apparent paradox head-on in a case now more famous for his concurring opinion than for its own legal or factual background:

Those who won our independence believed that the final end of the state was to make men free to develop their faculties, and in its government the deliberative forces should prevail over the arbitrary. They valued liberty both as an end and as a means. They believed liberty to be the secret of happiness and courage to be the secret of liberty. They believed that freedom to think as you will and to speak as you think are means indispensable to the discovery and spread of political truth; that without free speech and assembly discussion would be futile; that with them, discussion affords ordinarily adequate protection against the dissemination of noxious doctrine; that the greatest menace to freedom is an inert people; that public discussion is a political duty; and that this should be a fundamental principle of American government. They recognized the risks to which all human institutions are subject. But they knew that order cannot be secured merely through fear of punishment for its infraction; that it is hazardous to discourage thought, hope and imagination; that fear breeds repression; that repression breeds hate; that hate menaces stable government; that the path of safety lies in the opportunity to discuss freely supposed grievances and proposed remedies; and the fitting remedy for evil counsels is good ones.

In short, individual freedom of speech leads to a stronger society. But knowing that principle is not enough. You have to know how to put it to use on the Net.

A Call to Action: Freedom Fighting on the Net

Okay, this is the hard part. Everything up to now is just theory—about how to *react* to the issues raised by the interplay of the Net and society. The real challenge is learning how to *act*—how to use what we know about both old and new media in order to make things happen. The purpose of cultivating this expertise is not merely to benefit ourselves, although at the very least we'll be able to do that. Instead, our obligation as Netizens (citizens on the Net) is to use this expertise to help protect freedom of speech on the Net. Equipped only with these two tools—the Net and a basic understanding of how the mass media work—any citizen of the Net has the potential to influence public thought and action. This potential gives each of us more power than any of the framers of the Constitution had to change the world. The changes wrought by the Net will require all of us to become media-smart social philosophers. We no longer have any excuse for waiting for someone else to step in and think about media for us.

Since the Net is a world essentially built on communicative technologies and communicative acts, it should come as no surprise that most of the problems and issues emerging in the online world are also communicative in nature: distorted news items, false rumors, disruptive uses of the Net that deny freedom to others, defamatory statements, threats, offensive sexual content, copyright infringement, and so on.

In the past, we've handled such problems and issues by delegating them away—either to the industry players who controlled most mass media or to the government. But on the Net, there is no higher private or public authority with reliable means of resolving these issues. Yet many of these issues, if they remain unsolved, could result in long-term damage to freedom of speech that is central to the highest and best uses of the Net.

So if neither the corporate media nor the government can be relied on always to be effective (or, for that matter, always to have our best interests at heart), we've got to get out of the habit of delegation. What's more, we have to become smarter. Sure, the Net theoretically gives each of us the power of a newspaper or TV station, but having that power is not enough; we need to learn to think like journalists or broadcasters to use it well. This means paying more attention to how other communications media work and to how they interact with the Net.

I wish I could say I'm a media expert; at best, though, I'm just a media hacker—a hobbyist with more enthusiasm than expertise. Over the years, as an advocate for freedom of speech, I've done just enough work in media myself to have developed some instincts about how to talk to traditional media and how to leverage the strengths of the Net to maximum effect. So, at some points in this book, I share what I think I've learned about leveraging the media and the Net to affect the world in which we live. But be warned: my education is incomplete. That is, I still make my share of embarrassing screw-ups. I'm hoping, though, that what little I've learned is teachable and that certain stories in this book—notably the story about the Steve Jackson Games case and the sections having to do with *Time* magazine, Martin Rimm, and the cyberporn panic—will give you a running start at cultivating your own media savvy.

Want proof that the Net has leveled the playing field? All you have to do is look at the *Time*-Rimm cyberporn scandal, detailed at length in chapter 9 of this book. In that instance, a few concerned individuals and I discovered that when you know how to use the Net and have the truth on your side, it doesn't matter quite so much that the other guy has sheer media muscle. That period was a rough ride for all of us. But what we learned then about freedom of speech and the power of the Net turned out to be invaluable—a source of renewed hope about free speech in an open society.

In short, the Net has brought to fruition *precisely the promise of freedom of speech that Brandeis wrote about:* free speech that gets heard, free speech that makes a difference. "[The founders of the United States] believed that freedom to think as you will and to speak as you think are means indispensable to the discovery and spread of political truth," Brandeis wrote, adding that "public discussion is a political duty." Once you know it can make a difference—that it does in fact lead to truth after all—it becomes even more of a duty.

Not that it's an easy duty. When it comes to learning good Netizenship, you have to be willing to make your painful mistakes and keep on learning. Exploring and understanding the Net is an ongoing process. Cyberspace never sits still; it evolves as fast as society itself. Only if we fight to preserve our freedom of speech on the Net will we ensure our ability to keep up with both the Net and society.

Slippery Slope: Legal Cases and Controversies

Article III, Section 2, of the U.S. Constitution extends the federal courts' jurisdiction to "Cases and Controversies." This section has long been interpreted by the courts as a limitation on the power of the federal judiciary to interpret the law and the Constitution (including, of course, the First Amendment). The "Cases and Controversies" entry in the *Oxford Companion to the Supreme Court of the United States* states this limitation succinctly: "Federal courts may consider only issues that are presented in an adversary context. They may not answer merely hypothetical or abstract questions: their power is limited by law to questions that arise out of an actual dispute. The most widely cited reason for that requirement is to ensure full development of cases. When parties contend in a real dispute, each side is permitted to be zealously represented and the court may consider the legal issues against the backdrop of real facts." (p. 129)

Not being a federal judge, I'm not so limited in my jurisdiction. So in some parts of this book, especially when talking about issues that may arise in the future of the Net, I do consider "hypothetical or abstract questions." More often, however, I'll be talking about real cases or controversies, because I too believe that it's "against the backdrop of real facts" that we learn how the law works and how it should work.

It turns out that just about all of the cases and controversies surrounding the Net raise First Amendment issues. (This is easy to understand, given that communication is central to just about everything anyone does on the Net.) Take libel, for example. How does libel law, which supposedly provides protection to our reputations, apply in a world where anyone can send a lie about you to a national or global audience? Two cases discussed in this book—*Cubby* v. *CompuServe* and *Stratton Oakmont* v. *Prodigy*—underscore an important way in which online forums, while they may partake of the freedoms of the traditional press, are nonetheless different from the traditional press. They provide a springboard into discussion of how the Net itself, by providing its own remedy for libel, may eventually render libel law (as we have traditionally understood it) obsolete.

What about intellectual property, such as copyright and trade secret law? These areas of the law function (to oversimplify a bit) by prohibiting the unauthorized copying of certain kinds of protected information. Yet in a real sense, the Net is, among other things, a huge and immensely powerful copying machine, able to ship millions of copies to millions of readers in minutes. Can copyright interests and trade secrets survive the Net? One criminal case, *United States* v. *LaMacchia,* and several civil cases involving the Church of Scientology give us insight as to how intellectual property issues play out against the free speech framework of the Net.

Does the fact that everyone has the potential to be a publisher mean that there is a new need for government to step in and monitor for illegal or otherwise harmful content? It's well settled that the First Amendment doesn't protect certain kinds of sexually related material—those materials a court can judge to be legally "obscene" in a given part of the country because, among other things, they violate the "community standards" of that geographic locality. What happens when people in any locality can access such "locally obscene" material from anywhere else around the country or around the globe? Central to these cases is the issue of defining obscenity according to "community standards" when every geographic community may be connected by the Net to every other community.

Nor is obscenity the only kind of problematic sexual content. What about material that's acceptable for adults, but that many, and perhaps most, of us would prefer to keep from our children? Is there any way legally or technically to keep such material from our kids while preserving the rights of adults to read or view it? We will explore this issue as I discuss the controversy surrounding the proposal and passage of the Communications Decency Act (see chapters 8, 9, and 10).

And sexual content isn't the only kind of content on the Net that people have begun to worry about. So-called hate speech, online "threats," and the online publication of "dangerous information" (such as how to build a bomb) are issues that have been raised in Congress and in the news. Does the Net give individuals so much power that it is necessary to step in and strike some kind of new balance between the rights of individuals and the concerns of society? Many policymakers have argued that it does, but it's hard to see how such a new balance can be found without departing, at least to some extent, from the very free speech protections that the Net, with all its ability to empower individuals, seems to call for.

Is information about how to make explosives somehow worse or more dangerous if available on the Net than when it is available in magazines or books? Is a frighteningly violent piece of fiction more harmful if published online? Is sexist speech or hate speech less deserving of protection when it appears on the Net? Plenty of people are ready to say yes to these questions, and we must be ready to respond to them. We will examine the Jake Baker case (in which a student was prosecuted for publishing a "threat" on the Internet), which tells us much about how willing the government can be to perceive expression on the Net as threatening when the same material, published in a more traditional manner, would be understood to be protected by the First Amendment. And the Santa Rosa Junior College case we'll review demonstrates how even the most well-intentioned protectors of equality can become so eager to fight one battle (sexism on campus) that they overlook the applicability of the First Amendment to online forums.

Still another area of the law likely to be changed by the growth of the networks is criminal law. Consider, for example, how the development and dissemination of cryptographic software enables individuals to keep their communications private even from the nation's law enforcement and intelligence agencies. One of the legal norms in this country, buttressed by the First Amendment's free speech guarantees, is that under most circumstances, you can be prosecuted only for things you *do,* not for things you *say.* But the world of global computer networks is one in which your decision to use language relating to cryptography—not just the computer language a cryptographic program is written in, but even public discussions of the technology—might turn you into a lawbreaker. Where will the courts draw the line between speech and action? Is the person who writes an encryption or decryption program a criminal? What if she disseminates it accidentally? What if she does so on purpose? What if her activities are part of an academic study program focusing on cryptographic? Can merely explaining how a computer program works make you a felon? Should that even be possible? We'll review the actions of the Department of Justice against Phil Zimmermann, the developer of Pretty Good Privacy (a freely available cryptographic package), in the light of these First Amendment issues.

Here in the United States, the government has frequently used the fear of Net crimes and Net criminals as justification for imposing greater control on the Net as a whole. I've met a number of computer hackers in my time—whiz kids and otherwise. If I've learned anything from them, it's that the threat of malicious hackers and computer intruders is vastly overstated. Once you look into the hacker phenomenon, you discover that very few so-called hackers qualify as genuine threats to society. But this doesn't stop the government or the press from fomenting a backlash against freedom of speech on the Net, and fear of malicious hackers is just another tool for inciting that backlash.

Much of what people are told about cyberspace is wrong, and much of what they're told that's wrong is also frightening. We hear that people don't really communicate well on computer networks, or that something about using computers makes people act badly to each other, or that what some people call virtual communities are little more than consensual hallucinations—fantasy lands without any real meaning.

Regardless of what the critics say, it *is* possible to communicate in cyberspace as well as, or better than, we do in the physical world. In this book I show you why. It *is* possible to form virtual communities that are just as "real" as any other community you've ever been a part of—and I describe a framework you may use to design such a community yourself. What's more, while you're more empowered in this world than any individual has ever been before, the power you have in cyberspace is not, for the most part, merely neutral in impact. Give people a computer and access to the Net, and *it's far more likely that they'll do good than otherwise*. This is because freedom of speech is itself a good. The framers of the Constitution were right to give it special protection, because societies in which people can speak freely are better off than societies in which they can't.

But let's take this step by step. There's a lot to know, and it helps us understand this new world if we learn about the parts of it before we try to assemble those parts into a whole.

2

Where the "Virtual" Meets the "Real": Free Speech, Community, and Ethics on the Net

One need not be a constitutional scholar, or even a lawyer, in order to regard freedom of speech as a fundamental tenet of any society that most of us would find minimally acceptable.

—Melville Nimmer, *Nimmer on Freedom of Speech*

I care about what happens in cyberspace, and to our freedoms in cyberspace, because I dwell there part of the time.

—Howard Rheingold, *The Virtual Community*

The voice on the other end of the phone line was patient yet puzzled: "Mike, could you tell me again why you think we have to have Howard Rheingold appearing for us in court?"

The questioner was Chris Hansen, the sharp constitutional litigator who was the lead attorney for the American Civil Liberties Union (ACLU) in *ACLU* v. *Reno,* the case in which several individuals and organizations, including my own organization, the Electronic Frontier Foundation, challenged the constitutionality of the so-called Communications Decency Act (CDA). Chris was calling me that March afternoon in 1996 because he needed to be clear, for both himself and the other attorneys involved in this case, about why I thought Howard was such an important witness that he needed to be physically present in Philadelphia during the trial.

It wasn't a question of whether Howard would get to be a witness at all. Like most of our other witnesses, Howard had already drafted a statement that spoke of his concerns as a citizen and as a father about the negative effect he believed the Communications Decency Act would have on freedom of speech in general and on the Net's virtual communities in particular. (The CDA was passed as part of the Telecommunications Reform Act of 1996. Although it was marketed by its supporters as an antipornography bill, the CDA by its terms would have criminalized a wide range of nonpornographic, constitutionally protected speech.) Chris had always agreed with me that Howard, widely recognized as an expert on cyberspace and society, should be one of the witnesses for our First Amendment challenge to the CDA. But now he had asked for reasons that it was necessary for Howard to show up in Philadelphia and talk to the court in person.

To me it had seemed clear, since I first had an inkling that we'd be going to court to challenge the CDA, that Howard ought to play a role. I'd solicited his involvement as a witness as soon as we started putting together a witness list. I knew him from the WELL, a Sausalito-based conferencing system that he'd been a member of almost since its beginning in 1985. Through his writings in a number of publications, as well as through the publication of his book, *The Virtual Community,* in 1993, Howard had become identified with the very concept of virtual communities, which he defines as "social aggregations that emerge from the Net when enough people carry on . . . public discussions long enough, with sufficient human feeling, to form webs of personal relationships in cyberspace."[1] He was (and still is) the best-known popularizer of the concept and one of the most gifted at persuading people that a virtual community is just as real as any other kind.

Not that everyone needed that much persuasion. I'd always taken to the concept of the virtual community myself. But for some people, the concept is troubling, since "virtual" is often used to connote the opposite of "actual" or "tangible"; as a result, many people think that whatever a virtual community is, it can't be as real as, say, a community that grows out of a neighborhood or village. As a lawyer, however, I've never had much trouble with the concept that virtual communities are both real and intangible. The same can be said about the First Amendment itself. What we call "the First Amendment" is not something that depends on the scribbling of words on a piece of paper or parchment. Burn every copy of the First Amendment in the world, and it will still exist in the minds and hearts of Americans, many of whom have memorized the forty-five words of its text. Law students learn that those words represent, in turn, some additional virtual entities: fundamental principles, plus some rules of interpretation. The rules arise when the language, the history, and the underlying principles of the First Amendment interact with the *material* world. The world of these abstract, virtual entities and the concrete, tangible, material world of cases and controversies are shaping each other constantly. And the world of law is filled with countless other examples of virtual entities that are taken quite seriously in the material world.

Thanks to some special procedures for this case set out by Judge Stewart Dalzell (a member of the trial court's three-judge panel), only a few witnesses would be appearing in court; the rest would be "present" on paper. Those who would be present would only be cross-examined by the opposing side's attorneys. Their "direct" testimony would be submitted as a printed "declaration" to the court days or weeks prior to the trial.

I knew Howard to be capable of eloquent writing. The declaration he submitted was, for me, a compelling example of his gift for communicating the essence of complex truths in simple terms:

In my life, the virtual community became my real community. The people I first got to know in open, group conversation online have become my friends in the real world where real things happen to people. I sat with two people when they were dying, spoke at two funerals, danced at two weddings, passed the hat quietly among other virtual community members to help out a member in dire circumstance. The community I know takes place among people who matter to me, and online communication is what enables thousands of geographically dispersed interest groups to build communities. For people who live in remote areas, who share certain special interests, from mathematics to politics to problems of being an Alzheimer's caregiver to the civic affairs of a small town or large city, to being a gay teenager in a rural area, virtual communities enable people to form associations that can enrich their lives and often carry over into face-to-face society. In modern society, it is often difficult to find people who share interests and values; the virtual community enables people to find and get to know one another and to establish relationships they might otherwise never have formed, relationships that often carry over into face-to-face friendships. Indeed, I know of many examples of people who met [their spouses] online. In other cases, online friendships, become intense and meaningful whether or not the people ultimately meet in real life.

Howard's words alone would normally be enough to convey important thoughts or feelings (more on this later), but even when I'm most enthusiastic about the Net, I still have to admit that there are times when cyberspace is no substitute for being there. A kiss is one such situation; a cross-examination is another. I had two reasons for thinking that Howard had to be there in the courtroom, answering tough questions as the government took its best shots. Chris, who'd had to educate himself in a hurry about the Net to prepare this case and who now faced the task of educating three judges about it, listened patiently as I tried to spell them out.

The Seven Dirty Words: Censorship in Cyberspace

First, I knew the judges in Philadelphia were going to be doing a lot of reading in the course of this case. Howard's declaration, often needle sharp in its poignancy, might nevertheless get lost in the paper haystack of briefs, motions, submissions, transcripts, and references that would be cluttering these judges' desks. They'd read it, sure, but they might be too overworked to take much notice of it. I wanted Howard to be there in the courtroom, to be the human face of cyberspace. If he could get across to the judges a tenth of the depth of feeling he'd communicated on paper, he might catch their interest. He might even cause them to take a second look at his declaration, to give it more emotional weight.

The second reason had to do with a case called *FCC* v. *Pacifica Foundation.*[2] In this 1978 case, the Supreme Court upheld the Federal Communication Commission's (FCC) authority to sanction a radio station for broadcasting one of comedian George Carlin's most famous comedy routines, popularly known as "The Seven Dirty Words You Can't Say on Television." As it happens, the Supreme Court decided that you can't hear that content on the radio either. Writing for the majority, Justice John Paul Stevens had held that the FCC had the power under the First Amendment to impose sanctions on the Pacifica radio station airing the Carlin broadcast. The broadcaster's offense? It had broadcast material that was not legally "obscene" (and therefore unprotected) but merely "indecent" or offensive (and therefore presumptively protected under the First Amendment). In basing his opinion on the ostensible "pervasiveness" of the medium, Justice Stevens asserted that "broadcasting is uniquely accessible to children, even those too young to read"; a majority of the Court agreed with the justice's opinion that broadcasting is "unique" in its ability to reach into the home and (presumably) offend and even harm adults and children. *Especially* children. Therefore, he argued, the government had a constitutionally justifiable role in regulating the content of broadcasting.

You may agree with that argument about TV and radio, especially when it comes to children. But regardless of whether you agree about the dangers of broadcasting in general, it has always seemed to me that something else was going on in the *Pacifica* case. Justice Stevens was trying to create a little more flexibility under the First Amendment for government to regulate speech that is *constitutionally protected*. That is, he wanted government to be able to regulate, at least sometimes, speech that doesn't fall within the narrow categories (such as obscenity, perjury, fraud, conspiracy, and libel) understood to be unprotected under the Constitution.

Stevens's idea was that sometimes we can balance the social good we're trying to achieve by regulating speech against the value that speech has to society. To him, the Carlin monologue was of relatively little social value compared with things like political speech. Therefore, it would follow, society wouldn't be hurt much if they were regulated, at least as far as broadcasting went. "While some of these references may be protected, they surely lie at the periphery of First Amendment concern," Stevens wrote in section IV-A of the opinion.

Justice Stevens apparently did not realize (or was not willing to acknowledge) that Carlin had designed his monologue to make a deeply political point about what the comedian believed to be the silliness of censoring language because of the words one uses. And as I worked on the CDA challenge, I came to believe that the Court itself had made a similar point a few years earlier in *Cohen* v. *California* (1971).[3] In that case, a defendant had been convicted for disturbing the peace after he had entered a California courthouse while wearing a jacket on which the words "Fuck the Draft. Stop the War" had been (as the Court phrases it) "emblazoned." The Supreme Court voted to reverse that conviction, recognizing that Paul Cohen's jacket, regardless of its offensiveness to some people, was expressing *political* ideas—and if the First Amendment protects anything, it surely protects political speech. Justice John Harlan, writing for the majority, observed that "one man's vulgarity is another's lyric."[4] Harlan also argued that it's not just the ideas that are protected by the First Amendment. "In fact," he wrote, "words are often chosen as much for their emotive as their cognitive force. We cannot sanction the view that the Constitution, while solicitous of the cognitive content of individual speech, has little or no regard for that emotive function which, practically speaking, may often be the more important element of the overall message sought to be communicated."

To me, Harlan's argument in the *Cohen* case was easier to justify than Stevens's "social value" approach to First Amendment issues. If the government were to get into the business of deciding on a case-by-case basis whether a given instance of speech had value, I'd long ago decided, the First Amendment would soon be little protection at all. It's easy for a senator or a government official to blur the line between speech that's offensive and speech that lacks social value, yet in practice it's often the offensive speech that's the most valuable. The "emotive" content of Cohen's "speech," for example, expressed the depth of anger he and others felt about the government's Vietnam policies in a way that a more neutrally worded slogan could never have done.

What's more, even if many Americans favor government regulation of TV and radio content, I was convinced that any kind of general expansion of the ability of the government to censor speech, based on what the government thinks its social value is, was something some Americans might have a lot of problems with, especially if this censorship were applied to a mass medium with the potential to empower everyone to speak as well as listen.

Certainly six of Stevens's colleagues had some problems with his social value approach to regulating speech, and their reaction to his argument on this point is one of the things that makes *Pacifica* an unusual case. You see, Stevens had divided his opinion for the *Pacifica* case into four sections and had gotten a majority (six of the nine justices) to support three of them entirely, as well as a part of the fourth. These parts of the opinion—in which the Court held that there's something special about broadcasting that makes governmental regulation of its content constitutional—thus became the law of the land.

But when it came to parts A and B of the fourth section, only two other justices (Warren Burger, chief justice at the time, and then–associate justice William Rehnquist) were willing to agree with Justice Stevens. As a result, no majority of the Court supported those parts in which Stevens had attempted to define a sort of multitiered hierarchy of protected speech, based on its social value.

In short, it seemed to me Stevens had written against freedom of speech in this case, and for the government, for two underlying reasons. First, the mass medium in question (broadcasting) was more harmful than older, more traditional media (such as the press), in that it was more invasive and more likely to do harm to the sensibilities of children. Second, the kinds of speech at issue in this sort of regulation were, in fact, of less value, so it would do little harm if more restrictions were imposed on it than on such things as newspaper editorials and political speeches. Besides, the justice argued in a footnote, we have plenty of access to the same sort of (nonobscene, constitutionally protected) content in other media, so what harm would it do if the government restricted broadcasting content a bit more than other kinds?

That was just what I was afraid the courts might do with cyberspace. They might decide either that (1) the Net posed threats that other media don't, or (2) it didn't matter if the government restricted otherwise legal content on the Net, since adults would have plenty of other conduits for the kinds of information that might be banned from the public areas of cyberspace.

Chris Hansen, who's been dealing with free speech issues for a long time, had begun with a traditional approach for First Amendment challenges. The CDA, our side was prepared to argue, is unconstitutionally "vague" and "overbroad," two terms of art in constitutional analysis, in violation of the First Amendment's protections for freedom of expression.[5]

These traditional arguments would be solidly grounded in First Amendment scholarship, but I worried that this wouldn't be enough. Stevens in the *Pacifica* case had hinted that he might be willing to find the content of the George Carlin routine artistically valuable in another context, yet he'd ruled in a way that (as it turned out) opened the door for years of litigation about the content of broadcasting—not about obscenity or threats, but about relatively harmless, and sometimes even beneficial, content. Stevens is still on the Court, I thought. We could take up this issue for Supreme Court review, and Stevens could hold that this medium too was sufficiently different or dangerous to justify a special role for government in controlling content. And this time it wouldn't be just radio station owners who felt the heat. It would be everybody on the Net.

I wanted to make sure we had a witness who made a positive case for the benefits of freedom of speech on the Net—someone who, unlike many of our other witnesses, wasn't tied to a particular publication or a particular cause, but who had lived the full range of experiences a person could have online. We needed someone who would stand authoritatively for the intimate connection between an individual's free speech and a community's health. The Net censors would argue that the Net is dangerous and marginal. I wanted a witness who could say, based on a lot of personal experience in a broad range of contexts, that the Net is a fantastic benefit to individuals, parents, and communities, that the harms are overblown, when they exist at all, and that far from being marginal, the Net would become increasingly central to American public life—a mainstream phenomenon, in fact. I wanted the judges to see that we had more to lose than just another information pipe into the home if the CDA were found constitutional. We would be losing freedom of speech in the first medium that truly empowers each of us to be heard, and in the process, we'd be losing the very roots of a new kind of community, not to mention a tool that could reinvigorate the traditional kind.

I was a bit frantic as I argued these points to Chris over the phone. (Even half a year later, Chris and I had met face-to-face only twice during our entire collaboration on this case—that's what comes of being based on opposite coasts. A few days after our trial victory in Philadelphia, I sent Chris and the other folks at the ACLU a congratulatory note. Chris responded by thanking me for "being there" when they needed me. I thought it was a clever note, given that in one sense I was hardly ever there, but that in another I was working in the same online "space" with the team nearly every day. It was as my office had been just a bit farther down the hall.)

Despite my frenetic manner, Chris credited my argument: that we had to persuade the judges there was a lot more at stake in regulating freedom of speech on the Net than there has been in previous "indecency" cases. And to do so required an expert of Howard's caliber. During the trial, when the government sought to exclude Howard's testimony as an expert witness on cyberspace issues, Chris described Howard as "an expert in the part of cyberspace that involves the formation of communities, news groups, chat rooms, other conversation." Furthermore, Chris continued, "It is the plaintiffs' position that cyberspace is not just about [the World Wide Web], it is not just an electronic library, it is also a place in which people meet and converse and carry on conversations and form close friendships. Mr. Rheingold is being offered for the purpose of describing that sector of cyberspace, and his declaration suggests that that section of cyberspace, the community-forming, the friendship-forming part, will in fact be affected by the act."

In my opinion, Howard was a successful witness. Some court watchers worried that the government attorneys' attempts to discredit him during cross-examination—to make it look as if his love of the Net were little more than the enthusiasm of an overgrown kid with a beloved hobby—would be successful. But Howard's testimony is specifically cited in paragraph 24 of the court's factual conclusions, which were used to justify a decision favoring our side. "Another plaintiffs' expert, Harold Rheingold [*sic*], participates in 'virtual communities' that simulate social interaction. It is no exaggeration to conclude that the content on the Internet is as diverse as human thought."

Forget the judges' cautious use of the word *simulate,* their misspelling of Howard's name (attributable to the court reporter's error), or the quotation marks around "virtual communities." That second sentence, flatly imperative and universal in its scope, demonstrated that Howard had helped make the promise of the Net—a place where freedom of speech and community complement each other—something the three district court judges viewed real enough to be worth protecting.

But in order to have something worth protecting, you've got to work at it. And when it comes to building a community worth preserving—whether it's a virtual community or one of the more geographically oriented varieties—freedom of speech is essential, and free speech online is essential to constructing the kinds of online communities and social forms in which our grandchildren will build their lives.

My worries about *ACLU* v. *Reno* were just a smaller version of my ongoing worries about the general public perception of the Net. A lot of people, including a lot of policymakers, see the Net as marginal or out of the mainstream, illusory or unreal, or even lawless and immoral. If we're going to save freedom of speech on the Net, we have to make these counterarguments to the rest of the world:

• Our interest in, and love of, the Net, freedom of speech online, and virtual communities represent mainstream human concerns.

• What we experience online, even mediated primarily by language, is as real as anything else we experience.

• Most of us can be trusted to act responsibly with the freedom and expressive power the Net gives us.

On the Edge of the Virtual City: What We're Looking for in Cyberspace

The scope of cyberspace is as unlimited as the mind, but it can be hard to find a place to "live" there. That's why the time has come for planned communities in cyberspace. And those that are built on, and with, freedom of expression are precisely the ones likeliest to last.

If Howard Rheingold is the best-known popularizer of the notion of virtual communities, their earliest and most influential theorists are Starr Roxanne Hiltz and Murray Turoff, two social scientists who pioneered the study of what academics have come to call computer-mediated communication (CMC). Their book, *The Network Nation,* first published in 1978, was the first effort to assemble a comprehensive exploration of the design, functions, and consequences of online communication.

The book turned out to be prophetic—there's hardly an aspect of anyone's experience in the online world that is not prefigured to some extent in *The Network Nation.* Yet because Hiltz and Turoff began by attempting to find out what makes online conferencing systems work, they often focused on what kinds of design decisions have to be made if the system is going to work efficiently. It turns out that one of the key tools for improving system design is the fostering of community and that this in turn is connected to speech: "The designer of [computer communication] systems has to give as much weight to the behavior of his users and the social psychology of their particular communication process as he or she does to the internals of the computer system. . . . A designer wants to foster a user community in which users aid one another and actively exchange information on ways to do new and useful things they have discovered."[6]

Nowadays it seems a bit backward to think of building communities in order to improve the tools. If we've learned anything since the start of the twentieth century, it's that building tools is easy but constructing communities is hard. Still, Turoff and Hiltz did much to explore what it takes to make online communities work. Over time, they discovered that the social dimension of what they were doing kept intruding on their studies of the technology: "Some years after the book was first published we began to recognize the full import of what we were doing. We were not merely designing and investigating tools to improve human communication, but we were, in fact, designing 'social systems.' "[7]

Okay, think about what you want in a social system. If you're like First Amendment scholar Melville Nimmer, you see freedom of speech as a necessary feature for any society you'd want to live in. But what you may not realize at first is how necessary it is for building that society. The most successful online communities, however, seem to be those that tolerate the greatest freedom of expression.

That freedom is never limitless. Every society, even an online society, has norms and taboos that simultaneously protect and define the culture. In many virtual communities, for example, it's considered exceedingly bad-mannered to open to public view the content of someone's private mail, especially when the person e-mailed you with the expectation that you'd keep it private. This is true almost all the time, even when you might feel perfectly justified in exposing the other person to ridicule or criticism for the nasty thing he or she said to you privately.

The WELL, the virtual community I know best, has adopted that norm, but it's generally accepted that there may be times when it's okay to violate it—as when someone is being threatened in e-mail. (Public repostings of such private mail are incredibly effective at encouraging the sender to stop.) Another taboo is the reposting or republishing of someone's WELL postings in some non-WELL venue (either print or another online forum) without the original poster's permission. Cross that line on the WELL, and you'll be shocked at the sudden, steep (but usually temporary) down-turn in your social fortunes. Many journalist WELL members have crossed that line early in their tenure on the system. After all, they ask, what's wrong with quoting people who say something in a public forum? (I have no answer to this, except to say that I pay a lot of attention to the rule myself if only because the WELL is the place I live when I'm online, and I'm willing to sacrifice a little freedom to quote people in order to stay a part of the WELL.)

Still, the primary principle that keeps the WELL strong and growing is not the forsaking of freedom of speech but the exercise of that freedom. (And it's important to recognize that few people on the WELL think violating its social norms should be a crime.) Talking to other people singly and in groups—sharing what you're thinking and feeling and what matters to you—is the social glue that keeps long-term WELL users coming back. It is the sense of being connected to others—a sense created and mediated by freedom of expression.

If you talk to a friend who's not yet online and you start to wax poetic about the pleasures and rewards of your online community, your friend may think you're living in a wish-fulfillment fantasy. After all, if you look around, those communities are hard to spot. But one of the ways you know that virtual communities are not just wishful fantasies—that they're "real"—is that it's so hard to find a good one.

Oh, sure, it's easy enough to get an e-mail address or to find an online service where you can discuss *Star Trek* or health care issues or sexuality. But it's far more difficult to find true communities of people to which you feel a sense of belonging. The root of this problem lies in the fact that few people are *planning* virtual communities.

There still isn't enough talk about how one builds such communities. Howard's book focused on one of the chief benefits of online conferencing systems: they can restore a sense of community to a society that's been feeling alienated and disempowered by the lack of that feeling of connection. But for all that he explored the varieties and benefits of virtual community, he didn't address what may turn out to be its most pressing problem: How will the explosively growing cyberspace population find its way into such communities? How can such communities be designed and constructed?

To get an idea of how fast the move to cyberspace is occurring, compare the growth in suburban housing in postwar America, as documented by Pulitzer Prize–winning journalist and historian David Halberstam in *The Fifties*. "In 1944," he writes, "there had been only 114,000 new single houses started; by 1946 that figure had jumped to 937,000: to 1,118,000 in 1948; and 1.7 million in 1950." Halberstam attributes the growth to home-building magnate Bill Levitt's innovations in mass-produced housing, coupled with the immense postwar demand for such housing.

Over the two decades, a similar boom has occurred in what Internet demographer John Quarterman calls "the Matrix" and defines as "a worldwide metanetwork of connected computer networks and conferencing systems that provides unique services that are like, yet unlike, those of telephones, post offices, and libraries."[8] In this book I refer to Quarterman's Matrix as "the Net" and define it a little differently—I think of the Net as the global web of connected computer networks and conferencing systems whose largest component is the Internet—but in practice the two terms mean the same thing. In 1980, liberal estimates of the number of people online were in the hundreds of thousands. Now it's in the millions or even the tens of millions. Perhaps the soundest estimate is that of Vanderbilt marketing professor Donna Hoffman, who e-mailed me the Web address for her latest Net statistics in August 1996. Using the data from a number of separate studies, Hoffman and her coauthors "estimate that 28.8 million people in the United States 16 years and over have access to the Internet, 16.4 million people use the Internet, 11.5 million people use the Web, and 1.51 million people have used the Web to purchase something."[9] (Those figures have of course multiplied several times since 1996.) (I noted as I read her paper how much the Web has changed academic research methods since I was a graduate student in the 1980s. Rather than going to the library to find the paper or asking Hoffman to mail or fax me a copy, I simply pull it off the World Wide Web. Like many other academics these days, Hoffman and her coauthors normally opt to publish their work on the Web before it appears in the traditional "ink on dead trees" format of academic journals.)

Some estimates are significantly higher or lower, but most demographers agree that the movement of the general public to the Net is accelerating.[10] Still, of the people who've already taken steps toward integrating cyberspace into their daily lives, only a fraction have found a place in a virtual community. For many, freedom of speech on the Net means little more than access to e-mail, and it may be that only a few of these people actually spend much time online. Lots of folks simply acquire an e-mail address for its social value, just as many people in the postwar world saw value in owning a house. "If a new car was a status symbol, a house was something else," Halberstam writes. "Owning a house came to be the embodiment of the new American dream."

But in cyberspace, the dream increasingly is not just owning a house; it's living in the right neighborhood. One of the reasons the WELL, which has only about ten thousand registered users, is such a tony address in cyberspace is that the perception of community is so strong. (The WELL is located physically in the San Francisco Bay Area, but a high percentage of its users live elsewhere in the United States. A smaller but still significant contingent lives in other countries.) A few WELL users argue that this perception is illusory, but these skeptics ignore the fact that the power of a shared hallucination lies in the fact that it's *shared*.[11] The "virtual community" perception derives directly from the WELL's commitment to individual freedom as a necessity for community building.

Howard Rheingold reports the following about the WELL's original design goals (the ellipses are Rheingold's):

Kevin Kelly had been editor of *Whole Earth Review* for several years when the WELL was founded. The Hackers' Conference had been his idea. Kelly recalled the original design goals that the WELL's founders had in mind when they opened for business in 1985.

The design goals were

1. That it be free. This was a goal, not a commitment. We knew it wouldn't be exactly free, but it should be as free (cheap) as we could make it. . . .

2. It should be profit making. . . . After much hard, low-paid work by [Matthew McClure and Cliff Figallo, the first two directors of the WELL], this is happening. The WELL is at least one of the few operating large systems going that has a future.

3. It would be an open-ended universe. . . .

4. It would be self-governing. . . .

5. It would be a self-designing experiment. . . . The early users were to design the system for later users. The usage of the system would co-evolve with the system as it was built. . . .

6. It would be a community, one that reflected the nature of *Whole Earth* publications. I think that worked out fine.
7. Business users would be its meat and potatoes. Wrong.[12]

But to really understand what makes places like the WELL different, you have to compare them to the experience of logging on to CompuServe or America Online for the first time—it's a bit like being dropped in the middle of Manhattan without a map or a guide and trying to find a place you want to live. You may grasp the pattern of the streets and avenues, and you may eventually find a simpatico neighborhood on the Upper West Side or in the Village or in SoHo, but it will take you a while to learn enough about the city to make intelligent decisions. And unless you're very lucky, you won't have much control over the building you live in, or over your neighborhood, for a long time, if ever. The same thing is true of large commercial conferencing systems and especially true of Usenet. It's no wonder that so many people try these systems for a while and then give up. This doesn't mean that Usenet or the larger commercial systems don't foster community as well; often they do. But for the most part those communities aren't *designed;* they're merely instances of good luck.

A community built around the principles of freedom of speech and individual autonomy, however, has to be planned. WELL's pervasive sense that this is a community freely constructed, shaped, and reshaped by its users has to be planned, and as Hiltz and Turoff's research showed more than two decades ago, that planning has to foster free communication, which feeds back into the design of the community.

I think this "planning for freedom" is why the WELL seems to have gotten disproportionate press for its size, why it's regarded as one of the "great good places" of cyberspace. True, there's a significant degree of attrition of new users, as with all other online conferencing systems, and the WELL has yet to come to terms with how it wants to handle growth. But the WELL does enough things right that I'm comfortable using it as a model for understanding the rules for planning virtual communities around free speech principles.

Working from this model, I've come up with a set of principles that provide a good starting point for building these communities. Some other folks in cyberspace seem to agree. After I published an earlier version of these rules in *Wired,* I was frequently asked for permission to republish them elsewhere online. I've changed them a bit since then, so here is the updated and improved version.

Ten Principles for Making Virtual Communities Work

1. *Use software that promotes good discussions.*   In the days before the WELL's one-time owner (Rockport Shoes founder Bruce Katz, who bought the WELL from the Point Foundation in the early 1990s) invested in the development of a Web-based interface for the system, WELL users made a habit of complaining about "PicoSpan," the system's text-based conferencing software. PicoSpan may seem like a dinosaur in today's world of GUIs ("graphic user interfaces"—typically software in which you point and click with a mouse), but in fact it remains rather advanced in comparison with the slicker interfaces you can find on other systems. PicoSpan still does several things right, often by using what software de-signers call "constrained choices." For example, no one can start a new topic merely by responding to an old posting, so discussions and topics tend not to fragment the way they do on Usenet and CompuServe and certain Web-based conferencing systems. Also, you can't respond to indi-vidual postings unless you either read everything that's been posted pre-viously in the topic or make a deliberate decision to skip those earlier postings. This tends to reduce the amount of redundancy and make threads of discussion more coherent.

2. *Don't impose a length limitation on postings.*   Some systems limit the length of postings to twenty-five lines. This doesn't matter much if what you're interested in is banter and short tidbits, but it puts a crimp in discussions of history or politics or literature. Sometimes issues require serious space in order to be discussed fully. Individuals should be able to post essays as well as one-liners.

3. *Front-load your system with talkative, diverse people.*   The WELL made a strategic decision early on to give free accounts or complimentary time to individuals and hosts who could be counted on to make interest-ing and provocative comments. In a way, the thing that made the WELL work is not that there are like-minded people, but that there are *different-*

minded ones—users who inspire conversations and, sometimes, controversy with the strength and heterodoxy of their views.[13]

4. *Let the users resolve their own disputes.* On the whole, WELL management has taken a hands-off position when it comes to users' interpersonal disputes and conflicts on the WELL. Experienced users don't turn to management to complain. They choose instead to hash out their differences in public. And the WELL has imposed few rules on public discourse: the result has been that the user population has developed or adopted its own norms about quoting each other and publishing e-mail that are enforced largely by social pressures.

5. *Provide institutional memory.* Some of the WELL's conferences have postings dating back to the founding of the system in the mid-1980s. New users can come online and read about things that happened on the WELL early on. It helps new users get a sense of the WELL as a community to read how users helped one another during the 1989 earthquake or the 1991 Oakland fire.

6. *Promote continuity by keeping old postings available.* Of the WELL's core users, a significant number were active in the early days of the system, and most have been on the system for years. What makes the WELL feel like a community is what makes any other place feel like a community: you "see" the same "faces," know the same personalities, and have ongoing relationships. At the same time, continuity of communities requires that new users and their contributions be made to feel welcome. Not everybody is a Welcome Wagon type, but it's important to have at least a few of that type on any system to build community.

7. *Be host to one or more interest groups.* The WELL is the cyberspace home of Deadheads—Grateful Dead fans regularly congregate on the WELL to share information and converse about their favorite band. Their participation provides important cash flow to keep the community operating, and it also provides diversity as Deadheads go "over the wall" and converse on non–Grateful Dead forums. Some commercial services, notably systems like CompuServe and America Online, have attempted to be host to such communities for most of their existence, but for systems that big, no single community is necessary for financial survival. This rule is meant less for commercial providers than for smaller start-up systems,

some of which may be nonprofits or even run by hobbyists. If you can be host to a stable but enthusiastic interest group, it can provide the backbone to your system, financially or otherwise.

8. *Respect children.* Like many other systems, the WELL has provided links to the KidLink networks for ten- to fifteen-year-old kids, but more important, it has a tradition of treating young people with respect in grown-up forums on the assumption that what they say is as worth reading as anyone else's contribution.

9. *Commit the system to maintaining public spaces for public communication and public events.* What gives communities a sense of connection is shared experience, and that inevitably means experiences shared by some large percentage of the membership—a public experience. The common assumption that communities define themselves by closing out others with divergent views is, I think, a distortion of what really happens. The vital communities, virtual or otherwise, are those that give new or potential members something to share with the veteran members from the moment they log on. That's why lively public discussion spaces remain important and why basing those public spaces on the principle of free speech is absolutely necessary.

10. *Most important: Confront the users with a crisis.* Okay, it's hard to stage-manage crises. But it seems to be the case that events like the censorship dispute surrounding the Communication Decency Act or the search and seizure of Steve Jackson's BBS crystallize users' sense of belonging to a place they care about.[14]

There are probably some other rules I haven't thought of, of course. But I think the ten I've listed here amount to a blueprint for successful cyberspace communities, and the systems I know that have a truly "communal" feel (the WELL, ECHO in New York City, several MOOs and BBSs, and a few little pockets of Usenet) abide by most of these rules.[15] All of these places manifest what I take to be one of the best indicators of a healthy virtual community: they remain *stable over time.* I'm reminded of Robert Frost's observation: "Home is the place where, when you have to go there / They have to take you in." The real virtual community is the digital place where, when you need to go there, its members will be there to take you in.

We should remember that Bill Levitt's Levittown community was only the first attempt at solving a population boom, and few consider it the most successful one in terms of building community. Subsequent developments, like George Mitchell's famous "The Woodlands," a planned community in Texas, recognized that housing was only part of the picture. Schools, police, and well-designed public spaces were all essential to create a place you want to be.

If all that cyberspace gives you is an e-mail address—a place to hang your virtual hat and chat about your hobbies—you've been cheated. What most of us will want in the future, I think, is a place where we're known and accepted on the basis of what Martin Luther King, Jr., called "the content of our character." But without planning, without a deliberate architectural vision about shaping virtual communities—and, most of all, without true freedom of speech—the incoming hordes of cyberspace inhabitants will continue to be alienated, isolated, without any sense of belonging. Virtually homeless.

Up Close and Personal: The Intimacy of ASCII

Making the case for community is not enough, of course.[16] Once we explain that the Net is not merely a hobby or a game (or, worse, an addiction), but instead an opportunity to meet a very real need—the desire for community—that still won't get us past the objections of some anti-Net skeptics. "Sure, your motivations are legitimate," they'll argue, "but what you're experiencing here *isn't real*. Mostly it's just *words on a screen*."

That skeptics think the phenomenon of "words on a screen" is something cool, distant, inhuman, and illusory shows me they have overlooked just how powerfully expressive, how utterly human, how intensely hot, that experience can be. To get a feel for that intensity, consider one of the most common experiences of the Net—being "flamed."

Imagine how it might be (or remember how it was): You're a newcomer to the Internet, but you've learned the basics. So here you are, floating along in cyberspace, dropping the occasional bon mot or learned exposition into Usenet discussions and jetstreaming e-mail through T3 backbones.[17] Suddenly you jump back from your monitor with adrenaline nausea and the irrational sense that your eyebrows have been singed. You've been flamed (typically defined as the posting of e-mail or public messages designed to insult or provoke).

Not to worry, your e-friends and e-mentors will assure you. Flaming is an occupational hazard of the Net. Mere text, they'll tell you, is too narrow a communications medium for human beings—it doesn't carry body language or emotional nuance—so misunderstandings are all too probable.

Sometimes they'll go even further. When the information superhighways are all built, they say, and we're able to transmit live, full-motion video to one another, we will enter a "Golden Age of Telepresence," and online misunderstandings will evaporate.

They're wrong. Wake up, online belletrists everywhere. The golden age is already here, and flames, far from signaling some crisis caused by too much freedom on the Net, are the proof that the golden age has arrived.[18] The problem is not that ASCII is too restricted a medium but rather that text is so powerful that it often reveals too much, creates too much intimacy! Flames are the result of the friction that comes of minds rubbing too closely together.

Think about it for a minute. If you're face-to-face with someone, you're exposed to countless things over which the other person may have had no conscious control—hair color, say, or facial expressions. But when you're reading someone's posted ASCII message, *everything you see is a product of that person's mind.* As science-fiction author Neal Stephenson has remarked, "There is something about the process of translating events into words that clarifies what is really going on and filters out the glamorous irrelevancies." The problem of flaming is not that we don't understand each other. It's that we understand each other all too well. We're mainlining each other's thoughts.

Before I became a lawyer, I was a graduate student of literature. And it's hard to read many of the classics of English literature without being overcome by the immense capability of language to express emotional states, complex ideas, sensory experience, and humor. In a way, text is almost telepathic in its power. Who needs *Star Trek* or *The X-Files*? If you really want to experience the thoughts of a spooky alien mind, try reading some Emily Dickinson or William Blake! You'll learn more about their strange souls in an hour's reading than you would in a week of videoconferencing.

So you can imagine what I thought when I first read long-time Usenetter Chuq Von Rospach's advice to new users about the "need" for smileys. "Without the voice inflections and body language of personal communications," Von Rospach wrote back in 1984, "it is easy for a remark meant to be funny to be misinterpreted. Subtle humor tends to get lost, so take steps to make sure that people realize you are trying to be funny. The Net has developed a symbol called the smiley face. It looks like ':-)' and points out sections of articles with humorous intent. No matter how broad the humor or satire, it is safer to remind people that you are being funny."

Safer? Tell it to S. J. Perelman! Or Maureen Dowd! Or Dave Barry, for heaven's sake! You don't see any of those folks using so-called smileys. In fact, sometimes smileys are used to obscure meaning rather than reveal it. Stephenson, whose award-winning science-fiction novel *Snow Crash* is based in part on the premise that the written word has an unusual sort of power, wrote a compelling essay for the *New Republic* a couple of years back about the use of smileys. When I asked him later how people had responded to the piece, Stephenson told me he'd observed a telling phenomenon: "After I wrote the smiley piece I started noticing that people would say something intentionally obnoxious and then tack a smiley on at the end. They weren't afraid of being misunderstood—they were afraid of being correctly understood." Just so.

But flames aren't the only proof of ASCII's uncanny power. Just talk to a couple that's ever fallen in love online. In, uh, *face-to-face mode* (one hesitates to coin a term like "real reality"), these two people might never have broken the ice. But online they revealed their deepest secrets to each other, and each discovered a kindred spirit. Even the often disappointing first meetings of would-be online lovers tell you something of the power of text. It's those face-to-face distractions (his weight problem, say, or her acne) that prevent the union of those who otherwise might be soulmates.

This problem of too much sensory bandwidth is not a new one. Listen to John Schwartz, a WELL user who writes on science and technology issues for the *New York Times:* "That's part of the reason that filmmakers like Woody Allen or Steven Spielberg shoot their movie in black and white. When you narrow the bandwidth, you focus the message." And Jerry Michalski, managing editor of the computer society–computer industry newsletter *Release 1.0*, tells of a child who had her own response to a researcher who asked a child which she liked better, TV or radio.[19] "Radio," she told the researcher. "'Cause the pictures are better."

Electronic Frontier Foundation cofounder John Perry Barlow came across a different take on this old problem when he saw a demonstration of a videoconferencing system. Feeling oddly disappointed by what he saw, Barlow asked the system's project director what was missing. The problem, said the director, a native of India, is that the system cannot transmit *prana*, that almost mystical sense of life force or presence that one wants in a true meeting of minds.

The problem, I submit, is that video is constantly reminding you that it *is* video. Sophisticated TV viewers have learned not to take video seriously and to appraise it more for production values than for content. We no longer expect TV to tell us the truth; we expect it to entertain us. (If you doubt me, check the TV ads in any election year.) So when we see bosses or coworkers on video, trying earnestly to work through a meeting agenda, we can't help thinking that, well, this show ought to be cancelled long before thirteen weeks.

The language of Shakespeare, in contrast, admits no impediment to the marriage of true minds. And the WELL is decidedly low-tech as far as user interfaces go. Almost all communications there are in plain ol' ASCII. Yet it's no accident that users of the WELL tend to think of themselves as a virtual community. Subjectively, at least, many of them feel more truly connected to one another than they do to their next-door neighbors. When I lost a major part of my household, including my library, in a moving fire, countless fellow WELLbeings pitched in and sent me replacement volumes. A few books were more valuable than the ones I'd lost. I'm inclined to think they did this because they had a sense that they *knew* me from my postings. I wasn't a stranger, but, rather, a familiar person who happened to be in trouble.

It's a measure of how efficient ASCII is that one has been able for years to punt text versions of whole novels—*Howards End*, for example, or *The Remains of the Day*—across the Net, and it's a rare novel that requires more than a standard floppy disk of storage. Yet it will be a long time before we can so easily ship around the movie versions of those books (which are often regarded as inferior to the texts).

Of course, not everyone who uses text online is a Forster or an Ishiguro. "It takes some time to learn how to use text properly," Stephenson says. "I'm still learning every day—but once you've got the hang of it you can create extremely complex webs of metaphors and allusions that deliver vast cognitive bandwidth over minimal informational bandwidth." Still, even the poorest writers manage to invest something of their souls in what they send out to the Net. It's not the kind of claim you can easily make about video.

So you can see why I'm somewhat skeptical about the wonders of the new broadband information highway that so many have begun reflexively to demand. As a practical matter, everyday folks prefer technologies like the camcorder, which allow you simply to point and shoot, to technologies like desktop publishing, which require serious work if you're going to be any good at them. When everyone can send a memo or love letter in full-motion video, why take the trouble to learn to write well?

On the other hand, the inevitable irrelevancies and distractions that video and sophisticated computer graphics will introduce into everyday communications may mean fewer flames and more online peace. By distracting Net users from the irritating presence of other minds, video will have a placating effect—a digital Valium. Then, perhaps, the world of ASCII communications will become a preserve for the edgy exchanges of tense text maniacs. Like me.

Culture Wars: How Good and Bad Memes Change the World

Even if society gains some understanding that the Net will be a central channel for public and private life and for freedom of speech, and even if there's a consensus that computer interactions are real, there will still be the temptation to call for increased government control over free speech on the Net (perhaps far greater than its control over newspapers, books, and public speech). Since the Net makes everyone who uses it potentially very powerful, don't we need the guiding hand of government to step in and ensure that we use our First Amendment rights wisely and well?

Keeping the Net largely free from government regulatory hands, at least when it comes to what we say to each other on the Net, may be the toughest sell in the long run, but I also think it's the most important. Remember how the WELL turned out to be a successful community by building from the individual up—that is, by bringing in the individual user as a full participant in the planning and design? I think that in the world of words we call the Net, the same individual can (and often must) play the same role on a larger scale. The individual citizen on the Net— *Netizen* is as good a word as any—can do little physical harm to others, to the world, or to himself or herself just by exercising First Amendment rights, but to say that is to make a weak defense of the First Amendment.[20] A stronger defense can be found in Justice Brandeis's principle that "the fitting remedy for evil counsels is good ones."

Say you've found your community in cyberspace and you want to be a good citizen—maybe even take an ecological interest in the health of your community and of the Net at large. But in a world that's composed largely of talk, what can you do that makes a difference? One answer is to be on the lookout for "evil counsels" and respond to them with "good ones."

I had a clue as to what might be an appropriate "good Netizenship role" back in 1990, when I set out to experiment with what might be called "memetic engineering"—the design and construction of informational "genes," a.k.a. "memes."

But what exactly is a meme? One way to think of it is as a "genetic" conception of how human ideas work. Douglas Hofstadter provides a good analogy for understanding the concept of the meme in his 1983 book, *Metamagical Themas:*

In 1976, evolutionary biologist Richard Dawkins published his book *The Selfish Gene,* whose last chapter develops this theme further. Dawkins' name for the unit of replication and selection in the ideosphere—the ideosphere's counterpart to the biosphere's gene—is meme, rhyming with "theme" or "scheme." As a library is an organized collection of books, so a memory is an organized collection of memes. And the soup in which memes grow and flourish—the analogue to the "primordial soup" out of which life first oozed—is the soup of human culture.

In short, you can understand meme as an infectious (or otherwise self-reproducing) idea that propagates from mind to mind, much as a gene transmits itself from an animal to its offspring. But with a neologism as new and slippery as *meme,* sometimes a single definition isn't good enough. So here are some more examples from Dawkins himself:

Examples of memes are tunes, ideas, catch-phrases, clothes fashions, ways of making pots or of building arches. Just as genes propagate themselves in the gene pool by leaping from body to body via sperms or eggs, so memes propagate themselves in the meme pool by leaping from brain to brain via a process which in the broad sense, can be called imitation. If a scientist hears, or reads about, a good idea, he passes it on to his colleagues and students.

As for the second term, *memetics,* Keith Henson helpfully writes that memetics is a field that "takes the age-old saying 'ideas have a life of their own' literally, and applies models from biology to the evolution, spread, and persistence of ideas (memes) in human culture." Just as a body is built on a substrate of genes, a mind is built on a substrate of memes— ideas that provide structure, points of reference, fulcrums of thought.[21]

Back in 1990, I decided that what might be called "the Nazi-comparison meme" had gotten out of hand. In countless Usenet newsgroups, many conferences on the WELL, and on every BBS that I frequented, the labeling of some poster or his ideas as "similar to the Nazis" or "Hitler-like" was a recurrent and often predictable event. It was the kind of thing that made you wonder how debates had ever occurred before World War II, when speakers lacked that handy rhetorical hammer.

Of course, not everyone saw the inevitable comparison to Nazis as a "meme"—most people on the Net, as elsewhere, had never heard of memes or memetics. But now that we're living in an increasingly information-aware culture, it's time for that to change. And it's time for Net dwellers to make a conscious effort to control the kinds of memes they create or circulate.

Memes are not anchored to the minds they reside in. An infectious idea (call it a "viral meme") may leap from mind to mind, much as viruses leap from body to body. Like viruses, which may become a permanent part of a host's genetic structure, a viral meme may become part of a person's (or a culture's) value system or worldview.

Sometimes a viral meme is a word or phrase. In the early summer of 1994, when I was living in Washington, D.C., the big memetic phrase on Capitol Hill was "big hat, no cattle"—denoting some policymaker who talks the talk but can't deliver. The memes that Al Gore is a prevaricator, or that George W. Bush is unintelligent, were so virulent in the 2000 presidential campaign that the several articles countering each proposition could get no traction at all in the general press coverage.

When a scientific meme catches on, it may crystallize whole schools of thought. Take the "black hole" meme, for instance. The term *black hole* has been defined as a "region in space-time from which nothing can escape because gravity is too strong. Even light travels too slowly to escape; hence the region does not emit any radiation and appears black."[22] Physicist Brandon Carter has commented, "Things changed dramatically when John Wheeler invented the term [black hole]. This wasn't the first attempt; other terms had been used, but they hadn't caught on. The magic is when something does catch on. Everybody adopted it, and from then on, people around the world, in Moscow, in America, in England, and elsewhere, could know they were speaking about the same thing. And not only that: suddenly the whole range of concepts got through to the general public—even science fiction writers could talk about it."[23] Once the "black hole" meme became commonplace, it became a handy source of metaphors for everything from illiteracy to the deficit.

By 1990, I had noticed, something similar had happened to the Nazi comparison meme. Sure, there were obvious topics in which the comparison recurred. In discussions about guns and the Second Amendment, for example, gun control advocates were always reminded that Hitler banned personal weapons.[24] Birth control debates were invariably marked by some pro-lifer's insistence that abortionists are engaging in mass murder, worse than that of Nazi death camps. And in any newsgroup in which censorship was discussed, someone inevitably raised the specter of Nazi book burning.

But the Nazi-comparison meme popped up elsewhere as well—in general discussions of law in misc.legal, for example, or in the EFF conference on the WELL.[25] A certain subset of libertarians were ready to label any government regulation as incipient nazism. Invariably, I felt, the comparisons trivialized the horror of the Holocaust and the social pathology of the Nazis. It was a trivialization I found both illogical (presidential candidate Michael Dukakis a Nazi? Please!) and offensive—not just to Holocaust survivors and their families, but to any decent human being who had ever reflected on the magnitude of that crime. Sometimes I'd even get angry. Surely the millions of concentration camp victims did not die to give some Internet blowhard a handy trope!

So I set out to conduct an experiment: to build a countermeme designed to make discussion participants see how they were (and are) acting as vectors to a particularly silly and offensive meme and perhaps to curtail the glib Nazi comparisons. I engineered my meme to sound like a scientific principle and gave it my own name so I could trace it whenever it turned up. Here it is in its original form:

Godwin's Law of Nazi Analogies: As an online discussion grows longer, the probability of a comparison involving Nazis or Hitler approaches one.

Once I'd come up with something that sounded appropriately authoritative, I seeded Godwin's law in any newsgroup or topic where I saw a gratuitous Nazi reference. Soon, to my surprise, *other* people were citing it—the countermeme was reproducing on its own! Then it propagated like the informational virus I'd hoped it would be, generating corollaries like the following:

Gordon's Restatement of Newman's Corollary to Godwin's Law: Libertarianism (pro, con, and internal faction fights) is *the* primordial Net news discussion topic. Anytime the debate shifts somewhere else, it must eventually return to this fuel source.

Morgan's Corollary to Godwin's Law: As soon as such a comparison occurs, someone will start a Nazi-discussion spinoff thread on alt.censorship.

Sircar's Corollary: If the Usenet discussion touches on homosexuality or Heinlein, Nazis or Hitler are mentioned within three days.

Van der Leun's Corollary: As global connectivity improves, the probability of actual Nazis being on the Net approaches one.

Miller's Paradox: As a network evolves, the number of Nazi comparisons not forestalled by citation to Godwin's law converges to zero.

In time, I noticed, discussions in the seeded newsgroups seemed to show a lower incidence of the Nazi-comparison meme. And the counter-meme mutated into even more useful forms. (As Cliff Stoll once asked me: "Godwin's law? Isn't that the law that states that once a discussion reaches a comparison to Nazis or Hitler, its usefulness is over?") By my standard, the experiment in countermemes turned out to be a success.

However, its success had given me much to reflect on. If it's possible to generate effective memes and countermemes, is there any moral imperative to do so? When we see a bad or false meme go by, should we take pains to chase it with a countermeme? Do we have an obligation to improve our informational environment? Our social environment? (Improving our social environment seems to be the function of the Anne Herbert meme, now ubiquitous: "Practice random kindness and senseless acts of beauty.")

Although human memes are at least as old as language, mass media give infectious memes a far greater reach. Keith Henson, writer for the *Whole Earth Review,* points out that the spread of Nazism seems in retrospect to have been grounded in the power of Hitler's radio broadcasts. (Leni Riefenstahl's film *Triumph of the Will* didn't hurt either.) And the truly groundbreaking aspect of global computer communications networks is that they put the power of mass media in everyone's hands. You don't have to be AOL Time Warner or Gannett (the nation's largest newspaper publisher) to reach a mass audience.

But this immense power to do good may also be an immense power to do ill. Anyone on the Internet has the power to affect stock prices (or worse—a fraudulent re-creation of the Tylenol poisoning scare could cause a national or international panic). And truly destructive viral meme epidemics—racism and sexism are two examples—are capable of doing social damage that takes lifetimes to correct.

On the other hand, the continually increasing connectedness of everyone may ultimately blunt the effect of dangerous memes. In his *Whole Earth Review* article on memetics, Keith Henson argues that destructive cultural memes often depend on self-isolation: "In the case of the Soviet Union, the communist meme survives in a society largely isolated from the rest of the world."[26] Two years later, the USSR as we'd known it was dead. I can't help thinking that regardless of whatever other theories one might offer for this empire's implosion, the real cause was the increasing connectedness generated by global communications networks—not just computer networks, but telephone and fax, broadcasting, and satellite networks together with traditional mass media, such as the printing press and films. Economic forces are important, of course, but I think it was the USSR's increasing exposure to the outside world that ultimately caused its downfall.

Just as global mass media may prevent the isolation of a culture, they may also prevent the isolation of individuals, especially when they're most vulnerable to infection. Once you're on the Net, it's harder to remain isolated, stewing in your bad memes. The Net is filled with diverse critical thinkers who are ready to challenge your self-indulgent or self-aggrandizing memes.

Even so, we can't rely on the Net culture's diversity and inertia to answer every bad meme. The Nazi comparison meme has a peculiar resilience, in part because of its sheer inflammatory power ("You're calling me a Nazi? *You're* the Nazi in this discussion!"). The best way to fight such memes is to craft countermemes designed to put them in perspective. I'd like to think the experiment with Godwin's law is one example.

Keith Henson sees a moral dimension to meme consciousness: "If this article has succeeded in infecting you with the meme-about-memes," he writes, "perhaps it will help you be more responsible about the memes you spread and less likely to be infected with a meme that will harm you or those around you."[27]

Perhaps we needn't be so passive. The time has come, I think, for good Netizens and committed First Amendment supporters to commit ourselves to memetic engineering: crafting good memes that improve society as well as "anti-viral" countermemes that may neutralize and even eliminate the bad memes floating around out there on the Net and in society at large. (In a sense, a good meme is no more than a good idea, but it often helps you keep focused on your memetic engineering to visualize the dissemination of good memes into our informational environment.)

Here are a few of the viral memes I hoped to make some headway against in 1996. Each one is followed by some of the countermemes I've been working on. (As you can tell, some of my countermemes are still under construction.)

Bad meme 1: "The need to protect children is opposed to the need to protect freedom of speech."

A possible countermeme: "Protect your child by supporting free speech." Children are actually better protected in pro–free speech societies. It's easier in such societies to talk without shame about the bad acts committed against children by adults. And children who grow up in free speech societies are less likely to be disturbed by so-called offensive speech. Their society has taught them that learning to deal with the offensive speech of others is part of what becoming an adult is about.

Bad meme 2: "Bomb-making information on the Internet is an increasing threat in the United States and around the world."

Countermemes: "In cyberspace, no one can blow you up." "You can't download a dynamite stick." The idea is to underscore the fact that in the intangible world, there is no such thing as a fatal explosion. What it takes to cause physical harm is real people doing real crimes in nonvirtual space.

Bad meme 3: "Child pornographers and child predators lurk online, looking for children to victimize."

Countermeme: "The safest place is cyberspace." It's impossible for a child predator to reach through your monitor and grab your child. And it's possible to prevent any unwilling child from being exposed to sexually oriented materials online.

Bad meme 4: "Broadcast media, and particularly TV, are inherently harmful, and the Net is a lot like TV."

Countermeme: "In the digital world, you're the chief programmer." Television and radio are seen as problems because the programming decisions are made by corporations whose executives may not have any sense of accountability to the viewing or listening public. On the Net, in contrast, the "programming" you're most likely to encounter is the kind you make a deliberate choice to see. Or create.

But I'm not just building countermemes—I have a few positive memes of my own that I've already committed myself to spreading:

• The meme of virtual communities

• The meme that communities depend on individual First Amendment rights in order to function

• The meme that the Net is arguably the safest of all mass media

• The meme that freedom of speech resides in the individual and not in the medium he or she happens to choose

• The meme that individuals can use the Net to level the playing field against government and big media

• The meme that the First Amendment was crafted to protect unpopular speech, because nobody ever tries to ban the pleasant or undisturbing kind

One of the ways I'm trying to spread these memes, of course, is by writing this book. But you may be immune to my attempts to infect you with the First Amendment memes. You may decide that you have no duty to preserve and promote the health of the memetic ecology we're all destined to become a part of. You may have pessimistically convinced yourself that *plus ça change, plus c'est la* **meme** *chose.* But you have no excuse for being so discouraged. One of the great things about combining freedom of speech and the power of the Net is that everyone has the potential to make the world a better place through ideas alone. Although I don't insist that everyone adopt the same priorities I have, the moral imperatives to generate good memes and fight bad ones are pretty compelling. For me, at least, there is no higher or better way to exercise one's First Amendment rights.

Plus, doing so can be a hell of a lot of fun.

A Primer on Talking to the Traditional Press

Most lawyers will tell you that it's not a good idea to talk to the media when you've got a legal problem. But if you know what you're doing, sometimes talking to the press can be a powerful way to get the leverage needed to solve your problem. This is certainly true with the Steve Jackson Games case, an incident that not only helped put the EFF on the map but also reshaped the way the American law enforcement community handles computer searches and seizures.

It's now more than a decade since Steve Jackson and his Austin, Texas–based role-playing games company were raided by the U.S. Secret Service. Because Jackson was both a traditional publisher and BBS operator, the federal raid (which was motivated by an alleged threat to the nation's emergency 911 system) raised important First Amendment as well as Fourth Amendment questions. For me, it also raised a practical question: What can one person do to get the facts about government misconduct into the local and national news?

I was lucky enough to be the right guy in the right place at the right time to answer that question. I was a law student who knew computers and science fiction and who had had a long (although somewhat bumpy) association with Jackson in the Austin BBS community over the years. More important, I'd worked as a journalist and had even taken a year off from law school to edit my university's student newspaper, the *Daily Texan*. When it came to correcting the injustice done to Jackson and his company, I had a few ideas.

Enter Usenet

Some history: In the middle of my last year of law school (1989–1990), I was getting bored with the local BBS scene in Austin. I decided to get an account on a University of Texas system and participate in the huge, distributed, free-floating conference system called Usenet. (These were the days before the World Wide Web had become a household term— synonymous, in some people's minds, with the Internet itself.)

By sheer chance, this decision came at a time when the Net was particularly hungry for information about hackers and the law. Usenet was still abuzz with discussion about Robert Morris's Internet Worm, and there was a lot of talk about the so-called Legion of Doom search and seizures, which focused on three alleged hackers in Atlanta. As a third-year law student preparing to become a Texas prosecutor, I had plenty of answers to the legal questions that flooded Usenet newsgroups like misc.legal and comp.dcom.telecom.

As I continued to answer questions, I found myself talking from time to time about the "hacker cases" that were being reported on Usenet and in the news media. What I kept seeing were cases in which law enforcement agents and prosecutors were making obvious misinterpretations and mistakes and damaging people's rights in the process. The Legion of Doom hackers, for example, were accused of stealing the source code for the emergency 911 system from a BellSouth computer. Yet to anyone with even a rudimentary knowledge of what a computer program looks like, the emergency 911 "source code" was nothing more than a bureaucratic memorandum of some sort, with a list of definitions and acronyms thrown in.

My growing interest in these hacker prosecutions influenced my postings on Usenet. Whereas before I'd limited myself to fairly dry and academic expositions in answer to abstract legal questions, I found myself getting emotional about some of these cases. The more I learned about how the seizures and prosecutions were hurting individuals and chilling free discussion on the Net (I even lost an account when a system administrator ended public access to his system to minimize the risk of having it seized), the more I found myself arguing with those whose understandable anger at computer intruders led them to justify, uncritically, any and all overreaching by law enforcement.

Then the war on hackers struck closer to home. On March 1, 1990, Illuminati, an Austin BBS run by the nationally known role-playing-game publisher Steve Jackson Games, was seized by the U.S. Secret Service. Although neither Jackson nor his company turned out to be the targets of the Secret Service's criminal investigation, Jackson was told that the manual for a role-playing game his firm was about to publish (called GURPS Cyberpunk and stored on the hard disk of the company's BBS computer) was a "handbook for computer crime."

The seizure shocked Austin's BBS community and threatened to put Jackson, an innocent third party who himself was never charged or even suspected of wrongdoing, out of business. The sheer magnitude of the effect on Jackson and his business outraged the members of an Austin BBS called Flight, which numbered Jackson and me among its users.

Sound of Silence

Even more disturbing was the failure of the media to pick up on the injustice that had occurred. One Flight user asserted that this was because the mainstream press had no interest in BBSs, which publishers saw as potential competition. My own journalistic experience, however, told me this theory was crazy. I started arguing on Flight that the media hadn't covered the story because they didn't know about it, or at least didn't understand the issues.

Then a startling question hit me: Why am I sitting at my terminal talking about reaching the media, when what I should be doing is making sure the story gets publicized? With a certain aggressive singlemindedness, I set out to see that the story of the Steve Jackson Games raid and the other cases did get reported in the mainstream press. I gathered together several postings from local BBSs and from Usenet and drove down to the *Austin American-Statesman* office to talk to Kyle Pope, a reporter I'd been referred to by a friend who worked on the newspaper's copy desk. I took along photocopies of the statutes that give the Secret Service jurisdiction over computer crime and lots of phone numbers of potential sources. At the same time, I modemed materials to John Schwartz, a friend and former colleague at our college's newspaper, who was then a writer at *Newsweek*.

The story made the front page of the *American-Statesman* the following weekend. And John Schwartz's story, which covered the Steve Jackson Games incident, as well as the Secret Service's involvement in a nationwide computer crime "dragnet," appeared in *Newsweek*'s April 30, 1990, issue. When the second story appeared, I realized that (in a much smaller way, of course) I'd managed to do to the media what the Legion of Doom was rumored to have done to the 911 system: I'd hacked it.

Fortune Smiles

More important, I'd proved that anyone who knew enough about how traditional news media worked could be effective in getting a story out, especially a killer story like the Steve Jackson Games seizure. It seemed important to share that media-hacking knowledge, so I posted "Talking to Media" to the Flight BBS under "Johnny Mnemonic," my science-fiction-inspired "handle" on Flight:

Talking to Media
3/18/90
As I've promised on another message base, here's the beginning of discussion of how to bring stories to the media. Since I keep thinking of different things people ought to know about how to take a story to the media, I'm going to make this a multipost discussion.

 1) Try to think like the reporter you're talking to. One of the things that happens when people know about an event that may make a good news story is that they assume the importance of the story will be obvious to anyone. Sometimes this is true (when the tipster knows about a murder, for example). Often it's not.

So, when I tell a reporter about a story I think he or she should cover, I make sure to stress the aspects of the story that are likely to interest that reporter and/ or the readers of the publication.

For example, when I spoke to Kyle Pope about the Illuminati seizure, I stressed the following:

a) Steve Jackson Games is an Austin business that may end up being damaged by the seizure.

b) Nobody has given this story anything like major coverage in the national media, or (so far as I knew) in other geographic areas. (I was telling him he had a major "scoop" opportunity.)

c) There are some very dramatic aspects to this story. (I told him about the 20-year-old LoD member who woke up on the morning of March 1 with a gun pointed at him by a Secret Service agent.)

2) If you're going to meet the reporter in person, try to bring something on paper. There are lots of good reasons for this rule:

a) Believe it or not, people take stuff on paper more seriously than the spoken word. It's nice to give the reporter something that lends substance to what you're saying, even if the substance is a printout from your own computer.

b) It makes life easier for the reporter, who doesn't have to write down everything you tell her. Reporters like to have materials they can use for reference as they research and write their stories.

c) It helps you remember to say everything you want to say. Nothing is more frustrating than trying to get a reporter interested in your story, getting inconclusive results, and then realizing later that you neglected to tell the reporter about something important (e.g., "Damn! I forgot to tell him what 'cyberpunk' means, now he won't know how the federal agents misinterpreted the manual").

When I went to the *Statesman*, I took edited printouts of discussions from Flight, from SMOF (another Austin BBS), and from comp.dcom.telecom on Usenet. I also took some private e-mail I had received (with the names of the senders deleted). And I took my copy of the *Whole Earth Review* with the article on Usenet. My object was to convey to him the scale of concern about the seizures and give him enough background to be able to ask reasonably informed questions of the people he talked to.

3) If possible, give the reporter other people to talk to. There are two main justifications for this rule: First, it helps your credibility (especially if you don't already know the reporter personally). Second, multiple sources or witnesses usually enable the reporter to filter out what is mere opinion or speculation from what everybody knows for a fact.

4) Don't assume the reporter will cover the story the way you'd like him or her to. Reporters' accuracy and focus in a story are constrained by several factors:

a) The amount of available time. Reporters have to be quick studies and often have to assimilate a complex story in a hurry. This necessarily increases the risk of inaccuracy in a story, and gives you an even greater reason to follow Rules 1 through 3.

b) The reporters' obligation to be fair. This means they have to talk to people on the other side of the issues from you. This in turn means you're unlikely to get a story that represents or promotes your point of view at the expense of those who oppose you.

Once the Jackson case was in the public eye, it became a cause célèbre. Mitchell Kapor, the founder of Lotus Development Corp., and John Perry Barlow, a journalist and Grateful Dead lyricist, took the case as a sign of the need to start an organization that would defend and promote civil liberties in cyberspace. That organization would become known as the Electronic Frontier Foundation, and one of its first efforts was the initiation and support of *Steve Jackson Games Inc. v. The United States Secret Service.*

EFF's financial and legal support got the case off the ground. We won the lawsuit in 1993, and its influence has been significant: law enforcement personnel at the state and federal levels now take greater pains to respect the First Amendment rights of "searchees" (who, like Jackson, may not themselves be suspected of any crime). The case is cited in *Searching and Seizing Computers,* a federal guidelines sourcebook published by the U.S. Department of Justice.

This demonstrates, I think, how big an effect can spring from a small cause. At the time, all I thought I was doing was proving to the members of an Austin BBS that it was possible for a knowledgeable individual to ensure media coverage of an important story. As it turned out, I'd helped set in motion a sequence of events that resulted in the Secret Service's being called to account for its breach of Jackson's rights. (I'd also contributed, unknowingly, to the formation of the EFF, which a few months later hired me as its first employee. But that was just dumb luck.)

Afterthoughts
What I could have added to that posting, even then, were three more rules I regarded as both pragmatically and ethically required of anyone who deals with the media—either traditional media or the new computer network variety:

Don't try to spin the story. Most people who attempt to shape how a story is told by the press end up shooting themselves in the foot. Efforts on the part of sources to be spinmeisters are obvious to most reporters, who encounter such attempts every day. (They're increasingly obvious to ordinary readers and listeners too.) Furthermore, the fact that you're trying to spin the story undercuts your credibility. Just tell the truth as you see it, as fairly as possible. (Your own biases will emerge in any case, but it won't seem to the reporter that you're actively trying to be manipulative.)

Don't hide the ball. This means you shouldn't withhold information from the reporter in the hope of shaping the story through a selective presentation of the facts. Tell the whole truth, even if there are parts of it that don't help your cause. What you lose in shaping the story of the day you gain in long-term credibility with the press. And there will come a day when you'll need that credibility.

Never lie. Sometimes the facts of a story are sufficiently damaging to your side that you wish the reporter would just go away, and nothing true you can say will make your side appear any better. In that event, don't ever yield to the temptation to say something you don't believe is true. Outside of the fact that this is just plain unethical, it also has immense potential to do you and your cause permanent damage. If you can't tell the press the truth, then shut up. Reporters respect a refusal to comment; they'll never respect anyone who has lied to them.

None of these rules is medium specific; they're good to follow whether or not you have access to the Net or any other mass medium. With so many people getting Net access today, the potential for stories to gain coverage is greater than ever. In the short term, this means learning how to use the Internet to increase coverage in the traditional media. In the long term, it may mean using the Internet in place of traditional media. In any case, the fact that more of us are able to reach larger audiences means we have no excuse not to be media savvy. Learn how to hack *all* the media. Then put that knowledge to good use.

3

The Net Backlash: Fear of Freedom

Fear and Loathing: An Activist Attacks the Net

Like all the best epiphanies, this one took me at a moment of relative calm. There I was, munching quiche in an Austin restaurant with a clutch of EFF-Austin members, listening to a dinner speech, when it hit me: the Internet free speech backlash had arrived! Although I'd been anticipating this backlash for a while, it was turning out to be far more fear driven and intolerant—and far more pervasive—than I could have guessed.

I was listening to Gary Chapman, who directs something called the 21st Century Project at the University of Texas at Austin. Like Chapman, I was set to speak the following day at the John Henry Faulk First Amendment Conference on the UT campus. And like Chapman, I'd been invited to an informal dinner gathering of EFF-Austin members in order to give a preview of the conference events. (Despite its name, EFF-Austin has no formal connection with the Electronic Frontier Foundation.)

There was only one problem: I had no idea what I was going to talk about. But Chapman, who's a good speaker, turned out to be a remarkable source of inspiration. By the time he was finished, I was certain about what I needed to say.

Chapman began by joking that his two recent *New Republic* articles, which criticized *Wired* magazine and Internet culture, respectively, had established him as the "anti-Christ of the Internet." It was clear that Chapman took a grim pride in his iconoclasm. But as he continued, his pride gave way to what I could take only to be a sort of fear and loathing of the Net. If the Internet is such a tool of democracy, Chapman wondered, why isn't it being used to organize activist projects?[1] If "the digerati" are so forward looking, why aren't they devoting energy to solving social problems? Instead, Chapman complained, Net folks too often choose to exercise their vaunted freedom of speech by focusing on "trivia and sleaze." This is troubling, he said, because the purpose of freedom of speech is to inspire and promote social and political progress—to "stimulate collective action." For Chapman, "effective, potent free speech"—the kind that leads to progressive political results in the physical world—is morally superior to the anarchic, selfish free speech of the Net, which is "palpably disengaged" from the crises facing our nation.

I was stunned to hear these Bork-like takes on the First Amendment coming from the mouth of someone who'd paid his dues as a civil libertarian. (Chapman had served as executive director of Computer Professionals for Social Responsibility for six years and was a founding organizer of the Computers, Freedom, and Privacy conferences.) I'd always thought "trivia and sleaze" were among the best reasons to have a First Amendment. Surely the framers of the Constitution hadn't intended that we pay for our liberty by being earnest and constructive *all the time*. Surely we're entitled to this freedom for our own enjoyment as well as for the benefits it may or may not provide for society as a whole.

In one sense, of course, I agreed with Chapman. I share his belief that one can make value judgments about speech, and I've done so many times myself. But the notion that speech has as narrow a purpose as Chapman ascribes to it and that frivolous speech is somehow contemptible struck me as the kind of attitude that takes a lot of the joy out of being human.

As I listened, the speech got more troubling. Chapman told the story of how one student had labored on the Internet to organize protests against the then-current Republicans' Contract with America, with little result. The lesson to be drawn from this failure, he said, is that the Internet is inadequate as a political tool.

It was an odd conclusion for Chapman to jump to. After all, there are lots of other reasonable explanations for the protester's failure. Maybe the student was a poor organizer. Maybe his message wasn't clear or powerful enough. Maybe he broadcast his appeal during midterms or over Christmas break. Or (much as it pains a yellow-dog Democrat like me to consider it) perhaps the country was a bit more conservative than either Chapman or the would-be protester thought. Yet for Chapman, the obvious culprit was the Internet itself.

That's when it hit me: Chapman of all people had fallen victim to the same fierce strain of reflexive technophobia that's responsible for the current hydra-headed social impulse to clamp down hard on the Internet. Behind Chapman's eagerness to condemn the tool, I detected the panicky thread that underlies virtually every new call for regulation or control of the Net. It's what I call "Net backlash"—dismissive contempt for Net culture in all its frivolity, diversity, and perversity, that is, the fear of freedom.

The Politicians, the Press, and the Backlash

It has been a trendy sentiment over the last few years. We saw it in Senator Jim Exon's vision of the Net as a glorified means of making obscene phone calls. We saw it in presidential candidate Arlen Specter's opportunistic Senate hearing in mid-1995 entitled "The Availability of Bomb-Making Information on the Internet." During that hearing, the nominally liberal Senator Dianne Feinstein (my own senator!) expressed her readiness to shut up anyone who *sounds* too much like a terrorist.[2] We saw it in the prosecution of University of Michigan student Jake Baker, whose twisted little sex fantasies about a fellow student would never have gotten the attention of a U.S. attorney had they been written in ink rather than in electrons. (You'll read more about Baker in chapter 5.)

Most important, we continue to see it in news reports from the traditional media, which, given their social role as educators and skeptics, ought to know better than to slip into this phobic frenzy about the imagined Net threat. I first became aware of this larger phenomenon in the wake of the bombing of a federal office building in Oklahoma City. In the days and weeks to follow, I got dozens of calls from the press asking me whether there was legislation pending to ban bomb information on the Net. "No," I'd say. "Have you heard of such legislation?" No, they'd reply, but they were *certain* somebody, somewhere, was drafting it even as we spoke.

It's been interesting to speculate why these journalists were calling me with the idea that there had to be a link between "dangerous information on the Net" and the Oklahoma City bombing.

I have a theory, and it goes something like this. The reporters knew that the chief suspect was a fellow named Timothy McVeigh. And they knew that McVeigh might be associated with militia groups. And they knew that some militia groups used bulletin board systems to communicate. And they knew that bulletin board systems were somehow similar to Internet. And they knew that this kind of information could be found on the Internet. In short, they had all they needed to "know" that there was a connection between bomb-making information on the Internet and the Oklahoma City bombing. It's interesting to observe these little memes about the connection between the Net and bomb-making information as they propagate themselves throughout the media.

(As far as we know, by the way, there is no significant connection between McVeigh and computer technology or between that technology and the bombing. Fairness, however, compels me to note what may be an exception to this generalization: According to some reports, McVeigh said he believe that during his service in the Gulf War, he had some kind of computer chip implanted in a sensitive part of his anatomy—the part he sits on.)

In reality, of course, the "Internet as threat" meme was generated and disseminated primarily by the press itself, and it was as a *response* to the media-hyped Net threat meme that Senator Specter held his hearing. Although it led to no significant legislative proposal that year, it continues to fuel debate about this issue in Congress and in the media. In short, the hearing reinforces the associational link between bomb making and the Net.

Now, I don't think the reporters were acting as conscious anti-Net conspirators. Individually, they were just trying to sniff out new angles or were writing on assignment. Regardless of their motives, in the wake of the Oklahoma City bombing, they collectively spread the meme that "dangerous information on the Net" is somehow connected to terrorist bombings—in spite of the fact that there seems to be no connection between that horrific event in Oklahoma City and anything on the Net.

Something about the computer revolution seems to have triggered deep-seated fears in the government, in the media, and perhaps in the public at large. These fears are simultaneously subtle enough that most people are unaware of them, yet pervasive and powerful enough to shape how nearly everyone in the news industry discusses the Net.

Even now I get questions from reporters about how troubling it is that someone can log on to the Net, then hunt around and find instructions about building a bomb—perhaps even a fertilizer bomb of the sort that blew up a federal office building in Oklahoma City. Yet we never seem to hear an equally important fact: that information of this sort has been available in public libraries for decades, yet society seems to have survived its availability.

Some reporters may argue at this point that the problem with the Net is not that it makes the information available, but that it makes it so much easier to access. I then point out that they've hypothesized some class of terrorist who is too lazy to take a bus to the library yet is industrious enough to learn how to build a fertilizer bomb, then build it, then place it, then plan a getaway. I can't help thinking that this sort of terrorist knows how to use a library.

When a bomb exploded near the site of the 1996 Olympic Games in Atlanta, this tendency to link a bomb attack to the Internet resurfaced. To my amazement, a TV station in my own neck of the woods, the San Francisco Bay Area, included this in its next-day follow-up segment about the Atlanta bombing: a clip of a guy looking up bomb-making information on the Internet. *This was on the first day after the bombing, when authorities hadn't even identified a suspect, much less any connection between the explosion and the Net!* And the people who produced that show are supposedly *professionals*—much better at sifting truth from falsehood and rumor than us amateurs.

Both broadcast and print journalists routinely reinforce this link in the public mind between bombs and the Internet, but when you ask them why they're doing so, they often can't explain it. And those who do attempt to explain themselves rarely communicate more than the vague sense that if this information is available on the Internet, it's vastly more dangerous to society than if it's available in a library.

Not that all journalists have adopted the Net threat hypothesis. The *Washington Post*, for example, hasn't lost its ability to think clearly about this issue. The paper's handling of a similar controversy is instructive. When the *Post* did its own follow-up stories on the Oklahoma City bombing, the editors decided to include an explanation of how the bomb was built. When it published this information, many readers wrote to the *Post* and said, "You shouldn't have published that stuff. People will get ideas! They will use that information to build bombs!" But the *Post*'s editors had concluded (correctly, I think) that the people reading the *Washington Post* were not the ones building bombs—and that the people who *were* building bombs already knew how to do it without any help from the *Washington Post*.

We could spend days arguing over the sources of current ambivalence about the Net among politicians, activists like Gary Chapman, or the general public. But I think a discussion of the traditional news media's ambivalence toward this new medium would be shorter, and perhaps more helpful, since the professional journalists seem to be the primary culprits in spreading the Net backlash memes, which range from "bomb-making information on the Net" to "the hacker threat" to "the 'pervasive' flood of cyberporn." I think the reason for this obsessive, fearful response to the Internet is that professionals who are used to having a lock on mass media are nervous about all these amateurs who now can reach mass audiences on the Internet. Suddenly everyone is in the mass media game!

For many journalists, however, "freedom of the press" is a privilege that can't be trusted with just anybody. Yet the Net does just that. At least potentially, *anybody* can say *anything,* and it's just about impossible to shut them all up. In my imagination, which has been shaped in large part by a childhood of reading comic books, I keep seeing a stereotypical newspaper editor—Perry White or J. Jonah Jameson, say—sitting in an office somewhere and asserting, sagely or gruffly, *This damned Internet thing is out of control!* After this compelling judgment from the editor, Clark Kent (or is it Peter Parker?) nods silently, then dashes out of the office to pursue the Net scare story of the week.

Conquering the Fear

Back in Austin in the spring of 1995, however, much of the backlash had yet to materialize. Still, I took Chapman's speech as a sign that it was coming. So when I had my own chance to speak at the EFF-Austin dinner and later at the Faulk conference, I decided to spell out a vision of freedom of speech rather different from the constricted versions embraced by Chapman or Senator Feinstein on the left and by Specter and the Christian Coalition on the right.

What I told my friends in Austin is something I've been telling other audiences ever since. I told them I couldn't buy this etiolated notion of a freedom of speech that privileges political speech over what Chapman was ready to dismiss as "trivia and sleaze." (Hell, Chapman's notion doesn't even allow that posting a sonnet might be worthwhile!) I also told them that I can't believe that anyone who's appalled by the range of opinion, temperament, and discourse on the Net has any gut-level understanding of what freedom of speech is all about. It means, for heaven's sake, that you can "fuck around on the Net"—and that you can use that very phrase on the Net to describe your frivolous, nonproductive activity. Free speech on the Net has to mean that we can say worthless things, have goofy opinions, and show our ire. Otherwise it means nothing at all.

Sure, real democracy—and the democracy that pervades the Net is one of the most real—is a frightening thing. Give an individual a voice, and you'll find all too often that he's irascible, unpredictable, even uncouth. Remember how we were taught in our high school civics classes to embrace the *theory* of pluralism? The Net forces us to come to grips with its *reality*. And the reality of freedom of speech is just another variant of William Gibson's observation that "the street finds its own uses for things." The "street"—that is, the rest of us who aren't the government or the traditional press—finds its own uses for mass media. While each of us is entitled (I'm inclined to say we're obligated) to make moral judgments about particular uses of free speech, we're always on shakier ground when we claim to know that whole classes of speech categorically deserve less protection under the First Amendment.[3]

In a real sense, the issue is bigger than the Net. It's even bigger than freedom of speech itself. In the long run, it's not really any fear of too much freedom on the Net that we have to transcend. It's fear of each other.

To give you another idea about the backlash against freedom of speech on the Net, let me tell you what happened when I set up my first home page on the World Wide Web. *Home page* is the standard term for the primary document through which Web users around the world normally access the text, graphics, movies, sounds, or other files that you, as a proud home page owner, have decided to make available to the world. If you have a home page of your own, or are about to get one, you probably won't be quite sure what to put up on it. Lots of people post scanned photographic images of themselves. I had some pictures of myself, but I didn't like them much. Still, I did have some photos I thought were quite compelling. My little girl, Ariel, is a good-looking kid, and I like her baby pictures a lot. Now that the Net has made me a global publisher, I decided, I can ensure that every Net surfer in the world is able to see her. So I had the photos scanned to create digital images of the Ariel prints, then put up those images on my home page. Shortly afterward, I got e-mail from a friend who in all seriousness asked me this: "Aren't you afraid that by putting a picture of your child on the Internet you're going to invite child molesters to target your child as a potential victim?"

That question tells us just how far we have come. My friend had somehow learned to be afraid of the Net and had defined it for himself (in part) as a haven for pedophiles. Now, no one can dispute that as the Internet and its tools become available to everyone, they become available to pedophiles and other criminals as well. But the evidence we have suggests that nothing about the Net has caused the total number of child molesters to increase or the total number of victims to increase. But this debate isn't really about evidence. It's about the (often secret) fears we have regarding "strangers"—you know, the guy from out of town who can't meet your eyes and whose name you don't know. And on the Net, there are millions of those strangers.

Once upon a time, the Net was seen as a boon to the nation and the rest of the world. Nowadays, it's likely to be seen by the press and public as a threat to social stability, a haven for the lawless, or a cornucopia of pornography. All the worst fears each of us might have when walking a city street alone at night and encountering someone we don't know are fears that we have begun to project to the entire Net and from there to the entire world.

This is not the kind of basic assumption that builds relationships and communities. It is the kind that kills them.

I'd like to take you back to the dim dawn of time: 1993. Remember the hype about the "information superhighway"? That hype made the cover of *Time* magazine that year. We were told that five hundred channels of all sorts of content would somehow make their way into our home. Every library, school, hospital, and home would have a connection to the Internet. And everyone, literally everyone, could potentially be a publisher.

A few measly years later, the Internet is widely perceived as a threat. Why? Because everyone is a publisher! Because there are way more than five hundred channels of this stuff! And because it will be connected to every library, school, hospital, and home! Many of the people publishing on the Internet will not have been to journalism school. Many of them will say things that offend other people. Many of them will publish their own opinions without any notion of what is fair play, or nice, or middle-of-the-road, or politically correct. They'll say what they think, strongly, perhaps abruptly, but maybe also clumsily or sloppily—and the mere fact that they're not polite, or well spoken, will reinforce our fear about all these . . . strangers.

But once you get out of the habit of treating the Net as a den of menacing strangers—if you can find it in yourself to focus past the scaremongering for a moment—it's possible to see the glimmer of fundamentally positive changes in the workings of art and culture, thanks to the Net.

Take poets, for example. It's rare that a poetry volume finds itself on the best-seller list these days. People who write poetry (you may not see that many of them, but the fact is, we have a lot of good poets around) don't often succeed commercially. They may be able to sell only a few thousand copies, if that. If you're a brilliant poet who hasn't been able to give the time and effort necessary to get a book contract or even to place a poem as a freelance contributor, you'll be even more invisible than the most unread of published poets. Compared to publishing a book of poetry, posting the same material to the Net is trivial. Even if you're afraid of computers yourself, a friend can do it for you. Suddenly your poetry may reach literally every single person who could ever understand your verse—the audience that in your wildest dreams before now, you could never have allowed yourself to hope for. To make it all even sweeter, you'll be "in print" for a very long time—perhaps for as long as the Net or any record of the Net exists.

(Worried about your copyright? Maybe you should be, since it's hard and perhaps ultimately impossible to control the making of copies on a computer network that operates primarily by making copies. But I'll tell you a secret: in this instance, at least, it's no loss: the odds are that your volume of poetry wasn't going to kick a lot of royalties in your direction in any case. Elsewhere in this book, we'll discuss other ways in which the Net has an impact on intellectual property law.)

That is a fundamental shift.

But the benefits for poets are eclipsed by the claims about porn.

I remember the immense national headlines surrounding the prosecution of a Milpitas, California, couple, Robert and Carleen Thomas, who operated a microcomputer bulletin board system through which they sold pornography. They were prosecuted in Memphis, Tennessee. It was a good story because prosecutors in Memphis had reached all the way across the country to get a gentleman who was selling adult material out of his California house on a computer. But the story launched a general problem of perception about the Internet. Suddenly the online world was seen by some people primarily as a conduit for broad transmission of pornography and obscenity.

This change in perception is widespread. Someone recently asked me how many hours a day I spend online. I said I spend six or eight hours, some days even more. And he actually said, "It must be bad with all that pornography."

"I never see pornography on the Internet," I said.

"You're kidding," he said.

"No, I guess there's some out there, but I never go looking for it. I have work to do."

My friend thinks that when you've turned on your computer and connected it to the Internet, pornographic images simply flood over the computer monitor into your face. What's worse, he thought that maybe they flood over the computer monitor into your *child's* face. To judge from the question I had about putting my child's picture on the Web, some people seem to think that child molesters can reach through the computer screen and grab your child out of your living room.

If this anecdote exemplifies a shift in how the general public perceives the Net, it surely means that we should seek a shift in how the press talks about it. As it stands, we can't rely on the press to think clearly about the Net, much less report clearly about it. One telling example of this problem has been Howard Kurtz, who writes a media criticism column for the *Washington* Post. Kurtz, who is widely regarded as an astute critic of the traditional media, wrote two strangely similar columns about the Net in the course of approximately a year.

The first story involved a *Los Angeles Times* article by a fellow named Adam Bauman that somehow conflated hackers, pornography, spies, and cryptography. It was as if Bauman had had a checklist of hot-button issues on the Internet, and lots of his readers complained about the essential irrationality of his story. The second Howard Kurtz column involved *Time* magazine's July 1995 "cyberporn" cover story and the subsequent criticism the magazine received when it was discovered that the study was sensationalistic. Many Net users criticized *Time* in the strongest terms for its professional and ethical failures in running the story. Yet when Kurtz, who might have had much to say about the questions of journalistic practice raised by these stories, wrote about these controversies, he scarcely said anything about the newspaper's and the magazine's respective screw-ups. He chose instead to criticize the Net's users for being so nasty to those poor, hard-working press folks. That the nastiness might reflect the most valid moral judgment one could reach about either story seems not to have occurred to Kurtz, who did not retrace the reporters' steps in their respective stories. (If he'd done so, he might have felt motivated to flame them himself.)

When I say that the Net backlash is all about freedom of speech and our fear of others' use of it, I'm not always talking about the *content* of the speech at issue. Sometimes the use of the technology itself is what scares the powers that be. Yet these two have been used to press our hot buttons about the Internet, to make us fear online communication.

Take cryptographic software, for example. This computer tool, which can be implemented entirely in software on your own desktop machine, makes it possible for any citizen with a computer to render his or her communications in a truly secret and secure way. Yet this potential privacy boon—the last thing, really, our parents might have been taught socially to expect from computer technology—is often eclipsed by the efforts made by the Department of Justice and the National Security Agency. Those two federal agencies, for a number of reasons, have set out to sell the American public on the notion that allowing an individual this kind of ability to keep secrets is likely to destabilize and perhaps even destroy our society, not least because it makes it harder for the government to wire-tap effectively.

As if cyberporn and cryptography weren't enough, we also have the third big C scare of the Net: copyright. Bruce Lehman, who headed the U.S. Patent and Trademark Office under President Clinton, authored a report that would turn practically everything anyone does with any copyrighted material online into an infringement. Designed to calm current copyright-driven industries in the face of a perceived Net threat to copyright, the Lehman Report (also called "The White Paper on Copyright") would recast American copyright law in ways that its critics claim would destroy the long-standing balance between copyright holders on the one side and readers and scholars on the other. Despite the administration's denial that these charges would have such a far-reaching effect, law professor Pamela Samuelson and other critics in academia believe the changes would have these effects. If you browse material published on the Net without a license, that's a potential infringement. If you download it, that's also potential infringement. And if you look at it on your screen, that's an infringement. Three strikes and you're out. Maybe you deserve a life sentence in federal copyright prison![4]

The Net as Broadcasting: The Final Scare Tactic

Over the past two years, I've seen several members of Congress follow the suggestions of certain social-conservative interest groups in arguing that the Net is very much like broadcasting and therefore deserves the kind of regulation that the Federal Communications Commission administers to broadcasting entities around the country. My own feeling is this: Why shouldn't anything that's legal in a Barnes and Noble bookstore or in the New York Public Library be legal online?

I ask this question again and again, and I've engaged in many public debates about this issue. My favorite was the radio talk show episode in which I debated Bob Peters of Morality in Media, a religious right organization that wants to increase broad content-based government-imposed censorship obligations on the Net and, eventually, on all other media that are now fully protected (in the United States, at least) by the First Amendment.

I raised this question, comparing the content available in bookstores and online, and Bob Peters responded: "But, Mike, computers come into our home!" And I said, "Well, you know, Bob, *books* come into my home!" Yet you wouldn't be able to limit the content of books the way you want to limit the content of computer networks. We would think it a violation of the First Amendment to impose on books the kinds of restrictions that Peters would impose on the Net.

How can one equate the Net and broadcasting? And what implication does the broadcasting paradigm have for the Net? The nicest thing we can say about the relationship between the broadcasting medium and the legal regime that governs it is that this control has been limited to that one medium and hasn't overflowed to others. The FCC doesn't have jurisdiction over newspapers or books, which most of us think is just fine.

The constitutional justification for special regulation of broadcast content—which covers radio, television, and cable and includes regulations like time-based restrictions (such as limiting material for mature audiences to distribution at certain times)—has been twofold. First is the concept of scarcity of resources. There is a notion that broadcasting frequencies are so scarce that the government is the only institution with a global enough perspective to step in, allocate them, and govern their use for the public good. Second is the notion that broadcasting is pervasive in some fashion—that it creeps into the home in a way that makes it unique.

Regardless of whether you accept these justifications for content control over the airwaves, the fact is that the Internet is nothing like broadcasting in either way. Internet communication is not scarce. Every time you add a computer node to the Internet, you've expanded its size. It is not pervasive because (with the arguable exception of "spam," e-mail advertising) you don't have people pushing content into your home; you have people logging on and pulling content from all over the world. Despite recent hype about so-called push content, it is mostly not the case that you log on and have stuff pushed at you that you don't want to see, except in the same sense that you may not want to see the advertisements that are placed beside the articles in newspapers and magazines. (These days, my spam-filtering software blocks most unwanted advertising sent to me in e-mail.) It is a fundamentally choice-driven medium for communication, very much like a bookstore, a newsstand, or a library, and therefore deserving of at least the same high degree of First Amendment protections.

Through these instances, as well as others we'll discuss in this book, we can see how the Net is misrepresented both to and by the media, the general public, and Congress. I suspect we'll continue to hear apocryphal stories about the mythical child who unwittingly and unwillingly encounters pornography online within thirty seconds of first logging on. Media professionals have a special responsibility to make these issues clear by presenting a fact-based, fair, and rational picture of the story. We simply cannot allow the traditional media to play to our fears anymore, because the reality of the situation is this: Americans are already nervous about sex, we're already nervous about our children, and we're already nervous about computers. So if you combine all three in a newspaper story, you could pretty much drive anyone into a frenzy of anxiety.

The human regulatory reflex is always with us. Still, we all have to think carefully before calling for new regulation, because even the most ill-crafted and ill-considered regulatory scheme may become the rules we are all going to play under in the twenty-first century. That's why it's important to understand that this is the first time in history that the power of a mass medium lies in the hands of potentially everybody. For the first time, the First Amendment's promise of freedom of the press will be kept for all Americans. A. J. Liebling famously commented that freedom of the press belongs to those who own one. Nowadays, a whole lot more of us own one.

The Net is an immense opportunity for an experiment in freedom of speech and democracy, the largest-scale experiment this world has ever seen. It's up to all of us to explore that opportunity, and it's up to each of us not to lose it. I'm a parent, and like other parents, I worry about my child and the Internet (she has just begun to explore the Web on her own). But here's what I worry about: I worry that ten or fifteen or twenty years from now, she will come to me and say, "Daddy, where were you when they took freedom of the press away from the Internet?" At the very least, I want to be able to say I was there—and that I gave everything I could, did everything I could, to keep that from happening.

We live in a transitional generation—the generation between those who lived and died without the Net and those who will have grown up with it. For us in-betweeners, the strongest and most immediate temptation will be to regulate, or even silence, the kind of free speech that troubles or scares us. But a real commitment to freedom of speech means showing a different kind of trepidation. Now's the time to be cautious when it really counts—not cautious about allowing people to speak freely on the Net, but cautious about shutting them up.

4

Libel on the Net

One of the reasons I like Brock Meeks's reporting is that he's so consistently fearless about it—or at least he makes a good show of being so, which in itself means a lot when the people he's reporting on are generally more powerful (by traditional standards) and frequently less principled than he is.

I can't do justice here to his career as a journalist, which ranges from the underground newspaper he published while he was in the military to reporting on the Afghanistan war in the 1980s for the *San Francisco Chronicle* to the mock gonzo writing of his self-published, computer-based *Cyberwire Dispatch*. He is now an online columnist for MSNBC. But you don't need me to tell you how good he is. You can find his work yourself all over the Net, should you have a free afternoon or two, a fast Net connection, and a little basic knowledge of Internet search engines.[1]

In fact, the only reason I've said even this much about Brock's background is to explain the shock I felt when he contacted me—first by e-mail and then by telephone—to tell me how worried he was about the hazard he now faced: one of the people he'd reported on in *Cyberwire Dispatch* had decided to sue him for libel.

At first, I didn't get why he was so concerned. Sure, anyone who gets sued for any reason is going to be bothered about it, even if he's certain he's going to win. But I also knew that Brock took pains to be accurate and even more pains to admit and correct his occasional error. Being courageous is no substitute for careful reporting, but Brock was also a careful reporter, and in practice it helps you stay brave when you know your research is bedrock solid. In general, reporters as careful as Brock are less likely to be sued than those who take accuracy less seriously. So, I thought, unless Brock had been uncharacteristically loose with his facts, he'd most likely win any libel lawsuit on the merits. The only kind of plaintiff a reporter like Brock would have to worry about is the plaintiff who is simultaneously hyperlitigious, rich, and willing to invest a lot of money pursuing a very expensive hobby.

Unfortunately for Brock, this was just the kind of plaintiff he'd made an enemy of. Brock had written about a mass-mailing king who'd just begun expanding his aggressive marketing operations into cyberspace. The article had been rather critical of this monarch of the mails and had drawn his ire. In the hope of finding a way to punish Brock, the king and his lawyers combed over Brock's article, looking for something questionable enough to base a lawsuit on. The result? Nothing terribly substantial. Rather than alleging any express misstatement of facts, the king's lawsuit (once he had ceased to commission lawyer-authored warning letters) seemed to focus largely on Brock's use of the word *scam* to describe the king's online offerings. Brock believed that word was the right choice for connoting the remarkable degree to which the king's hard-sell merchandising tactics (which had already been judged in Washington State and elsewhere to have crossed the lines drawn by consumer protection law) pushed the boundaries of the just-barely-legal.

The king's case wasn't the strongest libel case in the world, but it didn't need to be. The lawsuit itself was a kind of punishment, since the king knew what Brock and I also know: even if Brock were to win such a case, the cost of defending himself against a truly committed, wealthy plaintiff—a cost that would take a physical and emotional toll as well as a financial one—would cause many other reporters to think twice before publishing anything less than nice about this ruler of retail. So the king had lined up his warriors—oops, lawyers—and prepared to teach Brock a harsh lesson about how a libel lawsuit can be used to punish. The king hoped it would chill the speech of other reporters as well. What made things even scarier was that the piece in question had been written for and published in Brock's own online publication, *Cyberwire Dispatch,* Brock didn't even have the slim comfort that so many other reporters have in such cases. There was no highly capitalized codefendant (a newspaper, say, or a TV station) with the motivation and finances necessary to help defend him. His work on *Cyberwire Dispatch* had been simultaneously public-spirited and entrepreneurial. Distributed free, the *Dispatch* existed for the purpose of publishing stories whose significance might otherwise have been overlooked by publications of the more traditional ink-on-dead-trees variety. At the same time the online publication did much to increase Brock's reputation as a writer and a reporter; he'd even gotten some well-paying freelance assignments based on stories he'd broken in *Cyberwire Dispatch*.

But nothing he'd done with his online publication had been lucrative enough to offset the likely cost of a libel lawsuit. Brock told me of his worries: that he'd be unable to meet the mortgage payments on his house, that the lawsuit would consume whatever chance he might have of funding his children's college educations, that the cloud of a libel lawsuit might damage his employability as a journalist. He wondered whether the EFF could help.

Although I could think of a few ways we might be able to contribute—as a nonprofit, EFF might help by sponsoring a defense fund, for example—I wasn't sure what else we could do officially. I'd reviewed the facts of his case and was certain he had a much better case than the plaintiff did. Assuming he didn't go broke first, he'd win it sooner or later, I concluded. My instinct was to find a way to help raise money for the case—it wouldn't feel right not to do so—but I wasn't sure then that that was within our mission at EFF. Also, we had tight limits on our own resources, financial and otherwise.

In the past, lack of such resources had meant that for the most part, EFF had to focus on criminal cases, where the constitutional issues are clearest, and that we had to turn down virtually all requests for assistance in civil cases other than those we'd started ourselves.[2] In other civil cases, the risks for the party in need of help might be serious indeed, but they'd never include prison time.

Yet the sheer imbalance of the lawsuit—its obvious unfairness—made it impossible to ignore. Ironically, libel lawsuits are supposed to give little guys a chance to protect themselves, or at least seek justice, from big media. In Brock's case, however, the plaintiff was the guy with all the money and the resources. And Brock, now a media defendant, had to consider whether his legal bills would bankrupt him.

It was some days after Brock had asked me for help that I realized how important his case really was. I'd been talking for years about the future of journalism on the Net, a medium in which anybody can be a reporter, editor, or commentator, regardless of whether he or she had the kind of cash it took to fund a newspaper or broadcasting enterprise. If Brock, whom I knew to be a responsible, highly professional journalist, was going to be crushed beneath the wheels of a fully funded retaliatory lawsuit, thanks to an outdated libel law system that favors the powerful, why would anyone else be willing to risk doing self-published journalism on the Net? I had written about my vision of "citizen journalism" in the next century. Now citizen journalism might be strangled before it was born.

After clearing involvement in the case with the other folks at EFF, I contacted Brock and his lawyers and offered them whatever assistance I could. Institutionally, EFF had already volunteered to help set up a defense fund for Brock that Net users could easily contribute to.[3] First Amendment lawyer Bruce Sanford, of Baker and Hostetler, and the other lawyers at his firm who represented Brock, were interested in gathering whatever materials they could find that had dealt with libel law on the Net. As I prepared a collection of my articles to send on to Sanford, it occurred to me that I might already have at least one answer to Brock's current problem and to the long-term problem of reconciling libel law and the dynamics of the Net.

Why We Have Libel Law

In the course of my work at EFF, I'd been asked many times for advice about libel law. Some of the requests for advice had come from Internet providers and bulletin board system operators, and their concerns usually boiled down to one question: How responsible am I going to be if someone libels someone else on my system? Other requests came from ordinary users, who mostly wondered to what extent their postings online posed the risk of someday being sued (and perhaps financially ruined as a result).

In some ways this was a tough question; although the law of libel is very old, the law of the Internet is still forming. And the lack of direct precedents in computer-related cases was even worse in 1990 and 1991, during my first year as an employee of EFF. Yet that year gave us one case, *Cubby* v. *CompuServe* (1991, which we'll explore in greater detail later in this chapter), that compellingly suggested what the eventual answers about online libel might be. The case was not only good news for service providers, but also has been lasting in its general impact on the free speech law of the Net.

What exactly is a libel? The case law is explicit. Libel is a false, written statement of fact that damages someone's reputation—that is, that "defames" someone. Libel is considered a subset of the law of defamation, which also includes slander (defamation that is spoken rather than written).

The person who merely quotes a libel can be held responsible too. (Somewhat confusingly, the legal term for quoting a libelous statement is called *publishing the libel,* although the individual who quotes the statement may not be a publisher in any traditional sense.) So you can't get past libel liability by saying, "I was only quoting Mike Godwin!" News stories that report libel cases are generally an exception to this rule, but also a pretty narrow one.

The theory behind libel law is simple. It's possible to say or publish something so detrimental to someone's reputation that it measurably damages his or her life and livelihood. This is especially true, say the theorists, when one is talking about defamation in mass media, such as newspapers and TV. The courts are set up to award monetary damages to deserving plaintiffs to compensate for the damage done by the defamation. This remedy also supposedly acts as a deterrent to defamation in the future.

The theoretical scope of libel liability is pretty broad. This raised once again a question I'd been thinking about for years: Why is it, given the theoretical liability any user of the Net might have, there have been so few libel lawsuits before now? After a lot of pondering, I came to believe that the ease with which Net users can reply to arguably defamatory postings has more or less eliminated any actual "need" for libel lawsuits and has in fact functioned to significantly limit the incidence of such cases arising from postings in cyberspace.[4]

It's not that people never say mean-spirited or malicious things to each other in cyberspace, of course. Earlier in this book, I noted that if you express strong opinions online, the chances are you'll be flamed. And the more fervent the flamer, the more likely it is that he or she will say something defamatory about you—something that, if taken as a factual statement, would tend to injure your reputation or good name.

So this comparative absence of libel lawsuits had made me wonder: Why hasn't the Net seen more such cases? After all, the verbal savaging of those Net folks had even become a strong (if also oft mocked) tradition in some parts of the Net. Every day, it seemed, some large percentage of the flood of new Net users was learning that "flaming"—defined in Eric Raymond's *The New Hacker's Dictionary* (third edition, MIT Press, 1996) as posting e-mail or public messages "intended to insult and provoke"—is an occupational hazard of Net surfers.

Yet the annual number of libel lawsuits related to online media at the time of Brock's case was in the low single digits (even in 2002, it's still not a terribly high number). With this puzzle in mind, I began to think that this remarkable lack of libel litigation is linked to an important aspect of libel law—the definition of *public figure*.

Public vs. Private: A Pivotal Case

Libel law (in the United States, at any rate) sets different standards for private individuals and people who are defined as public figures, essentially creating a tougher burden of proof for plaintiffs who are public figures. This focus on public figures is grounded in a Supreme Court decision handed down just over three decades ago: *New York Times Co. v. Sullivan* (1964). Although this case could be considered a recent one when measured against the two centuries of the Court's history, the decision reached was almost immediately recognized by scholars, practicing lawyers, and historians alike as one of the most important First Amendment decisions ever decided by the high court. What made this decision, which won the support of every justice then serving on the Court, so important? Simply this: *Times* v. *Sullivan* brought the common law (the precedent-based, judge-made legal tradition we inherited from Great Britain) of libel into the free speech framework of the First Amendment.

Associate Justice William Brennan, then near the beginning of his decades-long tenure on the Court, wrote the primary opinion in the case.

(Although there were no dissenters, three other justices wrote separate opinions in support of Brennan's overall conclusions.) In his opinion for the Court, Justice Brennan articulated for the first time in American history a systematic way to strike the right balance between the individual's specific common-law right to seek redress when his reputation is damaged and the public's constitutional right to a free, open, and unfearful discourse about public officials and matters of public concern. That such a balance was long overdue was apparent from the beginning of the *Times* case.

The facts of the case were straightforward. The *Times* had published an advertisement called "Heed Their Rising Voices," which promoted the civil rights movement in the South and solicited donations. L. B. Sullivan, who was serving as elected commissioner of the city of Montgomery, Alabama, brought a civil libel suit against the *Times* and against certain individuals who were named as sponsors of the advertisement. Unfortunately for the *Times,* the advertisement contained a number of inaccurate statements of fact about civil rights–related incidents in Montgomery. The inaccuracies were not major ones. For example, the advertisement stated that certain students had been expelled from school for leading a protest on the steps of the Alabama State Capitol; although they had been leaders of that protest, they were in fact expelled for another incident in which they had demanded service at a segregated lunch counter at the county courthouse.

But the traditional law of libel not only cut little slack for small factual errors, it also made little errors an easy excuse to punish someone for publishing a troubling story that was essentially true. Following state law, the trial judge instructed the jury that the statements in the ad were libelous on their face, that falsity and "malice" (a legal term of art, usually defined as ill will or spite) on the part of the advertisers and the *Times* could be presumed, and that general and punitive damages could be awarded against each of the defendants, even in the absence of direct proof of monetary loss due to the alleged defamation. This last instruction was particularly handy for local officials who had been involved in quelling civil rights protests, since it would have been hard for them to prove that their reputations or businesses had been damaged. If anything, their antiprotest efforts *improved* their reputations in their conservative, pro-segregation communities. Even so, the jury found the defendants liable for $500,000 each (which in 1964 was "real money").

As Anthony Lewis has documented in *Make No Law,* his excellent book on the *Times* case, public officials had a strong incentive to resort to libel actions against major northern newspapers like the *Times:* the financial pressure created by numerous lawsuits and large judgments would provide newspapers with a major disincentive to do critical reporting of civil rights issues in the South. That, of course, was why the *Times* fought the case all the way to the Supreme Court.

When it got there, the Court found that the *Times* case had raised a genuine constitutional issue—that libel law, as applied by the courts of Alabama, conflicted with the First Amendment guarantee of freedom of the press. What, then, should the standards of libel law be? Justice Brennan's opinion began by noting, "We consider this case against the background of a profound national commitment to the principle that debate on public issues should be uninhibited, robust, and wide-open, and that it may well include vehement, caustic, and sometimes unpleasantly sharp attacks on government and public officials." (He could easily have been describing Usenet or the World Wide Web in 1994 or 2002.)

Brennan went on to write that "erroneous statement is inevitable in free debate" (reporters and editors and Web site authors are only human, after all) and that libel law must therefore accommodate a certain amount of falsehood "if the freedoms of expression are to have the 'breathing space'" that they need to survive. Since discussion of public officials and their work is central to democratic debate, Brennan reasoned, it follows that we should make special allowances for debate about such officials. A public official can win a libel lawsuit under the First Amendment, wrote Brennan, only if he or she can prove "actual malice" on the part of the defendant, where proof of "actual malice" is defined as proof that the statement was made with "knowledge that it was false or with reckless disregard of whether it was false or not." (In other words, the term *actual malice* is defined quite differently from the older term *malice,* meaning spite or ill will.)

This rule about public officials was extended in later cases to public figures in general. The Court recognized that sometimes news stories about highly public individuals are central to democracy even when the individual doesn't happen to be a public official. Ross Perot and Jesse

Jackson come to mind as recent examples of public figures who have never (yet) been elected or appointed to governmental positions.

While the expansion of the "public official" doctrine to apply to all public figures solved one problem, this extension of the ruling of *New York Times Co.* v. *Sullivan* led to new ones. The worst one is this: How can you tell whether someone's a public figure? Is anyone who has been written about in the press a public figure simply because some newspaper editor thought a story was newsworthy? If that were so, there'd be no distinction between public figures and anyone else. The minute your name appeared in print, you'd be a public figure, and you'd have to prove actual malice (and not, say, mere negligence or sloppiness on the part of the reporter) in order to win your case.

In practical terms, proving actual malice can be difficult—when a public figure brings a libel case against a newspaper or broadcaster, he or she puts the court in the position of asking how much a reporter knew or didn't know at the time of the story—not to mention asking about the reporter's attitudes at the time of the story. That's why libel lawsuits involving public figures (like the case brought by psychologist Jeffrey Masson against the *New Yorker*) often turn on the evidence found in reporters' notebooks.[5]

Defining Public and Private Figures

The Supreme Court revisited the public figure issue a number of times in the decade after the *Times* case. In fact, it was a full decade before the Court came up with a lasting answer to the problem of deciding who's a public figure in a given case. In *Gertz* v. *Robert Welch, Inc.* (1974), Justice Lewis Powell, writing for the majority, outlined the basic distinction between public and private figures and justified their different treatment in libel law. First, the definition of public figure: "In some instances an individual may achieve such pervasive fame or notoriety that he becomes a public figure for all purposes and in all contexts. More commonly, an individual voluntarily injects himself or is drawn into a particular public controversy and thereby becomes a public figure for a limited range of issues. In either case such person assumes special prominence in the resolution of public questions." In short, if you're not famous and if you haven't (in Powell's words) "thrust [yourself] into the vortex" of public debate, you're a private figure or individual. And in most states, private individuals bringing a defamation lawsuit face a less rigorous standard of proof than actual malice.

But *Gertz* is also an interesting case because it goes into greater depth in explaining why it makes sense to give public figures less protection under libel law than we give private individuals. Powell wrote that the Court has "no difficulty in distinguishing among defamation plaintiffs. *The first remedy of any victim of defamation is self-help*—using available opportunities to contradict the lie or correct the error and thereby to minimize its adverse impact on reputation. Public officials and public figures usually enjoy significantly greater access to the channels of effective communication and hence have a more realistic opportunity to counteract false statements than private individuals normally enjoy. Private individuals are therefore more vulnerable to injury, and the state interest in protecting them is correspondingly greater."

Under the First Amendment, in other words, the *preferred* response to a defamation problem is to fix it yourself. But until recently, only a very few private individuals have had the kind of access to mass media it presumably would take to correct the record at all, much less to undo the damage done by the original defamatory statement.

The Supreme Court has explained that this inequity in individuals' access to media is a major reason we have libel law. In short, when you can't effectively correct the record yourself—perhaps because you don't have a mass media voice that reaches as far as that of the newspaper or magazine or broadcaster who originally defamed you—then it simply won't matter that all the facts are on your side. Instead, what will matter is what the public remembers. And in any unequal (and out-of-court) media contest between you and, say, a TV station you think has defamed you, what the public will most likely remember about your case is the alleged libel itself, not so much what *you* said to challenge or balance that libelous statement. The First Amendment allows states to use libel law to level the playing field, making it easier for private individuals to counter the damage that can be done to their reputations by mass media.

It was this theory of how libel law was supposed to function that had had me studying that particular area of law for years—almost from the beginning of my tenure at EFF and long before Brock contacted me with his problem.

Star Power: Fame and Defamation in Cyberspace

In the course of my research, I'd concluded that these two factors—the definition of *public figure* and the rationale for treating public figures differently—play out in unique ways on the Net. First, far more people on Usenet and CompuServe (to take two examples) can be said to "thrust themselves into the vortex" of public debate. If online conferencing means anything, it means the fostering of outspokenness. In effect, every opinionated individual has a microphone and an audience, and regular participants in online discussions may even become generally famous in their virtual communities. It's almost trivially easy to become a public figure in an online environment.

Second, I'd found that the comparative openness of access to the Net means that a lot more people who feel they've had their reputations be-smirched have access to self-help. If some bozo writes a hundred lines of false statement and innuendo about your sex life or personal habits, you can write five hundred lines of point-by-point refutation. It occurred to me that these factors may be making libel law increasingly irrelevant, at least as far as online conferencing is concerned.

It's also worth remembering that relatively few people ever actually sue for libel. For one thing, it's expensive, which means you either have to be rich or have to have such a convincing case that you can persuade a lawyer to take your case on a contingency fee basis (highly unlikely). For another, the long, drawn-out process of suing someone for damage to your reputation is almost always wearying and very rarely satisfying.[6] On the Net, in contrast, calling your defamer to account is comparatively easy. Probably, if your message was online in some topical area, such as a mailing list or Usenet newsgroup, so were the corresponding flames. And while few flame wars ever end in a clear win for one side or the other, there's still the deep satisfaction that comes of knowing you're in the right and that you've responded to every false statement anyone has made about you. It's a day in court that you can have over and over again, and it normally comes cheap.

As I became more certain that this was the explanation for the infrequency of Net libel cases, I became increasingly willing to stick my neck out and predict that libel lawsuits would *never* be a significant factor when it came to heated online discussions. Now and forever after, it would always be far easier to hit the Reply key.

Brock's attorney, Sanford, and his colleague, David Marburger, liked these conclusions and predictions, they told me. But because much of what I'd written had been in terms of the prediction of future cases rather than the discussion of prior ones, I knew they would also need to show that the facts of the Net—from its technical structure to its diverse and rapidly evolving culture—were already forcing libel law into a different shape than it had ever had before. Fortunately, I'd been on the lookout for such cases myself since my first days at EFF; I had even researched and written about those as well.

These cases were not about the defamee's ability to correct the public record. Instead, they dealt with a traditional media entity's risk of being held legally liable for some individual defamer's published or quoted statements. This meant that these cases didn't resemble Brock's in their specifics. For example, by acting as his own publisher to the Net, Brock had unintentionally ensured that he'd have no editor or publisher co-defendant in court with him when he defended himself against the king's lawsuit.

Nevertheless, the cases did signal to lawyers and judges a larger (and arguably more useful) conclusion: applying First Amendment principles from the print and spoken realm to cyberspace can still lead to unexpected results.[7] To see how this happened with online libel and to understand why such a shift in legal thinking might be very important in cases like Brock's, we need to step back from Brock's troubles for a few pages and take some time to understand the two leading cases relating to online libel: *Cubby* v. *CompuServe* and *Stratton Oakmont* v. *Prodigy*.

A Great Leap Forward and a Step Backward

Cubby v. *CompuServe:* "Provider as Bookstore" Model
If you spent much time on Usenet or CompuServe or the WELL back in 1991, you heard at least something about the decision in *Cubby* v.

CompuServe, a libel case. Cubby was decided on summary judgment, which means the judge decided the case on the basis of legal principles alone, so it never went to a jury.[8] It was one of the most important cases for BBS liability of the time. What later became clear, however, was that even those who believed it to be an important case frequently misunderstood the legal reasoning behind it.

The facts of the case are relatively straightforward. CompuServe had contracted with a third-party user for that user to conduct a special-interest forum (called "Rumorville") on CompuServe. The plaintiff, Cubby, claimed that defamatory material about its business was posted by a user in that forum, and he sued both the forum host and CompuServe. CompuServe moved for, and received, summary judgment in its favor.

The plaintiff in this case arguably had good reason to believe that he'd win. The common law of libel is that a person who repeats or otherwise "republishes" defamatory material is just as legally liable for the defamation as the person who originally published it. By that reasoning, CompuServe should be held just as liable for any defamatory statements in Rumorville as the proprietor of Rumorville himself.

What is remarkable about this case is the conclusion that federal judge Peter Leisure reached regarding how to categorize CompuServe for libel purposes. Traditional libel analysis categorizes defendants by control, and there are only two categories: print media, such as a newspaper, or "common carriers," such as a phone company. Clearly, a newspaper has much more editorial control over its content than does a phone company, which does not and cannot exert a prerogative to prescreen what anyone says on the phone.[9] However, Leisure found (or created, depending on how you look at it) a third category—the provider-as-bookstore model, which was advanced by CompuServe's attorneys. When he applied that category, the judge concluded that only in cases where CompuServe had had some prior "actual knowledge" (or where a reasonable person in CompuServe's position could hardly have avoided knowing of the defamatory character of a user posting) could it be held liable for that posting in a way that was consistent with basic First Amendment principles.

Leisure's reasoning showed a then unprecedented jurisprudential grasp of the First Amendment dimension of most online communication services. And his opinion turned out to have both an immediate and a long-term effect on computer-related cases that were then in the courts or that afterward would arise.[10]

In his opinion in the *Cubby* case, Judge Leisure held that CompuServe is less like a publisher and more like a bookstore owner or book distributor. First Amendment law allows publishers to be liable for defamation, but not bookstore owners (absent proof they knew or should have known about the defamatory content). Why this distinction? The answer is obvious when you think about it Holding a bookstore liable when it hadn't preapproved every book's content would burden bookstore owners with reviewing every book they carry to see if it contained defamatory material. This burden would "chill" the distribution of books (not to mention causing most booksellers to get out of the bookstore business) and thus would come into serious conflict with the purposes of the First Amendment.

So although other civil libertarians and I had often asserted (in a sort of "civil liberties shorthand") that BBSs and Internet nodes have "the same First Amendment rights" as more traditional publishers and publications, the *Cubby* case centered on one key way in which online systems are different. Online systems are more like the neighborhood bookstore than the town newspaper. But what is it that makes publishers different from bookstore owners when considered in a First Amendment light? The answer is easy once you give a little thought to how bookstores do business. We expect a publisher (or its agents) to review everything prior to publication. Publishers typically have a staff of editors and writers and through them control the content they publish. But we never expect bookstore owners to review everything prior to sale. Similarly, in the *CompuServe* case, as in any other case involving an online service in which users freely post messages for the public, we wouldn't expect the online communications service provider to read everything posted *before* allowing it to appear.[11] The prescreening alone would seem to take, well, forever.

Judge Leisure's analogy of CompuServe to a bookstore, a model that turns out to be brilliantly apt, derives from a 1959 Supreme Court case: *Smith* v. *California*.

A Landmark Obscenity Case

The *Smith* case represents one of the early modern efforts to modify the older law of publisher and distributor liability so that it fit better with the First Amendment and with the principles underlying that amendment.

In *Smith,* a bookseller was prosecuted on obscenity charges for selling a book called *Sweeter Than Life.* Prior to the *Smith* case, it was considered constitutional to hold a bookseller or newsstand responsible for the obscene content of a publication it sold, even when the owners or operators of such "distributor" entities weren't proven to have knowledge of that content. In short, if you ran a newsstand and you sold a magazine that turned out to have legally obscene content inside it, you could go to jail even though you had no idea such content was there.

Justice William Brennan, writing for the majority in *Smith,* stated that the First Amendment does not allow the law to hold such entities responsible for the content of everything in the store. To do so would be to force the bookseller to market only those books he had read and had assured himself were not obscene. Said Justice Brennan, "The bookseller's self-censorship, compelled by the State, would be a censorship affecting the whole public, hardly less virulent for being privately administered. Through it, the distribution of all books, both obscene and not obscene, would be impeded."

Bookstores, libraries, newsstands, and the like, said Brennan, were in fact places of important First Amendment–protected activity: the dissemination of art and of ideas. Force the newstand operator to be responsible for everything he sells, whether he knows its contents or not, and you will force him to sell a lot less news (or perhaps even to get out of the newsstand business altogether). And public discourse as a whole would suffer.

Ultimately, Brennan concluded that the First Amendment requires, at the least, proof that the defendant knew or should have known (such a mental state is referred to as *scienter,* a legal term meaning "guilty knowledge") of the contents of the disputed publication. Absent such proof, a prosecution and conviction of bookstores, newsstands, and libraries under an obscenity statute would violate the First Amendment and chill the dissemination of free expression everywhere.

By requiring governments to prove that the defendant had scienter as to any obscene publication, the Supreme Court created the kind of legal breathing space necessary for bookstores and libraries to operate without fear of gratuitous, arbitrary, and unpredictable prosecutions for obscenity. (Note that although *Smith* was an obscenity case, its reasoning was extended to libel law only five years later, in the groundbreaking libel decision *New York Times* v. *Sullivan,* also authored by Justice Brennan.)

Judge Leisure's reliance on *Smith* v. *California*, an obscenity liability case, not a libel liability case, would turn out to mark an important legal connection between *New York Times* v. *Sullivan* in 1964 and the free-speech-on-the-Net cases of the 1990s. In *Smith*, a 1958 case, the Supreme Court determined that it is generally unconstitutional to hold bookstore owners liable for content they did not know about. This principle was central to the majority opinion in 1964's *New York Times* v. *Sullivan*, which established the "actual malice" requirement for potentially libelous statements regarding public figures, creating the central balance between libel liability and the First Amendment in the modern era.

Without realizing how soon I'd have to be making this argument in the public debates surrounding the Communications Decency Act, I noted that this connection in Leisure's opinion between the *Cubby* case and *Smith* v. *California* seemed likely to have long-term significance. It underscores the constitutional principle behind both *Smith* v. *California* and *Times* v. *Sullivan*, which is that you couldn't just assume a bookstore owner (or newsstand operator or Internet service provider) is at fault if he or she makes available to the public some libelous, obscene, or otherwise legally problematic content. Instead the applicable principle is this:

If you're going to hold such a redistributor of other people's content liable for that content, the First Amendment (alone and in combination with other constitutional protections) requires, at minimum, solid proof that any reasonable person in this "redistributor's" place would have been aware of the legally problematic content.

What the *Cubby* Case Really Meant

To understand fully the significance of judge Leisure's opinion, it is important to review what he does *not* say. Nowhere does he argue that CompuServe exerts *no control at all* over the content of its forums. And while the judge stresses Rumorville's status as an independent subcontractor to (rather than an employee or agent of) CompuServe, he does not articulate any general principle that if CompuServe were to assert any editorial control over the content of forums moderated by a subcontractor, it would suddenly be liable for all the content of the subcontractor forum.[12]

Nor, indeed, could he. Having reviewed one of the forum moderator contracts that CompuServe was using at the time of the *Cubby* case, I knew that CompuServe routinely reserved all sorts of rights to step in and censor or shape content in accordance with the company's terms of service restrictions.

Similarly, Judge Leisure states elsewhere in the *Cubby* opinion, "While CompuServe may decline to carry a given publication altogether, in reality, once it does decide to carry a given publication, it will have little or no editorial control over that publication's contents." That is, even while stating that CompuServe does not function as an editor-publisher along the *New York Times* model, Leisure expressly acknowledges that CompuServe does reserve the right to exercise certain broad controls, such as when it "decline[s] to carry a given publication."

Leisure follows directly the reasoning of Judge Brennan in *Smith,* the bookstore obscenity case. Brennan did not argue or even imply that bookstores, newsstands, and libraries exercise *no* control over their content. Obviously, newsstands make choices about what to carry, or what not to carry, all the time. So do bookstores and libraries. In Berkeley, where I lived for a while, there's a science-fiction bookstore called The Other Change of Hobbit; the store routinely chooses not to carry John Updike novels, Barbara Cartland novels, or the *New Republic.* It would be irrational to argue that the exerting of such editorial judgment by the owners of this bookstore would somehow deprive it of the First Amendment protections outlined by Justice Brennan in *Smith* v. *California.*

The point Judge Leisure was making was this: Although CompuServe may be said to have certain editorial powers and prerogatives with regard to the content of those who, as forum moderators or as ordinary users, post material to the system, CompuServe is nevertheless more like a library or a bookstore than a publisher. Therefore, he reasoned, the company deserves the same First Amendment–based protections afforded to traditional libraries and bookstores.

This meant that *Cubby, Inc.* v. *CompuServe* shed light not only on defamation law as applied in this new medium but on obscenity law as well. But the light didn't reach everywhere. Many lawyers misunderstood the lesson of the *Cubby* case, which was that it made no sense to force the classification of a forum-service provider like CompuServe into the common carrier versus newspaper distinction. Instead they interpreted *Cubby* as *requiring precisely that choice.*

Lawyers who don't read the precedents are bad enough. What's worse is a *judge* who fails to understand the precedents. Such judges can produce a tragic miscarriage of justice in the case over which he or she is presiding.

It's true that our legal system works in a way that tends to limit the consequences of these kinds of ill-reasoned decisions. Given that the Net is such a new development, however, the consequences of bad judicial reasoning can be far greater. In this new area of the law, in which just about any case in any jurisdiction may end up being used as a precedent in any later Net-related case, poor judicial scholarship can result in a disaster. That's what happened when Justice Stuart Ain, in *Stratton Oakmont* v. *Prodigy* (a 1995 case in a New York state court) demonstrated the hazards of assuming that one can understand a case like *Cubby* without having understood the precedents it draws on.

A Prodigious Mistake

The *Prodigy* case began when an unknown party, using the still active account of a former Prodigy employee, posted what were alleged to be libelous statements about Stratton Oakmont, an investment banking firm, and its president, Daniki Porush. It remains unknown who actually posted these statements, but it was well known that Prodigy is a big enough entity to pay handsomely if it lost a libel lawsuit. That explained why Prodigy was the defendant named first in the defamation lawsuit Porush and his company filed.

For the plaintiffs to win this case, it was important to deny the defendants the First Amendment protection as distributors of information, such as the bookstore in the *Smith* case and CompuServe in the *Cubby* case. Porush and Stratton Oakmont therefore decided to move for a "partial summary judgment" and get Justice Ain to declare that Prodigy is a publisher and not a distributor—that it is fundamentally different from CompuServe.

The problem is that at the time of the alleged libel, Prodigy was no longer fundamentally different from CompuServe. Sure, Prodigy was originally pitched as a highly edited online service, but eventually its forums became similar to those of CompuServe and America Online. Just as on AOL, postings in forums on Prodigy were not prescreened at all, except to the extent that Prodigy uses software to filter out postings with profane language. (AOL relies for the most part on their forums' human moderators to filter out that kind of language.) And the agreements between Prodigy and its forum moderators weren't much different from those between the other providers and their moderators.

Nevertheless, Justice Ain did not appear to put much emphasis on these facts. Arguing that Prodigy had not adequately proved its claims to distributor status under the *Cubby* and *Smith* cases, he held that Prodigy is a traditional publisher and therefore vicariously liable for the actions of its agents (the forum moderators) and its users (whomever they may be). It was on this point that Justice Ain unwittingly illustrated the hazard of failing to read and understand the precedents that establish the legal principle that "distributors" have different and special protections under the First Amendment. Here's the central passage from the *Stratton Oakmont* decision:

The key distinction between CompuServe and PRODIGY is two-fold. First, PRODIGY held itself out to the public and its members as controlling the content of its computer bulletin boards. Second, PRODIGY implemented this control through its automatic software screening program, and the Guidelines which Board Leaders are required to enforce. By actively utilizing technology and manpower to delete notes from its computer bulletin boards on the basis of offensiveness and "bad taste," for example, PRODIGY is clearly making decisions as to content . . . , and such decisions constitute editorial control. . . . That such control is not complete and is enforced both as early as the notes arrive and as late as a complaint is made, does not minimize or eviscerate the simple fact that PRODIGY has uniquely arrogated to itself the role of determining what is proper for its members to post and read on its bulletin boards. Based on the foregoing, this Court is compelled to conclude that for the purposes of Plaintiffs' claims in the action, PRODIGY is a publisher rather than a distributor.

It's clear from Ain's language here that the justice believed *any* exercise of editorial control would deprive an online service of the ability to invoke First Amendment protections under *Cubby* and *Smith*. He seemed to think that *Cubby* v. *CompuServe* created a sort of common-carrier principle, in which providers give up all control in order to get the First Amendment protections afforded to distributors.

But this can't be the law. Logically, Justice Ain's interpretation of *Cubby* v. *CompuServe* makes no sense. Judge Leisure's opinion in the earlier case holds that online service providers *need not* be forced to choose, in effect, between declaring themselves to be common carriers (total absence of editorial control, but overall immunity from liability) and the daily newspaper model (total control of content, but maximum theoretical liability for other people's content). Yet Ain had interpreted Leisure's opinion as *requiring* providers to face that forced choice between these two ill-fitting models.

If analyzing the *Stratton Oakmont* decision logically isn't enough to convince you of its flaws, take a moment to remember the facts about the science-fiction bookstore I mentioned earlier. In fact, think of any bookstore. They all exercise certain kinds of editorial control, yet they do so without necessarily having to say they "knew or should have known" of the content of all the material they included or excluded. The same can be said of CompuServe and AOL, both of which reserve the right to make post hoc judgments as to whether to censor offending or illegal material.

Justice Ain seemed to think that an information service provider can be only a common carrier like the telephone company (which has no liability for content) or a traditional publisher like the *New York Times* or Random House (which have the maximum possible liability as publishers). But the whole point of the 1959 Supreme Court case *Smith* v. *California* was to identify a third class of First Amendment–protected entities—distributors—and suggest how the law ought to be applied in that third class of cases.

A Legacy of Bad Law

Ain's legal blunder was bad enough. What compounded it is how seriously so many otherwise intelligent lawyers were taking the *Stratton Oakmont* decision. In the 1995–1996 debates over the Communications Decency Act, even law professors made the same mistake that Ain had— or to put it another way, they echoed Ain's reasoning uncritically. And I saw lobbyists for the online service providers attempt to add ill-crafted "safe harbor" provisions to Net censorship bills, in the foolish hope that the elimination of future *Stratton Oakmont*-like decisions will make more tolerable the legislation that would turn providers into the "indecency" police of the Net.

Nowhere more than in the *Stratton Oakmont* case had I ever seen the truth of the statement that hard cases make bad law. What made this case hard was that it was so novel, and the potential "bad law" stretched from justice Ain's courtroom all the way to the halls of Congress—and all because so many lawyers were unwilling to read the relevant cases— to understand the constitutional law that connects today's world with the free speech framework built by this nation's founders.

Because I had already seen those time-tested constitutional principles survive the attacks of those who feared the social change wrought by computers and networks, I knew to a moral certainty that it would be the *Cubby* case, not the *Stratton Oakmont* case, that would provide the guiding principle for future courts dealing with online issues. After all, even the *Stratton Oakmont* decision had to center on the *Cubby* case, which, more and more lawyers were beginning to recognize, marked a watershed in applying our oldest principles of free speech to our newest ways of speaking.

Logic Prevails: Goliath Decides to Settle

Fortunately for Brock, it was the *Cubby*-style logic that Brock's attorneys were able to apply in his case. During the course of my conversations with Brock's attorneys, Sanford and Marburger, I summarized the most important arguments:

• The nature of "public figures" was changing, thanks to the Net. Since all those with a modem and keyboard can now "thrust themselves into the vortex" of public debate online, many more of us now count as "public figures" for libel purposes.

• The Net was reducing, and perhaps erasing, the imbalance of power between mass media and private individuals. The power of the Net allows anyone with a will and the energy to write the opportunity to publish their ideas.

• These shifts had already begun to be recognized by the courts.

Brock's lawyers expressed interest in the work I'd done; they asked for copies of the articles in which I'd laid out these arguments more fully. And except for the occasional update from the lawyers or Brock, that was the last time in the course of Brock's case that I did much that could be characterized as legal work on the case. I continued with my other work at EFF and rejoiced the same time everyone else did when Brock and his lawyers announced (in August 1994) that the king of mass mailings had chosen to drop his damages claims against Brock as part of a token "settlement" agreement.[13]

On the WELL, Brock noted that the king had approached him seeking a settlement immediately after his lawyers had filed a brief that recited in some detail how the king's mass mailing operations had gotten the organization into a number of legal wrangles. The brief documented in some detail, I was told, the king's long history of lawsuits in the libel arena (almost always the plaintiff) and the area of consumer protection law (where he was rather more likely to be the defendant). I think the judge in Brock's case seemed likely to conclude that the king was misusing the court system to punish someone for exercising his First Amendment rights. (Judges tend to get upset when parties use the litigation process itself as a sort of punishment. Strangely enough, they believe that administering remedies and sanctions is the job of judges, not of plaintiffs.)

For me, the settlement and the discussion about it came and went very quickly. Since the case was settled, it did not generate any official published opinion that detailed how the law and the precedents applied, so I didn't bother to read the brief when the copy that Brock's lawyers sent me arrived in my mailbox.

It wasn't until nearly a year later that I discovered, thanks to a passing comment of Brock, that he credited my theory about how "public figure" doctrine applied on the Net for forcing the king into seeking a settlement. Me? All I'd done was forward some photocopied articles and participate in a few phone calls!

Eventually I took the time to dig up a copy of the lawyers' brief and found arguments and even choices of phrase that resonated with things I'd written, but I still couldn't quite accept Brock's statement that my research had made the difference. So in fall of 1996, I called David Marburger in Ohio and asked him what he remembered about the libel-related material I'd given him a couple of years before.

"Those articles were very useful," he told me, speaking a bit loudly to compensate for the static of his car phone.

"That's good to know," I told him, "but I'm feeling a little uncomfortable about the fact that Brock is giving me so much credit when I was hardly even there."

"But you *deserve* credit," he told me. "I liked your public figures theory so much that when I drafted the brief, I simply fleshed it out a little and combined it with my own argument that [the king] had assumed the risk of discomforting public speech about himself on the Net when he decided to take his marketing operation there. And right after that, we were contacted by the attorneys on the other side. They were so interested in coming up with a settlement that they never bothered to reply to our brief."

It was a strange feeling to hear all this—to discover that I'd contributed significantly to a person's defense of his constitutional rights without ever learning of the victory and without even a clear sense that I'd been truly involved in the case. This revelation from Brock and Marburger made me realize how much the teaching and application of good legal principles is like the generation of good memes—that, in fact, the two processes may be different aspects of the same thing.

Now, I don't think one's motivation to generate and disseminate good memes should be conditioned on the personal rewards one may get for doing so. But it's nice when every once in a while, by the purest chance, one of your own memes comes back to you after its trips around the Net—and perhaps even the larger world of human information and ideas—and surprises you with the happy news that you've done some good work.

Is Libel Dead?

It's not unusual for those of us who focus on the law in cyberspace to wonder whether the Net has the potential to render libel law altogether obsolete. And if the Net (or similarly distributed and accessible successor technologies) should become the primary mass medium of this century, it's hard to see why anyone should weep if libel lawsuits disappear altogether.

One school of First Amendment theorists—a school that has included some Supreme Court justices—has long argued that the ratification of the First Amendment itself rendered defamation law obsolete. With true freedom of speech, they argued, you need not resort to the courts to repair your reputation. Instead, you can simply correct the record through your own speech.

In general, however, most scholars and most courts have refused to accept this argument. Throughout our history, mass media access (and here the term includes even the printing press of colonial America) has been distributed unevenly throughout society. As a result, few defamees have had as loud a voice in public discourse as a newspaper editor or TV programmer. Thus, the majority of the theorists argue that the balances, incentives, and penalties of libel law are necessary to make individual citizens' reputations safer from false and damaging factual statements.

But surely the Net, which has the potential to empower everyone to answer injurious false statements, can change all that. Maybe the changes have already taken place, and this is why there are so few Net libel lawsuits.

Drudge Match

"Internet on Trial" was how *Vanity Fair*'s December 1997 issue billed its report on the lawsuit against Matt Drudge, the Internet's first political gossip columnist. What was really on trial, however, was not the Internet itself but two other things: the degree to which mainstream journalists demonize the Net and the usefulness of libel law itself.

Drudge, now in his mid-thirties, is a news junkie who decided to become a gossip columnist and, thanks to the Internet, succeeded beyond his expectations, if not beyond his wildest dreams. Starting from scratch in 1995, Drudge had built up a subscriber list of (he estimates) eighty-five thousand and won a substantial, if not princely, contract with America Online to publish his online newsletter there as well. In the late 1990s, he blazed a meteoric path—becoming, increasingly, a frequently read source for political journalists, if not always a well-respected one.

But whatever Drudge's dreams of success at Internet journalism, he almost certainly didn't anticipate the nightmare of a $30 million lawsuit. And that's precisely the amount of reputational damage White House aide and former journalist Sidney Blumenthal claimed that Drudge (and America Online, which carries Drudge) did to him when the online columnist published an item suggesting that Blumenthal has a history of spousal abuse. (Specifically, the item said conservative operatives were planning on exploiting a record of spousal abuse they claimed Blumenthal had—but as I noted at the beginning of this chapter, merely repeating a false claim can make the person who repeated it just as legally responsible as the person who originated it.)

And as it turned out, Drudge's report, which was based on information from an undisclosed source, adds up to a falsehood. There is no known evidence that Blumenthal ever engaged in anything like domestic violence with regard to Jacqueline Jordan Blumenthal, his wife of twenty-one years, who at the time of Blumenthal's appointement and Drudge's publication of the item headed the White House Fellowships Commission. Tellingly, Blumenthal read the Drudge item on the evening of August 10, the same day it was released—illustrating either the immediacy of Internet news or Drudge's must-read status or both. (Jacqueline Blumenthal received a faxed copy of it from a former congressional press secretary the following morning.)

Understandably incensed, Blumenthal had his lawyer, William McDaniel, send what *Vanity Fair* called a "strongly worded" letter to Drudge, who after quickly discovering that he could not verify his original story, published an apology and a retraction. Unsatisfied with this response, Blumenthal filed a libel lawsuit against Drudge and America Online, seeking an improbable $30 million in damages.

The case raised a raft of First Amendment issues, most of which were only casually addressed, if at all, by the legal commentators and media watchers, and all of which undercut Blumenthal's case:

• *Who's a public figure?*   Long-standing libel law principles hold that a public figure—someone who, as the Supreme Court put it in *Gertz* v. *Robert Welch Inc.* (1974), thrusts himself "into the vortex" of public debate—bears a heavier burden of proof than a private-individual plaintiff. Whereas the latter may need only to prove negligence (under some states' libel laws) in order to recover damages, a public figure must prove either that the publisher of the defamation knew the statement was false or didn't care whether he thought it was true. This posed a tough problem for Blumenthal, whose prominent work as a pro-Clinton journalist almost certainly would qualify him as a public figure even if he had not followed up that work with a new job on the White House staff. And while Drudge was (in my view) probably negligent in what he published, there's no evidence yet that shows he knew it was false or that he didn't care about its truth. Quite the contrary, in fact. This means he lacked the "actual malice" required for liability under the public-figure doctrine.

• *Vicarious liability.* Drudge was not the only defendant, of course. Surely America Online's assets are the main reason for the inflated monetary demands in the lawsuit. But while $30 million might have seemed a fair figure if Blumenthal had been publicly humiliated and fired from his White House job, press reports indicate that, if anything, President Clinton was quite supportive of Blumenthal in the aftermath of Drudge's erroneous report. He even expressly allowed Blumenthal to state publicly that he had the president's support in suing the online journalist. Still, this logic might have escaped a trial court appalled by the gravity of Drudge's spousal abuse implications, and if the case had gone to trial and a jury had awarded damages of $30 million, America Online is the only party to the case that might conceivably be able to pay it.

But once again, Blumenthal had a problem: America Online, which provided access to the Drudge Report but did not prescreen it, cannot reasonably be said to have had the kind of relationship to Drudge that the *New York Times* has to its reporters. A traditional news organization like the *Times* can be held legally and financially responsible for any libels its reporters generate because the *Times*'s editorial policies and editorial hierarchy ensure that nothing appears in the newspaper that its editors have not preapproved. And ever since the milestone Supreme Court case *New York Times* v. *Sullivan* (1964), the Court has grounded libel liability on the concept of scienter—a successful plaintiff must show that the publisher either knew or should have known about the offending content prior to publication.

Making things even worse for Blumenthal was section 230 of the recently passed Communications Decency Act. Although much of that law had been struck down as unconstitutional by the Supreme Court in 1997, Section 230, which exempted service providers from liability for content they did not originate, seemed clearly to protect AOL from being held responsible for Drudge's story.

Blumenthal's lawyer nevertheless hinted that he could sidestep this evidentiary hurdle by showing that America Online was reckless even to contract with Drudge. But this was, after all, Drudge's first and only libel lawsuit; it can hardly be said that AOL should have known Drudge was going to publish actionable material when there were no previous cases to show he had published a libel before. Given that the legal theory behind suing the provider was shaky at best, AOL's presence in the lawsuit was hard to justify legally.

• *Reputational damage.* Let's suppose I'm wrong about Blumenthal's status as a public figure and that I had turned out to be wrong about whether he could have keep America Online in the lawsuit. There remains the issue of whether Blumenthal ultimately suffered any damage to his reputation at all, much less $30 million worth. (I won't dispute that Blumenthal found Drudge's false story personally painful—he and his wife surely did. But the very raison d'être of libel law is damage to reputation, not to one's personal psychological well-being. That's why "publication"—legalese for the showing of the defamatory statement to a third party—is the sine qua non of libel cases: you can't have committed a libel merely by hurting someone's feelings privately.)

We can start by reminding ourselves that Drudge quickly retracted his false report and apologized for it—more than once, as it happens, and in more than one place. This means that at the very least, the same readership that saw the original erroneous report saw its retraction, which ought to be enough to reduce the reputational damage, whatever it might have been, to a significant degree. But that can't be the end of the inquiry, since Drudge's retraction, and Blumenthal's announcement of the $30 million lawsuit, were immediately reported and discussed all over the Internet to an audience far broader than Drudge's core subscribers. What's more, it was a headline grabber in lots of traditional media as well, including a story in the *Wall Street Journal* and multiple stories in the *New York Times*.

This raises a central question for the case—one that not only calls the whole underpinning of this case into question, but also underscores the extent to which both traditional media and traditional legal commentators have been willing to shut off their critical faculties when it comes to thinking about the Internet. Specifically, the question is this: *Is there anyone at all who knows (1) who Blumenthal is, and (2) what Drudge originally wrote about him, who does not also know (3) that Drudge totally retracted his story?* I'm willing to bet that the answer to this question is a solid no.

That answer might be different if Blumenthal were a public figure as widely known as, say, Bill Clinton—or even Conan O'Brien. But Blumenthal is well known only in those circles that pay attention to bylines in the *New Republic,* and you can bet that to anyone with whom Blumenthal even *has* a reputation, Drudge's flat retraction is already old news. In other words, this is one case in which the media, old and new, have functioned just the way they're supposed to in an open society—and just the way some First Amendment theorists always argued that freedom of speech and press should operate. Drudge's correction has caught up with, and even outpaced, the original defamation.

This fact is obvious to anyone who reflects on the Drudge case, but it is a fact that has nevertheless escaped virtually all the reports about the case, which, when not skewed by partisan comments (liberals tend to be anti-Drudge, and conservatives tend to defend him reflexively) were full of comments about the Internet as a no-man's-land of dangerous speech that is only just now being civilized by the legal system. In reality, the Net has always been subject to libel law (as well as other laws), and no reasonable person has ever supposed that he couldn't be sued for saying something libelous on the Internet. A good litmus test for the kind of nonsense one can find in legal commentators dealing with the Net is a statement that we "don't know what the rules of the road are."

The fact is that we do know what the basic rules are, but what most of the pundits have yet to grasp is how the old rules play out in new ways on the Net. For example, one of the reasons a newspaper can still be made to pay a libel defendant even when it has published a retraction is that the retraction (one may reasonably argue) never has quite the impact that the original defamation did—not even if it's printed on the front page and not even if the falsity of the report is further publicized by the filing of a libel lawsuit. That's why Richard Jewell, the hero of the Olympic bombing whose reputation was seriously damaged by the FBI's irrational identification of him as a suspect in the crime and by the press's exacerbation of that damage with its own wildly speculative reports, had the pleasure of extracting tidy monetary settlements from news organizations around the country. Publications like *Time* took months to clear the air, quite a contrast to the immediacy of Drudge's retraction.

This has not prevented would-be legal pundits from dithering about the Net. "If anything, a libel on the Web is more permanent in impact even though it is evanescent in form," law professor Robert O'Neil of the University of Virginia told *New York Times* reporter Carl Kaplan. O'Neil's comment is an odd one from someone who's also director of the Thomas Jefferson Center for the Protection of Freedom of Expression, but not an untypical one from a legal commentator in these days of the social panic about the Internet.

For that, Blumenthal has two phenomena to thank: the immediacy of news reporting on the Net and the willingness of the media to sensational-ize any story that makes the Net look scary. Operating in tandem, these factors have made the retraction a bigger story than the libel ever was, which made Blumenthal's lawsuit look a lot more like opportunistic over-reaching and a lot less like justice in action.[14]

This is not to say that there won't be a lot of talk about Net libel lawsuits in the near term. Much was made of the *Medphone* v. *DeNigris* lawsuit back in 1993, even though legally the case (in which a Prodigy user was sued for business libel based on a posting he'd made in a stock market forum) had virtually no legal significance at all. Lots of Prodigy users claimed to be shocked—shocked!—to discover that something they said online could be the basis of a defamation lawsuit. What was really shocking, however, was that anyone was under the impression that the online world gave users some kind of special legal immunity to say any-thing defamatory they liked.

Interestingly, the defamed have not been satisfied with merely suing those who uttered the allegedly defamatory statements. In fact, what makes the well-known online libel cases, such as *Cubby* v. *CompuServe* in 1991 and *Stratton Oakmont* v. *Prodigy* in 1995, newsworthy has noth-ing to do with whether a *user* can be sued for what he or she posts; that's a given. Instead the focus is on whether the *service provider* ought to be held responsible for the postings of its users. In our society, the First Amendment broad speech protections require that our government insti-tutions defer (in general) even to the speech rights of individuals. In such a society, it's somewhat perverse to impose a great degree of liability on those whose communications systems merely transmit or automatically copy and forward someone else's libelous content. The more you impose such liability, the greater the incentives you create for providers to become content police, and you undermine what for many and perhaps most users is the chief value of the Net: direct communication with the rest of the world.

It's true, of course, that if you don't impose broad liability on service providers, you make it harder for the defamed would-be plaintiff to find someone rich enough to be worth suing. But it may be healthier for us as a society to begin to break the habit of looking for what lawyers often call "deep-pocket defendants." This seems to me to be an experiment worth trying, in any case.

Surely these factors may make libel law increasingly irrelevant, at least as far as online conferencing is concerned.

Perhaps all these factors together add up to the most complete explanation for the question that first began bugging me back in 1990: Why is it that for all the talk of libel lawsuits on the Net, there simply haven't been very many of them?[15] The short answer? On the Net, it's far less common for someone to believe he cannot respond to hurtful factual claims made by others.

It's possible that my explanations for the low count in libel lawsuits is wrong. But even if it is, the simple fact that there are few such lawsuits remains indisputable. That's why, even given the vast and accelerating tide of citizens joining the Net—learning the basics, stumbling over each other's feelings in the course of creating new norms for community—I feel quite safe in renewing my prediction of a few years back: Despite the fierce invective, strong feelings, and often defamatory statements one frequently can find online, the Net will never give rise to many libel cases. Perhaps the only cases in which a libel lawsuit will seem justifiable will be those in which the plaintiff can show that the defendant deliberately set out to spread falsehoods or simply didn't care whether they were false.

Even for the most fragile or immature ego—the man or woman who can't simply turn the other virtual cheek—it's a lot more satisfying to use the Net itself to correct the record and to flame your attackers. And that is a remedy for defamation that doesn't take years. It takes only minutes. Depending on your typing speed, of course.

5

When Words Hurt: Two Hard Cases about Online Speech

It may happen at different ages for different children, but at some point in their lives, most American children face an unpleasant revelation. For me, it came when I was nine or ten and one of my schoolmates had deliberately said something intended to cause me pain. He succeeded. I was angry and tearful.

I've long since forgotten how that particular dispute was resolved or any other details about it, but I do remember one thing. It was then that I realized how the statement we'd heard so often from our parents, our teachers, or our friends—"Sticks and stones can break my bones but words will never hurt me"—was a flatly untrue.

As falsehoods go, the sticks-and-stones meme is a clearly well-intended one. After all, the problem of helping children learn to tolerate hurtful words is one that faces every parent, and getting children to distinguish between tangible and intangible assaults on their well-being is an important step down the road to that problem's solution. But it also may be the sort of misrepresentation that makes it harder for us to think clearly about freedom of speech when we reach adulthood. That so many of us never expect to be hurt by words alone may explain the impulse to take the other guy to court whenever we *are* hurt by someone else's speech. It seems to us that something truly outrageous, even criminal, has taken place. Yet in an open, pluralistic society, surely the individual citizen should expect to come into contact with offensive speech, and perhaps even a sense of injury, on a regular basis, if not (it is to be hoped) on a frequent one.

Even if you don't agree with me yet on that point, surely we agree on the underlying fact that words can and do hurt us. Sometimes a lot.

Sometimes even irreparably. That is why one can't pretend to be dealing honestly with free speech issues without acknowledging that hard fact.

The reason freedom of speech matters is that words *do* have power. They can inspire both pleasant and unpleasant thoughts and feelings in the minds of others. They can even rouse us to action. If speech and expression didn't matter—if they weren't able to have such a strong effect on us much of the time—far fewer of us would feel the impulse to ban or restrict what other people say.

But neither would so many of us defend free speech as vehemently as we do.

In this chapter, we'll explore two cases in which words written online *did* hurt others. In these cases, you'll see situations in which freedom of speech seems to be on a collision course with the legitimate needs of individuals and of society as a whole. These two are among the toughest cases I know of, because both involve speech that, while protected constitutionally, cannot easily be defended on any other basis. In both cases, the online speakers are people whose speech I personally both dislike and disapprove of strongly, and I think it's likely that you'll have similar reactions.

Yet I'm taking you through these hard cases because for once I disagree with the old adage that such cases make bad law. In a very real sense, these hard cases are *good* for us. They test our commitment to the principles on which we've built our society. Even if I don't convince you that these two cases turned out right, I hope to show at the very least how a principled person who disagrees with the speech itself can nonetheless believe that the best outcome is to prevent that speech—in the absence of any more tangible act—from being punished merely for its offensiveness or scariness.

In short, I'm trying to be straight with you—to make it clear to you that to commit yourself to freedom of speech, whether online or otherwise, is to take on a tough challenge. And the challenge doesn't always come from other people's opposition to you. Sometimes it comes from your own reactions and doubts.

That said, I think if you follow me through these two cases, you'll see that even when it's most difficult to defend the rights of a speaker, freedom of speech—albeit used in offensive and disturbing ways that seem to create a genuine problem for others—is usually the best solution to whatever problem we thought we'd allowed to happen.

Free Speech or Gender Discrimination?

For me, the SOLO (Super Oak Leaf Online) case began in the late spring of 1993, when a journalism student at Santa Rosa Junior College called me at my office to tell me that Roger Karraker, a journalist and college teacher I knew casually from the WELL, had been suspended from his duties at the college. Karraker, I knew from our acquaintance on the WELL, served as both a journalism instructor and the faculty adviser to the college newspaper. The charge? Linda, the student who called me, explained that some other students were claiming that Karraker had operated the newspaper's online forum illegally. It was charged that he'd organized the forum in a way that amounted to sexual discrimination. His suspension (technically an administrative leave) was standard procedure for a state-run educational institution.

From what little I knew about Karraker, this charge seemed unlikely. To me, his postings on the WELL showed he was deeply aware of the social responsibilities of his roles as a journalist and educator. Still, I didn't know nearly enough to make a solid judgment about the facts of the case, so I asked Linda, a woman of about my age (like many other of the college's students, she was returning to school to complete her education after having spent several years in another career), about the background of the dispute. Ironically enough, she told me, Karraker's current problems stemmed primarily from a decision he'd made at the request of the system's female users, who'd requested a virtual forum to call their own.

He gave them that women-only forum in March 1993, just about a month before I took the call from Linda. In the interests of fairness, he gave the male users a single-sex forum too. It was these two laudable impulses—his responsiveness to his students' requests and his insistence on fairness—that laid the groundwork for his difficulties that spring.

When he'd started the SOLO project in January 1992, Karraker had never dreamed that his online communications forum would lead to charges of sex discrimination, suspension by his employer, and the intervention of the U.S. government. Explaining his impulse to start the forum in the first place, Karraker describes himself as an "evangelist" who believes "that online conferencing can revolutionize our society and our schools." Adds Karraker: "It has changed my life for the better and for years I sought a way to bring it to my students."

At first the experiment was a compelling success. Says Karraker, "SOLO grew quickly. Soon there were nearly four hundred students online from a variety of disciplines. It wasn't an open access system: you had to be a student of a half dozen instructors who was using the system for academic purposes. On more than two dozen occasions I and other faculty had invited administrators to participate on the system. In its three years of operation none ever found the time."

He adds that the range of topics discussed on SOLO was as broad as that of any other general-purpose discussion forum: "SOLO's topics grew just as quickly. Soon we had over two hundred different conferences: a dozen or more about music styles, a half dozen on different aspects of behavior, a vigorous group of current events discussions. Unlike some other systems, the software we used for SOLO was somewhat austere: there were no games that could be played, no Internet e-mail, gopher, ftp. There were only two things you could do on SOLO: read and write. . . . Over half of SOLO's users were women."

Yet not much more than a year after starting a forum for his students, Karraker's experiment had triggered nationwide attention (not only reported in the *New York Times,* but also the subject of an Anthony Lewis column there) because of the questions it raised about the conflict between sexual discrimination and the First Amendment in online forums.

Appropriately enough, this First Amendment fracas started at a newspaper—the Santa Rosa Junior College student newspaper known as the *Oak Leaf.* When Karraker, who combined his experience as a journalist with years of participating in and writing about virtual communities and the online experience, started the online conferencing system, he called it "Super Oak Leaf Online"—aka, "SOLO."

The SOLO case raised complicated issues because of Karraker's decision to provide single-sex conferences as well as public conferences. He wanted to give his journalism students the full experience of participating in online environments, in which single-sex conferences (particularly women-only conferences) have frequently been successful, as have many other experiments in designing forums that focus on women's issues. After a long interval in which several women on SOLO approached Karraker and requested their own women-only conference, he decided to give them one. He then started a men-only conference as well, less because many men had requested one than because it seemed like the equitable thing to do. (The coed public conferences remained open to students who were taking journalism classes or to those who were taking other classes in which the instructors used SOLO, which was open only to students and faculty at the junior college.)

Behind Closed Doors: The War of the Words

At the time, Karraker thought his decision would be relatively uncontroversial. After all, single-sex forums were common in online environments in the early 1990s, and none had been the source of any particular degree of controversy. Systems like the WELL and ECHO created them in response to the wishes of female users who wanted digital spaces in which they could discuss women's issues and share their concerns without having to compete in the often rough-and-tumble male-oriented online environments that are the norm. Women who participate in these forums say there is less free-floating aggression and less confrontation.

Fawn Fitter, a journalist in Boston who participates in the WELL's primary women-only conference, once explained pithily how the atmosphere of Women on the WELL (often called WOW for short) is different. "It's not all 'Here's how cool I am, and here's how clever I can be,'" Fitter told the Associated Press during the press's focus on the SOLO case. "It's an attempt to connect, not to show off."

Once a system sets up a women-only conference, there's usually a call for a male-only conference as well. (The WELL's Men on the WELL conference started this way.) Typically, participants in single-sex conferences are admitted to a conference only after promising to keep the contents of the postings confidential. When Karraker set up the single-sex conferences on SOLO, he posted the following conditions for participation:

1. Private conferences, by definition, are *not* public. You gain admittance by sending e-mail to the conference moderator (Dave Witkowski for men;

Lynette Williams for women). Only persons of the appropriate gender may gain admittance.

2. To encourage frank, private discussion, persons who gain entrance to a conference agree that what is said there is private. It is a violation of the rules of these private conferences to show messages or discuss their contents (other than a general summary) with a nonmember of that conference. If you can't abide by that rule, don't ask for admission to the conference. If you gain admittance, then later violate that rule, you will be summarily thrown out of the conference. If your indiscretion is grievous enough, you may be tossed off SOLO as well. Violating others' confidences is a major sin; don't do it.

According to many who participate in single-sex conferences, it is only this condition of confidentiality—the assurance that no one in the conference will disclose the contents of these private postings to members of the opposite sex or to others outside the conference—that enables them to speak freely. To underscore this point, Karraker even barred himself from access to the women's conference.

Sometimes women-only conferences engage in what charitably can be called "male bashing," but more often the discussions are civil and friendly (or so I am told by reliable sources). The same goes for the male-only forums, whose participants often focus on discussions of "struggling with being male in this society and dealing with pain and emotional hurt"—the kinds of things men don't always find it easy to talk about publicly.

Occasionally, however, someone will use a single-sex forum to let off steam, and that's exactly what happened on SOLO's male-only conference, which had only ten student members at the time. (Karraker, in the interests of making his experiment in free speech forums valid, occasionally participated but played no "editorial role." He did not prescreen any of the men's messages' content before it was posted.)[1] Some of the men in the conference had nasty comments about Lois Arata, a student who'd led a protest of what she regarded as a sexist advertisement in the *Oak Leaf*. Another man, a fellow who'd recently been involved in a breakup with a student named Jennifer Branham, posted some mean-spirited invective about Branham.

Branham had previously posted some unpleasant comments about her ex-boyfriend in the public conferences, but nothing (my sources tell me) as extreme as what the men had said.

The posted remarks in the male conference weren't pretty. Their language was profane, and they included the nastiest kind of personal and sexual insults. But not all the men shared in the invective. In fact, the talk was so troubling to at least one of the participants, Dylan Humphrey, that he took it on himself to inform Branham and Arata about the insults. When Jennifer Branham complained to Karraker about what had been posted, he shut down the male-only conference immediately. Soon after, he shut down the female-only conference as well, largely to avoid complaints that he was favoring female users over males. Later, when Karraker learned that Humphrey had violated his pledge of confidentiality, he felt compelled to remove Humphrey's access to the system for violating one of its primary rules.

Arata and Branham, as you might imagine, were incensed. They complained to the college administration, with the immediate result that Karraker was put on administrative leave while the college investigated the case.

Pointing Fingers: The Search for a Crime

A major hurdle for the two women was that they couldn't easily find a legal or official remedy for their (undoubted) sense of injury—or at least not at first. Ultimately Karraker would not be officially punished. (He would be punished unofficially. It was several months before his standing was restored and his name effectively cleared of any wrongdoing, intentional or otherwise.) College administrators eventually concluded after their investigation that no sexual harassment had taken place.

Branham and Arata's primary strategy throughout the dispute was to attempt to find an argument that what had happened to them added up to a violation of their federally guaranteed civil rights. The women knew that the framework for judging discrimination as a function of their gender was the Civil Rights Act of 1964, a statutory system aimed at giving both the courts and the executive branch of the federal government the power to rectify long-standing discriminatory activities conducted against some Americans on the basis of race, gender, or other prohibited criteria.

This statute is the basis for federal civil claims seeking redress for sexual harassment and sexual discrimination. While there has long been some dispute about the extent to which the statute applies in many cases involving private discrimination against classes of Americans (that is, in cases in which no government agent or institution is directly involved), there was scarcely any dispute, comparatively, as to its authority to prohibit gender-based discrimination in the activity of federal and state agencies, including Santa Rosa Junior College.

Yet there was little sign that any of the nasty comments had been grounded in the women's gender *as such* (arguably, the comments would have been just as nasty if Branham and Arata had been men), and the comments on the male-only forum were meant to remain unseen by any women. It would have been hard for the women to argue that they were being harassed by comments they were never meant to see.

Finally, as I've already noted, the single-sex forums came about because of women's *requests*. Whatever one may think of the wisdom of Karraker's decision, there's little doubt that he was actively trying to give his female students a real and equal opportunity to explore this new kind of forum—an equal chance to found their own virtual community.

If the Civil Rights Act appeared to be useless, so did the prospects for any libel lawsuit. The problem here for the women was that invective (calling someone a *bastard* or a *bitch,* for example) is normally protected speech under the First Amendment. To be libel, a statement has to make a specific false *factual* claim about the plaintiff—one that is credible and that furthermore actually damages a reputation in a significant way.[2] Posting that "Mike Godwin is a lousy writer and a jerk too" is not libel; posting that "Mike Godwin is a dishonest lawyer who cheats his clients" very likely is. The first is primarily a statement of feeling, while the second appears to be a factual claim, and only false statements of fact can qualify as libel.

The comments made about Arata and Branham, childish and mean-spirited as they were, did not rise to the level of libel. But if they couldn't sue for libel and if no sexual harassment claim was appropriate, the women at least wanted to get access to the male-only forum to find out exactly what was said about them and to confront the men who spoke ill of them. (In a telephone interview with me, Arata later bitterly referred to the male name callers as "cowardly" for not openly confronting her and Branham. Interestingly, if the men had chosen to do just that, the open confrontation itself might have qualified more clearly as some kind of harassment than anything that happened in the online world.)

There were two problems with the women's demands, however. First, Karraker had shut down the male-only conference, so there was no meaningful way for the women to enter into the discussions. (As Gertrude Stein purportedly once said of Oakland, "There is no there there.") Second, and more important, Karraker had set up the single-sex forums with an understanding, insisted on by the users, that the postings would remain confidential. Karraker and the school felt they'd be violating a confidentiality obligation to let the women have access to those private postings.

This didn't deter either Branham or Arata. Branham, herself a journalism student, continued to have access to SOLO's public conferences and could post her responses about the incident there. The school gave Arata access to the public conferences as well, but Arata felt that merely being able to answer the criticisms of her in a public conference was inadequate. She wanted to be able to pierce the veil of confidentiality and call to account the particular men who'd reportedly insulted her. Plus, Arata found that the audience for her postings in the public forums of SOLO was conspicuously unsympathetic. Of the other women who participated in SOLO, most seemed to be angry that Arata had taken steps that resulted in the loss of the women-only forum. Other users criticized her logic and factual claims, while still others engaged in personal attacks. After two weeks, Arata abandoned her account on the system.

In the offline world as well, the two women, together with Dylan Humphrey (the male conference participant who passed on the derogatory comments in the first place), felt an increasing sense of antagonism from other students on campus, many of whom specifically charged them as being responsible for the abrupt removal of Karraker from his position. To make this turn of events sting even more, the three students could see that Karraker, far from being stigmatized by the incident, seemed to have become an even more popular professor. Arata in particular was furious, since she had demanded that Karraker be dismissed. The two women decided to take their complaints to the Office for Civil Rights (OCR) of the U.S. Department of Education. That's when things got really messy.

When San Francisco–based lawyers for the OCR began investigating the complaints, they looked for violations of Title IX of the Education Amendments of 1972—specific amendments to the federal Civil Rights Act that ban sexual harassment and sex discrimination at federally funded schools (and that ban retaliation against those who try to bring to light sexual harassment and sex discrimination claims). After several months of considering the case, the lawyers decided they'd found what they were looking for.

Although the OCR did not find that Humphrey had a clear claim for retaliation, it did conclude that Arata and Branham had been victims of sex discrimination because they had been *barred from access to the male-only forum*. Furthermore, to quote their preliminary report, they found that "the College's failure to abate the personal attacks denied [Arata] the opportunity to participate in SOLO." The lawyers also decided that the nasty comments directed at Arata on SOLO amounted to sexual harassment and retaliation against her for her outspokenness. The Equal Employment Opportunity Commission standard for sexual harassment is unwelcome sexual conduct, one form of which is conduct that creates a "hostile environment." For words to arise to the level of "hostile environment," they have to be sufficiently severe and pervasive to create an environment that inhibits the victim's ability to perform. It is hard to imagine how the mere repeating of gossip, all by itself, rises to such a level of conduct, but this is what the OCR found.

Branham's claim also received a sympathetic hearing. Branham told the OCR that she was met with increasing hostility at the *Oak Leaf* offices from the student newspaper's staff. The OCR characterized the angry statements staff members expressed to Branham as harassment and as retaliation against Branham, who was perceived by her fellow students as having triggered the junior college's decision to put the popular Karraker on administrative leave.

It was at this point that the Sonoma County Junior College District, which oversees Santa Rosa Junior College, made a disturbing (to the defendants) choice. Rather than risk protracted litigation with the students, the district offered a settlement: Lois Arata, Jennifer Branham, and Dylan Humphrey each accepted $15,000 in return for releasing the junior college district from any and all claims based on this series of incidents.

In the final analysis, that settlement, it seemed, satisfied the student claimants. But the OCR didn't think its job was over yet. On its own initiative, the OCR proposed a set of rules for SOLO that would seriously abridge the very freedom of expression the system was intended to promote. Here's a passage from the OCR's proposed Remedial Action Plan:

V. SRJC [or, more precisely, the Sonoma County Junior College District, acting through its agents at Santa Rosa Junior College] shall promulgate guidelines of appropriate conduct for users of the Super Oak Leaf Online (SOLO) computer network and any other computer networks or bulletin board established or operated by SRJC. The Guidelines shall also notify users of their right to be free from harassment on the basis of race, color, national origin, or disability and of their right to be free from retaliation for protesting such harassment. In particular, the SRJC proposed computing procedures shall be amended to read as follows:

A. Paragraph 4 of the SRJC "Administrative Computing Procedures" shall be amended to read as follows:

The computing facilities at Santa Rosa Junior College are provided for the use of Santa Rosa Junior College students, faculty, and staff in support of the programs of the College. All students, faculty, and staff are responsible for seeing that these computing facilities are used in an effective, efficient, ethical, nondiscriminatory, and lawful manner.

B. A new paragraph 14.2 shall be added to the SRJC "Administrative Computing Procedures" to read as follows:

14.2 Nondiscrimination—All users have the right to be free from any conduct connected with the use of SRJC computing systems which discriminates against any person on the basis of race, color, national origin, sex, or disability. Discriminatory conduct includes, but is not limited to, written or graphic conduct that satisfies both the following conditions: (1) harasses, denigrates, or shows hostility or aversion toward an individual or group based on that person's gender, race, color, national origin, or disability, AND (2) has the purpose or effect of creating a hostile, intimidating, or offensive educational environment. "Harassing conduct" and "hostile educational environment" are defined below.

"Harassing conduct" includes, but is not limited to, the following: epithets, slurs, negative stereotyping, or threatening, intimidating, or hostile acts that relate to race, color, national origin, gender, or disability. This includes acts that purport to be "jokes" or "pranks" but are hostile or demeaning. A "hostile educational environment" is established when harassing conduct is sufficiently severe, pervasive, or persistent so as to interfere with or limit the ability of an individual to participate in or benefit from the SRJC computing systems.

On one level, it's clear how the OCR reached these recommendations: the authors of the suggested guidelines expressly quote language ("harassing conduct" and "hostile educational environment") that is commonly used in federal gender discrimination cases. But the sheer breadth of the prohibitions and the inevitable uncertainty as to what might qualify as "harassing conduct" (the OCR seemed to be defining any negative speech as harassment) meant that students at the junior college would likely be afraid even to participate in a normal argument (between a woman and her boyfriend, say) for fear that frankly expressed feelings might get them disciplined.

The Case for Protecting Free Speech

To understand how the OCR's recommendations affect First Amendment rights, it's important to examine the interests the First Amendment is designed to protect. The first interest is what most Americans think of first when they think of the First Amendment: freedom of speech. But we're less often inclined to remember that the First Amendment was crafted specifically to stop the majority of us from using the government to regulate speech someone finds offensive. Governments never try to ban any other kind.

There's no doubt about the offensiveness of the words in this case, but there's also no doubt that if freedom of speech means anything, it means the right to vent your anger about a bad breakup with your girlfriend or boyfriend. It also means that universities, along with the rest of us, acknowledge and accept that mere offensiveness is not enough of a justification for taking someone to court. (When I hear complaints about how lawyers are burdening the courts with lawsuits, I like to remind people that lawyers can't take a case to court without a client's approval. If you don't like lawsuits, your best strategy to reduce the number of them is to be less eager to sue someone.) And freedom of speech surely means the right to voice your frustration about someone whose political views you find offensive. Free speech is there for Lois Arata as much as it is for the men she complained about. Her pointed comments to the press and the public about the boorishness of the men in the men-only conference surely caused them to regret having forsaken good manners. Free speech may have been the problem, but it was also the solution.

What bothered me and other civil libertarians about the OCR's proposed plan was that it referred to something called "written conduct" that expressed "hostility or aversion toward an individual or group based on that person's gender, race, color, national origin, or disability." Leaving aside the issue of whether the comments about Arata and Branham were grounded in hostility toward their gender (rather than hostility toward them as individuals), it seemed clear that what the OCR wants to ban here is not "written conduct" but speech. By classifying it as "conduct," the OCR hoped to bypass the First Amendment's protections.

It's well established that First Amendment–protected speech may be offensive and even profane. In the early 1970s, in *Cohen v. California,* the Supreme Court held that a protester who wore a jacket with the inscription "Fuck the Draft" was engaging in speech that, while offensively profane to many, couldn't be limited or punished under the Constitution. Justice John Marshall Harlan, who wrote the majority opinion in that case, also held that the emotional content of speech is just as protected as its intellectual content. That is, even when we're venting our anger—letting off steam in a heated expression of opinion—we're engaging in protected speech.

For the same reason, the nasty comments that some SOLO users made about Arata (the OCR focused on both the comments in the male-only conference and the later exchanges between Arata and other users in SOLO's public conferences), puerile though they sometimes were, were nevertheless deserving of protection. It violates the First Amendment for the OCR to require the administrators of the state-run college system to police against such speech.

Nor was speech the only First Amendment interest at issue. There was also the matter of something that constitutional lawyers refer to as "freedom of association." Since the late 1950s, the Supreme Court has acknowledged that the First Amendment protects our ability to associate with whomever we choose, to do so in privacy, and to engage in private conversations. Government efforts aimed at preventing that kind of privacy from occurring are inconsistent with freedom of association, and this includes a government insistence that males (or females) cannot associate for purposes of discussion with members of their own gender. One of the ironies of the OCR's insistence that single-sex forums no longer exist on SOLO was that the ruling hurt women more than men. As I noted earlier, it's women who most frequently request single-sex conferences. (In fact, women in online systems are normally more amused than troubled whenever men on a particular system respond to the creation of a women-only forum by creating a men-only counterpart. The joke is that men don't need such a place for themselves, since the whole public world is, in a sense, already a male-dominated forum.)

It wasn't that the OCR was wholly unaware of these First Amendment considerations. But the lawyers for the OCR took the position that the First Amendment had to be "balanced" against Civil Rights Act provisions, and SOLO is an educational facility and therefore must operate under more restrictive rules.

But here the OCR demonstrated that it missed the whole point of SOLO. The online system is indeed an educational facility in some sense, but it was designed to educate its student users about freedom of speech. And the problem is that you can't teach freedom of speech in the abstract; First Amendment rights have to be used if they're to be fully understood. Perhaps the best understanding you can gain from the First Amendment is an understanding of the need to be tolerant of expressions or views that offend you or even hurt your feelings. This understanding can come only from individuals' independent explorations of that freedom, which includes learning how to handle your emotions when others' exploration of that freedom offends you.

Rather than shutting up the offending person or violating his or her desire for private conversations, the best remedy for bad speech is more speech, and this was a remedy to which both Branham and Arata had access. Arata's complaint that she found the antagonism against her on SOLO's public conferences too much to tolerate says more about her inability to cope with criticism and disagreement than it does about whether SOLO's users were "retaliating" against her. Conversely, the character of the men's complaints about Arata's activities did not speak well of them either.

Yet I'm convinced that various debates were already on the way to finding their own balance before the forum's evolution was derailed, first by the college's actions and then by those of the federal government. This is because I've seen how online forums, when left to speak in freedom, tend to become more tolerant places over time.

Now this probably flies in the face of what you've heard about the Internet, whose disputatious denizens regularly appal some people (especially an oddly timorous subset of journalists, who then editorialize against the "flamers"). Certainly those of us who've spent a lot of time online can attest that the Internet is in fact a medium of strong opinions, strongly expressed.

But the fact that users can express their views in offensive language is not a weakness of the online world; it's a strength. The Net may not always teach tolerance directly, but it does teach us the nature of pluralism. This is a lesson we need to learn if we're to cope with a world in which those with divergent opinions are increasingly connected to each other via the national and global information networks—a world in which, as John Perry Barlow has said, the First Amendment is often regarded, at least by other governments, as a "local ordinance."

This lesson of tolerance is one we're all going to have to learn, and it was this lesson that Roger Karraker's SOLO was well positioned to teach—until the Office of Civil Rights stepped in and decided that true freedom of speech was too dangerous to allow.

But the fight wasn't over yet. Some of us hoped to answer bad government with good speech. From the moment Linda, the student who was also a newspaper staff member, called to tell me about Karraker's troubles, I was convinced that the way to stop Karraker from being sanctioned by administrators or government officials who simply had no idea how these online forums functioned was to take the story to the rest of the world. In my experience as both a lawyer and, years earlier, a student journalist, I had learned that college administrators hate bad press almost as much as they love rich alumni donors. I suggested to Linda, who was active in organizing the students' response to the college's actions regarding SOLO and Karraker, that she and the other students make a point of telling their side of the story to the press. Although there was no guarantee that press coverage would be positive (the *New York Times*'s first story, for example, struck me as a bit negative with regard to Karraker and the forum), I also knew from my own experience as a troublemaker on campus that press coverage tends to make university administrators more deeply concerned about adhering to proper procedures. And I wanted to make sure that no one in the administration reached any reflexive or punitive action decision about Karraker without reviewing all the facts.

Then I gave Linda some suggestions about how to talk about the story to the local and national press. For example, I suggested that she stress in her conversations with the press that a majority of the women on SOLO were more troubled by the shutdown of the women-only forum than by anything the guys in the men-only forum had said. The other suggestions I gave her about dealing with media were essentially the same as the ones I've followed myself, from the beginnings of the Steve Jackson Games lawsuit (see chapter 2) to the investigation of *Time* magazine's "cyberporn" scandal (see chapter 9).

In the next few days, I started calling journalists myself to tell them about the story and let them know what the students and I thought the issues were. (I made a point of giving them contact information for Arata and Branham so they would have a chance to air their side of the story as well. Journalists tend to prefer it, I've found, when you give them as much as you know and don't try to slant the story by withholding important facts, such as who your most articulate opponents are.)

The outcome of these efforts (both mine and the SRJC students') was fairly dramatic. Tamar Lewin, a reporter for the *New York Times,* did not write the first story on the dispute, but (unsurprisingly) the story she wrote was the most influential in terms of getting the issues discussed in the national press. As Roger Karraker tells it, Lewin's article triggered real attention. "Then national coverage really materialized," he told an audience at the Computers, Freedom, and Privacy Conference in March 1995, citing articles in the *Washington Post,* the op-ed page of the *New York Times,* the *Chronicle of Higher Education,* National Public Radio, the syndicated TV show *Freedom Speaks,* and the *San Jose Mercury News.* Never one to miss an idea for a column, I wrote an article about the case for *Internet World.*

It was a good thing that we'd made the effort to get the story out, as it happened. The fight was only beginning when we took it on in April 1993. It was more than a year before there was anything like a final resolution of all the issues. These issues ranged from Karraker's rights as a professor facing a complaint about sexual harassment and/or gender discrimination, to the students' rights to have access to this online forum, to the Office of Civil Rights' prerogative to impose its speech code on a junior college. And of course they also include the question of whether Arata and Branham had a right to redress for their sense of injury.

The administrators of the college system of which Santa Rosa Junior College is a part considered whether and in what manner they could challenge the speech restrictions the OCR wanted to impose. Ultimately, they did so rather successfully. Here's how Roger Karraker describes it:

While this episode was clearly the most unpleasant thing I've ever experienced, it has had its bright side. One of the things I learned was that very few people understand or use free speech. "Hey, how about those '49ers" isn't free speech. Consequently, when this free speech issue erupted, I found that all kinds of people—administrators, students, a minority of feminists, and even some faculty—didn't understand the issue.

Many people conflated the issue. Because the content of the speech itself was repugnant—something everyone agrees on—it was somehow conflated to the conclusion that such speech shouldn't be allowed.

Another discovery was that those who *do* use free speech, those who use computer conferencing, refuse to allow anyone else to control their words. They are quite willing to take responsibility for their own speech.

At times I'm pessimistic about the survival of our constitutional rights. The Clinton administration, for which I have had and still have so much hope, has a dismal record in the area of electronic rights and privacy.

But I've found that all you need to do to create zealots for individual liberty is to get people communicating online. Once they've tasted the freedom of free, responsible speech, they are, almost without exception, extremely supportive of unfettered free speech.

Here's the final chapter: The Office for Civil Rights, which had threatened to take away Santa Rosa's federal funding, has closed the case. There were no findings, no report, no conclusions, no remedial plan. Of course, there also wasn't an apology or an indication that its initial, tentative findings might have been full of hot air. Sort of like the United States in Vietnam, the Office for Civil Rights declared victory and went home.

The agency attempted to save face by claiming that a newly adopted college policy essentially complies with its proposed remedial plan. The new policy is a master stroke of double-speak. It adopts OCR's language outlawing "harassing conduct" and "slurs, jests, insults, and jokes" of a racial, gender, or ethnic nature.

But the college's attorney mischievously added a sentence: "Nothing contained herein shall be construed as violating any person's rights of expression set forth in the Equal Access Act or the First Amendment of the United States Constitution."

So a policy deliberately intended as a hate speech code has been somehow transmogrified into an affirmation of the First Amendment.

Ever the educator, Karraker extracted a lesson from his travails at Santa Rosa Junior College. And the lesson of online pluralism and tolerance is an important one. If we value free speech, we can't allow Karraker's lesson to be supplanted by the lesson that the OCR wanted to teach.

We can't accept the argument there's some set of *online* speech that, simply because it's too offensive, justifies an exception to tolerance or to the First Amendment. Toleration for mere words is something we have always needed, and now begin to require, from any society that claims to be a free and open one.

The Troubling Case of Jake Baker

How far should tolerance of "mere" words go? Law professor and feminist theorist Catharine MacKinnon has strongly criticized those free speech defenders who argue that "words"—which stand metaphorically for the full range of human communication the courts have said is protected by the First Amendment—ought to be defended because they don't add up to physical harm. She even titled one of her books *Only Words* (Harvard University Press, 1996)—a sly way of ridiculing free-speech advocates who choose (in her view) to ignore the real harm that words can do.

The courts' continuing insistence on classifying most kinds of "words that hurt" as presumptively protected speech under the First Amendment leads MacKinnon to what may seem a surprising statement: "In the United States, pornography is protected by the state." (The statement is also clearly designed to have a kind of rhetorical shock value, because it's so counterintuitive to those of us who are aware that pornography producers and vendors are often prosecuted by the government in this country.) But MacKinnon, who believes there is a direct causal link between pornography and violent or otherwise abusive treatment of women, is not merely saying that lots of pornography can't be prosecuted under prevailing interpretations of the First Amendment. (She's right in saying this. For example, it may be sexually explicit but not legally "obscene," a concept we discuss at length in chapter 8 and elsewhere in this book.)

Instead she's making a far deeper criticism. She argues in *Only Words* and elsewhere that this (to her) arbitrary or willful decision to treat pornography as protected speech until it's proven otherwise in a criminal court makes it almost impossible for those she sees as victims of the pornography to obtain any legal remedy or relief. Because anything classified as "speech" is presumed to be protected by the First Amendment, she says, the legal system puts an unjust burden on the victims of pornography to prove that their harm is real enough to deserve either a civil remedy or protection by the criminal laws, or both.

MacKinnon's conviction that pornography is a direct cause of immediate harm to particular women as well as to women in general (since it reinforces their lesser legal and political status in society) leads her to regard with heartfelt contempt any free speech defender who simply parrots some dressed-up version of the old lie about the difference between "sticks and stones" and mere words, which "will never hurt me."

On this particular narrow point, I find myself inclined to agree with MacKinnon. The argument that speech is protected by the Constitution because it has no real power to hurt people is not only inconsistent with just about everybody's experience, it also undercuts the very reason anyone should ever want to defend free speech, which is that the power of words themselves requires us to defend the right to speak them.

After all, why defend a right that is essentially ineffectual—a right that doesn't matter much, that has no force in the real world? When we take this approach, we raise the question of why we're even arguing for free speech.

MacKinnon's arguments have a real-world application, which is why I think that if we're to argue with her and others like her, we have to do more than simply echo the distinction academics have come to accept between words and actions.

Now, we still have to argue the particulars with the anti–free speech forces (by pointing out, for example, that the evidence doesn't much support any claim of a direct connection between sexually explicit speech and crimes against women or other groups). But I think we also have to acknowledge that words can and do hurt people and that the reason we oppose new restrictions on speech, whether online, on a college campus, or in the public square, is that we are convinced of that particular principle. Specifically, we believe that in the long run, a society that emphasizes individual freedom, even when that freedom is sometimes used hurtfully, gives us far more than even the most well-meant law designed to free us from fear or discomfort ever can.

This is why the Jake Baker case is such a hard one. What makes the SOLO case hard is that it's relatively easy to identify with either side in that dispute. (I can even see how the Office for Civil Rights must have felt, at least for a while, that they were doing the right thing in attempting to impose a speech code on a college newspaper's online forum.)

The Jake Baker case, in contrast, is one in which many of us find it impossible to identify with the person defending his online free-speech rights. We may believe on an abstract level that Baker was correct to challenge the federal prosecutor who hoped to make an example of him for posting repellent stories to the Net. At the same time, anyone who reflects on the horror the whole affair must have created for the woman whose name he used in a piece of fiction cannot help feeling at least some discomfort at the prospect of defending him.

Two Wrongs Don't Make a Right

Emotionally, it's still hard for me to defend Jake Baker, even though I believe that what happened to him is a far greater threat to the general welfare than any he was ever accused of making. At best, the University of Michigan undergraduate was an amateur writer with a repellently misogynistic imagination. At worst, Baker, using horrific rape-torture-murder stories, was posting his actual sexual fantasies in the Usenet newsgroup alt.sex.stories and revealing a kind of twisted psyche I cannot even remotely understand.

Still, when I first heard reports about the Jake Baker case, it was immediately clear that the constitutional issues raised by a Michigan federal prosecutor's decision to prosecute him for stories posted on the Internet were serious ones. The issue was not, and could never be, whether Baker was a nice person or even a healthy one. Instead the case underscored the broader question of whether the stories and e-mail he transmitted over the Net constituted a crime.

Baker, a twenty-year-old sophomore linguistics major at the time of the postings, doesn't look like much of a Hannibal Lecter. The five-foot-six student is estimated to weigh in somewhere between 120 and 130 pounds. But that featherweight frame was home to some Frankensteinian sexual fantasies, for which Baker thought he'd found an appreciative audience in alt.sex.stories. (Lest you take from this the impression that the Net is, as commonly represented, a cornucopia of porn, consider that there are many, many thousands of newsgroups—another word for discussion areas—on Usenet. Amazingly, however, it's the ones having to do with sex that get most of the press.)

In early October 1994, Baker posted "Gone Fishin'," a story in which a teenage girl and her boyfriend are raped, tortured, and murdered. Later that semester, he posted a second story, "A Day at Work," which described another rape, torture, and murder, this time of a randomly chosen victim. Although many readers of alt.sex.stories were appalled by Baker's fiction and said so publicly, Baker also found a fan, identifying himself as "Arthur Gonda," who posted from an Ontario, Canada, account. Gonda and Baker began exchanging e-mail in which they described sadistic sexual kidnapping-murder scenarios they'd fantasized about.

In the meantime, Baker continued to write for the public as well. His career as a Marquis de Sade wannabe culminated in a piece in which the narrator and his friend Jerry sexually torture a young woman, then douse her in gasoline, and flick a lit match at her. Posted on January 9, the story was unusual (even compared to Baker's other fiction) in this respect: Baker had given the story's female victim the same name as that of a fellow student. (In this chapter, I'll call her Jane Doe. Baker claims he chose Jane's real name, which included the syllable "staff," because it suggested a phallic pun.)

No mere summary of any of Baker's stories can do it justice. So in order to give you a feel for why people find Baker's writing so outrageous, here's one of the less explicit passages from the story:

> She's shaking with terror as Jerry and I circle her. She's almost completely nude now—we've made her take off all her clothes except for her bra and panties. As Jerry and I pass by her, we reach out and feel her velvety flesh, caress her breasts and ass through her underwear. Jerry and I snap pictures of her tiny trembling body from all angles.
>
> She says in a little, terrified voice, "Why are you doing this . . . I've never hurt you. . . . P-please stop!" I pause in front of her. Jerry smiles at her terror. He laughs at her pitiful pleas. I say, "Shut the fuck up, stupid whore!" and hit the side of her head, hard. She collapses onto the ground, crying, curling up into a little ball.

Baker's story gets worse from there. It gets so graphic, in fact, that ten days later, when a sixteen-year-old girl in Moscow read the story online, she reportedly felt moved to tell her father how troubling she found it. Her father told his friend Richard DuVal about what his daughter had found on the Internet. DuVal, a University of Michigan alumnus, was so offended by the story, posted from a University of Michigan account, no less, that he called up his alma mater to complain. That single action created a world of hurt for Jake Baker.

The day after the U of M officials were contacted, Baker lost his computer privileges. Soon after, he was met at his dorm room by officials from the university's campus police, who asked to examine his room. Baker consented to that search, as well as to a search of his computer account by university officials. He believed, mistakenly, that if he disclosed everything, it would quickly become apparent that he intended no harm to Jane Doe or to anyone else, and that his public and private writings about violent sexual fantasies would be recognized as fiction and regarded as First Amendment–protected activities. As Jesse Jannetta, his roommate, told the *Washington Post,* Baker "thought if he cooperated and gave the university what they wanted—told the truth—it would all work out."

Instead, what worked out is that university officials sought his voluntary withdrawal from the school. When Baker failed to agree, the administrators proceeded to suspend him. Baker learned of the suspension when he was met by armed university officers after class on February 2, given a copy of the suspension letter from university president, James Duderstadt, then taken to his dorm room and given fifteen minutes to gather what he could prior to being escorted off campus.

But if Baker thought the worst had happened, he was in for a shock. By consenting to have university officials look through his e-mail, he'd guaranteed they'd find his correspondence with Gonda, which he'd saved. And if the public postings to alt.sex.stories were hair-raising, the private mail was even worse. In December, Baker had sent Gonda a message that included the following:

I just picked up Bllod [*sic*] Lust and have started to read it. I'll look for "Final Truth" tomorrow (payday). One of the things I've started doing is going back and rereading earlier messages of yours. Each time I do, they turn me on more and more. I can't wait to see you in person. I've been trying to think of secluded spots, but my area knowledge of Ann Arbor is mostly limited to the campus. I don't want any blood in my room, though I have come upon an excellent method to abduct a bitch—

As I said before, my toom [*sic*] is right across from the girl's bathroom. Wiat [*sic*] until late at night, grab her when she goes to unlock the door. Knock her unconscious and put her into one of those portable lockers (forgot the word for it), or even a duffel bag. Then hurry her out to the car and take her away . . . what do you think?

Gonda quickly responded:

Hi Jake. I have been out tonight and I can tell you that I am thinking more and more about "doing" a girl. I can picture it so well . . . and I can think of no better use for their flesh. I *have* to make a bitch suffer!

It's still unclear that Arthur Gonda is a real person. Early reports from Canada asserted no such name is listed in the Ontario tax records and suggested that "Arthur Gonda" is a pseudonym, or perhaps even a wholly fictitious persona (invented, perhaps, to spoof Baker). Later it was discovered that there is in fact someone named Gonda who lives in the region, but the problems of drawing any evidentiary connection between that person and the one who talked to Baker were probably enough to discourage even the most assiduous policeman.

In any case, the message from Gonda, with its expression of a feeling of compulsion, is quite disturbing. But can we infer from the "Gonda" e-mail that *Baker* was actively plotting to harm someone? Or was he simply sharing his fantasies with a like-minded correspondent? University officials didn't think they could take any chances, which is why they suspended Baker and turned over the material to federal law enforcement officials.

When a Threat Is Not a Threat

When the feds stepped in, their actions regarding Baker transformed the case: they took what had begun as merely an interesting question about the authority of state universities to discipline students who say scary things and had "made a federal case of it." This new case raised fundamental questions of due process, criminal law, and First Amendment law. University administrators believed that in addition to violating university policies somehow, Baker seemed capable of and willing to commit a crime. But the FBI and the U.S. Attorney's office took it one step further: they were determined to find a way to prove that Baker had *already committed one.*

That's why, a week after Baker's suspension, FBI agents took Baker into custody at his lawyer's home, charging him with violating Title 18, U.S. Code, Section 875(c), which prohibits the transmission "in interstate or foreign commerce any communication containing any threat to kidnap any person or any threat to injure the person of another." Theoretically, a defendant convicted of this felony can be punished by a prison term of up to five years.

It was an interesting legal theory for the government to advance. Before they had Baker arrested, prosecutors had hinted they might charge him on a federal distribution-of-obscenity count. But that approach looked pretty iffy, for a technical reason: The likeliest federal obscenity statute (Title 18 of the U.S. Code, Section 1465), had been persuasively interpreted in 1987 by the Tenth Circuit Court of Appeals as "restricted in its terms to the transportation of tangible objects." (See *United States* v. *Carlin Communications,* 815 F.2d 1367.) Another federal statute that might be applied—Title 47 of the U.S. Code, Section 223, the obscene phone call statute that Senator James Exon of Nebraska later tried to amend with the Communications Decency Act—was just as disappointing, but for a different reason: the statute punished noncommercial distributions of obscenity with relatively light sentences (six months was the maximum).[3]

On the emotional side, too, prosecuting Baker for mere obscenity would have seemed to be missing the point. What about the sense that Jane Doe (or her name, at least) had been violated? Surely her genuine sense of injury and fear makes Baker's actions something more than mere speech.

What about the sheer scariness of Baker's writings? I imagine the government reasoned that prosecuting the guy for an interstate "threat" would be a twofer: the statute provided for appropriately severe penalties, and a successful prosecution would give the government an effective tool to police frightening speech on the Internet.

Yet while Baker's public and private writings on the Net were frightening in the broad sense (it *is* scary when you think about the fact that there are people out there who like dreaming up horrific scenarios of the Baker variety), does it make sense to classify them as a threat? In the specific sense of the word, Baker's writings, while certainly frightening, were nevertheless no "threat." After all, he took pains to ensure that his alt.sex. stories postings were identified as fiction. And his expression of sick desires in his messages to Gonda, disturbing as they are, don't seem to be threats, either.

But the government was relying on the theory that the commonsense notion of *threat* doesn't apply. Instead, they insisted, the *legal* meaning of the term is broad enough to encompass communications that the speaker never intended to be seen as threats. ("Legal meaning" refers to the theoretically precise legal definition given a term rather than the vernacular meaning of the term.) In a set of proposed jury instructions on defining what constitutes a threat, the prosecutors submitted the following language: "A transmission contains a threat if a reasonable person would have taken the defendant's statement as a serious expression of an intention to inflict bodily harm or kidnap. The government does not have to prove that a defendant subjectively intended to threaten the person of another."

In criminal law terms, the second sentence of the government's definition is essentially correct. Most of the federal courts of appeals have held that Section 875(c) is a "general-intent crime," which means the government needs only to prove beyond a reasonable doubt that the defendant intended to *communicate* the words in question. They don't need to prove that the defendant intended the words to be *understood as a threat.* And you can see why the courts have taken the general-intent approach: it keeps defendants from threatening to rob banks or hijack planes or kill people and then claiming at trial simply to have been misunderstood. ("I didn't mean for you to be threatened—I was just engaging in performance art!")

But the first sentence of the quoted language—the part that defines what a threat is—is more problematic. Since Section 875(c) is one of those rare statutes that can be used to punish pure speech (that is, you can be found guilty even though all you've done is say something), and since speech in general is protected by the First Amendment, there is a constitutional interest in making sure that such a "pure-speech offense" is narrowly and precisely defined. This explains the U.S. Supreme Court's 1969 decision in *United States* v. *Watts,* 394 U.S. 705. In that case, the Court had to interpret a statute (Title 18, Section 871, which prohibits threatening the president) that shares the meaning of "threat" used in Section 875, the statute under which Jake Baker was indicted. In *Watts,* the defendant remarked during a political debate at a public gathering that if he was inducted into the army and made to carry a rifle, "the first man I want to get in my sights is LBJ." He was arrested and charged under a 1917 law that made it illegal to "threaten" the life of the president. The justices concluded that a "statute such as this one, which makes criminal a form of pure speech, must be interpreted with the commands of the First Amendment clearly in mind. What is a threat must be distinguished from what is constitutionally protected speech." Since Sections 871 and 875 share the same tension between protected speech versus an unprotected threat, logically the same analysis holds true for both statutes.

Even if the government didn't have to prove that a defendant intended a threat, said the Court in the *Watts* case, "the statute initially requires the Government to prove a true threat." A statute aimed at punishing "threats" must be limited to "true threats," or else it is unconstitutionally overbroad. After all, a reasonable person might conclude from listening to a Marxist revolutionary's public harangue that the speaker was willing, or even eager, to kill specific people in order to bring about the revolution of the proletariat, but that wouldn't make the harangue a true threat. In that instance, what the government in the *Baker* case would define as a threat is something that would clearly qualify as speech protected by the First Amendment: political speech. This is true even though there are kinds of political speech that can be disturbing. In the final analysis, the First Amendment was drafted in order to protect whole classes of speech that a majority of the public might find threatening or frightening.

So with the reasoning from *United State* v. *Watts* in mind, how do you go about distinguishing the merely scary from the true threat? Normally this isn't much of a problem. A review of the reported cases under Section 875(c) reveals that the threats in question almost invariably meet the narrower, commonsense definition of the term as well as any legal definition. Only a 1976 case, *United States* v. *Kelner* in the Second Circuit, has addressed in any detail the interplay between the First Amendment and Section 875(c)'s "true threat" requirement. Kelner allegedly threatened a foreign political leader during an interview that was videotaped and broadcast. Kelner claimed the threat was "relating to the free trade of ideas," but the Court didn't buy his rationale and held his threat was not protected First Amendment expression. Relying on the Supreme Court's decision in *United States* v. *Watts,* the court of appeals in the *Kelner* case stated:

> The purpose and effect of the Watts constitutionally-limited definition of the term "threat" is to insure that only unequivocal, unconditional and specific expressions of intention immediately to inflict injury may be punished—only such threats, in short, as are of the same nature as those threats which are "properly punished every day under statutes prohibiting extortion, blackmail and assault without consideration of the First Amendment issues. . . ."
>
> So long as the threat on its face and in the circumstances in which it is made is so unequivocal, unconditional, immediate and specific as to the person threatened, as to convey a gravity of purpose and imminent prospect of execution, the statute may be applied.

Since the *Kelner* case happened in a different circuit, the *Baker* court was not bound to follow *Kelner* as a precedent. (Federal courts apply a hierarchical rule of law. A district court, the lowest federal court, must apply the law of the court of appeals in which it sits. There are thirteen circuits in the United States, with the Supreme Court sitting above all the circuit courts.) But the judge was perfectly free to find the *Kelner* case *persuasive* on the legal issue of what qualifies as a "true threat" under Section 875(c), and this must have been worrisome for the prosecutors, since no single communication by Baker—and no set of related communications, either—met all the elements of the Kelner definition of a "threat." For example, there was no doubt that Baker's Jane Doe story was "specific as to the person," but it was hardly "unequivocal," what with Baker's insistence at the time of publication that the piece was a "story"—a work of fiction. This probably explains why the feds, in a superseding indictment, abandoned their claim that the Jane Doe story itself amounted to a "threat." The new indictment focused on Baker's e-mail to Gonda.

Yet the new indictment had its own problems: even if you considered all Baker's e-mail together and interpreted the mail as the government did, it is neither "immediate" nor "specific as to the person" as the *Kelner* definition of "threat" requires. In order to accept the prosecution's theory of the case, you had to accept the novel argument that all of Jake Baker's public and private writings, even though they were addressed to different audiences and at least some of the time framed as fiction, could, when taken together, qualify as a "threat" for Section 875(c) purposes. Given that the *Watts* case also specifies that it's the judge, not the jury, that makes the basic determination whether a communication is a "true threat," it seemed highly possible as the case neared its first major proceeding that Baker's trial court judge would grant the defendant's motion to dismiss the indictment, which was argued on May 26, 1994. And, in fact, that's just what happened.

Absence of Malice

Baker had done a month in prison, in spite of psychiatric examinations indicating that he posed no real hazard to anyone, because the sheer nastiness of what he'd posted, together with the fact that he'd said it on the Internet, had upset a number of federal law enforcement agents and federal judges enough to stretch the law in order to punish him.

That sort of behavior is something that, even in the short run, I find far more frightening than Baker's literary efforts. I'd say this even if Baker had written those stories about me.

From a legal standpoint, and regardless of my personal feelings about Baker, it was easy for me as a constitutional lawyer to conclude, as Baker's own lawyers did, that "the government has abused the purpose of the statute in attempt to silence Jake Baker's admittedly controversial writings." While that makes it intellectually easy for me to defend Jake Baker, this intellectual argument—the legal and constitutional analysis—didn't settle all the issues for me. The fact is, I still had my emotions to contend with, and I don't like what I've read of Baker's writings. I find his words repellent.

You see, I couldn't really dispute the one thing that really mattered for most people troubled by Baker's writings: that he indulges in what to me are unquestionably vile fantasies (although I suppose that *could* be disputed; we can't say for sure what his motives are, and some people play a sort of "Can you top this?" game on the Net, competing to shock each other or gross each other out). And the consistency and obsessiveness of the kidnapping-rape-torture-murder theme in his writing made me wonder how I'd feel after he won his case, as I publicly predicted he would then, and as I felt certain he would in the long run.[4] What if he were to go on and act out any of his sadistic scenarios?

One thought that has given me a certain amount of peace is that Baker has shown no sign of doing so (even though it has now been several years since he was arrested and prosecuted). The people who know him best think him incapable of doing actual harm to anyone, he was declared harmless by three different psychiatrists, and he was reportedly quite mortified to learn that, thanks to university authorities, Jane Doe had read the story in which the victim bears her name. "I'm really sorry that this came to her attention," Baker is reported to have said. "I never meant to hurt her." Furthermore, Jane Doe was not without options for self-protection. Almost all states allow individuals to seek a restraining order against someone they feel threatened by. With a restraining order in place, the potential victim has the resources of the police and the court system to protect him or her.

Regardless of whether I take his expressed regrets at face value, I have to distinguish between (1) someone who has vile thoughts and writes fiction about them and (2) someone who actually acts on those thoughts. What little I know about sexual fantasies suggests to me that people don't make moral choices about what kinds of fantasies to have. Jake Baker apparently thought that as long as he was merely writing about this stuff, he wasn't doing any harm. Even if that oversimplistic notion is not true (arguably, Baker should have realized that posting a story about a real person might get back to that person and cause emotional harm), it doesn't translate into a malicious act.

And who among us can say he's never wished to kill or injure someone? Who among us can say that she has never expressed such a thought to another person?

When I wrestle with these emotional issues, here's how I justify defending Jake Baker:

It may well be the case that Baker is a human time bomb, just ticking away and waiting for an opportunity to kidnap and assault some woman. (That's certainly what two U.S. magistrates thought. In decisions based solely on Baker's writings, they denied Baker bail. He spent a month in jail until the federal judge in charge of his case, Avern Cohn, approved his release on $10,000 bond.)

But even "human time bombs" are presumptively innocent of any crime, they have the right to freedom of expression, and they have the capability of choosing, morally, not to act out their desires. In a free society, we begin with the assumption that human beings are in general responsible for their actions. We do not assume that they are responsible for their thoughts or that vile thoughts and desires by themselves make someone a criminal.

Finally, and most important, it was Baker's feeling that he could publish his sick fantasies on the Net that led to an immense outpouring of public criticism of Baker. I cannot help thinking he learned something from that. As long as I can tell myself all this and still believe it, I can get to sleep at night.

The Challenge of Writing Speech Law
But perhaps you can't.

It may be that you agree with me about how words are powerful both in their effects on others and in the extent to which they can reveal the inner nature of oneself. At the same time, you look again at Baker's words, and you are so convinced of his likely criminality—if not today or yesterday, then certainly tomorrow—that even approaching the case from the assumption that human beings are morally autonomous creatures is not enough of a reassurance. Maybe you find what he has written so repugnant that it surely ought to be a crime in itself, and if we don't have a law that makes it a crime, we should write one.

The problem is, it's very hard—maybe even impossible—to write a criminal law that singles out speech of the sort Jake Baker liked to post on the Internet without also criminalizing whole classes of people whose speech is far more easily defensible from a moral standpoint.

Suppose you argue that the real test for whether speech should be criminalized is not whether it's a "true threat"—as that term is used in the law we discussed earlier—but whether a reasonable person would feel threatened by it, as Jane Doe surely felt threatened by what Baker wrote.

Such a law would be indefensibly chilling of our freedom of speech for at least two reasons. First, there are many kinds of speech that any reasonable person would feel threatened by that we don't want to see banned, as it might be according to the literal language of such a law.

Perhaps it's a politician's discussion of his plans for the social security system. Perhaps it's an economist's predictions of a coming depression. Or perhaps it's the details (as related in a "true crime" book) of how easy it was for someone to assault and kill an unsuspecting victim. A reasonable person may find these and other kinds of speech particularly threatening, at least in the broad sense that the prosecutors in the *Baker* case tried to use the term. But none of us would want to see such speech add up to a criminal offense.

Second, and more important, any criminal law that aims to restrict speech and uses as its reference point for legal behavior the feelings of a "reasonable person" is going to cause a lot of us to chill our own speech—and sometimes well-intended speech—for fear that we may be facing a *risk* of prosecution. Few of us are willing to say we know what adds up to "feeling threatened" for any and every reasonable person in this country or in the rest of the (increasingly linked) world.

(It's no accident that these two considerations map roughly to what the constitutional lawyers call "overbreadth" and "vagueness," two factors the courts use in judging whether a law unconstitutionally restricts our exercise of a fundamental constitutional right. We'll take a more methodical look at these two concepts later in this book.)

"Okay, Mike," you may want to say at this point. "It may be that some poorly drafted, broadly termed law might be a problem for us, but surely there's a way to craft such a law more narrowly. A narrower law wouldn't hurt our freedom of speech much, if at all. Perhaps we could simply make it a crime—or simply define it as one kind of threat—to publish something that uses a person's name in a way that makes that person feel threatened."

Okay, that would make it possible for me to have Citibank personnel arrested if they discover I've underpaid my credit card charges and send me a letter telling me I'm about to lose my credit rating if I don't pay up. (Much as you may like the prospect of being able to strike back against a credit card company under such circumstances, it would be a strange thing for such notification to amount to a crime.)

But maybe we can make it narrower still, in a way that saves the author of that warning letter from Citibank but stops a Jake Baker in his tracks. Suppose we craft a law that prohibits

1. transmitting or publishing or expressing in any other way

2. any statement or work

3. mentioning another person by name

4. expressed in a way that any reasonable person whose name was used in such a manner would find threatening (or, alternatively, that the person whose name was used did in fact find threatening).

It would be an easy law for any competent writer to sidestep. All one would have to do is write a Baker-like story that avoids using someone's actual name but otherwise clearly refers to a particular, identifiable person. You could use a detailed description of that person instead, or his or her address, or a parodic transformation of the person's actual name (a story about a "President W" has a pretty obvious reference point). If you broaden the law to prohibit these kinds of sidestepping tactics, you also broaden the possibility that someone will get prosecuted when his or her writing is misinterpreted as such a threat.

Beginning to see how difficult it is to write the "right" kind of speech-restricting law? A law that prohibits speech that just about everybody finds troubling even as it protects those speakers who (we may think) deserve First Amendment protection far more than Baker does?

Do you notice how, as we walk through the effort it takes to write a law that we hope is narrow enough not to infringe on our freedom yet is broad enough to criminalize a kind of speech or behavior we disapprove of, what we write looks more and more like a statute? That it gets harder and harder to avoid sounding like a lawyer or legislator? What we're doing is going through a thinking process very similar to what legislators—or at least the competent ones—go through when they write a statute. Sometimes going through that process means you can't avoid the conclusion that *no* statute could be written that criminalizes Baker's speech without also criminalizing speech that even the prosecutors in the *Baker* case would have to agree deserves First Amendment protection.

Don't get me wrong—I'm not trying to argue that speech can never be banned or restricted. I have no trouble with laws punishing perjury or fraud or blackmail or true threats, for example, and all four crimes center on speech. But the *Baker* case tells us that when we try to classify some kind of offensive speech as *essentially* an act merely because of the psychological effect it has on us—I believe this is what MacKinnon asks of us in *Only Words* and elsewhere—we come across just the kinds of difficulty we found here when we tried to base a law on the *Jake Baker* case. That is, we end up criminalizing either too much of the speech we want to protect or too little of the kind we are certain should be banned. I believe that whenever we come across this degree of difficulty in responding to troubling speech, it's a sign that passing a new law is the wrong way to go and that we should ask instead whether other mechanisms are in place that give us all the protection we need.

On the Net, you'll increasingly find, the mechanism for responding to "bad" speech is almost always the same mechanism that the original "bad speaker" used: the Net itself. Lawmakers often speak of the framework of criminal laws as representing the will of the people—what society condemns as unacceptable. But well before Jake Baker had been visited by the university police, much less touched by the hands of the federal authorities, he was hearing that voice directly. Few other organs of literary criticism are so direct or so immediate as the discussion forums of the Net. As he surely must have expected at the outset of his adventures as a horror writer, Baker got a lot of negative feedback from those who read his stories. It was feedback that not only expressed his audience's disapproval but also might have helped him learn how to deal appropriately with what seems to be a lot of internal rage.

Here's why I think so: When I first looked at his fiction, it made me think about why I felt so disturbed by what he'd written. Apart from the difference in literary craftsmanship, what distinguishes Baker's icky scenarios from something by Stephen King or Clive Barker, it seemed to me, is that the latter writers normally play out their stories in a cathartic way. That is, both writer and reader use the narrative as a way of venting and rechanneling one's existing fears and aggressions in socially harmless ways.

This may have been what Baker was trying to do, at least at first, but if so, he seemed to have taken a wrong turn, since his writings leave most of us more troubled than less—the very opposite of catharsis. He seemed to be cultivating his rage and his fantasy rather than releasing it. If that's what was really happening, then surely the thing he needed most at that point was to hear from other people why what he was doing was disturbing. And no other environment is better at giving that kind of social and psychological feedback than the Net.

This is why the problem facing the Net now is not the occasional twisted imagination of a Jake Baker, but whether we can trust ourselves, on our own, individually and collectively, to solve the problem of words that hurt. For the first time in history, we've been given the tools to explore fully whether freedom of speech is the kind of remedy for social and individual ills that free speech advocates have always argued it is. We have to learn as a society what we learned as children: words *do* hurt, but learning to cope with those words rationally and without fear is part of what it means to reach maturity. That's true whether it's an individual who is reaching for maturity or a society like ours.

6

Privacy Versus Society?

It's well understood that freedom of speech means the right to say almost anything you choose; it's less commonly recognized that freedom of speech also means freedom to choose *how* you communicate what you want to say. The U.S. Supreme Court has held on more than one occasion, for example, that your right to speak anonymously—that is, without any requirement to identify yourself—is an important component of Americans' speech rights under the First Amendment. The Court has also recognized that sometimes freedom of speech means freedom to speak in true privacy, without being overheard by others.

Perhaps the best-known (and most hyped) feature of the Net is that everyone on it has access to a mass medium. Each of us, at least potentially, can reach audiences of thousands or even millions. Less discussed is the fact that many and perhaps most of the folks on the Net can access that mass medium anonymously. We can choose to say what we want to a mass audience in ways that obscure or conceal our real identities.

There hasn't been a lot of discussion of anonymity yet in the political and legal arenas. In the next few years, however, we can expect lawyers and policymakers to come to grips with the issue of whether anonymity on the Net is a good or bad thing and whether it should be tolerated or discouraged.[1]

In order to address the issues surrounding anonymity, it's important that we know what we're talking about. This chapter outlines the basics of anonymity on the Net and suggests some ways of thinking about the subject.

The subject of anonymity on the Net (the practice of concealing one's identity and background while participating in online forums) has long been a controversial one. Discussion of this subject in online forums is a perennial focus of interest and generally centers on two general types of anonymity that are commonly available:

• Apparent anonymity, such as that offered on systems like the WELL and America Online to celebrities and others. Such anonymity is only "apparent" because system management always has the potential of knowing who the users actually are, and there would be little difficulty tracing such a user in the event of legal action.

• True anonymity, such as that offered by anonymous remailers and "forged" postings. Such anonymity is "true" because there may be no way to learn the identity of the originator of the postings.

There has been a growth in anonymous servers on the Net that will accept e-mail messages directed at particular mail lists or newsgroups and then post these messages without identifying information of the poster. As former WELL director Cliff Figallo has written, "To some, this is outrageous. To some, this is free speech in action." It has been suggested that programmers create filters to delete such anonymous postings from the lists and groups. These folks argue that if anyone has something to add to the conversation, that person should be willing to attach his or her name to it. This is a theme we find resurfacing often in discussions of anonymity—the notion that anonymous messages are somehow inherently worth less or are less reliable than "signed" messages.

Creating anonymity or false identity on the Net is common and relatively easy. Instructions on the use of anonymity, as well as the ethics of such use, are available in a three-part "Privacy and Anonymity" FAQ (frequently asked questions) file available by anonymous ftp (of course) from rtfm.mit.edu. They are also routinely published to these Usenet newsgroups (discussion areas): news.answers, sci.answers, alt.privacy. anon-server, and alt.answers.

Many online forums routinely grant anonymity to some or all users. Hobbyist BBSs, for example, commonly grant anonymity (individuals log on under their "handles"), and larger forums may have particular policies for granting anonymity. Commercial forums generally don't support true anonymity (after all, you have to identify your users if you're going to bill them) but occasionally make exceptions (such as the celebrity exception).

They may also offer features such as chat and instant messaging that allow for effective anonymity, through the use of nicknames, which make it possible to show up in such chat forums, participate, and leave before other users or moderators can identify you.

In spite of occasional problems with malicious or disruptive anonymous postings, there is as yet no consensus that anonymity is sufficiently problematic to require an industry or legal response. Some newsgroups on Usenet promote anonymity to protect participants (such as alt.sex. abuse.recovery and alt.transgendered). And there is an increasing sense that whistle-blowing may be an important function of anonymous newsgroups.

Another kind of anonymity, "forging a message" on Usenet—creating a posting that seems to be from someone other than the person it's actually from—is almost unanimously frowned on but nevertheless occasionally occurs because of the way Usenet is designed and implemented. The ability to forge a posting on Usenet is now more than a decade old, and it is a function of the way Usenet's protocols work. Typically, neither the approved anonymous postings nor the disapproved "forgings" require any special expertise on the part of the person seeking anonymity. Nor do they require special tools. A nontechnical person can be taught how to use either type of anonymity.

Yet given the vast potential for abuse, publicized incidents of abuse are rare. I think this is true for the same reason that obscene phone calls are (comparatively) rare: that most people want to use communications tools to communicate, not to disrupt or harass, and most people want to be identified as the originators of their messages. (It's the same impulse that makes reporters care about their bylines.) Most Net users want to have their names linked to their postings, most of the time.

Forgeries and Pseudonyms

Most forgeries can be detected by investigation and inquiry (at least as far as we can tell—the "perfect forgery," by definition, remains undetected). This does not, however, prevent the damage that malicious forgery can cause. Sometimes conferences are disrupted by floods of anonymous or, more often, forged postings. This has happened in several areas on Usenet, most often in the politically oriented newsgroups, but also in the science newsgroups, where it has generated particular concern.

While anonymity has its champions on the Net, no serious argument has been offered in favor of a policy supporting individuals' ability to forge postings when such forgeries purport to be messages from other actual individuals on the Net or elsewhere. Sometimes the forgery capability has been used in a fairly innocuous way (there was an April Fools' Day prank some years ago involving a posting purporting to be from Mikhail Gorbachev), but few believe that this kind of comic relief justifies the forgery capability.

In contrast, forgery of cancellation messages (postings to the "control" newsgroup) is regarded by many as playing a necessary role in the maintenance of Usenet (for example, in the response to the first appearances of commercial mass mailing in Usenet newsgroups. But in these cases, the anonymity aspect is ancillary. The value comes not from any concealment of identity, but from the cancellation effect itself. If it were possible to cancel another's postings without forgery (through an "advisory deletion" function, for example), it wouldn't be necessary to "forge" control messages at all.

The potential for damage caused by forgery is clear to anyone who reflects on the issue. Among the harmful uses of forgery are the following:

• *Disinformation:* "Forgery" can be used to spread misleading information or to disrupt events on the Net and elsewhere by giving rise to misunderstandings. A forged posting from a person pretending to be John Smith can result in a mailbox full of angry e-mail for the real John Smith. Disinformation can spread, and the "Craig Shergold" phenomenon can extend the life of such disinformation. In the Craig Shergold solicitation, Net users are told that a dying child wanted to receive enough get well cards to be mentioned in the *Guinness Book of World Records*. (The child has actually recovered and reached adulthood.) But the story lives on, showing remarkable resilience.

• *Damage to personal reputation:* This can play out in two different ways: forgery may damage the real person (if any) whose name is used in the forgery header, or a person named in the content of a forged posting may be defamed and may not be able to effectively seek a remedy against the forger.

• *Other "communications torts,"* such as trade secret or copyright infringement, or business defamation, can be facilitated by forged postings.

• *Actual criminal activity,* such as the posting of long-distance access codes and credit card numbers.

Pseudonymous posting is a posting or e-mail in which the name of the originator is invented. Pseudonyms are common on smaller systems, such as BBSs, and are often used in playful, expressive ways that are commonly accepted as part of Net culture. They enable shy individuals to communicate and allow users to make personal statements about themselves through their pseudonym. Choosing a name like "Eric Bloodaxe" makes a different first impression, for example, than a name like "mnemonic."

There are arguably some advantages in allowing pseudonyms. One is privacy. Some posters don't want to be bothered by people who would trace them through their real names.

Alternatively, someone may want to uncouple his ideas from his name: a poster may feel either that her ideas will carry too much authority or too little authority if linked to her name. The poster may also believe, if he is well known for reasons unconnected to the content of his posting, that discussions are likely to be diverted into the issue of his identity rather than the issues he wishes to talk about.

As many BBS users, chat room habitués, and instant messengers already know, pseudonyms can promote frank discussion. The ability to use a pseudonym may facilitate discussions of sensitive matters such as sexual abuse, debates concerning strong or unpopular political beliefs, or even detailed reports of malfeasance by government or private employers with less risk of retaliation. At the same time, pseudonymity has most of the same potential disadvantages as forgery.

Privacy and Cryptography

The Net has brought anonymity and communications privacy to the forefront of telecommunications policy debates in the United States. Anonymity on the Net has become an issue in part because it is a fait accompli. The very way the Internet is structured creates many opportunities for informed users to speak or act anonymously. The same is true of the telephone system, or Federal Express, but because neither of these communications and distribution networks is identified with the computer revolution, the potential for anonymous speech and acts using these networks has generated less panic even though, as a technical matter, it may be easier to remain anonymous in those other media.

The development of the communications privacy issue has been different, largely because it has been driven by the relatively recent expansion of cryptographic science and technology into the private sector. "Cryptography" (or, more commonly nowadays, "encryption" or "crypto") generally refers to the methods and machines used to translate spoken or written language into a code that, ideally, is decipherable only by the designated recipient. Thanks to some pioneering work done by American cryptographers only a couple of decades ago, the knowledge and techniques necessary for encoding or scrambling the things you write or say are no longer the sole preserve of government intelligence agencies; in fact, they are easily reproduced and implemented and available at low prices to most Americans today.

Both developments have been associated, at least in public perception, but often in deeper ways as well, with the recent accelerated growth of the Net. Anonymous speech has been available since the beginning of online communication, but the growth of public awareness about the Internet has led to a growth of anxiety about the widespread ability to speak anonymously there. What kind of social threat does this new ability to speak anonymously and perhaps irresponsibly pose? The now widespread technology of cryptography, which enables a single human being with a personal computer to transmute a message with a cipher (the type of encoding used) so tough that even the strongest supercomputers cannot break it within any reasonable time, has reinforced our ability to speak anonymously on the Net.

In a world full of governments that have grown accustomed to—even comfortable with—their ability to keep track of their citizens, and to gather evidence about them when necessary, these developments may be disorienting. What happens in a world where one cannot guarantee that a working wiretap will recover anything useful because the message traffic on the phone in question is encrypted? What happens when the perpetrator of a criminal threat can easily disappear from an online environment because no one has the information necessary to identify him or her?

These are important and troubling questions. The people who argue against anonymity or against easy access to strong cryptography (the designator "strong" or "weak" cryptography refers to whether the cipher can be easily broken) are, for the most part, arguing in good faith just as much as the pro-anonymity, pro-cryptography folks are. On the pro-cryptography, pro-anonymity side is the argument that anonymity is a right guaranteed by the Constitution and the belief that privacy creates better social relations and improves society by enabling sensitive communications. On the flip side is the concern that law enforcement efforts necessary to protect society from criminals, such as drug kingpins and terrorists, will be stymied by law enforcement's inability to gain access to communications or identities.

What I have discovered over the past few years, however, is that the ways one may answer these questions depend less on any technical or legal analysis than on one's philosophical approach. In fact, the issues of anonymity online and cryptography for the masses raise precisely the same questions about what we choose to believe about human nature that Plato raises in *The Republic,* a book written two dozen centuries ago.

This means that the answers depend on how we choose to think about each other and about ourselves.

The Politics of Anonymity

Hidden Agendas

A Washington lawyer invited me to lunch in the summer of 1994, hoping to sell me on his pet project: a piece of legislation that "would effectively require online forums to abolish anonymity for their users, or else face increased legal exposure." By the time lunch was over, however, he had persuaded me of something rather different and startling: that the source of most of his well-meant resistance to online anonymity was grounded neither in his own extensive experience of the online world nor in anyone else's documentation of the supposedly destructive effect of such identity concealment. Instead, the real basis for his opposition to anonymity was, of all things, his somewhat cloudy memory of a short passage in Plato's greatest philosophical work, *The Republic.* I later discovered that quite a few other would-be policymakers who were beginning to focus on online legal and policy issues had similar recollections.

It was this fundamental mistake about what Plato was trying to say so many centuries ago that had inspired what for me was a troubling provision in the most recent drafts of the Electronic Communication Forwarding Act (ECFA). In effect, this provision would give online service providers strong incentives not to offer any services their subscribers could use to engage in anonymous speech.

This was an *intended result*. ECFA's supporters were dead certain that their pet legislation needed to include a degree of political horse trading in order to be credible on the Hill. They were also convinced online anonymity would have to be traded away to Congress in exchange for strong legal protections to Internet service providers against lawsuits based on the actions or speech of their subscribers.

Their position had a certain logic to it. If the large corporate providers were going ask Congress to be freed from the risk of legal liability for, say, copyright infringement or libel perpetrated by some rogue user, didn't it simply make sense to discourage or even ban anonymous speech from their forums? For one thing (they argued), wasn't this the only way providers could tell lawmakers that although America Online or Prodigy may not be bearing the legal costs of harmful actions by their users, they could at least guarantee that users—the individual subscribers who'd actually posted the legally troublesome content—could be quickly identified, rounded up, and made to pay?

For another thing, they reasoned, isn't giving up anonymous speech—which they took to be practically a formal invitation to users to engage in pranks, sociopathic behavior, or worse—a small price to pay for this kind of immunity? Life in American society, they argued, is built on the notion of being responsible for one's actions. Shouldn't the laws of cyberspace therefore impose social responsibility on citizens by discouraging anonymous speech, which seems presumptively irresponsible, since the speaker doesn't want to be forced to face whatever consequences his speech could have created? At the very least, shouldn't providers, in return for Congress's guarantee that they won't be sued for every routine civil wrong committed by a subscriber, promise to do nothing that makes it more difficult for the legal system to track down such malefactors?

The ECFA supporters felt driven to come up with passable, effective legislation and to do so fast. Like me, they could see the potential for a social backlash against the Net.

But despite their consistent, principled, and well-meaning commitment to this seemingly elegant scheme, I was troubled by it, for a few reasons. First, it was being negotiated without any input from those who might argue that there are social benefits to anonymous speech, both offline and online. Those interests didn't even have any seats at the table.

Second, one only had to take a step or two into the history of the United States to find positive examples of the use of concealed identity to speak out and to shape political change. These included the pseudonymously authored *Federalist Papers,* which explained to the newborn Republic how its Constitution and laws would work. They included the anonymous membership of certain antisegregation organizations in the Deep South in the 1960s—unnamed individuals who might never have been able to contribute to the end of racial segregation had their identities, families, and fortunes been exposed to retaliation. It even includes things like Alcoholics Anonymous and crisis hot lines, where anonymity provides troubled people with a way of taking the first steps toward solving problems ranging from substance abuse to spouse battering.

If online society is going to reflect the range of experiences and needs in American social life as a whole, I worried, does it make sense to deprive some significant segment of this new society of the occasionally necessary avenues for anonymous speech that have long been available in the non-virtual world?

Third, does it *ever* make sense to pass a law limiting a kind of speech on the *assumption* that such speech will be harmful rather than on an established factual record of cases showing the actual harm such speech has caused? Whenever lawmakers sit down and try to imagine the worst-case scenarios that may take place if this or that speech-restrictive legislation is not passed, they're consistently successful in coming up with reasons to vote yes on the restrictions, especially when the speech in question is of a relatively new kind. Even in the absence of statistical evidence that there is a significant problem for the legislatures to address, lawmakers are quick to assert that passing such-and-such a law is necessary to prevent "even one more instance of [X]" (where X is massive copyright infringement, or a flood of pornography, or online defamation, or online "threats," and so on). Did I really want to support trading away our speech rights *prospectively,* the way the ECFA supporters were doing, on the assumption that all the relevant policymakers already know what the issues will be, what's politically possible, and what the acceptable compromises are?

These questions, plus some independent research I had done on legal precedents relating to anonymity, led me to break ranks with the ECFA supporters, most of whom had assumed I'd be a natural ally. (I do care, after all, about protecting online service providers. Some are small in size and economically too fragile to survive even a single libel or copyright lawsuit, but they're also absolutely necessary if freedom of speech is to thrive in cyberspace.) But the more I looked into the anonymity debate, the more certain I became that the supposed social ills associated with public anonymity were an invented problem—a function less of our social experience than of our individual fear that human nature is just the way Socrates' debating opponent Glaucon describes it in the early pages of the *Republic.*

The Ring of Gyges

If you haven't read *The Republic,* or if, like many other intelligent people, you read it in college and promptly forgot everything about it, here's the scene in a nutshell. Socrates' friend Glaucon is among the small group of Athenian citizens who, at the opening of the book, are discussing with Socrates the nature of justice. Although the book is thousands of years old, the questions they're addressing are still fresh ones central to any civilized society: What is it that makes justice more desirable than injustice, and what is it that makes us want to call the just man a good man?

Glaucon takes it upon himself to state the most cynical view of justice: that it's an ill-designed compromise between what human beings most desire (the ability to do harm to others and not be punished) and what they most fear (suffering harm inflicted by others without any ability to defend oneself or to retaliate). In short, says Glaucon, the notion that the just man is any better than anyone else is a social fiction. If you gave both the just man and the unjust the power to do whatever they wished *without fear of detection or punishment,* says Glaucon, it is certain that each will act the same way: they'll be ruthless, even murderous, toward others, simply because they can get away with it.

As a thought experiment, Glaucon introduces the myth of the ring of Gyges. In the myth, a shepherd named Gyges discovers a magic ring that allows him to become invisible. Armed with the power of that ring, Gyges is able to sneak into the king's palace, seduce his wife, and conspire with her (successfully) to kill the king and replace him. Glaucon argues that anyone with the kind of irresponsible, unaccountable power Gyges has in the myth will act more or less the same way—that the only reason we act civilized toward one another is that very few of us can get away with acting otherwise.

When I read *The Republic* in college, I quite enjoyed the tale of the ring of Gyges for its own sake, but I remembered only dimly the larger purpose for which Glaucon was recounting the myth. In fact, it almost certainly had been years since I'd even thought of the myth itself when I sat down to a lunch in a Chinese restaurant with my lawyer acquaintance, the ECFA booster. He still hoped to persuade me not to oppose the drafts of ECFA, but when I asked him why it was so necessary to trade away anonymous speech in order to get these protections for providers, he tended to be evasive in his answers. It was "obvious" that Congress would insist on such a legislative deal; in fact, he said, it was even "necessary." But when I asked him how he knew this to be true, he could say little more than that he simply believed himself to be correct.

"Okay," I said. "If it's necessary to do this trade in order to get a free speech–related bill through Congress, why is it that you've picked anonymity to be the right you're giving away? Was there ever any discussion, any consideration, of other trade-offs you might have made?"

The lawyer began to look a little defensive, but he still had what he thought was a trump card. "It's just true, Mike, that in every civilized society there has been little or no tolerance for anonymous or unaccountable action. Why, this has been known even as far back as Plato, who tells the story of a person who finds a magic ring that makes him invisible. Once he has the power to get away with any crime and without any accountability, he becomes a killer and a thief. Anonymity is socially destructive, Mike, and everybody knows it."

"Excuse me?" I said, startled. "You're saying you've based this whole legislative solution on a *myth* retold by *Plato?* That's it? That's your case?"

To my astonishment, he essentially admitted that this was his case—that the deliberate decision he'd made (without any consultation with those who feel differently about anonymity) was grounded in his intuition, shared by other supporters of the bill, that anonymity is simply wrong. That it is essentially destructive.

At that point, I knew I had a duty to make the pro-anonymity case—if only because no one else involved in the debate seemed to be addressing the issue head-on. If Congress is going to abolish or regulate anonymous speech on the Net, I decided, at the very least I should make sure it doesn't go down without a fair fight.

The Case for Anonymity

A number of lawyers believed in the mid-1990s that legal liability for providers may ultimately turn on issues of anonymity. Their reasoning went something like this: "At some point in the future, lawmakers and the courts will have to carve out a legal 'safe haven' for online providers, since it would be both impractical and chilling to First Amendment interests if online providers were held to precisely the same standards of responsibility that print publishers are held to. But since lawmakers and the courts will be unsympathetic to any something-for-nothing argument in which providers get protections without responsibilities, any 'safe haven' will have to be conditioned on provider policies that discourage or eliminate anonymity. That way, if someone has a legal claim based on a particular message, the provider could turn over the poster of that message and let the plaintiff sue *him* rather than the provider, who would be legally immune."

I find this argument unconvincing. For one thing, plaintiffs normally want to sue people who can remedy the damage (be it libel, copyright infringement, or whatever) with money and with action. It's highly unlikely that such a person is going to be satisfied when the provider says, "Sorry, we won't remove the offending posting, but we'll tell you who you can sue," since the offender is probably unable to provide the monetary remedy desired.

I also believe that discussions of any industrywide policy regarding anonymity should take place with the awareness of a number of factors:

First, our culture has a tolerance of anonymity, and it is a time-honored tolerance. The framers used anonymity to make the case for the Constitution, and this type of advocacy was not regarded as harmful to society. In our own time, we see many avenues for complete anonymity, from coin-operated telephones to letters without return addresses. If anonymity were inherently destructive to civil society, we'd have seen policymakers address these anomalies. A related point is that there is no social consensus as to the harmfulness of anonymity. In support of this claim we need look no further than the debate over caller ID, which had privacy advocates on all sides.

Second, it seems well established that anonymity can be used to serve social as well as antisocial ends. Twelve-Step programs, for example, use anonymity to allow individuals to talk about troubling experiences. Whistle-blowers can report the wrongdoings of corporations or government institutions under cover of anonymity. Foreign nationals who might fear retribution from their governments can discuss controversial issues on the Net through the use of anonymous remailers. The Supreme Court explicitly recognized the value of anonymity in *NAACP* v. *Alabama ex rel. Patterson* (1958), a case in which the NAACP refused to turn over its membership list to protect the members from being harassed.[2] In that decision the Court held, among other things, that to require individuals to step forward and be identified to assert their free speech rights would, in effect, negate those rights. In *Talley* v. *California* (1960), the Supreme Court threw out an ordinance that required distributors of flyers to print their name and address on them.[3] The Court stated, "It is plain that anonymity has sometimes been assumed for the most constructive purposes. (The Court ruled similarly in *McIntyre* v. *Ohio Elections Commission,* a 1995 case regarding a state law that required political leaflets to include identifying information.)

Third, there seems to be no harm uniquely associated with anonymity. It has been argued that failure to identify speakers leads to irresponsible or disruptive behavior on the part of those speakers. In practice, however, online environments seem to witness disruptive discussions whether or not anonymity is allowed. Similarly, each of us has the capability, through the anonymity of coin-operated telephones or mail without return addresses, to act in antisocial ways, yet few of us do so. Given the vast potential for abuse of these media, actual incidents of abuse are comparatively infrequent.

Fourth, historically, it seems that no theory of legal liability in the online world has ever turned on issues of anonymity. It has been argued that no judge or policymaker will allow any safe harbor for online providers unless those online providers can guarantee identification of the originator of troubling messages. Yet there is no case that supports this view. As a practical matter, there are often wrongs without legal remedies. Moreover, there seems to be no liability issue uniquely associated with anonymity. Provider liability turns on factors other than liability—most important, whether the provider has somehow "adopted" the communications of the originator.[4] There seem to be few lawsuits based on Net communications in general, still fewer based on defamation, and none yet on which the outcome depended on whether any of the defendants were anonymous.

Fifth, there may well be practical problems with attempting to reduce or eliminate anonymity, and these problems may be exacerbated to the extent that interconnectivity with other networks is allowed. (Online providers, if they choose to do so, are within their rights to limit or forbid anonymity for their own users' accounts.) It has been suggested that providers might label certain areas of their systems as "not guaranteeing identification of postings" or some such (thus suggesting that those who enter those areas have "assumed the risk"), but this does not address the underlying problem. If we assume for the sake of argument that liability *is* linked to anonymity, then having areas on the BBS where anonymity is allowed would, in effect, create increased-liability zones. Online providers would have to forgo connectivity to other systems in order to avoid liability, since third parties (such as copyright holders) might have their interests infringed on in such zones, and the providers could neither guarantee a remedy nor point to an assumption-of-risk clause.

Sixth, online providers that attempt to limit or forbid anonymity on all systems (by, for example, conditioning connectivity to a system's guarantee of origination information for itself and for all other systems to which it is connected) may be flirting with antitrust problems.

The question then arises as to whether there are alternatives to establishing a legal regime that discourages anonymity. To answer this question, it's helpful to remember that in this context, identification is not an end in itself but a means to an end. Usually the real goal is to locate a human being; if there are other means to that end, we need not tackle the intractable problem of identification.

Keeping the Lawyers Happy

What might some alternatives be?

• Industrywide procedures for responding to copyright complaints. Providers would commit to removing copyrighted material upon a showing by a complainant that infringement was occurring on their systems.[5]

• Industrywide commitment to right of reply in defamation cases.

• Assumption-of-risk clauses in user agreements (in effect, warning users up front that if they participate on a system, they may encounter messages they don't like, including defamatory ones).

• Other nonmonetary remedies for other torts.

• Promotion of a code of ethics for those who provide and for those who use anonymity.

There may well be other remedies, but the only way we'll develop them is to commit ourselves to exploring alternatives and preserving the ability of individuals to speak anonymously by encouraging a legal regime in which those who provide anonymity have the same constitutional and legal protections as those who don't.

The whole experience of trying to work through the questions raised by anonymous speech online and preparing them for presentation in order to inform others helped clarify my own thinking on the issue. (I become much more strongly pro-anonymity.) At the same time, draft versions of my essay on this topic, which I circulated on the Net for comment, helped crystallize opposition to the anti-anonymity provisions of the ECFA proposal. BBS trade organizations and grass-roots groups that reviewed the document were disturbed to hear that their ability to engage in anonymous speech was about to be given away by policy wonks inside the Beltway. Suddenly, members of the ECFA discussion group were being challenged to justify their position. What had been a fairly closed policy process became a more open one. Although the new players did not manage to help craft a better version of ECFA, they'd shown up just in time to join their voices with those of the established players, and the result ultimately was a much stronger coalition of opponents to the Communications Decency Amendment of 1996.

Tales of the Cryptographers

Only in a police state is the job of a policeman easy.
—Orson Welles

While the issue of anonymity online continues to be a sore point for some policymakers and even a bit troubling to the general public, the concerns raised by the anonymity debate were nowhere near as widely (or rancorously) debated as the concerns raised by the increasingly available technology of cryptography. In the cryptography debate, pro-cryptography people found arrayed on the other side the entire Department of Justice, the White House, and the National Security Agency. That pro-cryptography forces continually succeeded in preventing the government from making it increasingly difficult for individuals to get their hands on strong, uncompromised encryption tools says something about the inherent strength of the Net. Thanks to the Net, it's just about impossible for any government, as a matter of policy, to halt the dissemination of the basic technological facts about encryption. To begin with, the basic information about cryptography is public, not secret. Add to that the fact that just about everyone who is seriously interested in cryptography has some sort of access to the Internet, a cheap yet global communications system, and you get a sense of a government's difficulties when it comes to keeping the lid on cryptographic technologies.

Still, at a deep level, the philosophical issues raised by cryptography are the same as those raised by anonymity. They center on the question of whether we believe that human beings, once empowered to speak anonymously and secretly, are more likely to use their new powers unjustly, to do harm to others, than to act with integrity. At a more immediate level, the official concern about this nation's cryptography policy can be summed up in a single sentence: Your government is deeply troubled by the possibility that you can keep a secret.

To put it more precisely, the government is disturbed by the prospect of widespread powerful encryption tools, which enable anyone to create uncrackable private messages, in individual hands. Once you can keep your communications and data truly secret, officials worry, the value of wiretapping, an important law enforcement and intelligence tool, will evaporate.

In my opinion, the government's ongoing efforts to prevent us from adopting powerful and uncrackable encryption technologies raise serious questions about personal liberty, the role of government, and the possibility of privacy in the twenty-first century.

If you're not already familiar with these efforts, here's a brief overview of this important debate. At the beginning of its first term, the Clinton administration embarked on an ambitious plan to prevent a mass market for uncrackable encryption from *ever arising*. The first step in this plan was announced in 1993: the administration called for the entire federal government to adopt the Clipper Chip—an encryption standard with a "back door"—for communications and data security. The "back door" component of Clipper is called key escrow. Key escrow is like hiding a spare key in the backyard; once you tell government agents where the key is located, anyone who can access that key can walk into your house or, in electronic terms, unlock and retrieve your private messages. In addition, the government declared its intention to use every legal method short of outright prohibition to discourage alternative forms of encryption technology (such as the popular and free Pretty Good Privacy, or PGP, the public domain versions of which have no "back door").

The Clipper Chip was a hardware-based encryption device, developed to National Security Agency (NSA) specifications, that would keep your communications and data secret from everyone *except* the government. To understand how the chip worked, you need to understand a concept the government called "the key escrow encryption method." Designed by a private company, Mykotronix, and manufactured by VLSI Technology, the chip used an NSA-developed technology, an algorithm called "Skipjack."[6] A key feature of the chip is the fact that its primary encryption key can be divided up mathematically into two "partial keys." The government proposed in 1993 that each partial key be held by a separate government agency—the administration picked the Department of the Treasury and the National Institute of Standards and Technology

(NIST)—so the keys could be retrieved when government officials obtained a wiretap order. If, for example, the Department of Justice wanted to tap your phone line today, it gets an order from a judge, and the phone company places a tap on your line. If your communications were encrypted, the government would hear only garbage. If your communications were encrypted with the Clipper Chip, the government could obtain your keys from the escrow agencies and decrypt the messages.

The NSA and the FBI loved this idea. With the Clipper Chip in your phone or computer, they figured, you'd have all the power you need to keep your information private from crooks and industrial spies and anyone else who wants to pry—except, of course, for law enforcement and the NSA. Theoretically, law enforcement and intelligence agencies would be barred from seeking those escrowed keys in the absence of legal authorization, normally a court order.

Chips off the New Block
The initiative had been a long time coming. It was in April 1993 that the Clinton administration first announced Clipper, and was met with a public outcry from civil liberties and industry groups. Civil libertarians were concerned about the government's insistence on its need to prevent citizens from having access to truly unbreachable privacy technologies. Computer and telecommunication industry leaders worried that such a standard might crush a potentially vital market in such technologies. Since the government owned the Clipper Chip technology, it would control who received licenses to build systems incorporating the chip. This would artificially constrain the market for encryption components, both hardware and software.

At first the administration seemed to show a willingness to listen. The Digital Privacy and Security Working Group, a coalition of industry and public interest organizations then headed by EFF, outlined its objections and expressed the hope of engaging in talks with the administration about the issue. In early February 1994, however, the Clinton administration and various agencies announced to the world that in spite of the grave misgivings of civil liberties and industry groups, it would be proposing the Clipper Chip's encryption scheme as a new Federal Information Processing Standard (FIPS). The standard, stressed the government, would be entirely "voluntary," but the government would use export control laws and other methods to frustrate the market for any competitive form of encryption technology.

Current export control laws restricted the sales in foreign countries of encryption hardware and software, on the theory that cryptographic hardware and software—and even information about cryptography—amounts to a "munition," since either can be used militarily. The laws have not been entirely effective in keeping commercial encryption technologies out of foreign hands, it's possible to buy encryption products in Moscow, for example. But the laws did succeed in deterring the American software industry from developing powerful and easy-to-use encryption products, since any company that did so was denied the right to sell the product on the global market.

Still, if Clipper was voluntary, you may ask, what did it matter to *us* what standard the government adopts? The government also adopted the ADA programming language, after all, yet people are still programming in all sorts of languages, from BASIC to C++. The answer is simple: freedom of choice is meaningful only if there are real choices. The government's export control strategy, in tandem with the Clipper initiative and its successors, was designed to make sure there wouldn't be any real choices. If commercial software companies like Microsoft and Novell and Lotus aren't allowed to sell encryption to the world market, they're unlikely to develop strong, easy-to-use alternatives to Clipper. That means that individuals who aren't technohobbyists will, in effect, be denied access to alternatives.

As several of us on the pro-crypto side pointed out at the time, it's perfectly possible in theory to thwart the government-approved Clipper scheme by using a noncommercial encryption application, such as PGP, to pre-encrypt messages before sending them through Clipper-equipped devices. But most of these noncommercial products, because of their slowness or difficulty, are never likely to expand beyond the circle of hobbyists who enthusiastically support them. For commercial encryption products to give rise to a large consumer market, they have to be quick and almost transparently easy to use. (Paradoxically, in order for these features to appear, their development has to be fueled by an existing market.)

So, for example, if I want to send my mother a private letter containing sensitive personal material, I can ship it in a sealed container and be pretty certain no one but my mother will read it. Until recently, if I wanted to get the same level of security with e-mail, I had to save the file in a special format, run a separate encryption program, and then convert the file again to another format (one that a mailer could read); my mother had to reverse the process on the other end. This is clearly too cumbersome, and time-consuming, for everyday use (either personal or business). Users need convenient tools that serve their legitimate needs.

Businesses wanted to be able to use the Internet for secure communications as well. This is why in 1996 a number of implementations of virtual private networks (VPNs), which provide the ability to encrypt traffic between my machine and yours over the Internet, came into being. Internet standards were also created to support the interoperability of VPNs.[7] Large corporate customers like Intuit (which makes tax as well as PC banking software) invested millions in their VPNs to provide the security that their end user customers (consumers like you and me) were demanding before the end user would consider using Intuit's online banking system. But these advances were slowed or undermined by the U.S. government's insistence on export restrictions and back doors.

The vast amount of corporate dollars available for purchasing security products (about $5 billion by 2000), and the assurance end users are demanding before they'll trust the Net with their personal and financial data, will drive entrepreneurs to invest in developing easy-to-use, strong cryptography solutions. The feds have always known this, which is why their focus is on nipping (clipping?) the commercial encryption software market in the bud. It's the commercial market that really matters.

The Government's Side

When asked to substantiate the need for Clipper or the threat of unbreakable encryption, the government often talks about crime prevention. As a practical matter, however, wiretaps are almost always used *after* crimes are committed—to gather evidence about the individuals the government already suspects to have been involved in a crime.[8] So the hypothetical cases involving nuclear terrorism or murder-kidnappings aren't really convincing; it's the rare case in which a wiretap prevents a crime from occurring. The single most important asset to law enforcement is not wiretaps but informants. And nothing about unbreakable encryption poses the risk that informants are going to disappear.

Still, better arguments could be made for the government's position; one of the more rational statements of the government's case for Clipper comes from my friend Trotter Hardy, a law professor at William and Mary. As Trotter has written:

> The government's argument, I take it, is that the benefit is law enforcement. That strikes me as at least as great a benefit as minimum wage laws; perhaps more, since it protects everybody (at least in theory), whereas [minimum] wage laws primarily benefit their recipients. Maybe EPA regs [Environmental Protection Agency regulations] are the better analogy: everybody gets reduced pollution; with Clipper, everybody gets reduced criminal activity. Is that not a reasonable trade-off?

Trotter's argument is essentially that the overall social benefit of reduced criminal activity justifies the loss of freedom to individuals.

The problem is that the government refuses to be forthcoming as to what kind of trade-off we're really talking about. According to government statistics in the early 1990s, there are only one thousand to two thousand state and federal law enforcement wiretaps per year. (Under the Clinton administration, the federal government dramatically expanded wiretap requests, as did state governments. That trend has continued in the Bush administration.) But whatever the number of wiretaps, it's well established that only a minority of these wiretaps lead to convictions. Yet we were still being asked to abandon the chance for true privacy and to risk billions of dollars in trade losses. We were also being asked to believe that the kinds of criminals who are smart enough to use encryption are dumb enough to choose the one kind of encryption that the government is guaranteed to be able to crack.

These reasons seem too thin to justify the government's position. Perhaps what we're not being told provides a more compelling answer. For example, how often are unprotected communications currently used to gather leads or intelligence by government agencies? Even if these communications can't be used in court, they may provide valuable clues that lead to convictions.

Moreover, there is a fundamental political issue at stake. This country was founded on a principle of restraints on government. A system in which the privacy of our communications is contingent on the good faith of the government, which holds all the encryption keys, flies in the face of what we have been taught to believe about the structure of government and the importance of individual liberty.

Trotter went on to write:

I don't think the government cares whether an accountant in India can password protect a spreadsheet. I would guess that even Clipper or DES [the government's previous standard, called the digital encryption standard] or whatever would be more than enough protection for such a person. I think the government cares that it be able to detect foreign intelligence that is relevant to U.S. security or interests. I am not sure where I come out on the question, but at the very least it seems to me that the government is reasonable in this desire.

Regardless of how you feel about foreign intelligence gathering, the real issue for the government is that to the extent that a mass market arises for encryption products, it makes the NSA's job—gathering and processing signal intelligence (communications signals) from any and every source around the world—more difficult. And it may at some future time make some law enforcement investigations more difficult as well.

When asked to quantify the problem, however, the government invariably begs off. Instead, government spokespeople say, "Well, how would you feel if there were a murder-kidnapping that we couldn't solve because of encryption?" My answer is, "Well, I'd feel about the same way that I'd feel if there were a murder-kidnapping that couldn't be solved because of the Fifth Amendment privilege against compelled self-incrimination." (I'm opposed to torturing suspects in such cases even for the purpose of obtaining vital information in kidnapping cases.) In other words, I understand that limits on government power mean a loss in efficiency for law enforcement investigations and intelligence agency operations, but we have to make a fundamental choice about what kind of society we want to live in. Open societies, and societies that allow individual privacy, are *less safe*. But we have been taught to value liberty more highly than safety. We became an independent nation because of that very sentiment.

Wagering against the Unthinkable
A key problem in this debate has been the government's unwillingness to engage with its critics on the issue of rational risk assessment. To debate this issue openly and objectively, we need qualitative and quantifi-

able statistical analysis of the risks and rewards for a free cryptography society versus a constrained cryptography society. However, the government resists this approach. Instead the government subscribes to the reasoning of Pascal's wager. Pascal, a French mathematician who was also a philosopher, argued that the rational man is a Christian even if the chances that Christianity is true are small. His reasoning was quasi-mathematical: even if the chances of Christianity's truth were small, he reasoned, the consequences of choosing not to be a Christian are (if that choice is incorrect) infinitely terrible: eternal torment, demons, flames, the whole works.

This is precisely the way that the government talks about nuclear terrorism and murder-kidnappings. When asked what the probability is of (1) a nuclear terrorist who (2) decides to use encryption and (3) manages otherwise to thwart counterterrorist efforts, they'll answer, "What does it matter what the probability is? Even one case is too much to risk!" The problem with this approach is that you can't balance the competing interests. For example, if the risk of such a terrorist act occurring is one in a billion with weak cryptography, but the risk of having our nation's industrial secrets, including military secrets, stolen through information warfare is one in a thousand with weak cryptography, would we choose to allow strong cryptography even with the risk of terrorists? After all, our counterterrorist measures are generally pretty good and often rely on physical evidence such as car rental records and chemical tracing for bomb components.

Fundamentally we can't live in a society that defines its approach to civil liberties in terms of infinitely bad but low-probability events. Open societies are risky. Individual freedom and privacy are risky. If we are to make a mature commitment to an open society, we have to acknowledge those risks up front and reaffirm our willingness to endure them.

We face a choice now. After a century of technological development that has eroded our ability to keep our personal lives private, we finally possess, thanks to cheap computing power and advances in cryptography, the ability to take privacy into our own hands and make our own decisions about how much we want and how well to protect it.

This prospect is frightening to a government that has come to rely on its ability to reach into our private lives when it sees the need to do so.

But I am committed to the principle that our society is not dependent on our government's right to mandate disclosure of our personal records and private communications—that a mature society can tolerate a large degree of personal privacy and autonomy. Isn't this a principle any American could endorse?

You'd think so—or at least you'd think that if our government's officials insist on disagreeing with us about encryption policy, they could at least acknowledge that our differences don't in themselves amount to a threat to the social order. What our leadership opted to do instead, however, was engage in a lengthy persecution by investigation of Philip Zimmermann, the programmer who first developed PGP, now a worldwide standard for software-based encryption tools.

Up against the Wall, Mr. Cryptographer
The fact that PGP is a worldwide standard was used by the feds to justify a lengthy, intrusive, and anxiety-generating investigation of PGP's author. When Zimmermann, an American, returned from a speaking trip to Eastern Europe in late 1994, he at first thought nothing of the fact that he was being detained by Dulles Airport customs agents. For a frequent international traveler, such delays are annoying but routine. But as Zimmermann soon found out, U.S. Customs was less interested in what was in his luggage than in what might be in his head: information about how PGP had found its way into the Eastern bloc, as well as elsewhere around the world, in violation of federal export control laws.

Zimmermann, who consistently and continually denied having exported the encryption software, was detained for twenty minutes of sharp questioning. When he asked for his lawyer, he was told, "We can just all wait here until we get this sorted out." But as the customs office's heavy-handed tactics with Zimmermann signified, the main thing that needed to be sorted out was the government's own increasing worries about encryption, which potentially renders wiretapping of phones and computers largely ineffective, and about computer-related crime in general. Yet must the government's efforts at promoting law and order on the Net come at the price of limiting privacy and free speech there?

As I've noted before, the technology of encryption has become exceedingly cheap and accessible. Thanks to advances in encryption technology, the average person with a home computer is now potentially able to en-crypt communications and data so well that not even the NSA's super-computers can decrypt them in a reasonable time.[9]

That Zimmermann was under investigation at all signaled, I believe, a growing panic on the part of the federal government about encryption. Although the feds had been proactive on encryption policy since the ad-ministration of George H. W. Bush, by 1994 the government was increas-ingly worried about the accelerating spread of encryption software at home and abroad. In large part, its concern was grounded in the percep-tion of an increasing need to police computer networks.

Not that policing computer crime is anything new in itself. In Califor-nia, for example, prosecutors had been pursuing high-tech crime in Sili-con Valley for a couple of decades. In the old days, law enforcement typically concentrated on so-called hacking—primarily computer intru-sion and vandalism and telephone and credit card fraud. Over the past five years, the computer crime focus of state and federal law enforcement agencies has changed, and the cybercops are expanding their attempts to police cyberspace.

Underscoring the general anxiety about encryption is the fact that there have been a raft of new high-publicity crimes on the Net: copyright in-fringement, child pornography, and various sorts of frauds and scams. This has fueled a natural tendency for law enforcement agencies to ex-pand their jurisdictions. Given that the commercial online services and public networks such as the Internet can be used by conspirators to plan such crimes, we may predict the following with reasonable certainty: this expansion of what law enforcement is willing to call computer crimes will fuel still more demands for a more restrictive national cryptography policy.

Scott Charney of the Department of Justice's Computer Crime Division went on record as to his conviction that cryptography is a top-priority problem for law enforcement.[10] He called the spread of unbreakable en-cryption a serious threat to "law enforcement's ability to do its job." Once this technology becomes commonplace, he predicted, crimes that can be planned or committed using the Net will be far more likely to escape detection. Like most other prosecutors, he views the ability of the government to implement working wiretaps as essential—whether it's a voice line or a computer line being tapped. In Charney's view, widespread use of encryption would "shift the balance" away from effective law enforcement.

Jim Thomas is one of many crime experts who disagree with Charney's assessment. "Most law enforcement personnel really aren't concerned about encryption—that's been generated from above, by [FBI director] Louis Freeh and others," he says. Thomas believes that the number of crimes involving encryption is insignificant and that, in any case, restrictions on encryption "are simply not worth the risk to our civil liberties."

That encryption technology raises civil liberties issues has never been debated much. Long before the revolution in cryptography, civil liberties groups took to the courts to vindicate individuals' privacy rights as against the government. Nowadays, public policy organizations like the EEF and the Electronic Privacy Information Center see encryption as (in the words of EPIC's Dave Banisar) an "essential central tool in preserving privacy in the information age."

What's more, cryptography is central to freedom of speech as well. By allowing individuals to speak with the assurance of confidentiality, it promotes precisely that freedom. The deep connection between privacy and freedom of speech is the central reason Zimmermann argues that the primary uses of unbreakable encryption—daily communications and data security and transactional privacy—vastly outweigh the significance of criminal uses: "This technology is used by lots of people for lots of good reasons."

Ordinary people are likely to have a use for this technology, says Zimmermann, which is why he wrote PGP in the first place. Back in 1992, Zimmermann, disturbed by indications that the U.S. government might try to restrict individuals' access to encryption technology outright, took several months off from his consulting job and wrote the first version of PGP. "I wanted people to have access to this technology in the United States before the crackdown occurred," he says.

Keeping the Feds at Bay

Domestically, there has been no true crackdown yet, but throughout the 1990s there was no reduction in the feds' attempts to suppress the development of unbreakable encryption by adopting the Clipper Chip (or some equivalent) to allow the government to keep a set of keys to encrypted communications. Although the various Clipper proposals as such are currently dead in the water, the notion of key escrow encryption remained very much alive. The idea is that if the government adopts a key escrow standard that ensures government access to encrypted communications, the private sector will fall into line. (After all, almost everybody has to talk to the government at some point.) Although the government occasionally cut back its plans for Clipper-like encryption implementations whenever a storm of political and technical criticism gets loud enough, the White House remained committed to the idea of setting standards that guarantee government access to encrypted communications.

At the same time, the government continued to restrict exports of even weaker varieties of encryption software, apparently in the belief that doing so will discourage the development of encryption products by the American software industry and thus make the NSA's job easier. (Sure, they've got supercomputers ready to decrypt coded message traffic, but it's nicer for them to work in a world in which most message traffic is unencrypted.) When it became apparent that Zimmermann's public domain encryption software had spread around the world, the government decided to investigate possible criminal action against the programmer. Customs investigators determined almost immediately, however, that there was no evidence of wrongdoing on Zimmermann's part. It is widely believed that the only reason the government took another year before closing the file on Zimmermann was to generate what IBM marketing strategists used to call FUD (fear, uncertainty, and doubt) in the cryptographic marketplace and in the online world in general. (Full disclosure: If I sound even more biased than usual in my discussion of this case, it's because I was one of several lawyers besides Zimmermann's primary counsel, Philip Dubois, with whom Zimmermann frequently consulted during the period of the investigation. From the beginning it was clear to me from the evidence that Zimmermann would be acquitted were he charged with the dissemination of PGP outside the United States or any related crime.)

Stewart Baker, a former general counsel for the NSA, put the encryption issue in apocalyptic terms when he spoke at a conference in 1995: "There is somebody proposing a brave new world here and it is the people who want people to go away and to have unreadable encryption installed on all of the communications networks in the United States," Baker told an audience of civil libertarians and privacy advocates. "We don't know what it is going to be like if criminals or terrorists or other people who are hostile to society can use that sanctuary to communicate . . . but it probably won't be as pleasant in terms of freedom from crime and terror as the world we live in today, which is not exactly a comforting thought."

But like Philip Zimmermann, I find myself fearing a very different world: one in which government and other powerful entities can guarantee their access even to our most private communications and can search for them more easily than ever before. "E-mail messages are just too easy to intercept and scan for interesting keywords," Zimmermann told a House committee in 1993, conjuring the image of a huge message-filtering effort to capture incriminating message traffic on the Net. "This is analogous to driftnet fishing," he says—one that makes "quantitative and qualitative Orwellian difference to the health of democracy." Zimmermann terms the spread of encryption "a matter of good civic hygiene."

Something of a hero in the former Eastern bloc countries, Zimmermann treasures a letter he received from Latvia at about the time that Boris Yeltsin was shelling the Russian parliament. Wrote the author, "Phil, I wish you to know: let it never be, but if dictatorship takes over Russia your PGP is widespread from Baltic to Far East now and will help democratic people if necessary. Thanks."

It's a measure of how far the computer revolution has taken us that something as basic as the concern for law and order now requires us to debate the merits of a formerly arcane discipline like encryption. And it's by no means always clear who the good guys and the bad guys are. People like Zimmermann and Baker are both making good-faith arguments about what they see as necessary to a healthy America. But although concern for civic safety and stability is more important than ever to American citizens, I find it difficult to believe that citizens are ready to give up any technological guarantees of privacy. Recent elections suggest, at the very least, a healthy skepticism of any government-knows-best policy, even when that policy is aimed at fighting crime on and off the Net. I suspect that once Americans get a taste for true communications secu-rity, not even the specter of crypto-using criminals will incline them to give it up.

In the short run, however, there's already plenty to be grateful for, including the fact that I no longer need to light any candles for Phil Zim-mermann. Thanks primarily to the exemplary efforts of his attorney, Phil Dubois of Denver, Zimmermann is no longer likely to be the first martyr in our government's war on encryption. In 1996, the U.S. Attorney's Of-fice in San Francisco formally ceased its investigation of Zimmermann, largely, experts believe, because there was no case to be made that Zim-mermann had himself exported PGP. Thank the Department of Justice for small favors, I thought when I heard the news.

A Word on Human Nature

The government's decision to drop the investigation of Zimmermann was no comfort at all to anyone who spent the amount of time I had in contem-plating the value system implicit in the federal government's less-than-forthcoming advocacy of Clipper and its successors and in the lengthy and gratuitous harassment of Zimmermann. So much of what the govern-ment has done in the encryption arena seems simultaneously dishonest and inept. Given that the policymakers involved are not stupid people (I know some of them and feel comfortable saying this much in their favor), how do you explain the sheer waste of the Zimmermann investigation? Or the stumbling advocacy of key escrow encryption, which assumes a set of "permanent" keys even though there are countless applications and tools already that generate temporary encryption keys and forget them after the job is done? Or (most of all) the unwillingness to share with the public the real reasons for the panic about encryption (if in fact there really is any substance behind the fog of government assertions)?

Over time, I have come to believe that with this issue, as with anonymity, it all comes back to Plato, *The Republic*, and the story of the ring of Gyges, which Glaucon argued was a proof that human beings, in the absence of external social constraints, are certain to act like amoral, unjust, preda-tory beasts. I know a lot of people—and not exceptionally cynical peo-ple—who believe that this is a more or less accurate summation of human nature. But I just can't see it this way. For one thing, there are other views of human nature that I find to be vastly more convincing. And on this point the guy who should be citing *The Republic* is me!

You see, what my lawyer acquaintance (the ECFA supporter) had forgotten when he reminded me of the ring of Gyges myth was that Glaucon's argument was meant by Plato to be an example of *a wholly invalid, inadequate view of human nature.* In fact, the *rest of the book* after that point is meant as a thorough refutation of Glaucon's simplistic and distorted characterization of human nature.[11] And whatever one thinks about Plato's views overall (the philosopher Karl Popper, for example, labels Socrates one of the enemies of the kind of open society we live in), there is no serious dispute that Socrates' vision of the just man, in which every component is in balance—and whose just behavior is a function of that inner balance rather than any outer constraint—is truer to the subtleties of what it means to be a human being. This is true in our era just as much as in Plato's.

I remembered this important fact when I went home after that lunch in Washington and picked up my ancient Penguin edition of *The Republic* and started to read it from the beginning. It wasn't long before a sense of the book as a whole came back to me. And I realized that while there is much I disagree with in *The Republic* (for example, Plato is sharply critical of democracies, while I'm a big fan of them), it is also true that in my experience, human beings in general are not merely amoral beasts on a leash who can't be trusted with true anonymity or true privacy. There are such people, of course, but far more commonplace are people with consciences—people who, whatever their flaws and failures, still feel the impulse to do the right thing, to be kind, to be generous, to be fair, and to contribute. In the great majority of them, anyone can see the potential for Socrates' "just man"—the balanced, rational human being.

Just knowing the potential is there is all the reassurance I need that allowing people the kind of power and autonomy that anonymity and cryptography can give them is the right thing to do. Yes, some people will use these tools to do harm. I could never dispute that. But this would be true in any era, about any generation with any powerful tool.

In an open society, we're all constantly learning and relearning our responsibilities together as well as individually. One of the truths any good parent knows is also true for any good government: that you bring out the best in people, you teach them how to act responsibly and, ultimately, morally, you give them what wisdom you can, and then you trust them with responsibility. If we are to grow as a society in the digital age, our governments must learn to trust us with these digital tools. If they cannot teach themselves to trust us, then it will be time, once and for all, for us to remove our trust from them.

A 2002 Update: The New Cryptographic Landscape

As he sat listening during the Clinton administration's encryption policy briefing to the Congressional Internet Caucus meeting on September 28, 1999, Congressman Curt Weldon (R, Pennsylvania) began to get visibly angry. The administration's representatives, who included privacy czar Peter Swire and Bureau of Export Administration director Bill Reinsch, were explaining at length how the new policy, which appeared to greatly liberalize the export of encryption products, would operate and what it would mean. Weldon finally couldn't contain himself any longer and felt compelled to question the administration panel.

Weldon asked how the administration could even consider implementing this policy change, given that it has sent lots of high-powered people, including Attorney General Janet Reno and FBI director Louis Freeh, up to the Hill on countless occasions to urge representatives to vote against SAFE (Security and Freedom through Encryption Act). After all, he said, the administration had been saying that if encryption is freely exported, it will create serious domestic security problems and hamstring our law enforcement and intelligence operations. Why, Weldon asked, is the administration changing its mind?

It was a question that the administration spokesmen were unable to answer satisfactorily. The fact is that the new encryption policy did indeed seem to mark a serious change from the policy regime that had been in operation since the cold war was in flower. But the full meaning and extent of the administration's policy switch remained less than clear, partly because of its ongoing initiatives in other arenas, partly because the government has a long history of overstating the extent to which it is liberalizing its encryption policies, and partly because it continued to send mixed messages about its attitude toward this new data security technology.

Not long before the government's encryption policy announcement, the administration had announced that it planned to seek passage of the Cyberspace Electronic Security Act of 1999 (CESA), which was aimed at providing new legal and technical tools for the law enforcement community to fight the threat posed by encryption. At the same time the government announced its new export policies, it reaffirmed its support for CESA. And the Department of Justice was continuing to litigate vigorously for export restrictions in *Bernstein* v. *Department of Justice*, a case concerning a mathematics professor's claim that his right to distribute encryption-related source code is protected by the First Amendment.

In short, whether you were a civil libertarian or consumer concerned about personal data privacy, a business interested in making its e-commerce and communications channels secure, or a software company hoping to sell encryption tools in the international market, you were likely to be confused by what some experts saw as the U.S. government's apparent inability to speak with a single voice with regard to cryptography and encryption tools.

A Brief History of Encryption Policy
Two decades ago, the United States had no general public policy on encryption to speak of. In general, cryptography (the term is now generally used interchangeably with *encryption* in policy circles to refer to both the science of scrambling messages to make them unreadable by third parties and that of unscrambling them) was the province of intelligence agencies and nobody else.

A little over a decade later, the political landscape concerning cryptography had changed massively. Now it was dominated by a single, monolithic policy: Stop the Spread of Cryptography At All Costs. The new policy was born in a panic driven by some pioneering work done in the late 1970s by American cryptographers—work that for once had not been done by individuals in the pay of the intelligence agencies and that therefore had not been instantly classified. This academic revolution—the development of a public science of cryptography and a resulting colloquy about it—was accompanied by a similar equally dramatic revolution on the microcomputer front.

The result? For the first time in history, ordinary individuals with desktop PCs had the potential to encrypt their messages or data to a degree that only governments had had the power to achieve only a few decades before. What this meant for American intelligence agencies as well as for the American law enforcement community was clear: the party was over. Thanks to cheap computing and publicly available encryption tools, we were looking at a new era in which interception of a terrorist's or criminal's communications was no guarantee that you'd be able to figure out what they were saying.

Complicating things was the fact that telephone companies were increasingly computerizing their networks and telephone services, raising the specter of a world in which not only would computer data be routinely encrypted but also every telephone call might be as well. Government wiretaps—or at least effective ones—might become a thing of the past.

The Bush administration's response in the early 1990s was twofold. As documented by a 1992 memo, released as the result of a Freedom of Information Act request by the Electronic Privacy Information Center in 1996, former national security adviser Brent Scowcroft outlined the linkage between the Bush administration's digital telephony initiative, which would require phone companies to structure their networks and services so as to facilitate wiretapping, with what Scowcroft characterized as an approach to "the encryption problem."

According to Scowcroft, writing to Secretary of Defense Dick Cheney and CIA director Robert Gates, President Bush endorsed this plan of action: "Success with digital telephony will lock in one major objective; we will have a beachhead we can exploit for the encryption fix; and the encryption access options can be developed more thoroughly in the meantime."

From Clipper Chip to Key Escrow
It was a plan that was adopted without significant change by the Clinton administration when it took over the White House in 1993. Within two years, the government's digital telephony initiative had become law in the form of the Communications Assistance to Law Enforcement Act (CALEA). But the encryption initiative turned out to be harder to implement.

In the spring of 1993, the Clinton administration introduced the Clipper Chip program in the hope that it would steer the growing market for computer security in the right direction.

By 1996, the Clinton administration had abandoned the Clipper Chip as such but continued to lobby both domestically and abroad in favor of software-based key escrow encryption standards that would enable law enforcement and intelligence agencies to recover encrypted data when they believed they needed to. This effort was marginally successful abroad. Thirty-three countries, including the United Kingdom, the Russian Federation, Canada, France, and Germany, adopted the Wassenaar Arrangement on Export Controls for Conventional Arms and Dual-Use Goods and Technologies. But in the domestic software market, there was little acceptance of the administration's push for key escrow standards, now relabeled *key recovery*.

Civil libertarians and privacy groups also complained that the United States was promulgating privacy-undermining standards in countries that lacked the strong legal and constitutional protections for privacy that exist in the United States. Partly as a result of industry pressure and public criticism, the administration moved the locus of export control authority from the Department of State to the Department of Commerce, but the export controls themselves remained largely unchanged by the switch.

The Panic Begins to Relax

The year 1998 saw the pressure for liberalization continue to increase, both within and outside the Clinton administration. Within the administration, several factors were responsible, according to Dorothy Denning, a Georgetown University computer science professor and cryptography expert who was a strong defender of the government's wiretapping and cryptography policies throughout the 1990s. On the export front, Denning says, the administration had begun to recognize "the futility of trying to force the whole market into a 'Clipper' kind of model." On the law enforcement front, she adds, as the police "started dealing with [more encryption-related] cases, they were learning how to handle them."

In short, law enforcement's panic about encryption, while still present, was beginning to relax a little. As a result, the Clinton administration announced on the last day of 1998 a further liberalization of export restrictions. This one flatly legalized for anybody the export of encryption products using 56-bit keys. The previous standard had been 40-bit keys, and the strength of encryption products is generally taken to be a function of key length. It also allowed for the export of stronger encryption products in industry sectors with what the administration deemed a special need for data security: the banking industry, the health and medicine sectors, certain online merchants, and foreign subsidiaries of U.S. companies.

Outside the administration, critics of the revised export policy thought the government had not gone far enough—that it had talked a good game about liberalization of encryption exports but had failed to deliver. Congressman Bob Goodlatte (R, Virginia) had been increasingly successful in getting support for SAFE, which would remove restrictions on the export of encryption technology while imposing a greater criminal sanction on those who used encryption to commit crimes.

First introduced in the 104th Congress, where it stalled, it had greater success in the 105th, where Goodlatte had garnered about 200 cosponsors. It was passed out of five separate committees before it was halted once again, in part due to the opposition of Congressman Weldon, who had accepted the administration's claims that unrestricted export of encryption would demolish the nation's law enforcement and intelligence capabilities. In the 106th Congress, the reintroduced SAFE had even more support. By May 1999, it had once again passed through five committees, as well as several subcommittees, and this time it had 258, more than half the membership of the House, as cosponsors.

And Then Came Bernstein

In the courts, the government's export policy was scarcely faring any better. On August 27, 1997, a federal district court in San Francisco struck down the Department of Commerce's export restrictions with regard to Professor Dan Bernstein, a faculty member at the University of Illinois at Chicago. Bernstein, who sought to publish the source code for an encryption-related algorithm on the World Wide Web, had asked the government whether he would need a license, since publication on the Web is effectively an "export" under the export control laws. He was told that his source code qualified as a munition under the export control regulations. The district court found that this restriction looked a great deal like the kind of prior restraint that is prohibited by the First Amendment to the U.S. Constitution.

On appeal, the trial court's ruling was affirmed, albeit on slightly narrower grounds, and while the Department of Justice continued to litigate the case, seeking an en banc rehearing (a rehearing with all the appellate judges in the circuit acting as a panel) in the Ninth Circuit, encryption policy mavens inside the government knew it was uncertain whether the government ultimately would prevail. Faced on the one hand with an aggressive legislative push for SAFE and on the other hand with the prospect of a further reaffirmation of a broadly worded ruling that struck down its export controls as unconstitutional, the administration knew it had to take affirmative action to regain control of the issue. As Jerry Berman, director of the Center for Democracy and Technology put it, "the government has realized that delay is no longer a policy."

A Further Shift in the Terrain

In late 1999, however, the landscape changed again. And what once was a monolithic American cryptography policy was reduced to fragmented and perhaps self-contradictory rubble. One not inconsiderable factor was the presidential candidacy of Vice President Al Gore, who sought to strengthen his long-standing support among the leaders of high-tech industries (but who had been one of the backers of the administration's previous efforts to control crypto). But a more important factor was probably the harm that export controls had been doing to American computer industry companies. To the extent that export restrictions have prevented these companies from developing domestic products that incorporate encryption features, the companies had been at an increasing disadvantage in the global marketplace.

Denning, along with former NSA general counsel Stewart Baker, served on the President's Export Council Subcommittee on Encryption and heard witnesses from European governments and companies. The former explained that they were embarking on liberalization policies themselves. The latter would say, according to Denning, "Look at what we've accomplished [as a result of your export controls]. We're really grateful. Thanks!" Denning adds: "That really brought it home."

Nevertheless, the government's long twilight struggle to prevent or at least slow the spread of encryption may have had its lasting benefits, according to some of those who have advocated a restrictive export-control policy. Baker, now a partner at Steptoe and Johnson, believes that to some extent, the government's attempts to restrict the spread of encryption technologies have been a success. Had it not been for the export control regime, he says, computer and software manufacturers would probably have incorporated encryption tools into the operating system of every mass market computer. Encryption would in effect have become standard equipment. That may still happen, Baker and Denning agree, but right now the market for encryption is an aftermarket, which means that its use is not yet ubiquitous globally. This gave the intelligence community some breathing space to adapt.

And how is the law enforcement community adapting to the change in administration policy? Berman notes that "the FBI has been strangely silent," and policy watchers believe there is still serious debate within the administration about the wisdom of the new liberalization. It is the opinion of many interviewed for this chapter that the administration's announcement of the export control changes—an announcement that also reaffirmed support of the CESA proposal—was meant to mollify those in Congress and in the executive branch who remain concerned about the law-enforcement threat they believe encryption poses. And it's equally clear to them that the Department of Justice is still engaged in a full-court press in the Bernstein case.

Render unto CESA?

Both Baker and Denning saw the administration's offering of CESA as a way of addressing law enforcement's ongoing concern about encryption at the same time that the administration was engaging in what was apparently its strongest liberalization of encryption-related exports to date.

The preamble to CESA endorses cryptography in one breath and then warns about its dangers in the next: "Cryptography . . . is an important tool in protecting the confidentiality of wire and electronic communications and stored data. Thus, there is a national need to encourage the development, adoption, and use of cryptographic products." In the very next paragraph, however, one learns that "while encryption is an important tool for protecting the privacy of legitimate communications and stored data, it has also been used to facilitate and hide unlawful activity by terrorists, drug traffickers, child pornographers, and other criminals."

CESA was proposed by the White House in August 1999 and again in September, but did not find a sponsor on the Hill, although sources on and off the Hill remained hopeful a sponsor could be found. The less controversial provisions of CESA would have established standard procedures and safeguards for government agencies seeking the disclosure of encryption keys held by "recovery agents," who are trusted third parties who hold such keys in key escrow. They would also have provided law enforcement with more funding to research how to recover the content of encrypted information from computers and networks, well within the scope of the law enforcement community's general mission to investigate and prevent crime.

The original version of the bill sought expansion of the government's authority to engage in secret searches and covert entry in order to install monitoring equipment on targeted computers. That provision didn't survive internal review—privacy czar Peter Swire says there was heated debate about it before it was finally dropped—but one provision that did survive was equally troubling to some: the provision that would prevent the government from having to disclose, in the course of a criminal proceeding, how it recovered the decrypted information that it is using against the defendant. The theory here is that if the government reveals its decryption secret, which may involve secret decryption techniques that the government has developed, industry trade secrets or software flaws that government researchers have discovered, criminals will be forewarned and able to thwart decryption in future investigations. Think of this as something analogous to the federal Witness Protection Program—a sort of Evidence Protection Program.

Civil libertarians and criminal defense lawyers saw the provision as one that raises evidentiary problems, particularly authentication, and perhaps even constitutional problems (e.g., the confrontation clause), but Baker argued that the provisions have a clear precedent. "The unspoken model here," Baker explains, "is CIPA—the Classified Information Procedures Act."

CIPA, says Baker, was designed to prevent defendants in national security–related cases from putting the government in the position of either having to reveal classified information or dismissing an indictment.

Similar to CIPA, the CESA provision would allow an attorney for the government to seek an order preventing disclosure of information about the decryption of encrypted content "if the court finds that disclosure is likely to jeopardize an ongoing investigation, compromise the technique for the purposes of future investigations, result in physical injury to any individual, or seriously jeopardize public health and safety, or if the court finds that disclosure could reasonably be expected to affect the national security. (Such an order may also be entered by a court in order to protect trade secrets associated with access to [decrypted content].)." But whether Congress will accept the notion that the government's need to keep its decryption techniques secret is on a par with its interest in keeping classified information secret remains to be seen.[12]

Code Warriors

Cindy Cohn and Lee Tien, lead counsel for the plaintiff in *Bernstein* v. *Department of Justice,* see the recent developments in the administration's encryption as perhaps more spin than substance. Cohn was cautious about celebrating the new policy until the new implementing regulations are published, given that previous announced liberalizations have been disappointing. "I'll be really happy to be the last one to the party" if the policy is as broad as the government says it is, Cohn says.

On its face, the liberalized export control policy looks like something that cryptography and privacy advocates can cheer about. The administration announcement on September 16, 1999, stated that the government was removing altogether the licensing requirement for "mass-market" encryption products, reserving for itself only (1) the right to a "one-time review" of any product before it ships abroad—or informational purposes only, according to Baker—and (2) a prohibition of the shipping of any encryption products to terrorist states.

But Tien and Cohn note that on its face, the export control policy did not address the facts at issue in *Bernstein*. Specifically, there was no liberalization of the export of source code in electronic form (on disk or in a computer file). Both the current export control regime and the appellate court in the *Bernstein* case employ a distinction between "source code" and "object code," a distinction that Bernstein's lawyers say is hard to defend in legal terms.

Source code, by the way, is humanly readable program language that, in general, does not become functional until it has been "compiled" by a computer into machine-readable "object code." Bernstein's case relies in part on the fact that mathematics and computer science educators may need to use source code to teach students about computer problem solving. The appellate court in *Bernstein* ruled that the First Amendment protects source code but did not rule at all with regard to object code. Yet the export control liberalization addresses only products (object code).

Apart from the First Amendment issues relating to the use of source code as a communicative tool, there are other problems with this distinction. For one thing, in some contexts, source code is as functional as object code. Cohn asks, "What about HTML? What about Java?" Both languages are used by computers in the same form in which they are read by human beings.

What may be worse is that some computer products are designed to include source code as part of the product—for example, the Linux operating system and other products of the Open Source movement, which ship with source code or ship "as" source code. The administration's liberalization of its export control regime, together with its holding the line on the export of source-code-in-electronic-form, puts companies like Microsoft (which ship only object code) at an advantage over their Open Source competitors.

"You have to ask yourself," says Tien, "what is the policy interest being protected here?" Baker and Denning insisted there may be valid policy interests here even if the administration hadn't expressly articulated them. Both said that if the goal of export controls has been to prevent foreign countries from gaining the ability to manufacture encryption products themselves, it makes sense to restrict source code even if the lid is off when it comes to exporting the products themselves.

Baker also argued that the government may have a separate interest in continuing to litigate *Bernstein*. The lower courts' language is sufficiently broad that, if unchallenged, it might be taken to preclude the government's attempting to prevent the spread of information about, say, the construction of weapons of mass destruction. On the other hand, Denning allows that the pursuit of the *Bernstein* case by the government may be merely a function of inertia. The Department of Justice has pushed this case this far, so they intend to see it to a conclusion regardless of the administration's export-control liberalization.[13]

In the aftermath of these developments, industry observers began to ask themselves and each other whether there is a consistent encryption policy framework now. Baker's view is that the current situation, even with the apparent inconsistencies regarding source code and the government's own expressed attitude toward encryption, "is as coherent as government policy gets." Jerry Berman, whose public interest group, the Center for Democracy and Technology, has been at the forefront of the lobbying process, is cautious in his optimism. Although he observes that Congress seems prepared to pass SAFE if the administration fails to live up to its promise to fully liberalize the export of encryption products, Berman also noted in 1999 that "one terrorist incident involving encryption could change the landscape," a warning that resonates even more strongly after the events of September 11, 2001.

Adds Berman, "It is not beyond the politics of conservatives [or liberals] on the Hill to reauthorize the export-control restrictions." And even if the government continues to follow through on its general promise to be more supportive of the development and export of encryption products, Berman says, "the devil is in the details."

7

The Battles over Copyright on the Net (and Other Intellectual Property Encounters)

The general rule of law is, that the noblest of human productions—knowledge, truths ascertained, conceptions and ideas—become, after voluntary communication to others, free as the air to common use.
—Louis Brandeis, *International News Service* v. *Associated Press* (1918) (dissenting)

Before I went to law school, I worked as, among other things, a freelance writer. All I cared to know about copyright law back then was how to avoid getting sued over it, and law school didn't cure me of this lack of interest. What I discovered as a law student was that the law of intellectual property, of which copyright law is a major part, managed to combine an equal mixture of the subtle and the dull. It seemed unconnected with the realities of day-to-day existence as most of us experience them.

I had no idea then that the law of intellectual property, its economics, and the social and political forces it brings into play would turn out to be so central in deciding the free speech issues raised by the Net. Maybe I should have seen it coming. We're building new societies in cyberspace, and every new society must figure out what balances to strike between the economic rights of some individuals and the civil liberties of others. And on the Net, economic interests are invariably interests in information, in the broadest sense in which that term is used. At the same time, the civil liberties at stake almost always include a citizen's interest in speaking freely or in protecting her privacy—interests that also are fundamentally about information.

Protecting both one's economic interests and one's individual liberties is important to anyone who wants to be a free human being in this era, so fights over issues such as the balance between copyright and free speech tend to generate a lot of strong emotions like anger and fear. The emotions are even higher when we're entering the digital age, when the same technology that enables each of us to become a publisher to a mass audience also enables countless people to engage in a massive infringement of intellectual property interests with a single keystroke.

Many of those who aren't worried about their particular intellectual property interests per se have perceived in the cloud of concern around these issues the opportunity to pursue independent agendas. The federal law enforcement agencies, for example, consistently play on our fears about economic losses on the Net in order to justify the passage of new criminal laws and regulations or the broadest readings of existing ones. Other parties may cloak in a respectable intellectual property theory what they're really after, which is the silencing of troubling opinion and the opportunity to shape the future of the Net more to their liking. This is just as much a reflection of the Net backlash as the overblown concerns about pornography or other purportedly harmful Net speech.

In challenging this aspect of the backlash, the first step we have to take is to understand copyright and how it applies to the Net. This requires understanding the history and philosophy of copyright (plus a small excursion into the law of trade secrets). Once we know what's at stake, we can, at a minimum, understand why copyright holders are in such a panic. If we're sufficiently diligent and lucky, we may even be able to circumvent the biggest intellectual property wars that seem to be brewing in the United States and in the world at large.

The Beginnings of Modern Copyright

For some people, the term *intellectual property,* with its built-in connotative paradox of the tangible and the intangible, seems to be an oxymoron, like "sweet agony" or "military intelligence" or "jumbo shrimp." But for the lack of a better legal term of art, *intellectual property* has come to represent a whole class of legal interests. (As University of Texas law professor Mark Lemley points out, the term *intellectual property* came into vogue only recently; Lemley associates the term's origin with the foundation of the World Intellectual Property Organization (WIPO) by the United Nations in 1967.) At the same time, it has confused countless lawyers and laymen who have unthinkingly conflated intellectual property with traditional property notions, with the results that include attempts to treat copyright infringement as the moral *and* legal equivalent of theft.

A look at the history of copyright makes clear why the Supreme Court has said that a copyright holder's interest is "no ordinary chattel" (that is, no ordinary sort of property interest).

A Short History of Copyright

Our copyright interests, like most of our other rights in the American legal system, have their roots in the English common law (the legal precedents set by English judges in deciding disputes). Our country's common law, like that of England, is the collective substance of the decisions of previous cases, which is why legal precedents matter so much in our respective legal systems.

But that's not the only kind of law that governs us, and it's not the only kind of law that governed English-speaking people in pre-Revolutionary times. Laws written by Parliament and by Congress, also known as statutes or statutory law, have played an increasingly important role in defining the rights of individuals. This is especially true of the rights of authors and publishers—what has since come to be known as copyright.

While copyright is almost three centuries old—it dates back to the English Statute of Anne, passed in 1709—it is still a fairly recent development compared with the rest of Anglo-American common law. (By comparison, a landowner's rights to his property can be traced back to the Magna Carta, as can the First Amendment–guaranteed right "to petition the government for a redress of grievances.") William Shakespeare had no formal, legal guarantee to royalties for printed copies of his plays. The Bard received his compensation for writing nearly forty plays and a large number of poems through the patronage of noblemen or the revenue generated by charging theatergoers for performances at the Globe Theatre.

Once the printer-publisher trade became widespread, however, both authors and publishers asked Parliament to provide some protection from those printers who saw no reason not to take a published book, copy it into movable type at their own press, and sell their own copies. Parliament then passed the Statute of Anne, which was described as "an Act to vest authors with their copies, for the times therein mentioned." Authors were given this protection for a period of twenty-one years, after which others could print their own copies.

In the early years of the United States, the Statute of Anne, with its balance of authors' rights against the rights of copiers, was understood to embody a principle that perhaps Congress ought to follow: designing laws that would encourage creators to create. Thus, the U.S. Constitution provides in Article I, Section 8: "The Congress shall have Power . . . to Promote the progress of Science and useful Arts, by securing for limited Times to Authors and Inventors the exclusive Right to their respective Writings and Discoveries." Despite the wording of Article I, when Congress got around to using this power—the first Copyright Act was passed in 1790—it was unsettled whether Congress's primary role in setting up an intellectual property framework was to protect authors or to serve the public. This was a question that remained unsettled for nearly forty years, and it took the complaints of a former Supreme Court employee to settle the issue.

When a man named Henry Wheaton—the third person ever to hold the position of reporter of Supreme Court opinions and the first ever to be appointed to that position by the Court—turned over his job to his successor, Richard Peters, Jr., he found himself at odds with Peters as to the extent to which the former's work for the Court could by used by the latter. The resulting lawsuit, *Wheaton* v. *Peters* (1834), forced the Court to articulate the philosophy behind American copyright law, and it is a philosophy that has persisted to the present day.

The Court settled many issues in its decision in *Wheaton* v. *Peters*. For one thing, it decided that the common law—the law of previous Court decisions—did not establish any copyright interest in Wheaton's work. From this case forward, only federal copyright law applied to any of the works listed in that statute. At most, there could be only a statutory interest created by the first Copyright Act. And the requirements of establishing a copyright interest under that law, the Court found, must be strictly, not loosely, followed. The Court also decided that the purpose of the Copyright Act was not to enrich authors and editors like Wheaton, but to promote science and useful arts. Finally, the Court held that even if Wheaton had been in strict compliance with the statute (he wasn't), he would not have prevailed because "no reporter has or can have any copyright in the written opinions delivered by this Court; and that the judges thereof cannot confer on any reporter any such right."

This is the philosophy that copyright scholars normally invoke when they talk about the theoretical underpinnings of copyright in the United States. Implicit in that philosophy is that the needs and concerns of the general public in an open society are paramount. The Copyright Act must be understood, therefore, as a means to an end (educating and enriching the public) and not as an end in itself.

It is this approach that explains one of the most common themes of American copyright law: that original expression of factual matters is protected, but the facts themselves, once they're published, can be used by anybody. This distinction was first clearly drawn in an 1880 Supreme Court case, *Baker* v. *Selden,* and more recently received a resounding reaffirmation by the Court in *Feist* v. *Rural Telephone* (1991), a case involving competing telephone directories.

In the *Feist* case, the Court held, consistent with the long-standing facts-expression distinction, that one could not copyright mere collections of public facts, like telephone numbers. It did so in order to correct a trend in some lower federal courts toward granting copyright protections to those who, without adding anything that could be called "original expression," had labored to create some sort of factual compilations. Legal scholars referred to this as the "sweat of the brow" or "industrious collection" theory.

In the *Feist* case, the Court held that this "sweat of the brow" approach was invalid, since it flew in the face of *Baker* v. *Seiden*'s emphasis on original expression. Sure, you may have worked hard to assemble some collection of facts (like phone number listings), the Court was saying in effect, and you may even deserve some kind of reward for that, but the Copyright Act doesn't provide protection for mere labor. In reaching this opinion, the Court also relied on the fact that when the Copyright Act was amended in 1976, Congress dropped the reference to "all the writings of an author" (which had helped to lead courts astray) and replaced the language with the phrase "original works of authorship." The *Feist* case has reaffirmed that the originality requirement remains the touch-stone of copyright protection today.

The Coming of the Anti-*Feist*

No less than the Internet (which, as I keep stressing, can be understood as a global collection of copying machines), the Supreme Court's decision in the *Feist* case has been troubling to those who seek protection under the Copyright Act for their labor (which may in fact be undeniably valuable labor). This has especially been true of businesses like West Publishing, whose whole revenue-generating enterprise centers on the company's recording and publication of court decisions—very important but not fundamentally creative enterprise, which raises the question of the degree to which West should be able to claim a copyright interest in those published decisions. (In effect, West, a Canadian company, is playing the role in the modern copyright debate that Henry Wheaton played more than a century and a half ago.) Companies like West would like Congress to undo the *Feist* case—to bring about what I like to call "the coming of the anti-*Feist*." What's more, they'd like other nations to implement similar protections for collections of facts, like databases.

Initially, at least, they were remarkably successful in their lobbying efforts. The European Union endorsed the protection of databases as copyrighted works in the spring of 1996. And Bruce Lehman, the controversial head of the U.S. Patent and Trademark Office, led an American delegation to a world conference on intellectual property rights in December 1996. One of his expressed goals was to implement the protection of databases.

Indeed, Lehman and other pro–database protection advocates have gone a few steps further than seeking amendments to the Copyright Act and suggested it has become necessary for what lawyers call *sui generis* (one-of-a-kind) protection of databases. In these proposals, including one bill that would have created a whole new form of intellectual property just for the protection of databases, the term *database* is so loosely defined that it's hard to imagine what kind of information doesn't qualify for protection under the proposals.

This means it's hard to imagine how your average scholar or journalist can avoid being a felon. The database-protection bill I mention above would punish those who use databases for commercial purposes without an express license from the owner with five years in Club Fed. For example, under the terms of such a law, any would-be historical novelist who uses facts gleaned from the *Encyclopedia Britannica* (on paper or CD) for the purpose of writing a best-selling book would be presumptively guilty of a felony, absent permission from the *Britannica* people. Even worse, and unlike infringement in copyright law, you'd be guilty even if the novel was never actually written, much less sold.

Why is it that given the willingness of some copyright advocates to protect databases by amending the various nations' copyright laws, Lehman, and others are so bullish on so-called new sui generis protection? I believe it's because Lehman (and the panicky information service providers like West and Microsoft, whose interests he regards as paramount) is impatient with the existing Copyright Act, which has all sorts of inconvenient provisions and exceptions and decades of case law in which defendants sometimes win. In the proposals for sui generis protection, there's nothing as clearly developed as the Copyright Act's fair use provisions, which allow scholars, for example, to engage in some unlicensed use of copyrighted works without being liable for infringement. In contrast with Lehman's proposed penalties under this new act, the Copyright Act's criminal provisions focus on monetary damages, not prison terms (which max out at one year in the U.S. Code). But Lehman's worry is that the next generation of "infringers" won't be deterred by huge fines (which, since they may just be individuals using the Internet, they may be unable to pay anyway), which is why he backs scary jail sentences to protect these companies' interests on the Net.

As a copyright holder myself, I understand why so many companies like West are afraid of the Net. Its very method of propagating content is copying packets of information from node to node across the globe. This fact perpetually scares copyright holders and database companies, not to mention trademark holders and companies with trade secrets. The information revolution can be pretty frightening indeed when one has relied heavily on and invested in the ability to control the circulation of information and the relative expensiveness of making copies of it.

But as a civil libertarian, there are things I find scarier—like the prospect that we might soon enter a world in which all facts, and all collections of facts, are presumptively *owned*. In a free society, we do not require that every citizen have the same economic resources, but we have long depended on the principle that every citizen has at least something like the same access to basic informational resources, such as public libraries—resources that provide each citizen with an ability to educate himself about the world, to use the facts of the world, which no one owns or should own, to better his situation.

It may well be that the potential economic threat to companies like West Publishing requires some tinkering with our intellectual property framework. Certainly it would seem unfair if a competitor to West simply copied the fruits of West's labor and started up its own legal database services. But intellectual property holders have faced challenges and adapted before. When the VCR was first released, movie companies rushed to the courts to prevent the distribution of the machines, claiming their copyrights would be infringed right and left. Fortunately, they lost their case, the consumer VCR was deployed, and movie companies adapted. The aftermarket in video sales and rentals has since generated huge financial rewards for the movie industry, and it has even made it possible for movies that fail in the theaters to be successes on the bottom line.

But as Justice Holmes said long ago, "The life of the law has not been logic; it has been experience." That is, the best guide to the way the law should work is to study the past and present, not to attempt to predict every possible future. As the history of the VCR shows, the appropriate strategy is to wait and see what problems emerge for West or for anyone else, not to panic about what *could* happen. Once we understand the *actual,* not *perceived,* risks, we can legislate accordingly and with full regard for the competing interests at stake.

The greatest interest at stake is not that of the copyright holders or that of the database companies. It's the interest in a free and open society of ensuring that everyone, regardless of his or her economic background, has access to the facts. We should regard our nation's investment in the knowledge of its citizens, and in their ability to participate knowledgeably in an open society, as the highest and most precious intellectual property we can ever protect.

It turns out that a lot of Americans feel that their investment in this kind of open society is a personal one. Thanks to the combined outcry of civil libertarians, librarians, educators, scientists, legal scholars, and—by no means the least influential—Netizens themselves, the database protection treaty proposal advanced by Lehman in 1996 was defeated, as were the more outrageous suggestions for amendments to the international law of copyrights. Although some critical provisions regarding digital copyrighted works were in fact adopted as part of the treaty, as we shall see later in this chapter, the facts of the world are still free for the public at large to learn, build, and discuss without fear of legal penalties, at least for now.

Copyright on the Net in the Mid-1990s

Modern copyright law in the United States is laid out in Title 17 of the U.S. Code. The last major restructuring of the Copyright Act took place in 1976, but the fundamental approach to copyright law in this country can be found in a passage from the legislative report on the Copyright Act of 1909: "In enacting a copyright law Congress must consider . . . two questions: First, how much will the legislation stimulate the producer and so benefit the public, and, second, how much will the monopoly granted be detrimental to the public? The granting of such exclusive rights, under the proper terms and conditions, confers a benefit upon the public that outweighs the evils of the temporary monopoly."

In short, the idea behind copyright law is to encourage creators to generate expressive works because it benefits society to do so. The kinds of works that can be protected by copyright law are listed in Section 102 of the Copyright Act. Here's the list:

1. Literary works

2. Musical works, including any accompanying words

3. Dramatic works, including any accompanying music

4. Pantomimes and choreographic works

5. Pictorial, graphic, and sculptural works

6. Motion pictures and other audiovisual works

7. Sound recordings

8. Architectural works

To be protected by copyright law, works have to have been fixed at some point in a tangible medium, and they have to be original. Note also that according to Section 102 of the act, copyright law protects the particular expression of an idea or theme, not the idea itself. You can't copyright the idea of boy meets girl (not even if you fix it in a tangible medium by writing it down somewhere), but you can copyright the movie *Before Sunrise*. (Again, you can see this distinction between unprotected facts, standing on their own, and the protected work that may express those facts, which we saw in the *Feist* case.)

For the most part, the Copyright Act addresses, appropriately enough, the right to make a copy. (There are ancillary rights as well, such as the right to control who publicly performs your performable work, or who displays it, but the right to make copies is the central protected interest.) If you make copies of a copyrighted work without a license granted by the copyright holder and you can't avail yourself of any defense, such as fair use (discussed later in this chapter), you're a copyright infringer.

Can Copyright Infringement Be Theft?

Copyright springs into existence the moment a work is captured in a tangible medium. So as soon as I write these words on my PowerBook, my copyright interest in these words is created. Thus, in theory, if I e-mailed a draft of this chapter to a colleague and he printed that draft without my express or implied permission, he'd have engaged in a copyright violation.

As you might imagine, when it comes to the huge copying machine we call the Net, there is tremendous tension between the copyright law's monopoly on creating copies and Netizens' insistence on making electronic works copyable and therefore more useful. But common sense does provide some guidance. For example, when I e-mailed my colleague, I would not consider it harmful, or even unusual, for him to print out the chapter in order to review it. I would probably consider it a violation of my copyright, however, if he chose to publish my work under his own name. But I wouldn't consider it a theft, no matter how angry I was. After all, I still would own my copyrighted work, and neither my rights in it nor my ability to use it would be diminished (I could still publish it under my own name, for example). By comparison, if someone steals my car, I can't use it, even though I still have the right to do so.

Unfortunately, not everyone is familiar with the legal distinctions between so-called intellectual property and everyday tangible property. This means that, thanks to misunderstandings about the operation of and policies behind copyright law, there will be more and more claims that online infringement, including unintentional or unknowing infringement, of intellectual property amounts to "online theft or fraud." Sadly, these claims will be used not only to justify ill-considered expansions of the copyright laws, but also for expansions of law enforcement authority generally. That's what happened in the case of David LaMacchia.

Inventing New Crimes—The Feds to the Rescue

For LaMacchia, then an MIT undergraduate, Christmas 1994 came four days late. It was December 29 when federal judge Richard Stearns decided that LaMacchia, who'd been charged by the U.S. government with conspiring to trade millions of dollars of illegal copies of software over the Internet, because he managed a BBS where illegal copies of software had been found, had in fact committed no crime at all.

It had been nearly a year since LaMacchia (the kind of intellectually gifted student whose dorm room is nevertheless so cluttered that he can barely make it from bed to computer terminal) had been notified by officials at MIT that he was under federal investigation. "I guess I got really scared when they told me I was responsible for thirty million dollars worth of software violations," LaMacchia later said. (Subsequent estimates put the figure at closer to $1 million.)

LaMacchia's case had been touted as the largest single incidence of software piracy ever reported. According to the government, he had set up a bulletin board system on some MIT workstations that could be used to trade unauthorized copies of commercial software. But the question of whether LaMacchia had in fact committed any crime at all turned out to be a difficult one for authorities to answer. Said LaMacchia's lawyer, Harvey Silverglate: "The government is attempting to assert control over this burgeoning thing called the Internet." As a result, he says, it "spasmodically overreacts in order to set an example, to deter behavior the government doesn't like."

The problem for the feds was that the copyright law (as it existed in 1994) didn't criminalize LaMacchia's conduct. Section 506 of Title 17 (the Copyright Act) does offer a criminal provision, of course: "(a) Criminal infringement.—Any person who infringes a copyright willfully and for purposes of commercial advantage or private financial gain shall be punished as provided in section 2319 of Title 18." The language is straightforward enough, but it was difficult with the available facts for the government to show that LaMacchia had ever received, as a result of his BBS operation at MIT, any "commercial advantage or private financial gain." So, as a fallback measure, they chose to indict him on a charge of conspiracy to commit wire fraud.

I first learned about the case early in 1994, when Brian LaMacchia (David's brother, then also an MIT student) called me at the EFF, looking for a referral. Although no charges had then been filed, it was clear to me after talking to Brian that the government would have some trouble making a case against his brother. A few years previously, I had written about the many difficulties the government has faced in computer crime contexts when it tries to go beyond the Copyright Act to prosecute an alleged infringer with a more general criminal statute, such as the interstate transportation of property statute or the wire fraud statute. In particular, I'd pointed out that the Supreme Court had held in a 1985 case, *Dowling* v. *United States,* that copyright infringements must be prosecuted, if at all, under the criminal provisions of the Copyright Act. Specifically, the Court had held that Congress's well-deliberated penalty provisions under the copyright laws precluded any attempt by prosecutors to "fill the gaps" with more general-purpose criminal laws. Yet it was precisely this sort of gap filling that the Boston U.S. Attorney's Office seemed to be attempting in the *LaMacchia* case. What on earth were they thinking?

The difficulties the feds were going to have with the Dowling decision would be compounded, I knew, by the difficulty with their alternate theory involving wire fraud. In fact, I doubted they could even prove that what we classify as wire fraud had taken place.

Let's look at the elements of wire fraud as defined in *United States* v. *Lemire,* a D.C. Circuit case decided in 1983:

The elements of wire fraud are (1) formation of a "scheme to defraud," and (2) use of interstate wire communication to further that scheme. . . . Congress did not define "scheme or artifice to defraud" when it first coined that phrase, nor has it since. . . . Instead that expression has taken on its present meaning from 111 years of case law [since the phrase was first used in the mail-fraud statute of 1872]. . . .

At the core of the judicially defined "scheme to defraud" is the notion of a trust owed to another and a subsequent breach of that trust. But "not every breach of a fiduciary duty works a criminal fraud." . . . In their attempts to delineate which breaches of duty rise to the level of criminal fraud, courts have used various limiting doctrines. Some, including this court, have required that the fraud be "active"—that the fiduciary utilize his trusted position to obtain a benefit for himself at the expense of the person whose trust he breaches. . . . Other courts have required that the breach be accompanied by some material nondisclosure or misrepresentation to the party owed the duty. . . . The crux of these requirements is that the wire fraud statute makes criminal only breaches of duty that are accompanied by a misrepresentation or nondisclosure that is intended or is contemplated to deprive the person to whom the duty is owed of some legally significant benefit.[1]

It's clear from the discussion of wire fraud in the *Lemire* case that a defendant, to be convicted of wire fraud, must be shown beyond a reasonable doubt to have made a misrepresentation or to have failed to disclose material facts that he had a duty to disclose. Yet the LaMacchia indictment did not allege either a misrepresentation or a nondisclosure, and the facts as related in the indictment didn't even imply one. To me, as well as to other criminal lawyers who know the federal law of mail fraud and wire fraud cases, the case looked lousy for the government. It wasn't because the government had written its indictment badly (that's a problem the feds can correct with a superseding indictment). Instead, it looked as if the government had no case at all—no criminal copyright case and no scheme to defraud. In the absence of a fraudulent scheme, LaMacchia couldn't be convicted of conspiracy to carry out such a scheme.

It seemed clear to me after reviewing both *Dowling* and the federal fraud cases that the government shouldn't have brought this case at all—that LaMacchia had broken no law regardless of the claim that his BBS had been used for large-scale software copyright infringement. So I then had to ask, How do we explain the government's decision to prosecute David LaMacchia?

After some reflection, I came up with five theories to explain the government's actions. Feel free to pick any of them (or any selection of them) that you find credible:

1. The government was just dumb. The wire fraud statute is so broad and so routinely used as a catch-all that the prosecutors didn't seriously question whether it actually fit the conduct.

2. Prosecutions are in themselves punitive. The government may have thought it was going to lose, but prosecutors figured they were doing a public service by making the defendant have to go through hell to get acquitted.

3. Federal indictments of any sort, even flawed ones, put immense pressure on defendants to settle—to cop a plea—and if the defendant yields to that temptation, it doesn't matter whether the legal theory of the case is weak. The outcome is still a successful conviction.

4. The feds hoped to narrow the meaning of the *Dowling* case. Since 1992 or so, I'd heard one or two prosecutors argue that *Dowling* v. *United States* should be interpreted narrowly—as precluding the prosecution of infringement under the interstate transportation of stolen property statute, but not as precluding such prosecutions under more general criminal statutes. The only problem with this interpretation, which may sound good at first, is that the actual reasoning of the *Dowling* case is too broad to fit so narrow an interpretation. Dowling says that when it comes to infringement, if you want to do a criminal prosecution, it's the criminal copyright provisions or nothing.

5. There was too much political pressure to bring the prosecution. When I spoke about the case early on to one Department of Justice official, I was told that the department felt they couldn't just ignore what seemed to be a massive software-infringing operation. Politically speaking, it would be hard to explain to the software industry why it hadn't tried to take some kind of action.

A sixth argument—that the government was trying to make the case that copyrighted software is inadequately protected under current law— did not occur to me until much later.

When I started posting these five theories on the WELL and explaining how I thought that under the law LaMacchia had committed no crime, I was surprised at how much criticism I received from people who couldn't accept either that the government was mistaken to bring the case or that I seemed to care so much about it. After all, they said, even if the laws don't quite reach LaMacchia's (alleged) conduct, shouldn't he be punished anyway? Surely (they argued) this case raises no important issues for a civil libertarian!

The questions assumed that LaMacchia had deliberately set up the BBS system to facilitate software piracy. But I knew that in addition to claiming the indictment was legally flawed, LaMacchia and his attorneys steadfastly denied the government's factual allegations. David LaMacchia characterized himself as a "sysop" (the BBS term for system operator) who was being blamed for conduct of his users. To LaMacchia, his case illustrated a serious risk to system operators on the Net: To what extent will they be held criminally responsible for the acts of their users? As we've already seen, computer networks, public and private, have become an important forum for public discourse and activity. Make sysops responsible for their users' actions, and you may give them a powerful incentive to quit operating forums altogether.

Similarly, there's a fine line between legitimate deterrence and a chilling effect on constitutionally protected speech. A prosecution like the one in the *LaMacchia* case may deter some software pirates, but at what price? Even some law enforcement officials (notably Scott Charney of the Department of Justice) have expressed concern that well-meaning efforts to police cyberspace may have an undue chilling effect on First Amendment prerogatives. Will we feel free to speak freely if we think there's a cop constantly inspecting what we say for criminal content?

For all that the government says it's concerned about constitutional rights, the *LaMacchia* case illustrates how government also responds to pressure to put the lid on activities that are regarded as undesirable even when the laws don't directly make those activities a crime. While some copyright holders were pleased to see the government step in and attempt to convict LaMacchia of copyright-related offenses, civil libertarians were disturbed at what they saw as a tactical use of the government's ability to prosecute. "This prosecution represents another attempt to mold the criminal law according to what the Justice Department wants rather than what Congress has intended," said Silverglate. In his decision to dismiss the *LaMacchia* case, Judge Stearns cited a Supreme Court opinion to similar effect: "It is the legislature, not the Court, which is to define a crime, and ordain its punishment." Stearns, who assumed for the purposes of his decision that LaMacchia had committed the actions alleged in the indictment, suggested that Congress, if it wishes, could amend the copyright laws to enable prosecutions of cases like LaMacchia's. But although he disapproves of LaMacchia's alleged actions, he also noted that expansive interpretations of the criminal law "would serve to criminalize the conduct of not only persons like LaMacchia, but also the myriad of home computer users who succumb to the temptation to copy even a single software program for private use. It is not clear that making criminals of a large number of consumers of computer software is a result that even the software industry would consider desirable."

Stearns's opinion reminded me a bit of the dialogue between Thomas More and his son-in-law in the Robert Bolt play *A Man for All Seasons*. The son-in-law says he'd willingly cut down every law in England to get at the devil. More responds: "And when the devil turns on you, what protections would there be, every law in England being cut down?"

A lot of the arguments I saw on the WELL reminded me of More's son-in-law: some users hoped to find some way to stretch the law (which, it turns out, isn't much different from cutting it down) to make it fit LaMacchia (whom they assumed to be guilty of *something*). When I pointed out that LaMacchia was denying the factual allegations and had some pretty good legal arguments as well, I got a lot of grief: "You're just focusing on technicalities!" "You're simply trying to pick apart this indictment on technical grounds!"

What some people called a concern with legal technicalities and legal pedantry is what civil libertarians call a concern with due process. I simply can't accept that it's a merely "technical" argument to say that Congress didn't make the defendant's behavior a crime.

In the years following the dismissal of the *LaMacchia* case, Congress attempted to correct its "omission" with an amendment to the Copyright Act's criminal provisions. The motivation behind the law is a typical example of Net backlash. It was Congress's perception of a problem, rather than the existence of any problem itself, that gave rise to this amendment, which might as well have been called the LaMacchia amendment. How can I say there's no problem? Well, for one thing, there doesn't seem to have been any wave of similar infringers either before or after the *LaMacchia* case. (If there had been, we'd have had to call them copycat criminals, I suppose.) In fact, it's hard to point to a single company that can claim that copyright infringment on the Net has driven it out of business. Nevertheless, Congress amended the Copyright Act in 1997 to address what it called "the LaMacchia problem."[2]

But the very fact that the government attempted to stretch the law to fit the *LaMacchia* case keeps that line from Thomas More echoing in my head: If the government stretches the law and ignores precedent to reach every instance of conduct it disapproves of, what protections will be left for us? And that's only one of the temptations the government will be faced with as it struggles to come to terms with the Net.

Nor is it only the government that faces these temptations. Sometimes the copyright holders manage to do their own overreaching in the course of participating in the Net backlash. Certainly nothing has done more to bring home to me how willing private entities are to reshape the Net into a world safe for *their* interests—regardless of the cost to others—than the efforts of the Software Publishers Association in the fall of 1996 to engage in "warfare by lawsuit" against the Net.

The SPA and the ISPs

It wasn't the pleasantest phone conversation in the world. In the course of my investigation of a legal campaign by the Software Publishers Association (SPA) against Internet service providers (ISPs), however, the call I took from Sandy Sellers one Monday afternoon in Fall 1996 turned out to be one of the more useful phone calls I received.

Sellers was then vice president of the SPA, a trade organization that claims to protect the copyright interests of many of the nation's largest software manufacturers. Sellers finally called me back after I'd made a number of attempts to contact her and SPA chief Ken Wasch the previous week. She knew I was on the warpath about the lawsuits the SPA had recently filed against three Internet service providers, including

Community ConneXion, which operated in the San Francisco Bay Area (my stomping grounds) and provided Internet access to local residents. I was looking into their charges against Community ConneXion, and I wanted the facts.

Perhaps Sellers delayed in calling me back because she worried that no matter what she had told me, she'd never be able to refute my suspicion, which was that the cases were unfounded. The SPA's goal, I believed, was to generate what long-time CompuServe attorney Kent Stuckey calls a "pattern settlement"—the kind of lawsuit settlement that cascades through an entire industry and changes the way players in that industry respond to a legal problem. In particular, I believed that the SPA hoped to force most or all of the defendants in these cases into "settlements" that establish what kinds of measures the industry should take in response to complaints about copyright infringement—and make it look as if the SPA had been justified in suing these (allegedly) infringing companies. It was a strategy with which the SPA could advance what I suspected was its agenda of turning ISPs into copyright police without appearing as though it had bullied the ISPs into that role.

I was pretty sure of my theory even before Sellers called me that Monday afternoon. But what made me certain about it was Sellers's subsequent refusal during the call to tell me anything about the SPA's case against Community ConneXion. Despite SPA chief Ken Wasch's earlier e-mail telling me that all I needed were the facts to understand why the SPA's lawsuits were justified, what I found was that the organization seemed afraid to disclose anything. In my own investigations, I'd found reason to believe that the SPA cases were at best very weak.

After interviewing people at Community ConneXion, as well as a number of other individuals who'd encountered the SPA, I was unable to find any evidence of clear civil or criminal wrongs by the small Internet access companies SPA was suing. What was equally disturbing was the extent to which the SPA seemed to be using these cases for the purpose of advancing a copyright policy that could cripple the growing ISP industry and create a chilling effect on speech by forcing ISPs to filter and monitor postings (and possibly even Web links) for potential copyright violations.

You may wonder why a civil liberties lawyer cares about the ISP industry. To me, the connection is obvious and necessary. While it may be true that the Net, as Villanova University law professor Henry Perritt has commented, "can realize its potential only if it protects private property and makes it possible to offer something for sale or license," the Net's potential is more than merely economic. It's also democratic: it lies at the center of what it will mean to us socially, in the extent to which it provides the greatest number of voices an opportunity to speak and be heard. And freedom of speech on the Net depends on the existence of a market that provides access to the Net. If you can't buy access to the Net or can't opt to become a service provider yourself, your free speech rights there are strictly theoretical.

As former Vice President Albert Gore, among others, has noted, one of the great developments in the growth of the Net has been the ability of small companies with little initial capital to set up shop as access or forum providers. Like Gore, I have long believed the government's telecommunications policies ought to be designed to preserve that immense, already existent opportunity, not just because it's good for business but also because it's good for freedom. We have to look carefully at any policy regarding copyright, and other areas of intellectual property, that could cripple or kill the growing market in providing low-cost access to this newest of the mass media, the Net.

The Would-Be Reformers of Copyright

This expand-the-laws-and-increase-deterrence approach, stupid and dangerous though it may be, was precisely what the Software Publishers Association was pinning its hopes on. As I learned when I researched the SPA's public announcements about its lawsuit strategy against alleged copyright infringers, the organization explained that its legal theories of copyright infringement derived in part from a highly controversial document released in 1995: the U.S. Patent and Trademark Office's "White Paper" recommendations on copyright, which would expand the scope of the Copyright Act's protections and its definitions of infringement.

The White Paper has been bitterly criticized by legal experts and public policy analysts. Some of the criticisms are grounded in concerns that librarians and educators have typically raised whenever copyright policy is revisited. For example, the White Paper omits in its summary of copyright law any significant discussion of the first-sale doctrine (which allows you to resell the copy of a copyrighted work that you bought—say, a college textbook) or of the fair use principle (which outlines the circumstances in which you can reproduce some or all of a copyrighted work without being liable for infringement). The White Paper, authored by Patent and Trademark Office director Bruce Lehman, was only the first step in the administration's major push toward aggressively expanding intellectual property rights in this country and worldwide.

But not even the broadest reading of the much criticized White Paper would create the kind of liability the SPA was arguing for, which includes liability for the provider even when one of its users has not infringed directly or otherwise, but merely has a Web page that includes a link to a site containing information that might be used to facilitate infringement. (It's a little like charging someone for theft because he or she published a book whose index contained a reference to Abbie Hoffman's *Steal This Book*.) But the SPA was not prepared to deal with a service provider that refused to cave in to SPA pressure.

Unsuspecting Infringers

It was Sameer Parekh, founder and president of the San Francisco Bay area ISP Community ConneXion, whose principled, courageous stand compelled me to look into the details of the SPA's strategy. Parekh maintained to me that both he and his company were innocent of any wrongdoing. Thus, even though his company is a small one, Parekh refused to agree to any settlement offer from the SPA and instead decided, as a matter of principle, to hire a lawyer in spite of the potential costs of defense. Shortly after it became clear that Parekh and his company wouldn't settle, the SPA formally dropped its case against Community ConneXion. This happened after my first e-mail to Ken Wasch but before my phone conversation with Sellers. So when Sellers finally called me, I had something new to talk about.

"Are you going to apologize to Community ConneXion?" I asked her.

"No," she said after a pause. "Why should we?"

"Well, you and I both know that your case against them was a dog that wouldn't hunt—that there's no evidence they ever infringed against anyone. Shouldn't you apologize for saying otherwise?"

That's when Sellers stunned me by aggressively asserting that the SPA would do no such thing, that it still had a case against Community ConneXion, and that if the ISP failed to negotiate with SPA, they'd file suit again. Despite what I already knew about the weakness of their case, Sellers was responding to criticisms of its actions against Community ConneXion by repeating the original charges that Parekh and his company were liable as "contributory infringers" under current copyright law.

Parekh's attorney, Terry Gross of San Francisco, has since criticized the SPA's refusal to admit its mistake in suing Parekh and has suggested that under the circumstances it would be appropriate for the SPA to clear the air by admitting its mistake and paying Community ConneXion's legal expenses.

Sellers seemed remarkably defensive during our phone conversation, even before I found myself raising my voice in disbelief and anger at her disregard for Parekh and his company. Her defensiveness turned my attention back to the question of what the SPA was really after. For example, she continued to claim that the SPA sent an e-mail message to Parekh that gave him due and proper notice about copyright infringement taking place on or through his Web site. But when I pointed out that the e-mail in question could not possibly constitute notice because it contained no specifics and asked her what that evidence was, she wouldn't tell me even in the most general terms what it might be, even as she reasserted the claim that the case could still go forward and that it would in fact go forward if Parekh refused to meet the SPA representatives. In short, Sellers was claiming that the SPA had disclosed the basis of its case while still refusing to disclose the basis of the case.

Parekh maintains that he never received the SPA's original notice e-mail in the first place and that he received a copy of it only after the suit had been filed. It was impossible to determine from the e-mail's text what content on his site could be infringing. He is correct to believe that vague allegations do not constitute due notice as the law requires. The federal courts require that the complaint (suit) state the cause of action with sufficient detail to allow the defendant to prepare a response. In addition, the defendant must receive adequate notice that he or she is being sued. Sellers claims that it was reasonable to assume that Parekh had received the notice because the SPA's e-mail to Community ConneXion "didn't bounce." However, the burden is on the plaintiff to ensure that the defendant is on notice, which is why, in the paper world, notice is usually delivered physically through a traceable means, such as certified mail.

It was Sellers's reluctance to disclose any information, including information that might improve the credibility of the SPA's assertions, that caused me to take a closer look at the details of the SPA's dealings with Parekh and other defendants. My research raised troubling questions. It began to look as though the SPA had never built any real case against Parekh and that it had done little, if any, research on him.

The Bigger Picture

What I was able to learn about the other cases instigated by the SPA suggested a similar pattern, even though "settlements" had already been announced in two of the other cases involving ISPs. But even in these cases, the evidence of any infringement was never made public. It began to look to me as if the real focus of these lawsuits was not to remedy any *past* infringements, but to lay the groundwork for far broader infringement lawsuits in the future. The real goal seemed to be to force some significant number of providers to agree to the SPA's own code of conduct, an "education" effort that was announced at the same time as the litigation campaign. Among its provisions was that ISPs agree to appoint a "compliance officer" to make sure that no one using their services is engaged in infringement of anyone's copyright. Because copyright infringement is rarely evident at first glance (how do you know that a copy of WordPerfect or Novell Netware on my computer is a licensed copy just by looking at it?), the compliance officer empowered by the code becomes a sort of all-purpose copyright policeman working for the SPA (but paid out of the ISP's payroll).

I also believe the SPA had targeted smaller companies because they would be more likely to settle than to take on the cost of litigation. In criminal law terms, the cost of mounting a defense would push these companies to "cop a plea" and accept a kind of "probation." If the SPA could get enough companies to adopt a "voluntary" code of conduct (itself drafted by the SPA), then in future copyright litigation against ISPs and other access providers, they could say that these "voluntary" codes amounted to an industry standard of due diligence. A defendant's failure to adopt such a code could then be characterized as proof at least of negligence, and perhaps even of complicity, in copyright infringement. In the long run, the establishment of such an "industry standard" would provide the SPA with a powerful legal tool to use against larger providers like Netcom and America Online. And in the short run, suing these little companies would have a chilling effect on the First Amendment rights of other providers, as well as on their users, because the providers would feel intimidated into adopting the role of copyright police.

Not long after Parekh started getting news play for his resistance to the SPA strategy, SPA spokesmen were quoted as saying it was considering a revision of the code in response to the outpouring of public criticism about its original wording. That wording seemed to put each provider in the role of policing not only every user's content on the provider's own site, but also every Web link to any other site that had infringing information. In effect, the code as it was originally worded would put each provider in the position of having to police content on the Web as a whole.

This would have been a deeply wrongheaded policy. It's as if someone sued B. Dalton's bookstores because a certain number of books in their huge inventory contain infringing material, then ordered the chain to hire a compliance officer for every store to make sure that it didn't happen again. Even if there were serious copyright enforcement problems, you couldn't solve them by turning bookstore employees into police. After all, even the most assiduous copyright police can't normally tell by reading a book whether it contains infringing works. Doing so would give people a strong incentive to get out of the bookstore business altogether. Yet even if you're a service provider that disapproves of software piracy and even if you steadfastly refuse to engage in it yourself, the SPA has declared its right to sue you for not choosing to be one of its designated copyright cops.

That's the substantive criticism of the SPA's proposed code of conduct, but it doesn't address the questions raised by the organization's litigation strategy. Most of the companies that support the SPA have great track records as corporate citizens. It would be a shame to see companies like Apple and Adobe have their positive public images marred by the SPA's excesses. I also believe that some, and perhaps most, of the SPA's backers would nix this sort of strategy if they were fully informed about it in advance, opting instead for a more straightforward debate in the policy arena rather than in the courts.

Although there are some real issues facing the world of copyright in the digital age, there's no reason they can't be debated publicly and honorably. As to the merits of the proposed copyright reforms, the companies that want to increase legal protection for intellectual property think their arguments are compelling enough without needing to sneak policymaking through the back door of a lawsuit. I don't agree with some of the software providers' arguments, but I do agree that the arrival of the Net as a central force in public life presents an occasion for a full examination of intellectual property issues. And the only unassailable consensus about copyright on the Net will be the one that comes from fair and open public debate.

The Aftermath of the SPA Skirmish

The SPA has revised its suggested "code of conduct" for ISPs into something almost reasonable. The revised code looks much like the current terms of service agreements outlining the rules under which subscribers may participate through a particular ISP—agreements that ISPs already impose on themselves and their subscribers. (Strangely, no one has yet argued convincingly that any update of those terms of service was necessary.) So settlements adhering to this code of conduct really amount to business as usual for an ISP.

After the publicity surrounding Community ConneXion's resistance to the SPA threats, two of the three Internet service providers that were named defendants in the SPA's October 1996 lawsuits announced "settlements" with the organization. A close look at those settlements suggests that the SPA backed down from its original aggressive approach in order to salvage some good press from what was turning into a PR disaster. Once it had become clear that Community ConneXion was going to hang tough by refusing to settle or to admit any wrongdoing on the copyright front, the other defendants began to question how much they had to give up in these "settlements." So the SPA began to back-pedal about its code of conduct and claims of infringement, especially after the press began to ask some pointed questions of SPA spokespersons. For example, one SPA representative told the press he hoped that one outcome of filing the lawsuit against Community ConneXion would be to "start a dialogue." Not long after, another representative stated that "starting a dialogue" was the reason SPA had *dropped* its lawsuit against Sameer Parekh's company. It seems fair to say that the organization probably needs to work a bit more on its ideas about starting dialogues.[3]

Holy Wars: Using IP Law as a Weapon

In one of the earliest widely publicized sets of cases involving intellectual property on the Net, the Church of Scientology has been exploring the uses of copyright and trade secret law when it comes to silencing its critics, many of them former members of the church. Although the underlying facts of these cases are not particularly mainstream, they did play a significant role in shaping what eventually became SPA's litigation strategy.

I uncovered this last fact when speaking at a legal education seminar held in San Jose in the fall of 1996. I spoke about the problems raised by the Communications Decency Act (discussed at length in the next few chapters). But it wasn't "indecency" I was thinking about. No, it was obscenity—the obscenity I saw in the SPA's decision to go after small providers in an attempt to impose its industry standard regarding copyright infringement. I mentioned this to a number of the other lawyers who were lunching with me after a few of us had participated in a discussion panel.

Interestingly, one of the lawyers there, who I later learned represented one of the larger software publishers, had heard about the case and had a different take on it from me. Said the lawyer, "This case [against Parekh and Community ConneXion] isn't so much about copyright as it is about *notice*." The truly interesting question, he argued, was what degree of notice a provider had to have before it could be said that the provider had a duty to remove infringing material from his site. Or if it couldn't be easily determined whether the material in question was infringing, what kind of duty did the provider have to respond to infringement complaints?

He then noted that although it is true that sometimes litigation can be used destructively, as I had been complaining, it is also true that litigation about things like proper notice and the duty to respond will nevertheless lead to industry standards about them. "Surely you agree that this is what's happening in the Netcom case," he said.

What the lawyer referred to as the Netcom case was known officially as *Religious Technology Center* v. *Netcom* and unofficially to countless Netizens (together with related cases) as *Scientology* v. *The Net*. (The Religious Technology Center is a secular arm of the Church of Scientology.) The facts of the case are simple. A number of critics of the Church of Scientology were once members of the church, and in the course of their involvement they (or their sources) received access to a number of church documents that either discussed policies promoted by the church or laid out some of the church's religious and metaphysical doctrines. The church's critics felt that the publication of these documents on the Net, in news groups such as alt.religion.scientology, would expose the church to public ridicule and criticism. At the same time, the critics no doubt knew that church officials would be furious at the fact that their secret documents had been made public.

The church responded to these provocations. It sued the critics and the ISP, Netcom, for copyright infringment and trade secret theft. But the legal argument that had the greatest public impact was the church's attempt to establish that service providers have a duty to police the content of their digital realms, at least when responding to a complaint that some of the posted content is infringing on someone's alleged copyright violation (or another intellectual property interest). The parallel between what the church wanted to do with regard to its critics and what the SPA wanted to do with regard to infringers was clear: both the church and the SPA hoped to create a legal framework in which service providers would have the primary responsibility to step in and halt or prevent infringing acts on the Net.

The logical connection between the two legal disputes seemed obvious to me once the software company lawyer pointed it out during that lunch in San Jose. But previously I'd missed the connection altogether, in part because the Church of Scientology and its agenda seemed very different from the likely motives of the SPA (which was concerned more about copyright than about criticism) and in part because the two cases reached their fruition at different times. After my colleague had pointed out the connection, however, I began to wonder whether the similarity might be more than coincidental. Could it be that the SPA had been following the Scientology case all along and taking notes for its own campaign?

It's especially important to understand that the focus of the church's concern was not on infringing material that the service provider or its agents may have posted themselves. Instead, it was on the duty of providers to police the content of their subscribers. Since many providers enable their customers to run their own Web sites, the logic of the church's position was clear: it wanted to choke off their critics' allegedly infringing acts at a strategically crucial point—the point of access (for example, the Internet service provider).

Ultimately, the church was trying to establish that the provider has some kind of legal duty to take potentially draconian action, like shutting down an entire Web site even though only a piece of it may be infringing, once that provider has notice of a possible infringing act on the site.

At first glance, it may seem that the church was seeking nothing more than for the courts to require that providers—once they've been given notice—have a duty to remove infringing materials posted by their users. But it's not so clear to me that it would be good policy to impose this duty on providers, and in fact we do not normally impose such a duty on other kinds of businesses that sometimes carry infringing content, even when they know about it! Furthermore, it is better for legislatures, rather than the courts, to create such framework of legal obligations.

Think about how we deal with infringement in other communications media. Consider, for example, that most of us connect to the Net these days over ordinary voice-grade telephones. Suppose I posted something infringing to a Web site with my laptop and modem. Do we really think that Pacific Bell ought to be legally responsible for my act of infringement? Even if they've received a complaint (that is, "notice") about it?

To take another example, suppose I publish a magazine and infringe on some other writer's copyright. Now suppose my magazine is delivered directly to subscribers by Federal Express. Would it make sense for a court to hold Federal Express legally liable for my act of infringement simply because someone was industrious enough to inform FedEx representatives about it?

Historically, our legal system has opted until now to focus primarily on the originator of the infringing content—the guy who posted the infringing message or software in the first place. What's more, we've always put the primary burden of protecting one's interest in intellectual property on the person who actually holds the IP interest.

But on the Net, there's no guarantee that a copyright holder will be able to find a defendant that's worth suing or even find a defendant at all. Since one of the revolutionary dimensions of the Net is the low economic barrier to participation in a mass medium, we're entering a world in which not everyone who can reach a mass audience happens to be rich enough to sue, or even cares very much about whether he or she *is* sued. A $10 million verdict against some Netizen in a Net copyright lawsuit, for example, may not mean much to him (other than the trauma of being sued itself); such a laughably large verdict is so far beyond what the normal individual can pay that he's likely to ignore it altogether. You can't get blood out of a stone, after all.

But for a company like Netcom, an expanding nationwide ISP, such a verdict could be a real threat to business. What's more, Netcom, like all other Internet service providers, plays an active role in administering the Net. So the church may well have wondered, Who better to put in the role of defendant in these infringement cases than a provider, and who, if it lost, could be ordered by the court to help stamp out infringement elsewhere on the Net?

Thus, at the core of all the legal conflicts collectively (and unofficially) referred to online as *Scientology* v. *The Net* were two basic questions. First, does it make sense for a court to impose on online service providers a duty to stop infringements of the church's intellectual property—infringements that will occur every time individuals post church documents and other information about the church? Second, if there is to be such a duty for ISPs, what kind of legal notice should be required? Is e-mail enough? A phone call? A registered letter? As the lawyer suggested to me at that lunch in San Jose, these are the kinds of legal nuances that typically arise from the "common law" of judges' decisions in particular cases, not the statutory law that Congress writes. I'm inclined to agree with him.

Infringement or Freedom of the Press?

The defendants in the Scientology cases fell primarily into two basic groups: (1) publishers and posters and (2) providers of online services. The first group includes people like Dennis Erlich, a former minister of Scientology who is now an outspoken critic of the church; Arnie Lerma, who has published controversial court documents concerning one of the many cases that the church, a famously litigious organization, has been involved in; and Lawrence Wollersheim, who runs a BBS called FactNet. Also in the first group is Scamizdat, an anonymous Usenet poster who has distributed dozens of Scientology documents. Arguably, the *Washington Post* also belongs in this group because it was sued over Scientology materials it received (some of which it published as part of its coverage of the *Lerma* case).

In the second group are companies like Netcom and Digital Gateway Systems, two major Internet service providers, as well as support.com, a bulletin board system run by Tom Klemesrud. These three services were sued by the church as part of an effort to establish a legal duty for them to act as copyright cops. A different sort of online service provider, anon. penet.fi, an anonymous remailer operated in Finland by Johan Helsingius, was also targeted by the church. Helsingius was legally compelled in 1995 to surrender the identity of one of his anonymous users whom the church believed to be circulating secret documents.

What were the documents in question? Mostly they were writings by the late L. Ron Hubbard, the former pulp science-fiction writer who founded the church. Hubbard's writings include documents that recount the church's mythology, describe practices for dealing with "thetans" (entities that can cause mental or physical problems), or state the church's internal policies. Church officials refer to these documents, and to the information contained in them, as "sacred scriptures."

Although the church has relied on other legal theories, ranging from trademark law to the First Amendment's freedom of religion provisions, in the course of its thrashes with net.critics, its primary rationales for its legal action against these parties were two rather distinct areas of intellectual property: copyright law and trade secret law. Interestingly, these legal theories seem to have been chosen less for the substantive merit of the lawsuits than for their tactical value in silencing, either temporarily or permanently, the church's critics.

The Secret Weapon of the Copyright Act

Perhaps the most startling stories of the various *Scientology* v. *The Net* cases are those in which lawyers for the church, accompanied by local law enforcement personnel, raided defendants and seized their computers. It's not the kind of thing one normally expects to happen when one is accused of copyright infringement, on the Net or anywhere else.

But Section 503 of the Copyright Act provides an unusual remedy for immediate infringement that was used dramatically against several of the publisher defendants in the *Scientology* cases: "At any time while an action under this title is pending, the Court may order the impounding, on such terms as it may deem reasonable, of all copies or phonorecords claimed to have been made or used in violation of the copyright owner's exclusive rights, and of all plates, molds, matrices, masters, tapes, film negatives, or other articles by means of which such copies or phono-records may be reproduced." In other words, the plaintiffs in a copyright case can conduct a search and seizure at the alleged infringer's premises, ostensibly in order to prevent further infringement. In the Scientology cases, this has meant that Scientology lawyers showed up at defendants' homes, law enforcement agents in tow, to seize their computers and many of their other possessions as well. It's the kind of utterly disconcerting, frightening event that few people, even vociferous critics of a controversial and litigious church, really expect, given that this kind of seizure can take place before an infringement case goes to court or even before the defendant's lawyer has had a chance to talk to the judge. It's a tactic that was designed to handle commercial infringers, but it's one that the Church of Scientology has adapted to its own purposes—a sort of legal scare tactic aimed at certain critics of the church. (Ironically, the church in its own publications has classified some of the critics as "copyright terrorists," an eye-joltingly incongruous notion.)[4]

Although the defendants were being treated under the Copyright Act as presumptive infringers, were they truly infringers? They claim that even if they are making unlicensed copies of copyright-protected Scientological works, their copying is protected by the principle of fair use. Under Section 107 of the act, an otherwise infringing use of a copyrighted work can qualify as a "fair use." It all depends on how a court weighs factors such "the purpose and character of the use" and "the amount and substantiality of the portion used in relation to the copyrighted work as a whole." There's no easy test as to whether a use is fair use. Sometimes use of the entire work can qualify, and sometimes use of only a small part of a work is too much. But given that the church's critics claimed to be using Scientology materials in order to engage in both public education and criticism of the church's activities, it seems likely that at least some of the defendants' uses of the materials would qualify as a fair use.

The possible applicability of the fair use doctrine, together with the fact that copyright law doesn't protect ideas or facts, but only particular expressions of ideas or facts, created a problem for the church. Although the Copyright Act's seizure and impoundment provisions give the church an excellent tool for silencing critics over the short run, the act's careful balancing of authorial rights with the public's rights (that's what fair use is all about, really) means that the church can never totally control its documents through copyright. Similarly, the idea/expression distinction of Section 102 of the act means that copyright law can't be used to stop critics from *paraphrasing* material they find in church documents. The act protects only the actual words used, not the information they convey.

This is why the church chose to characterize its materials as trade secrets as well as copyrighted works. It was a second legal theory that might effectively plug the gaps in the first one.

Religious Trade Secrets?

The first thing you need to know about the trade secret branch of intellectual property law is that although copyright law is created by federal statute, there is no corresponding federal law of trade secrets. There have been federal cases, including Supreme Court cases, that discuss the legal concept, but for the most part, trade secrets are defined by state law. This means that the definition of *trade secret* varies somewhat from state to state.

Still, most definitions of *trade secret* have certain elements in common, which is one reason federal courts can talk sensibly about the concept. Let's look at how the U.S. Supreme Court defined the term in a 1974 case, *Kewanee Oil Co. v. Bicron Corp.*: "[A] trade secret may consist of any formula, pattern, device or compilation of information which is used in one's business, and which gives one an opportunity to obtain an advantage over competitors who do not know or use it. It may be a formula for a chemical compound, a process of manufacturing, treating or preserving materials, a pattern for a machine or other device, or a list of customers."⁵ This isn't the sort of material one normally associates with a religion, but let's go on.

In *Kewanee Oil*, the Supreme Court also listed the particular attributes of a trade secret:

1. The information must, in fact, be secret—"not of public knowledge or of general knowledge in the trade or business."

2. A trade secret remains a secret if it is revealed in confidence to someone who is under a contractual or fiduciary obligation, express or implied, not to reveal it.

3. A trade secret is protected against those who acquire, through unauthorized disclosure, violation of a contractual duty of confidentiality, or "improper means," which includes such things as theft, bribery, burglary, or trespass.

The holder of a trade secret may take a number of steps to meet its obligation to keep the trade secret a secret: (1) labeling documents containing the trade secret "proprietary" or "confidential" or "trade secret" or "not for distribution to the public"; (2) requiring employees and contractors to sign agreements not to disclose whatever trade secrets they come in contact with; (3) destroying or rendering illegible discarded documents containing parts or all of the secret; and (4) restricting access to areas in the company where a nonemployee, or an employee without a clear obligation to keep the information secret, might encounter the secret.

In some respects, trade secret law seems made to order for the church's efforts to silence these defendants. For example, most of the material in question really is secret (or at least it was until it was posted on the Net). Normally, a member of the church would have to be a member for a long time—and would have to have paid a lot of money—before the church would disclose some of this material to that person voluntarily. And church members can be routinely required to sign confidentiality agreements that ensure that any "trade secrets" retain their legal status if a disgruntled former member should choose to reveal them.

What's more, while there's no "fair use" exception when it comes to trade secrets, anyone who discovers a trade secret without violating a confidentiality agreement can disseminate it freely. For example, if you board a commuter train in Atlanta and discover that a Coca-Cola employee has left the secret formula for the company's flagship product on one of the seats, you have no obligation not to reveal it to the world. More important, this means that newspapers often may legally publish material that may have been obtained illegally, as long as they did not induce the illegal taking or know about it beforehand and as long as no one was induced or solicited by the newspaper to steal the material in question.[6] And trade secret law protects the information itself, not merely its particular expression. Trade secret law, unlike copyright, can protect ideas and facts directly.

But did the material in question really qualify as "trade secrets"? Among the material the church has been trying to suppress is what might be called a "genesis myth of Scientology": a story about a galactic despot named Xenu who decided 75 million years ago to kill a bunch of people by chaining them to volcanoes and dropping nuclear bombs on them. (Apart from anything else, this sort of aggression on Xenu's part strikes me as excessive—volcano chaining *or* nuclear bombing, but not both!) You may recall that part of the definition of "trade secret" in the *Kewanee Oil* case is that it "gives one an opportunity to obtain an advantage over competitors who do not know or use it." Does a "church" normally have "competitors" in the trade secret sense? If the Catholics get hold of the full facts about Xenu, does this mean they'll get more market share?

It seems likely, given what we know about the case now, that even a combination of copyright and trade secret law wouldn't accomplish what the church would like it to accomplish: the total suppression of any dissemination of church documents or doctrines. But the fact that the church was unlikely to gain any complete legal victories in its cases didn't mean that they wouldn't litigate. It's indisputable that the mere threat of litigation, or the costs of actual litigation, may accomplish what the legal theories alone do not: the effective silencing of many critics of the church.

That this was in fact the real goal of the litigation was apparent to federal judge Leonie Brinkema, who, while refusing to dismiss the copyright claims against the church's individual critics, dismissed the church's lawsuit against the *Washington Post.* "The Court finds the motivation of Plaintiff in filing this lawsuit against the *Post* is reprehensible," she states in her opinion. "Although the [church, through its secular arm, the Religious Technology Center] brought the complaint under traditional secular concepts of copyright and trade secret law, it has become clear that a much broader motivation prevailed—the stifling of criticism and dissent of the religious practice of Scientology and the destruction of its opponents." In a subsequent order in which she addressed a free exercise of religion argument that the church had newly raised, Judge Brinkema tied together the intellectual property threads that have been the focus of most of the *Scientology* cases:

We recognize that the RTC [Religious Technology Center] has installed extraordinary measures to maintain the secrecy of its . . . AT documents and that they have zealously pursued any reported leaks of information. However, it is a quantum leap to claim that Scientology's endeavors to enforce the secrecy of these documents thereby prohibits secular organizations from undertaking legally permissible criticism of Scientology including quotes from these documents as long as possession of the documents was achieved lawfully. In their effort to enjoin the *Post,* the RTC is essentially urging that we permit their religious belief in the secrecy of the AT documents to "trump" significant conflicting constitutional rights. In particular, they ask us to dismiss the equally valid First Amendment protections of freedom of the press. Furthermore, RTC asks that we allow the free exercise clause to deflate the doctrine of fair use as embodied in the copyright statute, one of the very status laws upon which the RTC has based this lawsuit.

In short, the fact that the *Post*'s "possession of the documents was achieved lawfully" defeats any trade secret claim, while the *Post*'s limited quotation of the documents is allowed under the Copyright Act's fair use provisions.

Like the case against the *Washington Post,* most of *Scientology* v. *The Net* cases seemed to be moving toward eventual de facto victory for the defendants, even though they might have lost the lawsuits. (Judge Brinkema was skeptical about defendant claims that the publication in full of an original church document, followed by only a line or two of commentary, added up to fair use.) None of the legal theories advanced by the church seemed adequate to stop the hemorrhaging of Scientology's secrets on the Net. In the past, the threat of litigation itself would be enough to silence at least some individuals, but there is every indication that the church has underestimated what it is dealing with when it chooses to tackle the online world.

In the case against Netcom, however, the parties opted not to wait for a trial verdict; they opted instead for a settlement. The terms of the settlement itself were secret, but observers did notice that Netcom decided shortly afterward to revise its "terms of service" to specify response and review procedures in the event of a claim of infringement. While one can't criticize Netcom for wanting to settle the case and thus end it, the news of the company's decision to settle has had a lasting impact. For one thing, providers began looking to Netcom's new terms of service for guidance as to how to avoid a lawsuit from the Church of Scientology or from other publishers. Second, it seems to have given some other parties, like the SPA and the software company that employs the lawyer I spoke with that day in San Jose, some ideas about how to make the legal environment in cyberspace a bit friendlier to their interests (though less friendly to ordinary users).

The problem for the church is that in cyberspace, nobody is really isolated. Once the church seizes on a defendant like Dennis Erlich, or the SPA targets someone like Sameer Parekh, this tactic can create a backlash in the online community, which is zealous in its regard for the free speech rights of everyone, including both the Church of Scientology and its critics. Countless individuals who never would have given the church a second thought otherwise have been motivated by the heavy-handed legal tactics in the *Scientology* cases to take part in organized efforts to frustrate the church's efforts to keep its secrets. And a number of system operators and concerned Netizens have begun sharing information about the SPA's strategy and tactics for reducing infringement and shaping the legal system's notions of duty with regard to copyright.[7] The sheer power of the Net as a mass medium, together with its decentralized character, make this potentially impossible to stop. The church of Scientology, with its millions of dollars and legal resources, may be the modern equivalent of King Canute: they seem to be discovering that the law of copyright and trade secrets, even when used together, cannot prevent the Net tide from coming in.

But whatever long-term balances may be struck in the intellectual property arena, we need more people like Parekh in the short term. As these cases have shown, the uses of intellectual property law, either substantively or strategically, to suppress or constrain freedom of speech on the Net will be a hot topic in the months and years to come. The cases will be coming from the government, from private parties, and from lobbying groups, and each will be couched in terms of the threat the Net poses to intellectual property.

This means we can no longer be as complacent as I once was about how little I had to know of intellectual property law. Those of us who find ourselves spending more of our time in cyberspace have already learned that we need to know the basics of this area of the law in particular, not only to make sure that in our own exercise of freedom of speech we treat our fellow citizens fairly, but also to make sure that we can continue to speak freely.

Since this discussion of intellectual property and the Net backlash has been pretty long and involved and has dealt with some pretty arcane matters, it's possible that you may have lost sight of what you as a user or publisher may do on the Net—and in particular on the World Wide Web—to avoid copyright liability. I'd feel pretty guilty if I left you confused about these issues, so my research assistant Tess Koleczek and I have worked up a set of commonsense guidelines that while not guaranteeing that nobody will sue you, will almost certainly reduce the likelihood that someone will want to. The philosophy behind them is not to tell you what you can get away with. Instead, we aim to encourage you to treat copyright holders in the online world not as likely adversaries, but as friends and coparticipants in this great democratic experiment we call the Net. Since we believe in virtual communities, and we hope you do, too, you may be interested in what we think it takes to make someone a good neighbor when dealing with other people's copyright interests.

A Good Citizen's Guide to Copyright on the Web (Or, How to Link Friendly and Influence People)

You probably already have a pretty good idea of the ways you can use the World Wide Web to benefit your business or enhance your personal enjoyment of the Internet. And you likely know something about how powerful and flexible the Web can be when it comes to capturing material from the Net and reshaping it for your own use. But when you're staring at all that exciting potential, you may find it easy to forget something very important: just because new tools empower you to use the Web in creative new ways doesn't mean you should be using it in ways that hurt other people's rights and interests. It especially doesn't mean you automatically have a legal right to do anything you want with the material you access.

We can't be your lawyers, so you shouldn't take what we're about to tell you as the legal advice that will help you out of your particular fix. But we can help you be aware of how to avoid some common pitfalls in copyright law. We'd like it if you followed the rules we've come up with, not only because they'll help you keep out of legal trouble but also because it would help show the world that the Internet- and Web-exploiting software can be used wisely and responsibly. We can't guarantee that these rules will keep all trouble from your doorstep, of course. But we're hoping that if we can start a general movement to treat copyrights with a little bit of extra niceness, the Web and the Net will be a better place for all. So think about the following guidelines and about the ways you can be a friendly linker:

1. Linking to other sites, even without express permission, is generally okay.

But it is important to distinguish linking to a Web site from making a copy. Absent some explicit restriction on the part of the copyright holder, you can link to his or her page and you have an implied license to those copies that are made automatically when you use your browser or other software tools to view this material. Making copies beyond that, however, is generally verboten, absent permission from the person who holds the relevant copyrights. (See the following rules for some exceptions.)

If you do happen to receive a request from the copyright holder of the page asking you to "unlink" from his or her site, it is generally good Netiquette to respect that request for whatever reason and remove such link. But this needn't be a hard-and-fast rule. For example, your link to a political opponent's page may be used to illustrate a particular criticism. If you are pro-choice, for example, you might want to link to an antiabortion page (or vice versa) to make your point. Such criticisms, even with the attendant links, and absent any defamatory or threatening remarks, are generally okay.[8]

2. Don't try to pass off someone else's material as your own.

It doesn't matter whether you're linking or just plain copying. Copyright law is all about making sure the person who holds the copyright for a particular work has the primary control over it and gets the primary benefit from it.

3. When in doubt, ask permission.

If you would like to use someone's material, the most logical step is to ask permission. Be sure that the person from whom you are obtaining permission is authorized to give it!

4. Don't just assume that reusing material is okay.

It is rarely a bad idea to ask permission to use material in order to avoid problems down the road, especially if the material you are copying to your hard drive, floppy disk, Web page, offline publication, and so on is something that the copyright holder might not want you to use. There is a great amount of leeway in copyright law that would allow for use of material without permission, provided you stay within the rules. Sometimes it is not necessary to ask for permission in using copyrighted material, but you might want to ask anyway. And in copyright law, it often does matter if you can show you tried to find the copyright holder.

5. Use of ideas or of information that you may have learned from a copyrighted work is also generally okay.

Copyright law doesn't protect ideas or information; it just protects the *particular expression* of ideas or information once they've been "fixed" in a tangible medium (like paper or a hard disk). So if you see the movie *Love Story* and you write your own story about preppy finds girl, preppy loses girl, preppy really loses girl, you probably haven't violated anyone's copyright. But the minute you start posting actual dialogue from the book to your Web site, you increase the risk that you'll be hearing from Erich Segal's (or his publisher's) lawyers.

6. The mere possession of material does not make you the copyright owner.

Sure, the guy sent you the e-mail out of the blue, and it's something you feel like publishing. Nevertheless, the copyright to the material you are using may still belong to the author or someone else who has acquired it. Use of the material may still require their permission.

7. Look at the purpose and character of your intended use.

If you are using the material for educational purposes, limited use of it may be acceptable, even without permission. However, if copyrighted material is to be used for a commercial purpose or to derive some economic benefit, you will likely have to gain permission from the copyright holder and comply with certain conditions for use.

8. Compare the proportion of the work you are using to the work as a whole.

It is one thing to quote a few paragraphs of a twenty-page essay. It may be another matter to take eight hundred words of a thousand-word newspaper story. The amount and substantiality of the work you can use without permission is not carved in stone (or even set out in the law books), so be aware of how large a proportion of the work you are taking. This is a gray area, but if you're even slightly embarrassed by how much of the work you're, uh, repurposing for your own use, it's probably something you should ask the copyright holder about.

9. In general, try to make sure that your unlicensed use of any copyrighted work does not significantly affect the potential economic market of the original work.

Okay, you can break this rule—maybe—if you've got a copy of the latest equivalent to the Pentagon Papers and you think the world has a right to know. But in general, a copyright holder has an exclusive right to use his material for economic gain. That's the assumption you have to begin with. So unless you have obtained permission to use someone else's work, usually in the form of a license, the impact you have on the copyright holder's market by your use of the work could expose you to an infringement lawsuit. And who needs that? (It's true that sometimes a court will rule in your favor anyway, as when other factors, such as educational or journalistic uses, are important enough to outweigh the economic impact on the copyright holder.)

10. Don't assume that your use of copyrighted material on intranet systems is not an infringement or will not be seen outside the company.

Intranet Web pages may be limited in circulation, but they're not exempt from the copyright laws. And don't circulate infringing material within your intranet on the assumption you won't get caught.

Don't treat other people's copyright interests as if they were necessarily opposed to your own. "Link friendly" instead. (As a native Texan, I'm paying homage here to the Texas Department of Transportation slogan "Drive Friendly" by slightly rewording it for the information superhighway.) Often the owner of a copyright will discover his or her work being used without permission and simply request that the infringing work be removed from the publication or Web site. And since you're a nice guy (or gal), you'll want to comply. But you can't count on every copyright holder to be so understanding. Don't risk a lawsuit for copyright infringement by assuming you will not get caught.

If you have real legal problems, you'll need to talk to your own lawyer, and cribbing from our (copyrighted!) guidelines here won't suffice. But our experience is that if you basically do your best to be a nice gal (or guy) when it comes to someone else's copyrights, you're unlikely to have serious legal problems in the first place. And since part of using the Net is finding new ways to connect with people and to work cooperatively with them, it's better if everybody acts nice enough so that no one even thinks about going to the courthouse. Or at least not before it's absolutely necessary.

2002 Update—The Digital Millennium Copyright Act and the New Battles over Copyright

Riding the DMCA Bullet

The war going on over the state of copyright law in this country has been heating up in the past four or five years, but it's a war whose battles are largely being fought covertly. On the occasions when the conflicts are made public, they have not been recognized for what they signify. What has gone mostly unseen and unremarked on is the effort by industries that benefit from copyright law to shift the balance of the law forever in their favor and away from the public interest that, according to Article

I of the U.S. Constitution, is supposed to be the beneficiary of copyrights. (The Constitution, we may remind ourselves, expressly says that copyright and patent laws are designed "to promote the Progress of Science and useful Arts.")

But try to talk to any normal American about how this country's copyright law has gone off the rails, and you'll likely witness a new speed record for how quickly her eyes glaze over. That's why, when I want to communicate the horror of modern copyright law, I use the example of horror writer Stephen King, who (at least in theory) is a potential victim of the current state of the law. In mid-2000, King decided to experiment with online distribution of his fiction. His first experiment involved a novella called *Riding the Bullet*, which Simon & Schuster distributed in formats that could be read only on Intel-based PCs running the Windows operating system. This troubled King a bit because he (like me) is a devoted Macintosh user. King told reporters at the time that as a dedicated and long-term Mac user, he was "surprised and a little unhappy at how hard it is for Mac users to access the story." Even in its Wintel versions, there were limits on users' access. Someone reading it through Glassbooks' or Netlibrary's proprietary e-book technology, as required by the official downloadable versions, was prevented from copying any of the text or from printing it out. Simon & Schuster explained that it disabled the reader software's printing and copying functions to prevent piracy.

This odd state of affairs—a book offered in electronic format that cannot be easily read on the author's own computer—gives rise, when looked at in the context of current copyright law, to an interesting thought experiment. Suppose a Stephen King fan purchased a copy of the Wintel-based downloadable story and asked a friend to reverse-engineer a way of reading the story on his Macintosh computer. That bit of inventiveness might create a liability for the friend under the Digital Millennium Copyright Act. Or suppose that a King fan offered King himself a software tool that might enable the author to sidestep the e-book's encryption and extract the story for easy readability on the author's own PowerBook. According to the reasoning of recent court decisions, that too is a violation of the DMCA, an omnibus copyright bill passed in 1998 to implement the 1996 "Internet treaties" promulgated by the United Nations' World Intellectual Property

Organization (WIPO). Both the WIPO Internet Treaties and the Digital Millennium Copyright Act represent the successful efforts of Bruce Lehman to expand the rights held by copyright interests. Although, as documented earlier in this chapter, Lehman failed in his attempt to create a new intellectual property interest in mere facts (the "Anti-*Feist*" of database protection) and although his White Paper did not result in creating a widespread duty for Internet service providers, Lehman succeeded on other fronts. The result is that it is now illegal to exercise many of your substantive rights under the Copyright Act if doing so involves using, making or selling tools that defeat copy protection or access control technologies.

What the DMCA does generally is broadly prohibit use or dissemination of "circumvention technologies"—digital tools that can be used to defeat the (typically encryption-based) technologies that copyright holders may use to protect and control their digital works by preventing copying or controlling access, or both. You can't even use or disseminate such tools if you're doing so to engage in fair use of the copyrighted work, or if you're using them to access works that are out of copyright, or that are unprotectable under copyright law.

But if the purpose of copyright is to benefit the public, how is it that the DMCA punishes members of the public for using circumvention tools even when exercising their otherwise lawful prerogatives? The explanation, according to Wayne State University law professor Jessica Litman, has to do in part with the shift in copyright theory from the bargain-with-the-public theory interpretation of the Constitution's copyright clause to a new doctrine stressing the importance of the copyright holders' maintaining control over copyright works. Because the new theory stressed the importance of control over almost any other policy goal in copyright, Congress was persuaded to outlaw circumvention tools altogether rather than merely outlaw their use to perpetrate infringement. The very existence of such tools is too threatening to the control the copyright industries feel they must have over digital versions of copyrighted works.

The guts of that shift have to do, Litman explains, with a longstanding disagreement among copyright theorists as to what the underlying rights of copyright are and ought to be. According to one view, copyright interests are the product of a kind of bargain between the government and creators—a bargain that Congress, pursuant to the "copyright clause" of Article I of the U.S. Constitution, has the right to shape. Under that bargain, Litman writes in her compelling exploration of the topic, the book *Digital Copyright,* "Authors are given enough control to enable them to exploit their creations, while not so much that consumers and later authors are unable to benefit from the protected works."[9]

But exactly what rights remain in the creators' control—or, as is most often the case, the publishers' control—has now become a matter of some controversy. The constitutional language itself is no unambiguous guide. It simply grants Congress the power "to promote the Progress of Science and useful Arts, by securing for limited Times to Authors and Inventors the exclusive Right to their respective Writings and Discoveries." What does "exclusive Right" mean? And what does "limited Times" mean? Litman spells out the controversy: "Some people insist that copyright owners are entitled to just enough control to provide an economic incentive for their creation, since the broad purpose of copyright is to promote knowledge by encouraging authors to create and disseminate their works. Others argue that the only uses of a work that are properly excluded from the copyright owner's control are the ones that have no significant economic value."

It is the latter view that has come to dominate the shape of American copyright law in the course of the past quarter-century. The fundamental explanation, according to Litman, is that Congress has essentially delegated the business of writing copyright law to the copyright industries, which consistently have used technological advance as a rationale for expanding their protected interests under the law.

This was not always the case. "The first U.S. copyright statute," she reminds us, "gave authors exclusive rights to 'print, reprint, publish, or vend'—in other words, to control the reproduction and sale of copies." At its heart, that law concerned commercial copying and commercial distribution of creative works—a fairly limited set of government-created rights that did not address things like performances and recordings. For a while this was okay for (to take one example) composers of popular music. Under the then-current copyright law, they had no copyright interests in performances, but performers had to buy the sheet music, so composers got their revenue indirectly. But technology changes things: "Once it became possible to record a musical performance on a piano roll or phonograph record and to make and sell hundreds of those, or to broadcast performances over the radio, however, composers could be excluded from the additional proceeds generated by the recording or broadcast. . . . Thus, each technological advance inspired a dispute about whether it entitled copyright owners to expanded rights over their works."

That pattern in itself was neither remarkable nor particularly threatening to the balance of rights then built into copyright law, but at the turn of the twentieth century, Litman writes, "Congress got into the habit of revising copyright law by encouraging representatives of the industries affected by copyright to hash out among themselves what changes needed to be made and then present Congress with the text of appropriate legislation. By the 1920s, the process was sufficiently entrenched that whenever a member of Congress came up with a legislative proposal without going through the cumbersome prelegislative process of multiparty negotiation, the affected industries united to block the bill." What we have been left with is industry-written legislation defining the terms of the copyright bargain—and the purported beneficiaries of that bargain, the public, have not been at the negotiating table. As a result of this legislative pattern, which has been consistent for each of the major revisions of American copyright law since 1909, the resulting legislative efforts have certain predictable characteristics. They expand copyright owners' rights, both by extending copyright interests expressly and by characterizing existing law in ways that have the effect of extending copyright interests. And they appease other groups that might otherwise be troubled by these extensions. They do this by crafting special exceptions: librarians are appeased by a special copying privilege for libraries (which requires a legislative definition of *library*) and broadcasters are appeased with a special broadcaster privilege (which requires a legislative definition of *broadcaster*), and so on. The result is statutory law that expansively defines copyright holders' rights but is also riddled with special exceptions and definitions and provisions—and more or less impossible for normal citizens to grasp.

Perhaps more important, the increasing expansiveness of the copyright law has led to a shift in the theory behind the law. What began as a government-created monopoly established in the public interest has increasingly come to be understood, especially by the copyright industries, as a kind of natural right. Copyright policy is discussed less in terms of where the rights interests should be split between creators and the public and more in terms of preserving creators' livelihoods, or their "fundamental" rights to their creations.

Added to this quasi–natural rights approach to copyright has been anxiety about the Internet, which has been widely characterized (by me and others) as a global network of copying machines. Suddenly the threat to the copyright holder is not primarily competing commercial interests (although the drumbeat over the threat of commercial infringers never lets up in the policy arena). Instead, it's ordinary citizens, whose use of new technology to trade copies of copyrighted works, such as songs reduced to MP3 files, not only makes those works easier for foreign and domestic commercial infringers to find, copy, and sell, but also may have a commercial impact all by itself, as Internet users cease buying new CDs and other copyrighted products. (Whether Internet users have actually quit buying CDs and the like in significant numbers is a matter of hotly contested debate.)

This panic led, by a somewhat circuitous path, to the Digital Millennium Copyright Act, whose provisions lead to anomalous results of the sort that might affect Stephen King's rights to read his own published works on his own computer. That path began in the early 1990s when the incoming Clinton administration set out to shape policy for the "National Information Infrastructure," its name for what had been termed, for a brief period at the beginning of the decade, "the information superhighway." Content policy was ultimately delegated to a working group on intellectual property that was chaired by Bruce Lehman, the newly appointed patent commissioner and a former copyright lawyer for the computer industry. Not surprisingly, his senior staff included former lobbyists for the copyright industries. After hearings that included testimony from major information industry players, the working group came up with the "Green Paper"—a draft report on the state of copyright law that made recommendations for what it characterized as minor changes and clarifications in the law, but which critics like Litman, Berkeley law professor Pamela Samuelson, American University law professor Peter Jaszi, and others saw as seeking fundamental changes in our copyright law. And the changes looked to be bad ones.

At the core of that radical shift, Litman explains, was "the assertion that one reproduces a work every time one reads it into a computer's random-access memory." In fact, a few cases had held that such an event qualified as copying for copyright purposes, but the Green Paper treated this relatively new and controversial doctrine as if it were settled law. Those cases, transmuted by the Green Paper authors into dogma, may be the central cause of what Litman terms "the transition from an incentive model of copyright to a control model." The Green Paper also set out to regulate transmission of a copyrighted work (e.g., across a computer network)—both because such transmission should be interpreted as a public performance or display (which was already included in the copyright holders' bundle of exclusive rights) and because if it *weren't* counted as a copy, it would in effect be a "distribution," which meant that "first sale doctrine" would end copyright holders' interests. (The first sale doctrine is what makes it legal for you to sell your used paperbacks to a friend or to a used-book store without paying the copyright holder a dime. It's a policy that all but the copyright industries regard as a benefit to the public.)

Finally, the Green Paper endorsed the copyright holders' right to use copy-protection and access-control technology to prevent unlicensed copying and use of their work. In addition, the paper called for new laws that would prohibit the circumvention of such technology and outlaw the creation or distribution of tools that could be used to circumvent it. The Green Paper authors could not make all unlicensed copying illegal. That would directly contradict the public policy that allows some unlicensed copying, such as fair use copying of copyrighted works for scholarship, education, or review. (I'm engaging in fair use copying in this article by quoting Litman's book without asking her for a license to do so.) But if they couldn't make it illegal, they could make it (legally) impossible, at least in the digital sphere.

The Green Paper evolved into a "White Paper," whose characterization of current law was less disturbing rhetorically but no less radical. Writes Litman: "Using the tools that good lawyers use when engaged in such tasks, the White Paper carefully explained that just about every ambiguity one could imagine, properly understood, should under the best view of current law be resolved in favor of the copyright holder."

As a result, she further writes, "That approach enabled the authors of the White Paper to come to conclusions that would strike anybody but a copyright lawyer as extravagant. . . . Since any use of a computer to view, read, reread, hear, or otherwise experience a work in digital form would require reproducing that work in a computer's memory, and since the copyright statute gives the copyright holder exclusive control over reproductions, everybody would need either to have a statutory privilege or the copyright holder's permission to view, read, reread, hear, or otherwise experience a digital work, each time she did so." Because these seemingly extravagant claims of right energized academics, librarians, and, perhaps most significant, communications service providers (telephone and Internet service providers that might themselves be held liable for users' infringements under the White Paper's reading of the law), the reforms recommended in the White Paper stalled in Congress in 1996. But the ever-resourceful Bruce Lehman discovered a workaround by pitching a version of the White Paper to the World Intellectual Property Organization (WIPO), which was crafting a new copyright treaty. While most of the White Paper recommendations, such as the call for database protection, were either diluted or not adopted at all, the anti-circumvention recommendations made it, albeit in much more moderate form, into the final treaty.

And with the treaty language in hand, Lehman and the copyright interests were able to come back to Congress and ask for implementing legislation, lobbying for anti-circumvention language that was far more draconian than anything demanded by the treaty. The result of this effort was the Digital Millennium Copyright Act, which became U.S. law in 1998. Although the DMCA includes many provisions—notably safe-harbor provisions for service providers whose services are used by subscribers in infringing ways—its most controversial aspects were its anti-circumvention provisions. As Litman writes, "Lehman argued to Congress that other nations would not act to prevent piracy of United States works until the U.S. Congress demonstrated leadership by enacting tough anti-piracy laws, that, for example, made it illegal to defeat copy protection (or to market devices or services that do so) for any purpose whatsoever. Representatives of the motion picture and recording industries backed up the commissioner's arguments with prophecies of widespread international piracy unless Congress acted quickly. The world's eyes, they said, were on America."

And Congress did just that: it passed broad anti-circumvention provisions with narrow and not entirely clear exemptions. (Stephen King arguably has the right under the DMCA to write his own software to extract the text of *Riding the Bullet* for reading on his Mac. But nobody can sell or give him a tool that does this for him.) The result was legislation that, as Litman writes, "is long, internally inconsistent, difficult even for copyright experts to parse and harder still to explain." Even worse, the law "seeks for the first time to impose liability on ordinary citizens for violation of provisions that they have no reason to suspect are part of the law, and to make noncommercial and noninfringing behavior illegal on the theory that it will help prevent [copyright] piracy."

Litman does see, in the very awfulness of the DMCA, the potential for redemption. Because the DMCA is a crazy and contradictory set of laws that will increasingly be applied to individual citizens, one likely outcome is that citizens will simply opt to ignore it—to choose noncompliance. Plus, she writes, "The more burdensome the law makes it to obey its proscriptions, and the more draconian the penalties for failing, the more distasteful it will be to enforce." As a result of noncompliance and nonenforcement, the copyright lobby may be forced to revisit the DMCA and the Copyright Act in general. "Laws that people don't obey and that governments don't enforce are not much use to the interests that persuaded Congress to enact them."

Litman also sounds this slightly hopeful note: "Even if copyright stakeholders refuse to give the public a seat at the bargaining table, they may discover that they need to behave as if they had." I just hope that if and when that turn of events comes about, policymakers are reminded that the public is the biggest stakeholder. But in 2001 and 2002, even as the DMCA continued to receive more criticism from academics and from public policy groups, copyright interests had moved their attention to a new front: ensuring that our computers and other digital tools can't be used to make copies of commercial content.

Hollywood Versus the Internet

If you have a fast computer and a fast connection to the Internet, you make Hollywood nervous. And Tinseltown is nervous not because of what you're doing now, but because of what you *might* do: grab digital Hollywood content with your computer and broadcast it over the Internet. Hollywood, along with other content companies, from book publishers to the music industry, has begun a campaign to stop you from ever being able to do such a thing, even though you may have no intention of becoming a copyright "pirate." That campaign has pitted corporate giants like Disney and Fox against corporate giants like Microsoft and IBM, but the resulting war over the shape of future digital technology may end up with computer users suffering the collateral damage.

As music software designer and entrepreneur Selene Makarios puts it, this campaign represents "little less than an attempt to outlaw general-purpose computers." Internet security and cryptography expert Bruce Schneier puts the matter a little differently: "If you think about it, the content industry does not want people to have computers; they're too powerful, too flexible, and too extensible. They want people to have Internet Entertainment Platforms: televisions, VCRs, game consoles, etc."

Let's get one thing straight: when I say there's war looming in cyberspace over copyright, I'm not talking about the struggle between copyright holders and copyright pirates who distribute unlicensed copies of creative works for free over the Internet. Maybe you loved Napster or maybe you hated it, but the right to start a Napster, or to infringe copyright and get away with it, is not what's at issue here. And in a sense it's a distraction from what the real war is.

What I'm talking about instead is the war between the content industries (call them the "Content Faction") and the information technology industries (the "Tech Faction"). The Tech Faction includes not only computer makers, software makers, and related digital-device manufacturers (like CD burners, MP3 players, and Cisco routers). Allied with the Content Faction are the consumer electronics makers—the folks who build your VCRs and DVD players and boomboxes. The Tech Faction, which makes smarter, more programmable devices and technologies than the consumer electronics guys do, may count among their allies many cable companies and even telephone companies.

But what's the "collateral damage" exactly? Perhaps the most likely scenario is this: At some near-future date, perhaps as early as 2010, individuals may no longer be able to do the kinds of things they routinely do with their digital tools in 2003. They may no longer be able, for example, to move music or video files around easily from one of their computers to another (even if the other is just a few feet away in the same house) or to personal digital assistants. Their music collections, reduced to MP3s, may be moveable to a limited extent unless their digital hardware doesn't allow it. The digital videos they shot in 1999 may be unplayable on their desktop and laptop computers—or even on other devices—in 2009.

And if they're programmers, trying to come up with the next great version of the GNU/Linux operating system, for example, they may find their development efforts put them at risk of criminal and civil penalties if the tools they develop are inadequately protective of copyright interests. Indeed, their sons and daughters in grade school computer classes may face similar risks if the broadest of the changes now being proposed becomes law.

Digital television is the thin entering wedge for the Content Faction's agenda. Here's why. Unlike DVD movies, which are encrypted on the disc and decrypted every time they're played, digital broadcast television needs to be unencrypted, for a couple of reasons. First, the federal government requires that broadcast television be sent "in the clear"—in unencrypted form—as a matter of public policy. The argument here is that broadcasters are custodians of a public resource—the part of the broadcasting spectrum used for television—and need to make whatever they pump into that spectrum available to everyone. Second, digital broadcast TV has to reach the existing (albeit relatively small) installed base of digital television sets, which wouldn't be able to decode encrypted broadcasts.

But digital broadcast television also poses a special problem: it's just too darned high-quality. A home viewer who can find a way to copy the content of a digital broadcast can reproduce it digitally over the Internet (or elsewhere), and everybody can get that high-quality digital content for free. This would have a particularly harsh effect on the movie and TV studios, which currently repackage old television shows for resale to individuals as DVDs or videotapes and also syndicate the rights (resell broadcast rights) to cable networks and individual broadcasting stations. If everybody's trading high-quality digital copies of *Buffy the Vampire Slayer* or *Law and Order* over the Internet, who's going to view the reruns on, respectively, Fox's FX network or the Arts and Entertainment channel? What advertisers are going to pay to air those shows when their complete runs are available online to viewers, commercial free, through some successor to Napster or Gnutella peer-to-peer file sharing?

The Content Faction has a plan to prevent that world from coming about—a plan they hope will work for music and every other kind of content. One guide to a different future is the "marking" solution proposed for digital broadcast television.

Essentially, there are two parts to the scheme. The first part is this: the digital broadcast TV signal will include a "broadcast flag" and/or a "digital watermark" containing information that tells a TV watcher's home entertainment system whether to allow copying at all, or to allow limited copying, or to allow unlimited copying. The "flag" is just a bit or set of bits that's sent along in the digital TV signal. The so-called digital watermark is not like a normal watermark in stationery; instead, it's "steganographic." That is, it's contained in the content itself, but the normal viewer isn't able to see it without special tools. Not all of the bits in a digital bitstream have to be used to communicate images or sound; the remaining bits can be structured in a way that adds up to a "watermark" or a "broadcast flag." Both measures have the effect (it is hoped) of marking commercial content so that it can be recognized as such by consumer digital devices. (The "digital watermark" is purported to have the additional feature that it will survive digital-to-analogue and analogue-to-digital conversions—as, for example, when a digital TV signal is received by your old-style analogue color TV (which would have to be retrofitted with a converter box of some sort). In a nutshell, the broadcast flag, which can't survive digital-to-analogue conversion, is designed to prevent copying from digital TVs and TV receivers, which never convert anything to analogue signals. The watermark is designed to prevent copying when the signal is transformed by analogue devices, such as legacy analogue TVs and TV receivers.)

But the first part of Hollywood's fix—adding a mark—doesn't work without the second part, which is that the components of the home entertainment system have to be designed to receive those watermarks and flags and limit copying accordingly.

If the digital TV guys put together a working watermarking scheme for television, then at least in theory they've come up with a solution that will apply to all other digital media. After all, bits is bits.

There are some problems with this scheme—perhaps intractable ones. If Princeton computer scientist Edward Felten is right, when you design your marking system so that it is invisible to normal viewers or listeners yet easily detectable by machines, it's probably going to be relatively easy to strip it out. To put it simply, if you can't see it, you won't miss it when it's gone. Which is why, when you think through how the marking systems will work, you realize that in the long term the components of new home entertainment systems will also likely have to be designed not to play unwatermarked or unflagged content. Otherwise, all you've done is develop an incentive for both inquisitive hackers and copyright "pirates" to learn how to strip out the marks. So much for your legacy digital videos. So much for your MP3 collection.

What will the components of a new home entertainment system be? Mostly standard consumer electronics: a VCR, a DVD player, maybe a CD player, speakers, a TV receiver. Yet what tech-industry pundits call "convergence" means that one other component is increasingly likely to be part of home entertainment setups: the personal computer. Says Business Software Alliance special counsel Emery Simon, "That's the multipurpose device that has them terrified, that will result in leaking [copyrighted content] all over the world."

This is precisely what Disney CEO Michael Eisner, in a speech to Congress in the summer of 2000, was referring to when he warned of "the perilous irony of the digital age." Eisner's statement of the problem is shared by virtually everybody in the movie industry: "Just as computers make it possible to create remarkably pristine images, they also make it possible to make remarkably pristine copies."

Because computers are potentially very efficient and capable copying machines and because the Internet is potentially a very efficient and capable distribution mechanism, even in the hands of ordinary individuals, the Content Faction has set out to restructure the entire digital world we have today. They want to rearchitect not just the Internet but every computer and digital tool on or off the Net that might be used to make unauthorized copies.

Ask them about their goals, though, and they'll tell you they don't quite want to turn back the clock. If you use your VCR to record a favorite program so you can watch it later, why, then, the Content Faction says, we'll let you do something similar in the future—but we're also going to make sure, with our watermarking scheme or something similar, that it won't be possible to do more than that.

The Content Faction is proceeding on many fronts: legislative, of course, but also in standards groups, industrial consortia, and global business policy forums. A recent legislative proposal floated (but not formally introduced) by Senator Fritz Hollings (D, South Carolina), which would require that all new digital transmission technologies have built-in copyright protection—built-in watermark-scheme compliance, in other words—generated a significant public backlash after being leaked to the press. But that proposal caused a backlash because it was itself public. In reality, it's only one small part of a mostly unpublicized global effort to include digital rights management in every digital technology. "Digital rights management," known to both factions as DRM, is the generic term used to characterize any technology—software, hardware, or both—that prevents unauthorized copying of or controls access to copyrighted materials.

At stake in this war, says Eisner, the acknowledged leader of the Content Faction, is "the future of the American entertainment industry, the future of American consumers, the future of America's balance of international trade." The lobbyists at News Corporation and Vivendi Universal S.A. and pretty much any other company whose chief product is content agree with Eisner about the magnitude of the issue (although the foreign-based ones, like Bertelsmann AG, are understandably less concerned about the U.S. balance of trade). All of them tend to talk about the problems posed by computers, digital technology, and the Internet in apocalyptic terms.

The companies whose bailiwick *is just* computers, digital technology, and the Internet—whose focus is more technology than content—take a different view. These members of the Tech Faction, which include Microsoft, IBM, Hewlett Packard, Cisco Systems, and Adobe, also value copyright. (Adobe, for example, instigated in 2001 the prosecution of a Russian computer programmer who cracked the company's encryption-based e-book security scheme.) And many of them, particularly those that have been developing their own DRM technologies, want to see a world in which copyrighted works are reasonably well protected. Yet if you ask a Tech Faction member what he or she thinks of the Content Faction's agenda for the digital world, you invariably get something similar to Emery Simon's judgment of the scheme: "We are strongly anti-piracy, but we think mandating these protections is an abysmally stupid idea." (BSA is an antipiracy trade group whose members include the major players of the Tech Faction, from Adobe to Microsoft to Intel to IBM.)

You can't overestimate the extent to which the two factions are both pro-copyright: their shared view of the importance of protecting copyrighted works online makes them awfully uncomfortable to be on opposite sides now. One thing the Tech Faction and the Content Faction have in common is that both supported the passage of the Digital Millennium Copyright Act in 1998; both like the DMCA pretty much as it is. That act, which was framed as the implementation legislation for the WIPO's Internet treaties, prohibited the creation, dissemination, and use of tools that circumvent digital-rights-management technologies.

Where the two sides differ is on the issue of whether the DMCA is enough. BSA's Simon views the DMCA as a well-crafted piece of legislation, but thinks that efforts that would build DRM into every digital device are overreaching at best. And in taped remarks presented at a December 4, 2001, business-technology conference in Washington, D.C., Intel CEO Craig Barrett spoke out against legislation like the Hollings bill, which would have the government mandating a copyright protection standard to adopted by the entire information technology industry. Yet the Content Faction, as represented by their lawyers and lobbyists in Washington, as well as by their West Coast technologists, say that failure to standardize on a universally built-in DRM technology will in effect lead to the destruction of the digital content industries.

A few companies are so big and so diverse that they don't fall easily into either the Tech or the Content faction. Take AOL Time Warner, for example. The movie companies and other content producers under the AOL Time Warner umbrella tend to favor efforts that lock down copyrighted works to some extent, but AOL itself, as well as some of the company's cable subsidiaries, opposes any effort to mandate DRM in all digital technologies. "We like the DMCA," says Jill Lesser, AOL Time Warner's senior vice president for domestic public policy. "There isn't from our perspective a need for additional remedies of copyright violations," Lesser says. AOL's reluctance to embrace the Hollings bill explains why the Motion Picture Association of America, of which AOL Time Warner is a prominent member, remained officially neutral on the bill at least at first.

But Lesser needs only to take a breath before she adds that something like the Hollings bill, at least with regard to digital broadcast television standards, may be a good idea, since industry progress toward an agreement for copyright protection in digital television hasn't proceeded as quickly as the content companies would like. "Maybe a mandate is the way to get there more quickly," she says.

The specter that's haunting the Content Faction is Napster. Although the free version of Napster has been essentially wiped out by the music company litigation against it (a new version of the file-sharing system is purportedly being developed by Bertelsmann AG), the Napster phenomenon still casts a long shadow. One technologist for News Corporation who's working on a DRM scheme told me he thinks Napster already signals the end of the music industry. Because most record companies have most of their catalogues available on unprotected CDs, which can be "ripped" and duplicated with CD burners or distributed over the Internet as MP3 files, music lovers have already gotten out of the habit of paying for records, which means an end to big profits and thus an end to big record companies. "Within five years," the technologist says, "the music industry will be a cottage industry."

Matthew Gerson, the vice president for public policy at Vivendi Universal S.A., which produces and sells both music (Universal Music Group) and movies (Universal Studios), is quick to dispute the prediction that the music companies face cottage industry status. "We know that if we build a safe, consumer friendly site that has all the 'bells and whistles' and features that music fans want, it will flourish. My hunch is that fans will have no trouble paying for the music that they love, and compensating the artists who bring it to them—established stars as well as the new voices the labels introduce year after year."

But maintaining that model—the model of the big music company that plays an important filtering role for music audiences—depends on both large streams of revenue and control of copyrighted works. The Internet and digital technology could change all that, cutting off the revenue stream by moving music consumers to a world in which trading music online for free is a norm. At the same time, a technical-legal scheme that perfects control of content in the digital world creates new revenue opportunities. The music companies, for example, could "rent" or "license" music to us in a protected format rather than sell copies outright to us in unprotected forms.

And that, says Simon, is why the Hollings legislation is so broadly drafted: it's designed to close up all the leaks that digital technology might pose. In the drafts made available in fall of 2001, the Hollings bill, then titled the Security Systems Standards and Certification Act (SSSCA), would create a civil offense for anyone who developed (for example) a new computer that did not include a federally approved security standard preventing the unlicensed copying of copyrighted works. The SSSCA also would set up a scheme under which private industry met and approved the security standard. It would require that the standard be adopted within eighteen months of passage; if that deadline passed without an agreement on a standard, the government would step in and impose one itself. In at least one version, the law would also felonize the act of removing the watermark or flag from copyrighted content, as well as the act of attaching a computer to the Internet that removes or sidesteps the copy-protection technology. In the spring of 2002, Senator Hollings introduced a slightly altered, renamed version of the SSSCA, called the Consumer Broadband and Digital Television Promotion Act.

It doesn't take a close look at the provisions of the Hollings measure to see that its scope extends far beyond digital television. And you can see why the crafters of the proposal want it to reach so far. If the watermark scheme works for digital TV and results in an established standard for both labeling copyrighted works and designing consumer electronics not to allow unlicensed copying of those watermarked works, it ought to be adaptable to the rest of the digital world, especially that most troubling sphere of the digital world: the Internet. This explains why the draft of the proposal, under its own terms, applies to any digital technology, and not just television. The big music companies like the Hollings bill too because they have been laboring for years through a group called the Secure Digital Music Initiative to agree on a digital music watermarking standard.

The many fronts of the DRM standards push include DRM proponent groups like 4C Entity (promoting a standard for building DRM into mass-storage devices, such as hard drives), the 5C Consortium (developing a copy protection standard for digital television), interindustry forums like the Content Protection Technology Working Group (CPTWG), and a growing number of conventional standards-setting groups. And as we've seen, they also include legislation like the Hollings bill, whose genesis, according to sources on the Hill close to the legislative process, was Eisner's summer 2000 speech to Congress.

Those close to the process that drafted the Hollings proposal don't couch the legislation in terms of protecting embattled copyright interests. Instead, they frame it as a proactive measure designed to promote both digital content and increased use of broadband, high-speed Internet services. The theory here is this: consumer adoption of broadband services (like cable modems and DSL) has been slower than predicted. This means the cable companies and the phone companies have too small a consumer base to justify building out their broadband capacity very quickly or very far. But (the theory goes) if Hollywood could be assured that its content would be protected on the broadband Internet, the studios would develop more compelling content and make it available on the Internet, which would spur greater consumer demand for broadband.

There are problems with this theory—it assumes that what people really want from the Internet is more TV and movies—but it's the theory with the most currency in Washington policymaker circles. And Congress wants to find a way to take credit for a quicker rollout of faster Internet service.

It's the Hollings legislation that has brought the existence of the war between the Content Faction and the Tech Faction out into the open. Before the draft legislation was circulated, "we didn't know how broad this was," says one lawyer for cable company interests. (Some cable companies have aligned themselves with the Tech Faction partly because they see themselves as technology companies too and partly because they see DRM, which might define the conditions under which subscribers could use and copy content, as interfering with their own ability to package content for their subscriber base. Other cable companies, however, are owned by Content Faction players. Officially, they favor measures like the Hollings bill.) And, initially at least, it's the Hollings legislation that is likely to be the flash point for the debate about widespread copyright protection standards in the near future. The first hearings on the measure took place in March and April 2002.

Although the Hollings legislation is controversial, some folks in the Content Faction remain bullish on its passage. Preston Padden, the executive vice president for government relations for the Walt Disney Company, traces the impulse behind the Hollings bill to recommendations from the Global Business Dialog on e-Commerce, a CEO-led public policy group that tries to shape global business policy. Since the GBDeC includes members of both the Tech Faction and the Content Faction, the argument is that there is, at some very high level, a global business consensus on the need to protect content.

Padden says the group approached the issue of content protection with an attitude of "let's get together and identify the daunting, unprecedented global issues that are represented by the Internet and see if we can come to a common view as to how these issues should be resolved." The group's intellectual property subcommittee is chaired by Michael Eisner, who shepherded through language favoring government "facilitation" of standards for copyright protection, after much give and take with Tech Faction members. With the group's recommendations in hand. Eisner could go to Congress and say there was a general business consensus favoring the passage of new laws to protect content on the Internet.

But although companies like IBM and Disney officially agree on the need to protect content on the Internet (and it's really the Internet that is the focus of DRM efforts, not digital broadcasting), the devil is in the details. IBM, Microsoft, and other Tech Faction members each want their own DRM technologies to be adopted, they don't want design mandates, and they want technology-based copyright protection to be the special case rather than the rule.

Both Padden and News Corporation vice president for governmental affairs Rick Lane say the reason for the Tech companies' recalcitrance represents a "philosophical problem" those companies have with design mandates. Lane says the Tech companies oppose technological mandates because "they've never been subject to them before, except for export controls [on encryption]." Lane and the other Content Faction lawyers think the computer companies need to grow up and get over it. After all, they say, technology mandates have been a fact of life for the consumer electronics industry, particularly radio and television equipment, for many decades. (The consumer electronics companies generally don't like government regulation either, but they sometimes see value in it. As EFF technologist Seth David Schoen points out, the Content Faction often can get the major consumer electronics companies to adopt new standards without resorting to lawmaking. But if the new standards limit what their devices can do, that makes the established consumer electronics companies vulnerable to competition from an upstart company that produces a more capable machine. Better to have a law in place that prevents that from happening.)

But the philosophical war really runs deeper than mere resistance to government control. One way to understand this is to look at how the Content industries talk about individuals as compared to how the Tech industries do. The Content industries refer to "consumers." The Tech industries refer to "users."

In general, if you see the world as one of consumers, you think, "Nobody gets products to consume for free, but price it appropriately and consumers will come." You control access to what you offer, and do everything you can to prevent theft, for the same reason that supermarkets have cameras by the door and bookstores have electronic theft detectors. Allowing people to take stuff for free is inconsistent with your business model.

But if you think of the world as one of users, you see the market as one in which you give people more features and powers at cheaper prices. The impulse to empower users was at the heart of the microcomputer revolution. Steve Jobs and Steve Wozniak, for example, wanted to put computing power into ordinary people's hands, and that's why they founded Apple Computer. If this is your philosophy—one of empowering users to do new things—it's harder to wrap your mind around building in limitations. Plus, at some basic level, moving bits around from hard drives to RAM to screen and back again, with 100 percent accuracy in copying, is simply what computers do. Building DRM into all of this— limiting how computers perform their basic functions—seems to the Tech Faction almost to be an effort to make a computer something other than a computer—a digital appliance maybe, or something special purpose like a toaster. It's an approach that would have the effect of undoing the user empowerment philosophy that drove the PC revolution in the first place.

It's important at this point not to overstate the differences between the Tech and the Content Factions. The Tech companies are arguably just as adamant about protecting intellectual property as the Content Faction is. And as Schoen remarks, "Some of the IT folks can occasionally ally themselves with particular parts of the content faction, often in order to try to deflect something they see as worse."

But because the Tech Faction's approach to their customer base is different, they find the universal DRM approach anathema. To them, the digital world is one in which users are generally empowered to do whatever they want with digital tools, except to the extent that copyrighted works are walled off by DRM. But to the Content Faction, the digital world isn't safe unless every digital tool also functions as a kind of copyright policeman.

Still, the Content Faction's approach to the issue shouldn't be easily dismissed. They may be right to say that what individual citizens really want is compelling content over broadband, and it may even be the case that a majority of citizens would trade away the open, robust, relatively simple digital tools they now have for a more constrained digital world in which they have more content choices. But the important thing to note is that until recently, few ordinary citizens have had any voice in this particular debate about the digital future. Few are even aware the debate is going on. (It doesn't help, for example, that the Hollings proposal was first pitched as a "security standard" rather than as a new copyright-related law.)

The consequences of the outcome of the struggle between the Content Faction and the Tech Faction fight are huge. At the heart of the fight are two questions: Whether computer users can continue to be allowed to have the abilities that computers have had since their invention and whether the content companies can survive in a world in which users have that power. What's been seriously lacking in the debate so far has been participation of the users themselves. It seems safe to say that most computer and Internet users like to have choices—choices of the content they consume and the kinds of tools they should get to use. Still, maybe citizens would say they're willing to give up general-purpose computers and instead use systems designed to prevent them from engaging in willy-nilly copying if that is the price you have to pay for compelling music and movies and television over the Internet. Maybe they'd say so if you asked them. But until just recently, nobody's been asking.

8

A Bad Spin and a Cyberporn Primer

Here's an interesting experiment. Try combining the topics of sex, children, and the Net in a magazine or newspaper story or even in an online discussion. This combination will almost invariably cause ostensibly intelligent people to shut down their higher thinking centers.

For me, the most prominent example of this rule appeared on America Online in *Time* magazine's online forum, Time Online, in September 1995, just three months after its cyberporn cover story—based on what turned out to be a phony study of online porn—had blown up in *Time*'s face and seriously damaged its reputation in the online world.[1] In the years just prior to the cyberporn story scandal of 1995, *Time* had done a good job of creating a lively and interesting discussion forum on AOL, but sometimes the corporate interests of the magazine skewed the discussion. Take, for example, the following post by "RPTime" (Robert Pondiscio, an in-house public-relations person for *Time*) in the topic dedicated to discussion and criticism of the magazine's cyberporn cover story. Shortly after the national press reported (in a story unrelated to the *Time* scandal) that the U.S. Justice Department had announced a dozen arrests in a two-year investigation into the use of commercial online services to distribute child porn and seduce minors into sex, the following message appeared in the cyberporn topic in Time Online:

Subj: Arrests 95-09-14 10:20:08 EDT
From: RPTime
Posted on: America Online
Looks like the FBI has arrested a dozen people in connection with the biggest non-problem in cyberspace. The feds have reportedly seized digitized pornographic images of children as young as two years old from members of this very online service.

I'll be interested in the reactions of our First Amendment absolutist friends. Perhaps they will argue the arrested should be released, and the parents of children involved should be charged with neglect for not adequately supervising their kids' online activities.
Robert

Analyzed rhetorically and legally, this was a fascinating posting. In Pondiscio's defense, it must be said that he'd had to work overtime in defending *Time*'s decision to hype in a cover story the now notorious cyberporn study authored by Martin Rimm. Given the flood of criticism of both the story and the study itself, you could understand if Pondiscio was feeling a bit fried. So you may be able to forgive his over-the-top rhetorical strategy of classing critics of the cover story as "First Amendment absolutists" who, as such, must be blasé about child pornography or the victimization of children.

From a legal standpoint, however, the posting is even more interesting, and far less forgivable, given that Pondiscio, in his public role and as a private individual, had touted *Time*'s strength in explaining the issues to its readers. You see, by posting this message in the topic dedicated to discussion of the cyberporn cover story, Pondiscio was implying that the FBI raids somehow vindicated *Time*'s decision to run that story. Yet even if we accept the (false) implication that the cover story was not primarily about Marty Rimm and his *Georgetown Law Journal* article, Pondiscio's post demonstrates confusion about what the legal and factual issues relating to porn, the Net, and children really are. And since much of the rest of this book deals with the law centering on this subject area, it's probably a good idea to do what we can to avoid the kind of confusion that Pondiscio's posting exemplifies.

Defining the Terms

When talking about pornography and child safety on the Net, you'll often see several different terms bandied about as if they were interchangeable. They're not. Here are some basic definitions.

Pornography   In general, this is material that presents sexual content of some sort, with the intent of being arousing. *Playboy* and *Penthouse* could be included under this definition, and, like any other uses of the press, such material is presumptively legal under the First Amendment. To be illegal, pornography either must be found to be "obscene" or "child pornography."

Obscenity   To be "obscene," pornography must meet all parts of a three-part test designed by then Chief Justice Warren Burger in 1973 in *Miller* v. *California*. This is normally a question of content. As I normally frame them, the three parts of the so-called Miller test are as follows:

1. The state law requirement: Normally, there must be a state statute or state case law in place that describes with specificity the particular sexual (or excretory) acts that cannot be depicted.

2. The community standards test: The depiction of the sexual acts must be "patently offensive" and "appeal to the prurient interest," as judged by a reasonable man applying the standards of the community.

3. The escape clause: To be obscene, the material must lack "serious" literary, artistic, scientific, political, or other social value.

Child pornography   This material is illegal regardless of whether it is obscene, which means you don't even bother to ask any questions about community standards. At the time of Pondiscio's posting on America Online, "child pornography," under federal law, was any visual material that depicts a child either engaging in explicit sexual acts or posing in a "lewd and lascivious" manner, when the manufacture of such material involves the actual use of an actual child. Thus, verbal or textual material could not be child porn under federal law, although it could be obscene.

By the same token, it was the law in 1995 that computer-generated material that seems to depict children engaged in sexual activity but does not use real children would not be child porn, although it might well be obscene. In short, the category of child pornography was legally defined at the time of Pondiscio's posting not primarily in terms of content ("offensive" depictions), but in terms of conduct (the victimization of actual children). Since the child pornography statute was fundamentally a prohibition against *conduct against children,* rather than a prohibition against *obscene content,* the child pornography law stood quite properly outside the First Amendment–obscenity framework.

Strangely, this relatively unassailable distinction between obscenity and child pornography was undermined by Senator Orrin Hatch, of all people, in 1996. In an effort to capture some of the momentum of the Panic of Cyberporn Summer for his own ends, Hatch introduced legislation in 1995 that amended the child porn statute by classing computer-generated, simulated child pornography as the same sort of crime under the child porn statute as *real* child pornography. While this may have been satisfying to Senator Hatch (who seemingly had forgotten that federal obscenity statutes already would reach any legally obscene images of the sort he professed to be concerned about, regardless of whether children were used in the making of those images), it created constitutional problems for the child porn statute (Title 18 of the U.S. Code, Sections 2252 and following) by reclassifying that crime in terms of content (which is presumptively protected by the First Amendment), not conduct (which isn't).[2]

Child sexual abuse   Sometimes children are abused sexually, yet no one takes any pictures of it. This is not child porn, although of course it is, and should be, illegal.

Child seduction   Sometimes child abusers attempt to seduce new victims, including trying to contact such victims by an online service. Despite the commonly repeated claim that pedophiles rely on pornography to seduce children, it is possible to engage in child seduction without ever using pornography, obscenity, or child pornography.

Exposure to inappropriate materials   Most states make it illegal to expose minors to sexually explicit material, even when such material is otherwise legal. It is this issue that has been the primary subject of the "indecency" and "harmful to minors" legislation that we've seen so much of in Congress.[3]

Indecency   This is a special term for content that up to now has been regulated only in two special areas of federal jurisdiction: broadcasting and so-called dial-a-porn services, both currently under the jurisdiction of the Federal Communications Commission (FCC). In those contexts, *indecency* normally means "patently offensive" sexual content or profane language.

When you're talking about media that are not under FCC jurisdiction—newspaper and book publication, say, or the movie industry—the term *indecency* has no legal meaning. One of the strategies that lobbyists for the Christian Coalition and associated groups have been employing to limit sexual content online has been to ask Congress to expand FCC jurisdiction (and the FCC's definition of *indecency*) to cover the Internet. But in the absence of a historically accepted justification of a special regulatory role for the federal government, such broad content control in nonbroadcasting media would surely be unconstitutional.

Children First

With our primer in hand, we can return to Robert Pondiscio's posting. Once you're clear on the different meanings of the terms and concepts I've outlined here, you can note that the FBI raids primarily involve material described as child pornography. Yet the critics of *Time*'s cyberporn cover story had been addressing issues of pornography, obscenity, child seduction, and exposure to inappropriate materials primarily as they relate to *Time*'s coverage or Martin Rimm's discredited study. What the critics were saying was a "nonproblem" was *Time*'s implication that children (and others) were routinely stumbling, unwittingly, across pornographic images, which *Time* had described as "pervasive."

They were also arguing that despite scary anecdotes about pedophiles e-mailing pornography to children online, it's common for minors to spend years online without ever encountering a child predator or having any inappropriate material sent to them. It was this argument that Pondiscio transmuted into a claim that child predation in cyberspace was a "nonproblem"— an especially adroit rhetorical move, given that Philip Elmer-DeWitt's story for *Time* had also said the danger was minimal. Elmer-DeWitt wrote, "While groups like the Family Research Council insist that online child molesters represent a clear and present danger, there is no evidence that it is any greater than the thousand other threats children face every day."

That consideration aside, no one has ever denied that child sexual abuse is a problem, whether in cyberspace or out of it. Neither *Time* nor its PR director is doing anyone any favors by distorting the arguments of the magazine's critics—by hinting that the critics were untroubled by child pornography or child abuse.

Instead of this weirdly hostile and irrational spin control, what *Time* could have done, if Pondiscio and his employers were interested in correcting the damage to public understanding done by the cyberporn article, would be to repeat a few basic and irreducible facts that have gotten lost in all the sensationalism, such as the fact that there's arguably less of a threat to your child online than there is on the corner across from the schoolyard. After all, even the most determined child predator can't reach through the screen.

Time also could underscore the fact that the National Center for Missing and Exploited Children (NCMEC) has developed some excellent guidelines for parents and children. The NCMEC pamphlet, *Child Safety on the Information Highway,* is available on America Online and just about everywhere else in cyberspace. For families that follow those guidelines, the Internet is a far safer place than Disney World.

Unfortunately, so long as government officials are intent on regulating the Internet in ways that the traditional press is not regulated, the Net still isn't a safe place for the Constitution. And that won't change until we solve two problems. First, we've got to teach ourselves to think clearly about the legal issues of online life, regardless of the willingness of anti-porn activists and the mainstream media, including *Time,* to confuse them. Second, we've got to remember, come election time, that we need to protect ourselves against the "clear and present danger" of politicians who, in their eagerness to say they have done something about pornography in cyberspace, have promoted such ill-crafted and ill-considered measures that they seem to have forgotten the meaning of the Constitution they've sworn to uphold.

2002 Update: Standards Issue—The Supreme Court, Community Standards, and the Internet

The law of obscenity in the United States is based on community standards, which shift from one jurisdiction to another: what folks consider obscene—that is, without any redeeming social, cultural, or aesthetic value—in one place may be unobjectionable somewhere else. This is no small matter, as material considered obscene can legally be censored, and its speakers and publishers can legally be punished.

But a recent federal appeals court decision called the entire community standards doctrine into question, and the U.S. Supreme Court agreed to weigh in on the matter. This set up the possibility of the first wholesale revision of obscenity law in decades. Although there are a few reasons to be optimistic that the ultimate outcome of the case in question will increase the realm of protected speech, there are also reasons to worry that we may end up with fewer speech rights if the community standards doctrine is applied reflexively (rather than thoughtfully) to the Internet.

Here's the background. In 1998, Congress passed the Child Online Protection Act (COPA), aimed at preventing minors from getting access to sexually explicit but otherwise legal material. COPA is based on the notion that the government has a role in preventing children's exposure to content that is legal for adults (that is, material that isn't legally obscene) but that nevertheless might be considered "harmful to minors" (sometimes known as "obscene for minors").[4]

Soon after COPA became law, the American Civil Liberties Union challenged it in court, claiming it overly restricted First Amendment–protected speech. A U.S. district court in Pennsylvania agreed that COPA ran afoul of the Constitution, and in June 2000, the Third Circuit Court of Appeals also agreed that COPA was too restrictive. The Supreme Court agreed to hear the case in the term, beginning in October 2001.

So why is the Third Circuit decision troublesome? In *Miller* v. *California* (1973), the Supreme Court came up with a way of dealing with so-called obscene content that got the high court out of the business of deciding at a national level what content is legal and what can be punished. *Miller* held that the definition of obscenity depends at least in part on the standards of local communities. Content that is acceptable in New York or San Francisco isn't necessarily going to be legal in Waco or Paducah, the Court reasoned. At the same time, the Court did carve out an exception for material that has "serious" literary, artistic, or other social value; such content, it ruled, can't be obscene no matter what local standards prevail.

Miller didn't address whether sexual content that's legal for adults is legal for minors as well, but subsequent federal and state court cases have suggested that community standards apply here too. This led to the concept of otherwise legal content that may be "harmful to minors." Thus, parents in Manhattan, New York, may think little of allowing their children access to content that would appal parents in Manhattan, Kansas. As the Third Circuit correctly noted in its decision, the statutory scheme of COPA is wrapped around that concept of "harmful to minors," which itself depends on the notion of community standards.

This, said the Third Circuit, is a big constitutional problem for Web site publishers. After all, when you put up a Web site, you can't tell who's going to access it or where they are, at least not with current technology. So even if you publish content on your Web site that isn't harmful to minors in your locale, you can't guarantee that a kid in a more restrictive community won't click his way to it. What COPA effectively requires, the court concluded, is that every Web site operator design his content so that it is acceptable—not "harmful to minors"—in every jurisdiction in the country, or else check everyone's I.D. at the door.

Either alternative is excessively burdensome on speakers, including relatively innocuous speakers such as the *Buffy the Vampire Slayer* fans who write erotic fiction featuring the show's characters or the keepers of racy Web logs whose content is not only legal for adults but also clearly protected by the First Amendment. (COPA purportedly addresses only commercial Web site operators, but the definition of *commercial* in the statute is so broad that it arguably includes even nonprofit and hobbyist Web sites.) Based on this reasoning, the Third Circuit concluded that the community standards doctrine, at least when applied to the Internet, is itself unconstitutional.

On the face of it, the Third Circuit's dismissal of community standards on the Internet should have pleased *somebody*. After all, the two basic sides in the various legal fights over sexually explicit material both dislike community standards. Civil libertarians find the doctrine too restrictive and variable, and social conservatives hate it because it allows too much to be published (plus, it has that annoying escape clause about "serious" value).

Despite such problems, the community standards doctrine has brought comparative stability to an aspect of law that prior to 1973 had become increasingly contentious, which is the main reason I expected the Supreme

Court to think long and hard before dumping the doctrine, Internet or no Internet. I wasn't the only one with that expectation, which is why both sides in the Supreme Court case, dubbed *Ashcroft* v. *ACLU,* had to wrestle with how to deal with community standards. Neither side really wanted to ask the Supreme Court to do what it is probably loath to do: set national standards and, potentially, have to deal with every obscenity case in the country. But neither party really wanted to defend the community standards doctrine either.

Despite its reservations, the government, along with various social conservative *amici curiae* such as the National Coalition for the Protection of Families and Children, did argue for a national "harmful to minors" standard, under which they believed COPA could survive a constitutional challenge.

COPA's challengers, despite having won in the Third Circuit on the community standards issue, mostly wanted the high court to avoid that issue altogether. After all, they had gotten COPA struck down in the district court on a different legal theory: the district court judged the law unconstitutionally overbroad and vague in its regulation of speech protected by the First Amendment. Not impossibly, they had hoped the Supreme Court would somehow look past the Third Circuit decision and focus on the trial court's reasons for finding that COPA is unconstitutional. But despite ACLU advocate Ann Beeson's best efforts to get the Court to focus on the trial court's reasoning, the Supremes remained tightly focused on the community standards issue at oral argument in November 2001. And in May 2002, the Court ruled on the narrow issue of whether the Third Circuit had been right to attempt to punt the community standards doctrine. In an eight-to-one decision, the Court held that the Third Circuit could not invalidate COPA solely on the argument that the community standards doctrine, as applied to the Internet, is unconstitutional. (This did not affect COPA's inactive status, however. The trial court's injunction against enforcement of the law, based on different reasoning from that of the Third Circuit, remained in place.)

In itself, the Supreme Court's narrow ruling, which sent the case back to the Third Circuit, wasn't particularly troubling: the overbroad COPA statute was still not being enforced, and the Third Circuit might well invalidate the statute again, this time citing the trial court's legal reasoning rather than sidestepping it. What *was* troubling to me, however, was the apparent willingness of some justices, as expressed in concurrences, to abandon community standards doctrine when it comes to the Internet and "harmful to minors" content and to adopt a national standard instead. It's unclear to me how either Congress or the Supreme Court could set out to define a national standard of what qualifies as "harmful to minors" without causing serious fear, uncertainty, and doubt about what can be published on the Net. Since what is "harmful" for a seven year old may not be "harmful" to a seventeen year old, any rational "harmful to minors" standard likely varies according to age as well as according to community.

That said, I think it's possible to revisit community standards doctrine and find something useful and pro-liberty in it. It helps to remember that when it comes to censorship, what lawmakers have been trying to preserve is not government authority to regulate content per se, but community integrity—the ability of groups to maintain the character of their public spaces without being confronted with, say, sexually oriented businesses such as adult bookstores and strip clubs.

In other words, one can reasonably argue that lawmakers are interested in public spaces, not private ones. That the government has no authority to invade the privacy of a home to root out obscenity—regardless of community standards—has been established at least since the Supreme Court's 1969 decision in *Stanley* v. *Georgia*.

With that case in mind, it seems certain that whatever the social interest is in regulating obscene and harmful-to-minors content, it has to do only with public spaces—spaces outside the home. The government's power to regulate obscenity and harmful-to-minors content has been understood, in the modern era at least, to be a function of that community interest in protecting public spaces.

So when we look at community standards, what we're looking at is a right that is vested not in state and federal police officers, but rather in the citizens of communities themselves. Yes, historically, that right has been delegated to the police, but the problem in the age of the Internet has been that police-centered content regulation, especially when it comes to content whose legality varies depending on what community you're in and what age the audience is, is too blunt an instrument. And retrofitting the Internet to implement a national "harmful to minors" standard may be, in a practical sense, impossible.

The Internet is a decentralized medium, so it makes sense that the primary arbiters of what's seen on the Internet ought to be individuals, including individual parents. We Internet users tackle this problem in different ways. Some of us may use filtering software to enforce our choices, while others, eschewing what they see as the clumsy world of commercial filtering tools, simply rely on their own ability to choose where they go and what they and their children see on the Internet. It's not a perfect system, of course, but it's better than having the cops make their own judgments as to what may be "harmful" to our minors, and it's better than balkanizing the Internet technologically and legally in order to make it easier for the cops.

Is this user-centered approach to community standards a First Amendment framework that we all can live with? In a sense it always has been— it's precisely the system that we parents are used to enforcing in the offline world. Parents may do what they can to control what their children encounter, but all parents know their children will encounter things in the real world that they'd prefer the children not see. What we parents have relied on historically has been our ability to instill our own community standards in our children—internalized values that remain with our kids when neither parent nor policeman is around.

In that sense, the Internet and the Web don't pose any new community standards problems, just a digital version of a very old one that we've been coping with for a long time.

9

Fighting a Cyberporn Panic

I have two stories to tell you here. The first is shorter and easier to tell—
it's the story of how the nation's most prominent newsweekly was lured
into promoting the Great Cyberporn Panic of 1995. The second story,
which is more significant, has to do with how a few of my friends and I
managed to correct the record, relying on the oft-demonized Internet to
counter the mistakes and the malfeasance of the traditional media.

First Story: The Lives and *Time* of Marty Rimm

In the summer of 1995, *Time* magazine had one of its covers hijacked
by a hype artist named Martin Rimm. Rimm, a thirty-year-old undergraduate at Carnegie Mellon University, concocted a "study" of pornography on computer networks and successfully promoted the "study" into
an article in the prestigious *Georgetown Law Journal*. From there, he
boosted it straight into a cover story for *Time*. When that story hit the
streets on June 26, the luridness of *Time*'s packaging was remarkable.
The cover featured an illustration of a wide-eyed child staring in horror
into a computer monitor. Interior illustrations included an image of a
naked man having sex with a computer and a picture of a child being
lured into a dark alley by a man holding a computer monitor. The only
things more outrageous than *Time*'s graphics were the sweeping conclusions of the Rimm study itself.

The "study" (as described by Rimm—no one other than Rimm has
ever purported to have seen the study itself as a whole) was misleading
in many ways. The most significant of these were Rimm's generalizations
about "the information superhighway" from a study based primarily on

data from a single adult-oriented computer BBS, seasoned with only a dollop of data about Carnegie Mellon University students' usage of the Internet. To anyone with even a smattering of statistical expertise, Rimm's *Georgetown Law Journal* article about the study raised more red flags than the People's Republic of China.

Yet *Time* chose to hype—and thus implicitly endorse—the study. In doing so, the magazine poured gasoline on the flaming national debate about Net censorship. Senator Charles ("Chuck") Grassley (R, Iowa) had the text of the *Time* story read into the *Congressional Record*. Grassley argued that *Time* and the CMU study proved the need for imposing stricter speech and content controls in cyberspace than in any other medium. In spite of Net activists' success in uncovering the truth about Rimm and his pro-censorship allies, Congress was primed by the Great Cyberporn Panic to pass into law the Communications Decency Amendment (CDA), a law that would restrict not only pornography but all sorts of "offensive" speech on the Net. If the law survived First Amendment challenges in court, material that would be constitutionally protected expression if carried by Barnes and Noble could get you two years in federal prison and a $250,000 fine if you published it on the Net. How did such a draconian bit of legislation become law? Who was responsible for creating a federal gag order for the Net?

(This Communications Decency Amendment did not have anything to do with obscenity law, and the subsequent challenge to the CDA did not challenge any prohibitions of obscene material. Instead, it addressed so-called indecent material, an undefined category of material discussed at greater length in chapters 8 and 10.)

All the threads of the Great Cyberporn Panic, it seems even now, lead back to Rimm, the long-in-the-tooth Carnegie Mellon undergraduate with an astonishing track record for finding allies in his quest for porn. Rimm is a man with an interesting history. Had *Time* investigated him instead of swallowing his law journal article uncritically, it would have uncovered his remarkable pattern of publicity seeking, stretching back more than a decade.

As a student journalist at Atlantic City High School in the early 1980s, Rimm claimed to have conducted a survey that showed epidemic rates of illegal gambling among the city's high school students. New Jersey was still anxious about having legalized gambling in Atlantic City, so Rimm's claims made headlines. Between spring of 1981 and the fall of 1984 (Rimm had finished high school and begun his undergraduate coursework at New College in Florida), the amateur pollster milked his new-found fame as an expert on teenage gambling for all it was worth. At only nineteen, he was a member of a state Council on Compulsive Gambling and had testified before New Jersey's gambling commission. "We are cultivating a generation of compulsive gamblers," Rimm ominously announced before the commission. "The more available it is, the more they will gamble." In response to Rimm's alleged exposé of the problem of teenage gambling, New Jersey legislators raised the minimum gambling age from eighteen to twenty-one. It wouldn't be the last time Rimm made legislators dance to his dubious music.

Was Rimm seriously involved in research into teenage gambling? Or was the whole thing just a grab for the spotlight? One reason to believe the latter is that neither the casinos nor the state commission was able to duplicate the results he reported. More telling reason was Rimm's fondness for PR stunts—his most famous being the occasion in which he dressed himself up as an Arab and managed to get served free drinks at a major Atlantic City casino.

That Rimm was less than sincere in his worries about gambling was apparent in his subsequent career. After dropping out of New College and spending several years in relative obscurity, he appeared again in Atlantic City as a casino worker. According to reports by Ray Robinson of the *Atlantic City Press,* the former teenage gambling crusader "returned to the United States in 1987, graduated from a craps dealers school, and went to work in the city's casino industry the following year." Rimm worked not only as a craps dealer, but also as a pit clerk and security guard. Casino work was a strange career choice for someone who had crusaded against gambling only a few years earlier. But this would not be the last time Rimm merged with the subject of his study.

In 1990 New Jersey's Division of Gambling Enforcement (DGE) investigated Rimm about some unusual gambling-related hoaxes, one of which involved bogus windshield flyers that purported to offer a free $25 in casino chips to anyone who bought a copy of Rimm's self-published book of autobiographical fiction, *An American Playground*, and presented the book at the Trump Taj Mahal casino.

Rimm also earned DGE's attention that year by sending a letter to a member of the Casino Control Commission, Valerie Armstrong, in which he claimed to have penetrated the computer system at one casino, uncovering evidence of special favors granted to government officials. "Given my extensive computer expertise," Rimm wrote Armstrong, "I managed to crack the standard security codes and access an astonishing amount of information." It wouldn't be the last time Rimm claimed to have extensive computer expertise.

Nothing came of the DGE's investigation of Rimm. Although he was the only suspect in a series of hoaxes, no one had lost any serious money as a result. Rimm had apparently been more interested in winning the spotlight than in lining his wallet. The investigators dropped the case after it became clear that Rimm had no plans to renew his casino worker's license.

Rimm then disappeared for nearly three years. He claims to have spent at least some of this time serving in the military, but he's evasive about what precisely he did during that service. After resurfacing in the fall of 1993, he parlayed his earlier college credits from New College into admission as a transfer student to Carnegie Mellon University, one of the nation's top five technical universities. He enrolled as an electrical engineering undergraduate. But once Rimm was at CMU, he demonstrated that his primary talents lay in what computer hackers call "social engineering"—manipulating others into giving him what he wanted.

Pornography, though, was his primary field of study, and Rimm found a mentor to support his "scholarship" in Professor Marvin Sirbu, his adviser. Sirbu maintained a World Wide Web home page at Carnegie Mellon that listed him as a professor in "Engineering and Public Policy, Industrial Administration, and Electrical and Computer Engineering." He was also the chairman of the Information Networking Institute, a grant-seeking research entity at CMU. Sirbu's wife, Barbara Lazarus, was a vice provost at CMU. In that position, she controlled the SURG (Small Undergraduate Research Grant, pronounced "surge") project, which awarded grant money to undergraduates working on independent scholarly projects. Rimm lost little time exploiting these connections. He told

Sirbu that he'd been collecting data about online porn, and planning a study of it, since he'd come to CMU. All he needed was sponsorship and a little funding to continue what he hoped would be groundbreaking research.

Rimm started receiving SURG money by his second semester at CMU, which is when his research project—supposedly an exhaustive study of the marketing of online porn—began to kick in. By as early as spring of 1994, Rimm claimed to have catalogued nearly a million items of online pornography. And he began claiming in public and private messages on the Internet to have discovered statistically verifiable patterns in the marketing of porn.

Although his claims were broad, they were also general, and Rimm was cagey about the specifics of his project. It was clear to anybody who reflected on the issue that a million images would be nightmarishly time-consuming to download.[1] Cataloguing them would take even more time.

Assume that you'd have to look at each image to classify it. If you then assume (optimistically) that one can examine, classify, and record five porn images per minute (12 seconds per image), it would take 200,000 minutes to complete the job. That adds up to more than 3,300 man-hours. At 40 hours a week, a researcher who devoted himself to nothing more than this task would face more than a year and a half of sustained, mind-numbing, lust-killing labor of the sort that would drive the most jaded porndog into the nearest monastery.

We know based on subsequently released correspondence, however, that Rimm had sold Sirbu on the notion that it was possible to analyze online porn quickly and even scientifically. We may imagine Sirbu nodding sagely in his office as Rimm, the ever-serious, ever-earnest undergrad, outlines his technique: what Rimm will do, see, is download the *descriptions* of the images that adult BBS operators used to market their wares. He'll then run the descriptions through a large computer running a text parser and sort the descriptions into various categories, based on keywords. After this, he can compare the images and image categories to the frequencies with which each image was downloaded. Sirbu begins to see where this is going and leans forward intently. Marty can tell he's got a big one on the hook as he then asserts blandly (and incorrectly) that all adult BBSs record image-download statistics in a consistent and reliable way. (He probably fails to mention that download statistics from Usenet, the Net's distributed global conferencing system, cannot be known or verified.) Winding up his sales pitch, Rimm explains that his new marketing research approach will give the world, for the first time ever, solid data about the kinds of online porn marketed and the types of online porn most successful in the marketplace.

Rimm may have convinced Sirbu that the undergraduate's pioneering techniques would support the professor's own agenda: getting grants for exploring the ways in which financial transactions can be implemented and tracked on the Net. Over time, Sirbu and Rimm's other faculty adviser, David Banks of the statistics department, would remarkably come to believe that the Rimm project could even be sold to the Department of Justice as a tool for the fight against obscenity and child pornography in the online world.

Sirbu became Rimm's chief champion when the entrepreneurial undergraduate triggered a censorship debate at Carnegie Mellon in the fall of 1994. It was then that Rimm e-mailed CMU president Robert Mehrabian and informed him that during his porn research, he'd discovered that some material available on the university's computers, themselves a part of the global Internet, had been found legally obscene in Tennessee that summer during the prosecution of Robert and Carleen Thomas, the proprietors of the Amateur Action BBS.

Rimm's message to Mehrabian came with an entertaining tag line. Since CMU had now been officially notified that its computers were part of a network on which legally obscene material could be accessed, Rimm asserted, the university was a potential defendant under state and federal obscenity laws. That Rimm was no legal analyst didn't faze CMU administrators. They'd been looking for an excuse to censor sexual content on university computers, and Rimm had given them one.

What followed was a censorship flap at Carnegie Mellon (students were incensed to discover that CMU was planning to censor any Usenet newsgroup with any sexual content, including alt.sex.safe and a forum for sex abuse survivors) that made the national press. In retrospect, given what we now know know about Rimm's taste for the spotlight, it seems certain that this was precisely the effect he hoped his letter to Mehrabian would have. He had used his connections to Sirbu—and through Sirbu to other CMU administrators—to put himself on the national scene as part of the CMU censorship story. It was the first step to the cover of *Time*.

The most prominent of the stories about the CMU flap was written by Philip Elmer-DeWitt for *Time* magazine in its November 21, 1994, issue. The *Time* piece showed Rimm in a favorable light. It omitted the fact that his "study" of online porn was an undergraduate project. The story also misstated his (purported) methods in a way that made it seem as if Rimm had done far more work than, in fact, he had. So it's no wonder Rimm saw quite the opportunity in Elmer-DeWitt. When the publication date for Rimm's law review article approached, Rimm offered the *Time* writer an advance "exclusive" on his study. Elmer-DeWitt leaped at the opportunity.

Thanks in large part to Elmer-DeWitt's efforts, *Time* magazine had led the newsweeklies in coverage of cyberspace issues for most of 1993 and 1994. But *Time*'s lead was slipping. *Newsweek* had hired Katie Hafner, a veteran of the cyberspace beat and coauthor of *Cyberpunk,* a book on computer hackers, to lead its coverage of cyberspace issues. Hafner succeeded in thwarting one of *Time*'s initiatives to beef up its staff by luring another veteran cyberjournalist, Steven Levy (author of the seminal book *Hackers*), out of a deal with *Time* and into a sweeter deal with *Newsweek.* While this was happening at *Newsweek,* a writer at *U.S. News and World Report* named Vic Sussman was almost single-handedly steering the third major American newsweekly into treating cyberspace issues as worthy of mainstream coverage.

Elmer-DeWitt and *Time* fretted about keeping their edge. They spent months planning a *Time* special issue on the theme "Welcome to Cyberspace," only to be undercut by a special issue of *Newsweek* focusing on a similar theme that beat *Time*'s publication date by weeks. Irritated by that small *Newsweek* coup, Elmer-DeWitt was praying for a cyberspace story that *Newsweek* couldn't get. Rimm, with his offer of an "exclusive" about his cyberporn study, was the answer to that prayer.

Elmer-DeWitt also wished to establish, once and for all, the legitimacy of the cyberspace beat for the readers of *Time*. Some of the magazine's higher-ups are said to have been skeptical of cyberspace reporting. The stories, interesting as they were, seemed offbeat, frivolous, and out of the mainstream. The Rimm story was tailor-made to prove the doubters wrong. Rimm was about to publish an article based on the study in the *Georgetown Law Journal*. That dovetailed nicely with the growing fervor in the U.S. Congress for some kind of new regulation of porn on the Internet—a fervor itself grounded in the stories surrounding the CMU censorship debate that Rimm had instigated the previous fall.

Rimm's success in cultivating Elmer-DeWitt was partly a function of his immense gift for flattery. According to an interview Elmer-DeWitt gave to the online publication *Hotwired*, "Rimm was hard to get ahold of the week that I was doing [the CMU] story, so I had to interview a number of people, Marvin Sirbu and others, to find out what this study was in order to fully report what had happened. Finally, late in the week he [Rimm] got back to me, and I went over how I had described the study, and he said, 'Geez, I can't believe you got that right!' He ended up being impressed by how I managed, he thought accurately, to characterize his [Internet porn] study."[2]

In reality, Elmer-DeWitt's report on the CMU censorship flap had been less than accurate. The November 21, 1994, *Time* story said that "research associate" Rimm (Elmer-DeWitt omitted Rimm's undergraduate status, just as he would the following June) had "put together a picture collection that rivaled Bob Guccione's (917,410 in all)" and had tracked 6.4 million downloads. In reality, Rimm had done nothing of the kind. Instead (if his descriptions of his methodology were to be believed), he'd simply collected descriptions of the images and statistics from BBS operators about the frequency of downloads.

Rimm appears to have been relentless in his use of Elmer-DeWitt as a conduit to *Time* and, through *Time,* the national spotlight. It's also known that within *Time*'s editorial ranks, Elmer-DeWitt was a champion of the idea of making the Rimm study the peg for a cover story on cyberporn. After all, he'd contacted Sirbu about Rimm, and the CMU professor had assured the *Time* writer that Rimm's study was a serious scholarly effort. What's more, the CMU administration thought Rimm was enough of a serious scholar that they relied on his and Sirbu's representations about the material on CMU computers when crafting their new censorship policy. Elmer-DeWitt also knew that Rimm had succeeded in placing an article purportedly based on his study in the prestigious *Georgetown*

Law Journal, where it would be accompanied by commentary on the article, or perhaps on the "study" itself, by legal scholars ranging from antiporn activist and law professor Catharine MacKinnon to anticensorship law professor Carlin Meyer of the New York School of Law. By the time Elmer-DeWitt was ready to write his second story about Marty Rimm—this time a cover story based on the Rimm study—he was sufficiently confident of Rimm's credentials that he relied almost entirely on e-mail contact with Rimm for his interview. According to one source, *Time* didn't send anyone to Pittsburgh to interview either Rimm or Sirbu in the flesh.[3]

What wasn't clear to Elmer-DeWitt until well after the *Time* cover story had been published was that Rimm was playing him like a fish. Thanks to the combined efforts of amateur Net activists and professional journalists at other publications, Elmer-DeWitt was forced to confront the irreducible fact that he'd been had. After Elmer-DeWitt and his editors at *Time* learned how mistaken he was about the reliability of the Rimm study, he was called on to write what many observers regard as the closest thing to a full-page retraction in *Time*'s seventy-year history. It appeared three weeks to the day after the original publication of the cyberporn cover story.

But it wasn't just Marty Rimm and his hunger for the spotlight that *Time* had been drawn into supporting. It was also the agenda of certain antiporn activists associated with the religious right.

On a Monday, June 26, 1995, Senator Charles Grassley (R, Iowa) rose in the Senate to denounce "computerized pornography" and praise the just released "study" of online pornography from "researchers at Carnegie Mellon University."

Clearly Grassley had captured the zeitgeist about so-called cyberporn. It was less than clear at the time that Grassley's anticyberporn crusade had its roots in the efforts of antiporn groups. Although there is still no smoking gun linking the "Carnegie Mellon study" and the antiporn activists, there is at least a bloody glove or two.

For one thing, interviews with Rimm acquaintances, together with internal evidence in his *Georgetown Law Journal* article, establish that Rimm had help in crafting and placing the law review article that caused all the fuss. Who gave him that help? The numerous links between

Rimm and a particular set of antiporn activists suggest a team effort to create the perception of a pornography problem on the information superhighway.

In the fall of 1994, one of those activists—John McMickle, a lawyer with the National Law Center for Children and Families—seems to have had advance, detailed knowledge of the Rimm study at a time when virtually no one else, including CMU's administrators, had even seen it. At the turn of the year, McMickle left his job at the National Law Center and took a new, higher-profile position as a legislative aide to Senator Grassley. McMickle became the architect of Grassley's anticyberporn campaign.

Grassley's speech on June 26 was hardly an opening move. The senator had introduced legislation earlier in the summer that supposedly aimed at regulating online porn. But what Grassley insisted on calling "the Carnegie Mellon study" was now being hyped on the cover of *Time*'s July 3 issue, which had just hit the streets that Monday morning. The senator simply had to seize this golden opportunity to surf the wave of nervousness about the Net. In his speech, Grassley took pains to establish that the "study" had the provenance of neutral, scholarly research: "Mr. President, Georgetown University Law School has released a remarkable study conducted by researchers at Carnegie Mellon University. This study raises important questions about the availability and the nature of cyberporn. . . . I want to refer to the Carnegie Mellon study, and I want to emphasize that this is Carnegie Mellon University. This is not a study done by some religious organization analyzing pornography that might be on computer networks."

That last comment reveals Grassley's own awareness that the study must be perceived as sound scholarly research and not as an effort driven by the antiporn-activist agenda, even as it advanced that agenda. But the links among Rimm, his study, and the antiporn activists put the lie to any claim of scholarly neutrality.

This brings us to the central question of this story and why it is relevant to anyone who follows the struggle for freedom of speech in cyberspace: Who were the principal forces promoting Marty Rimm's study of cyberporn? Primarily, these forces were the three antiporn organizations that at the time shared suite 320 at 3075 University Drive in Fairfax, Virginia:

1. *The National Coalition for the Protection of Children and Families.* Formerly the National Coalition Against Pornography, this organization renamed itself in 1994, perhaps in anticipation of its legislative campaign against online indecency (a broader category than pornography). H. Deen Kaplan, a vice president of the National Coalition, just happened to be a law student at Georgetown and an editor of the *Georgetown Law Journal*, where Rimm published his article, "Marketing Pornography on the Information Superhighway."

2. *The National Law Center for Children and Families.*   This organization was formerly headed by antiporn activist Cathy Cleaver. It is now headed by Bruce Taylor, formerly a prosecutor specializing in obscenity cases. Taylor is also the former general counsel of Citizens for Decency through Law, an antiporn group based in Phoenix, Arizona. That organization was founded by Charles Keating, himself a veteran of the Attorney General's Commission on Pornography (a.k.a. the Meese Commission) and later a veteran of the national savings and loan scandal.

3. *Enough Is Enough!*   Presenting itself as a secular effort, this organization provides a platform for former party girl and ex–No Excuses jeans model Donna Rice-Hughes, who has leveraged her notoriety as Gary Hart's close personal friend into a career as an antiporn zealot. In her new incarnation, Rice-Hughes had aligned herself with other religious right antiporn activists. In that role, she had already met with senior Republicans, including Bob Dole, in the summer of 1995 to lobby for censorship legislation.

These groups, along with several others associated with the religious right, saw (and still see) in the Internet an immense opportunity to steer the country away from what they believe is the too permissive framework of obscenity law. Outside the realm of broadcast media and dial-a-porn services, most nonobscene publication and expression in this country is fully protected under the First Amendment. But long-standing legal precedent says the First Amendment doesn't apply if the publication or expression has been found "obscene." As we saw in chapter 8, if a work is to be considered legally obscene, it must flunk a three-part legal test laid out in the Supreme Court's 1973 decision in *Miller* v. *California:* (1) it depicts sexual or excretory acts listed in a state obscenity statute; (2) it depicts those acts in a "patently offensive" manner, appealing to the "prurient interest," as judged by a reasonable person applying the standards of the community; and (3) it lacks "serious" literary, artistic, social, political, or scientific value.

The antiporn activists despise that test, especially the last part, which allows some erotic and otherwise explicit pictures and words to escape censorship if they are judged to be socially valuable in some way. They lust for a legal regime like that administered by the FCC over the world of broadcast radio and TV—one in which "indecency" can be regulated in the interests of protecting children from the nasty effects of exposure to a "pervasive" medium. The term *indecency* had never been precisely defined by Congress or the Supreme Court, but it was well settled that it signified a far broader concept than "obscenity." In fact, "indecency" has nothing to do with porn. In one of the few definitive statements ever made by the Supreme Court about "indecency," the Court has said the term does not depend on whether the material in question appeals to "the prurient interest." Even material that no one intends to be sexually arousing and that has "serious" artistic value can qualify as "indecent." All it has to do is offend the right people.

But how do you get such a broad, patently repressive, and possibly unconstitutional restriction on Net content passed into law? The best way, figured the antiporn activists, was to generate a panic. Rimm's "study" was these activists' way of falsely shouting "Fire!" in a crowded theater.

To make the connection between Rimm and the antiporn gang is to assemble a mosaic from many tiny pieces. But Rimm's law journal article, in both early and final versions, makes up a major section of that mosaic. Once you read both that piece as it was published side by side with an earlier draft from December 1994, two things are clear. First, the content of Rimm's legal footnotes was scarcely changed at all by the law journal editors. These footnotes appear in much the same form in the law journal's June 1995 issue as they do in the December 1994 draft. This means Rimm either had legal help or he had a highly unlikely natural talent at the specialized kind of research and writing required for law review articles. Second, the form of Rimm's legal writing is equally good. Rimm's first-draft handling of the special formatting for legal footnotes (lawyers refer to it as "citation form" or "cite form") is amazingly good for someone who once told me he didn't have a lawyer on his research team.[4]

Rimm's legal writing, while somewhat biased, is as astonishingly competent as his statistical methodology is astonishingly ludicrous. This, more than anything else, makes it clear that Rimm had assistance from someone who wanted to make his legal scholarship look good enough for a law journal.

Who helped Rimm get his article placed in the high-profile *Georgetown Law Journal*, where it would be read by countless lawyers and policymakers inside the Beltway? The editors of the *Georgetown Law Journal* at that time were mightily defensive about their publication of the Rimm article and officially denied that anything fishy took place. Although one source at the journal said that the Rimm study was brought in by Deen Kaplan, the prominent antiporn activist who was also a law student and editor of the journal, the editors' official story is that they got the idea of running the piece from reading about it in the November 1994 *Time* article. If that statement is true, the timetable for Rimm's and the law journal's interactions goes something like this:

On November 14, 1994, the *Time* article on the CMU censorship flap, written by Philip Elmer-DeWitt, hits the newsstands. (The cover date for that issue is November 21.) During the next twenty-one days, Meredith Kolsky, articles editor for the *Georgetown Law Journal*, reads about Rimm's study. She gets a copy from Marty Rimm, reads it, and suggests its publication to the *Georgetown Law Journal* staff. The *GLJ* editors meet and decide to accept the article. Carlin Meyer, a professor at New York Law School, is selected as a probable contributor. Kolsky solicits Meyer's comment on the Rimm article on December 5. Two days later, Kolsky thanks Meyer for agreeing to write the comment on the Rimm article and ships a copy of the draft of the study to Meyer.

This swift official timetable means that the law review editors had no time to change Rimm's article much before it was shipped to Meyer.[5] So it's certain that Marty had legal assistance prior to the official formal submission to the law journal. Who gave that assistance?

At this point in the inquiry, the likeliest answer appeared to be that Deen Kaplan, the *Georgetown Law Journal* staff member and antiporn activist, played a significant role both in placing the article and developing the legal scholarship necessary to justify its publication in a law journal.

When I asked Rimm in e-mail about the evidence that he received help from partisan forces in preparing his "neutral" study, he denied that Kaplan actually wrote the footnotes. The narrowness of Rimm's denials, however (he does not deny that someone else wrote the footnotes for him), suggests the truth of a more general claim: that Rimm's study was in part crafted by individuals and groups inimical to pornography who hoped the law review article and study would serve as a platform for new legislation to censor the Net.

When did Rimm make contact with his unlikely allies? It's possible that Rimm met Kaplan or another computer-adept antiporn activist as early as spring of 1994. Throughout the late spring and summer of 1994, Rimm publicized his study of pornographic imagery in a number of Usenet discussion forums, notably soc.feminism, where his postings were certain to be seen by Net-savvy antiporn activists. In April, Rimm joined the California-based Amateur Action BBS, whose proprietors, Robert and Carleen Thomas, were already under federal indictment in Memphis, Tennessee, on obscenity charges. The Thomases, whose prosecution was fervently promoted by antiporn activists, were convicted in July 1994. Rimm never revealed to the Thomases that he was planning to publish a study that relied heavily on data gathered from their BBS. And it was images from the Thomas case—images that Rimm said were also available on the Internet—that Rimm used to stir up the administrators at CMU. (A BBS is reachable primarily by dial-up phone lines and is not normally a part of the Internet.)

At about the same time that Rimm was writing the CMU administration about online pornography, the September 12, 1994, issue of *Christianity Today* magazine appeared. It contained one of the first magazine articles to use the term that *Time* made famous: *cyberporn*. The piece quotes Deen Kaplan of the National Coalition, who telegraphs the religious right's legislative goal: "We need to look at [computer networks] more in terms of a broadcast medium and some of the careful restrictions that go into that to protect children." This is precisely the legislative strategy embodied in the respective cyberporn bills of Senator Jim Exon (D,

Nebraska) and Senator Charles Grassley; each was aimed at online "indecency," a term used primarily in broadcasting regulation.

Exon's bill eventually passed the Senate and, in somewhat altered form, found its way into the omnibus Telecommunications Reform Act, itself passed and signed by President Clinton in early February 1996. Deen Kaplan is known to have provided Senator Exon with what reporters and legislators later referred to as "the blue book"—a collection of online porn that the senator brandished on the Senate floor during his last-minute, but successful, efforts to pass an "indecency" bill in the Senate.

Senator Grassley's indecency legislation was introduced on June 6, 1995, at approximately the time the issue of the *Georgetown Law Journal* was set to be published. Hearings on the Grassley legislation were set for July 24. Coincidentally, perhaps, that was four weeks to the day after *Time*'s cyberporn cover story hit the streets—or perhaps it wasn't purely coincidental: Rimm seems to have known in March that his study would be featured in a *Time* cover story.

Had it not been for the fast response of the Net activists, the Rimm study hype would have been a complete success. It was the online community that systematically critiqued Rimm's study, once it became publicly available, and that later led the investigation into Rimm's background. Net-savvy journalists and researchers, for example, uncovered the fact that Rimm had been planning the publication of a book called *The Pornographer's Handbook: How to Exploit Women, Dupe Men, and Make Lots of Money*. The book's mocking dedication to *Penthouse* publisher Bob Guccione was posted to the Net, whereupon it was discovered that this passage parodied Machiavelli's dedication to his patron in *The Prince*.

The revelation Rimm hoped to transmute his new fame into a remunerative literary career, or perhaps a career as a consultant to online porn vendors, got him yanked from the witness list for Senator Grassley's hearing on Net "indecency." Without Rimm as a star witness, the hearing fizzled.[6]

Still, the passage of the Exon bill into law shows how successful Rimm and his antiporn allies were in creating the Great Cyberporn Panic. Most senators and representatives, and much of the American public, are convinced that some high percentage of the content on the Net is pornography, when in fact only a small fraction of that content is pornographic.

(That it's an increasingly well-advertised fraction is a function less of the Internet itself than of the increasing use of "spam"—broadcast advertising—by vendors.) Civil libertarians are faced with the acute problem of giving the world a truer picture of the Net. But it's time to tell the truth: The Net is potentially the fullest flowering of freedom of speech that has ever existed, and the "crisis" of cyberporn has been, at bottom, little more than an attempt by those who fear this new medium to blast that flower into ash.

The Waste of *Time*

I had dinner back in 1997 with a friend, Lisa Brink, who asked me a question about the Rimm study that no one else, in the time since I'd first labored to expose it, had thought to ask: "If the study was as obviously phony as you say it was, why weren't there lots of people instantly on the case? Where were the other journalists? Why was it just you and your friends at first who were working to debunk it?"

The question was so right on the money that I was speechless for a moment. Then I fumblingly answered: "Uh, well, eventually everybody did see that it was trash. And by August, lots of people were helping to expose it."

I later came to a better understanding of the reason so few people caught on to the Rimm study at first. Even the people who claimed to distrust *Time* magazine had reacted to the news of the study by believing it was true. Most of us knew you could find hard-core pornography on the Net if you made an effort to look for it—even though if you weren't looking for it, you might never see it. And hardly anyone was ready to believe that *Time* and Philip Elmer-DeWitt could have gotten it so wrong, so they didn't even bother to read the Rimm article itself.

Lots of people on the WELL, where I first began criticizing the *Time* and Rimm articles publicly, were smarter than I was, or better connected, or better trained to detect Rimm's methodological fudging. But I was the one who took the trouble to get a copy of the study as soon as the *Georgetown Law Journal* would release it to the public, which was on the same day *Time*'s cover story hit the newsstands.

When I read it, there was so much that was clearly strange and wrong about it that the questions it raised were immediate and obvious. I pulled my law student interns off other work they had been doing for me and assigned them to make photocopies of the Rimm article, which I then sent by Federal Express to Donna Hoffman, a marketing professor at Vanderbilt whom I knew to be an expert on Internet statistics; to Jim Thomas, professor of sociology at Northern Illinois University, who was alert to the methodological and ethical ins and outs of research; to Brian Reid, head of Internet research at DEC; and later to Pete Lewis, then the Internet correspondent for the *New York Times*. I didn't try to tell them what to think about the Rimm article; only with Donna Hoffman did I discuss in detail what I thought was wrong with the article and what I was beginning to suspect might be the case: that the Rimm study might even be a deliberate hoax. A year later, after that dinner with Lisa, I sat in my bedroom, surrounded by my files, and tried again to remember what it had been like when I first read the study itself.

How much of what's wrong with this article is intentional? I had asked myself as I read the Rimm paper. Rimm's gift for obscuring the ambiguity he was generating with a patina of pseudoprecision was immediately evident. One finds it even in the title in the *Georgetown Law Journal* article, which appeared in the June 1995 issue: "Marketing Pornography on the Information Superhighway: A Survey of 917,410 Images, Descriptions, Short Stories, and Animations Downloaded 8.5 Million Times by Consumers in over 2000 Cities in Forty Countries, Provinces, and Territories." The very title is misrepresentative. For example, the article that follows includes no information at all about "short stories and animations" and precious little even about "images," even if one were to take every word in the article as true.

Yet . . . the sheer precision of the numbers! Those last 410 images! Not just countries, but "provinces and territories"! From a rhetorical standpoint, the title was jam-packed with verisimilitude.

Still, any alert reader needed only to get to the "overview" of the article to discover that Rimm's research, even if it were valid, could not be said to be very much about the "information superhighway" at all.[7] I'd seen the overview before; CMU student body president Declan McCullagh had e-mailed me a copy of Rimm's abstract in the fall of 1994 after I returned to Washington from Carnegie Mellon University. I later learned that Rimm had been sending it around to a number of people in that period. Here's the first paragraph of a late version of the abstract that Rimm sent to Michael Berch, then the editor of *Infobahn,* a start-up magazine that hoped to provide some high-culture competition to *Wired:*

> As Americans become increasingly computer literate, they are discovering an unusual and exploding repertoire of sexual imagery on the Usenet portion of the Internet and on "adult" computer bulletin board services (BBS). Every time they log on, their transactions assist pornographers in compiling databases of information about their buying habits and sexual tastes. The more sophisticated pornographers are using these databases to develop mathematical models to determine which images they should try to market aggressively. They are paying close attention to all forms of paraphilia, including pedophile, bestiality, and urophilic images, believing these markets to be among the most lucrative. They are using the Usenet to advertise their products, and maintaining detailed records of which images are downloaded most frequently.

As I read it, I could see a number of ways in which this overview blurred the apparent precision of the article's title. The use of the term *Usenet boards* to refer to Usenet newsgroups—a usage based on the CMU habit of referring to newsgroups as "bboards" (pronounced "Bee-Boards")—suggested a connection between the newsgroups and computer bulletin boards. (In reality, the Thomases' bulletin board system—the chief source of material for the Rimm article—could not be reached from the Internet or be considered a part of the Usenet distributed conferencing system.) This misleadingly suggested that whatever might be learned from the Amateur Action BBS (which Marty referred to, without defining the term, as "the market leader") applied to Usenet and the Internet.

But Marty wanted his article to have an even broader impact—to apply to the entire "information superhighway" of the article's title. Hence in footnote 7 of the article, he wrote that *information superhighway* and *cyberspace* "are used to refer to any of the following: Internet, Usenet, World Wide Web, BBS, other multimedia telephone, computer, and cable networks." It was a definition that allowed Marty to take his data from five Usenet newsgroups and subset of computer bulletin board systems and assert that he was talking about any electronic or digital medium you could think of.

This was the kind of "abstract" that, for me, raised more questions than it answered. These questions troubled me less because I'm a lawyer concerned with free speech on the Net than because once I had started graduate school on the road to becoming a research psychologist and had devoted serious time to studying research methodology and statistics. And it was my research alarm bells, not my legal ones, that Rimm's "abstract" first set off.

Even in his draft abstract, Rimm was making statements that he could not possibly support. "Every time [users] log on, their transactions assist pornographers in compiling databases of information about their buying habits and sexual tastes," he'd written. It was the kind of absolute statement that no responsible researcher dealing with human behavior would ever make. Given the range and unpredictability of human behavior, credible researchers will qualify both their hypotheses and their conclusions. The abstract was chock-full of categorical generalizations like the one I quote here—generalizations that, given the limits on the types of data Rimm purported to be studying, were wholly inappropriate.

As it happens, I knew that many of his statements were also flat wrong. In the course of my work, I had regularly been in contact with operators of adult BBSs (they often have questions about obscenity law, and they hope to stay on the right side of legality). The claim that they're refining their offerings of sexual material to focus on what Rimm asserts to be a more "lucrative market" in what he charmingly calls "paraphilias" (as Marty used it, this psychoanalytic term signified "sexual perversions") flew in the face of what I'd been hearing from the BBS sysops who called me for advice or whom I met at conventions like One BBSCon. Those sysops wanted to minimize the risk of angering their communities, especially their local law enforcement agencies, but the strategies Rimm was categorically attributing to them would *increase* their legal risks. Offering more extreme or bizarre sexual imagery would make them more likely to provoke law enforcement attention.

There were other potential methodological problems: the reliance on verbal descriptions of the images to characterize them, the apparent conflation of Usenet and BBS data, the conflation of "download" and "consume." Sure, it was possible that Rimm might advance, in his discussion of his methods, reasonable explanations for this peculiar approach, but even the most rigorous theoretical framework he could advance would not leave him in the position of generalizing with the certainty to which he was prone in the abstract. Given what I knew about Usenet and the difficulty of measuring user behavior there (I had long followed the pioneering research of Brian Reid at DEC), Rimm's implication that he might be able to determine "the percentage of all images available on the Usenet that are pornographic on any given day" was sheer fantasy.

Nor were these the only problems I had with the abstract. But the biggest howler was this one: "The research team at Carnegie Mellon University has undertaken the first systematic study of pornography on the Information Superhighway." Even from the abstract, it was apparent that the bulk of Rimm's data came from sixty-eight "adult" BBSs. To generalize from commercial porn BBSs to "the information superhighway" would be like generalizing from Times Square adult bookstores to "the print medium."[8]

There were other weirdnesses that were neither factual nor methodological (like Rimm's evident fascination with types of porn that are, to put it delicately, not mainstream). It was hard to avoid concluding that Rimm was, at best, an odd duck and that in any case he had some sort of agenda.

In his subsequent e-mail to me, Rimm renewed his request that I review his legal footnotes. He even sent me the text of the footnotes for my convenience. But even if I'd had the time to check on someone else's legal research (doing the job right would require many hours), I couldn't ethically approve of legal footnotes without seeing the text of the article they were footnotes *to*. I pointed this out to Rimm and suggested that if he were to send me the full article, I might find the time to review the footnotes for any obvious mistakes.

Rimm told me he'd get back to me on that. He never did. And the next time I heard about the Rimm study was when Philip Elmer-DeWitt of *Time* called me early in the week of June 19, 1995 (about nine months after my initial encounter with Rimm and his study) for comment on the study and on the conclusions Rimm, who by now had received his bachelor's degree, had reached.

I had long considered Philip a friend and believe he felt the same way about me. Earlier that year, thanks to Philip's recommendation, I'd contributed a "law and order" piece to *Time*'s special issue "Welcome to Cyberspace." The assignment paid well, and I'd gotten it on Philip's recommendation. To discover that the *Time* cover story touting Rimm's lousy study had been championed by Philip in an apparent lapse of journalistic professionalism was one of the worst things I've had to deal with emotionally in my work as a lawyer.[9] But I didn't realize immediately how much responsibility Philip and *Time* would have to bear for the successful hype of Marty's study. When Philip first called me, I figured this was another case like the Jake Baker case.[10] I might not like the impression it created about cyberspace, but I had no reason to believe at the outset that Philip was wrong in thinking there was a real story here.

Among Rimm's conclusions, Philip told me, were that tastes for online porn were becoming more "extreme," that adult BBSs were using Usenet to market their wares, that sysops had discovered that the more "violent" the language of a description, the more popular an image was, and that Amateur Action BBS, whose Milpitas, California, sysops had recently been successfully prosecuted in Memphis, Tennessee, was "the market leader" of online porn. As someone who'd written about that case, and who worked for an organization that had filed an amicus brief in the appeal of that case, I was quite familiar with the facts surrounding the Amateur Action BBS.[11] This was why I was so surprised to discover that this mom-and-pop computer porn store, reachable only by modem, a long-distance call from nearly everywhere, was "the market leader" of anything.

I wasn't even sure what "market leader" was supposed to mean. I now think Rimm took the term from a 1995 book, *The Discipline of Market Leaders*. The book's authors use the term to describe any business that aggressively and successfully identifies and shapes its market—precisely what Rimm said Amateur Action BBS had done. The only clear answer I could get at the time, however, was that "market leader" did not mean anything so simple as "largest business in the market."

Philip made it clear that *Time* was going to treat the Rimm study as a major story—perhaps even a cover story. This insight was the first part of what I'd later think of as Philip's triple whammy. Given what I already knew about Rimm's research, I was appalled that *Time* would publicize it. I immediately tried to warn Philip of the methodological and other problems I saw with the study. He told me that study was going to be published in an article in the *Georgetown Law Journal,* that *Time* had an exclusive, and that he (that is, Elmer-DeWitt) found Rimm's methodology convincing. I couldn't believe we were talking about the same study. Philip found it easy to dismiss my caveats. After all, he reminded me, I hadn't seen the study.

So I asked to see it. I promised Philip that if he showed it to me, I wouldn't leak it but instead would use it to frame more detailed and substantive criticisms (or, perhaps, be forced to admit that the methodology and conclusions were convincing after all). That was when Philip hit me with the second whammy: thanks to an arrangement with the law journal and/or with Rimm (Philip was vague about this), *no one* outside of the editors of *Time* and the law journal would get to see the study before the *Time* story appeared and the law journal issue was published. I was stunned. If there were questions about the study's reliability (and I still had every reason to believe there were), the arrangement Philip told me about practically guaranteed that those questions wouldn't be fully considered by *Time*'s editors, especially since Philip seemed to believe that the doubts I tried to raise weren't serious ones.

At this point I made two suggestions. First, I referred him to Donna Hoffman, a Vanderbilt University professor I knew from the WELL. I had become friends with Hoffman over the course of the preceding year and knew that she and her husband, Tom Novak, were among the most knowledgeable people in the world when it came to questions of surveying Net usage or modeling marketing strategies in this new medium. I assumed that Hoffman and Novak would raise the same methodological questions I had, plus some I'd no doubt overlooked. Perhaps that would convince Philip to look again at the reliability of the Rimm study.

My second suggestion was for Philip to contact whoever was insisting on nondisclosure of the article and ask them to grant me permission to see it for comment, with the proviso that I'd agree not to leak it in any way. This came to nothing. When I reminded Philip about it the following week, he professed not to remember that I'd ever proposed this arrangement.

Although Philip did have one of *Time*'s field reporters interview Hoffman, he never spoke to her himself. He did, however, read the "file" from the reporter's interview. We know this because he later argued on the WELL that the intensity of Hoffman's language in commenting on the Rimm study methodology (she knew about it from the abstract and—mirabile dictu!—from her own prior correspondence with Rimm, who'd solicited her advice and support months before) made her an unreliable source. After all, how could she be so critical *when she hadn't seen the study?* And, of course, she was barred from seeing it by the arrangement among *Time,* the law journal, and Rimm.

The more I thought about the study's imminent publication, the more troubled I was by the secrecy and lack of critical review. That was when I felt the first inkling of a suspicion that Rimm's study might represent something worse than an undergraduate's sloppiness. Was it possible that Rimm had deliberately chosen this sort of publication venue in order to achieve scholarly respectability while escaping the rigors of peer review that other kinds of journals would impose on him? I began to consider how odd it was that an article by an *electrical engineering major,* purporting to be a *marketing* study relating to the Internet, was appearing in a *law review*. Although Philip took this to be an index of the study's likely reliability, I knew something that, at least at first, he did not: that law reviews are unlike most other scholarly journals in that they're edited not by professors or professional editors, but by *second- and third-year law students*. While I have the highest regard for the ability of student law review editors at a school like the Georgetown University Law Center, I knew it was highly unlikely that the editorial staff had the expertise to question the claims and arguments Rimm would be making about his computer-mediated research into the information superhighway. Suddenly the legal footnotes, which Marty had been so worried about for so long, took on a new significance: they were the thin entering wedge that qualified Rimm's article as a fit piece for a law review.

In the course of the three or four weeks that followed *Time*'s publication of its cyberporn cover story, the story that emerged as the result of my investigations, the online reporting of Brock Meeks, and the investigative journalism of Ray Robinson of the *Atlantic City Press* turned out to be vastly more colorful than any of us could ever have imagined at the outset.

February–March 1996: Rimm's Last Gasp

By early 1996, the Rimm study was widely regarded as discredited. The most important single event in the exposure of the study had been Hoffman and Novak's posting of their critiques of the Rimm article and the *Time* cover story on their Project 2000 Web page at http://www2000. ogsm.vanderbilt.edu/. Second in importance only to the Hoffman-Novak effort was the "journoporn" page at *Hotwired,* which included an archive of the discussions from the WELL's media conference.[12] I picked this conference—the WELL conference most frequented by professional journalists—as the place to confront Philip about what was wrong with the study and the story; it was where an exposure of the problems with the Rimm and *Time* articles would have the most impact. As you can see when you look at that discussion, the other members of the WELL—the ones who had not at first seen what was wrong with *Time*'s cover story—quickly realized the magnitude of *Time*'s lapse once we began to outline it. And this realization triggered their own investigations and condemnations of the scandal.[13]

After only a few months, the scandal of the study was so widely known that many of us assumed we'd never have to deal with it again. We were wrong, though. In their first filing in *ACLU* v. *Reno,* the case in which we were challenging the constitutionality of the Communications Decency Act, passed into law by President Clinton in February 1996, the government's attorneys, led by Anthony Coppolino, *appended the full text of Rimm's law journal article.* I was horrified; then, when I learned from the other attorneys in our case that Coppolino and his team *knew* that the Rimm study had been discredited, I was furious. All lawyers are bound by the formal rules of legal ethics not to knowingly mislead a judge as to the facts. By treating the Rimm article as if it were valid research, the Department of Justice lawyers seemed to be doing just that. (A spokesperson later told the *Washington Post* that the study was included as "an initial reference" as to the kind of pornography available online.)

Like the stubborn vampire in the last reel of a horror movie, the Rimm study threatened to rise once more from the dead. I was prepared to file a formal ethics complaint with the Department of Justice and with the relevant state bar associations, but first I hinted at my intentions in quotes I gave to Pete Lewis of the *New York Times* and John Schwartz of the

Washington Post. These were the two newspapers I could be certain would be read by Coppolino and his superiors at "Main Justice" in the District of Columbia.

When my quote in the *Post* appeared the morning after the government filed its opposition to the ACLU's request for a temporary restraining order, Coppolino called Chris Hanson, the ACLU's lead counsel on the case, to complain. Hadn't we all agreed that we were going to avoid needless antagonism as we pursued this case? Coppolino asked. Certainly, Hanson told him, but I can't make any guarantees about this guy Godwin out in California. He seems to think you've crossed a line here.

But in the long run I never had to file a complaint. The Rimm study was dropped from the government's subsequent filings, and it never appeared again in their papers, except for a brief mention in passing by one of the government's witnesses at the trial in Philadelphia. The quote in the *Post* had been enough.

Second Story: Hacking the Media Coverage of the Cyberporn Study

Frankly, I think there's a good story to be done, probably by me, in what's gone on in the WELL. This might be self-serving, but it feels like poor Marty Rimm is being lynched there. He's not getting a fair trial; his study's not getting a fair trial. Mike Godwin has organized an attack, and there are precious few voices that are not already prejudiced to one side.
—Philip Elmer-Dewitt, senior editor, *Time* Magazine

The writer of the Time story, Philip Elmer-DeWitt, characterized the attacks as "a lot of rhetoric from a professional lobbyist and a professor who called it reckless and criminal before she had read" the study.
—Brock Meeks, editor, *Cyberwire* dispatch

This topic has been an amazing learning experience, and the best example I've ever seen of an online community in action. To me, what's happening on this topic is the story. It may be just a battle in the larger war, but if the work that comes out of this helps to cause Time to be more careful about the truth from now on, then it's a very important battle.
—Mark Frauenfelder, associate editor, *Wired*

To know what went wrong in the coverage of the cyberporn study is to know only half the story. What you really need to know, to appreciate what an effect the Net is already having on society and the media, is what went right. And this is the second story I want to tell you in this chapter.

When I look back on the summer of 1995 now and my desperate efforts to derail the bullet train of misinformation and panic about porn on the Net, I can see how it must have looked to Philip Elmer-DeWitt. In the week following publication of the *Time* cyberporn cover story, which he wrote, he was being assailed from all sides, but he could see how many of the attacks were traceable to my own criticisms of the *Time* story and of the "bizarre study" on which it was based.

But it seemed to me then, and it seems to me now, that *orchestrated* was not the right word. It implies a sort of strategic planning of which I, in my frenzy during the weeks between *Time*'s preparation and publication of its cover story and its quasi-retraction of that story, was wholly incapable. What I really did in those weeks during which the *Time* story and the Rimm study each began to implode may be better described not as "orchestration" but as "jamming." It was more as if I were doing riffs and other people were picking them up and improvising.

It may have been far more effective than a planned event would have been, however. It had vigor, spontaneity, and popular sentiment behind it and was driven by passion and not by calculated maneuvering. And it proved the power of online communities to take on the traditional media establishment, once the playing field has been leveled. The WELL and the World Wide Web and Usenet had leveled the field.

What follows is my account of those weeks in which the virtual communities wrestled with *Time* over the cyberporn cover story and with the censors, and won one small victory in the war between those who love the Net and those who fear it.

Monday, June 19, 1995

I was working in my office at EFF in Washington, D.C., that afternoon when Philip Elmer-DeWitt called and asked me if I had time to talk. I said I did, and in fact because of our good relationship, I would have made time for Philip regardless of how pressed I might have been. I considered him a friend—not just because he quoted me in his *Time* articles now and then, or because we were both denizens of the WELL, one of the strongest and best online communities, or even because he'd helped get me a writing assignment for *Time* a few months earlier. It was also because I admired his work (writing for newsmagazines is a tricky art) and because I believed he had a real understanding of the dynamic of the Net.

"Mike, I need some quotes from you, but I also need you to promise not to tell anyone about this story."

"Sure," I said. The newsweeklies are pretty uptight about whether it's known that they're going to run an item, so I routinely kept a lid on such things anyway.

"Do you know about the Martin Rimm study of pornography at CMU?"

"Yeah, of course. Supposedly it was what triggered all the censorship stuff there. I haven't seen the study itself, though."

"Well, it's about to be published in the *Georgetown Law Journal,* and we're doing a cover story on it for next week."

I was blown away. "You're doing what?"

Philip explained that he was planning to use the Rimm study as the peg on which to hang a story about pornography on the Internet. He wanted to know what I thought the general reaction to the study would be. I started blurting out all sorts of issues I had with the study. But Philip was inclined to think that my criticisms couldn't be that serious—after all, I hadn't seen the actual study myself, and lots of people at CMU and elsewhere had vouched for it. He referred to the three legal writers who were contributing "comments" (that is, short articles) to accompany the Rimm article in that issue of the law journal. Rimm's professors also vouched for him. So who was *I* to be telling *him* that the study wasn't good science?

"Okay," I said. "Can you get me a copy of the study? I could make more informed comments about it if I had it in my hands."

Philip told me that the law journal was embargoing the study prior to its publication the following week and that *Time* had also agreed not to show it to anyone. He explained to me that it wasn't up to him or to *Time.* It would be up to the law journal and to Rimm, one of which (he was unclear about this) had insisted on the secrecy.

"Can you at least ask them if I can see the study beforehand?" I pleaded. Philip was noncommittal.

Even without the study in hand, I thought I was on firm ground in voicing skepticism about it. I had talked with Donna Hoffman about the so-called Rimm study months before, when I had been e-mailed a copy of the study abstract by Declan McCullagh, student body president at Carnegie Mellon University, where early reports about the study's findings about porn on the Net had triggered some predictable overreactions by the university's administration.[14]

All by itself, the Rimm abstract raised a lot of doubts for both Donna and me. The problem with the abstract was twofold. On the one hand, it didn't say enough about the method or the data; you couldn't really tell much about Rimm's methods. On the other hand, as Donna had pointed out with some heat, what it did say about the study strongly implied that Rimm was taking a highly skewed sampling of content on the Net and then drawing overbroad conclusions from it.

But here it was, soon to be featured in a law journal, praised by legal scholars on the left and the right, with the full backing of a major technical university—and soon to be on the cover of *Time* magazine at a time when Internet censorship regulation was cooking up a storm in Congress.

I knew that Philip had an obligation as a journalist to report facts he didn't like, just as he reported the ones he liked, and I never expected to convince him not to run the story on the basis of his political druthers (or mine). My job at that point, I thought, would be to get as many facts in front of Philip as I possibly could, and that meant mobilizing Donna. I filled her in about the fact that the Rimm study was going to be in *Time* and that Philip (I thought) would be calling her.

I then tried to calm myself. It seemed to me that Philip had in the past attempted to make sure his stories were balanced. Surely he'd do so this time. And maybe the story wouldn't have much of an effect on the public debate. That a story appears on the cover of *Time* is no guarantee it will create a big public splash. (Yeah, okay, I was trying to fool myself a little bit. But I'd worked past setbacks before, and if this was going to be a setback, maybe it would just be a small one.)

Tuesday, June 20, 1995

The next afternoon, I met with several other civil libertarians in Danny Weitzner's office at the Center for Democracy and Technology to discuss the latest censorship legislation in Congress. Danny and I had worked together at EFF before former EFF executive director Jerry Berman had persuaded him and a number of other EFF staffers to join Berman's new group, the Center for Democracy and Technology. We were working together still. Also present were representatives from the Electronic Privacy Information Center (EPIC), ACLU, and People for the American Way. Professor David Post, a former Supreme Court clerk who was now teaching law at Georgetown University Law Center, also attended.

I was a bit drowsy—I hadn't slept well the night before. But I struggled to stay awake and pay attention as we discussed how best to frame civil libertarian concerns at a larger, industry-oriented strategy session the next day. Industry groups and civil libertarians tend to be suspicious of each other, but when it comes to online issues, we're all in the same boat. (The only problem is that we have to keep reminding each other of that.) And an industry–civil liberties coalition gets listened to on Capitol Hill in a way that neither group does individually. This kind of coalition is so broad that it's not easily dismissed as marginal or special interest oriented.

At the beginning of the discussion, Post said something that woke me right up. He announced what he'd been hearing about an upcoming publication at Georgetown. "They're running a study of pornography online, and *Time* magazine is doing a story on it. They're being very secretive about it."

Other people know about the upcoming *Time* story! I thought. What a relief! So it's not any breach of my promise to Philip if I talk about it, too. I had been torturing myself as to whether I had a stronger obligation to warn my own organization and our allies about the story or to keep my promise to Philip. But Post's announcement had freed me from that dilemma.

I asked Post whether he'd seen the article himself. "No," he said. "Some law students approached me with some questions they had about the Internet, based on statements in the article. I asked them whether I could see the article and read the statements in context." The students, Post said, denied him access to the article. He found this puzzling, since normally there's nothing very secret about upcoming law review articles.

I decided I'd raise the red flag at the Wednesday meeting.

Wednesday, June 21, 1995

It was a typically humid, uncomfortable summer day in Washington, D.C., as I made my way to the Piper and Marbury law office, where the Interactive Working Group was set to meet. By the time I arrived, the meeting had already begun. There was talk about how to respond to the House's proposals for counterlegislation that would promote filtering by parents as opposed to top-down censorship from the Department of Justice. (It was already the case that software filters like Surfwatch, though crude and deeply flawed, did more to bar children from inappropriate content than federal legislation, even in theory, ever could do.) "The important thing," said Jerry Berman, who'd organized the meeting, "is that we're all reading from the same page"—that the whole group, industry representatives, lawyers, and civil libertarians alike, stand together and respond collectively.

The discussion then moved to whether the industries represented at the meeting should take a united front in dealing with the press and, if so, what they should say. In the course of the discussion, I volunteered that *Time* would be coming out with a cover story about online porn the next week and that we all ought to be ready to respond to it—that we all should anticipate what we would say when asked about it.

I had some thoughts about that. I recalled a discussion from the WELL in which several folks had commented that by leading with the First Amendment in their opposition to censorship, anticensorship forces laid themselves open to charges that they didn't care about families—that they valued free speech more than they valued the protection of children. Of course, civil libertarians are often parents themselves, and they too care about their children; that fact gets little attention in these debates. I also remembered a Supreme Court opinion authored by Justice Antonin Scalia that interpreted a venerable Supreme Court precedent, *Wisconsin v. Yoder* (1972), as standing for "parental rights."

"When we simply say we oppose the legislation, we seem defensive, and if we start out talking about the First Amendment, the censors will eat our lunch. Why not say first that we stand for 'parental empowerment'?" I suggested. This didn't seem to have much of an effect at the time, but the People for the American Way representatives, as well as Don Haines of the ACLU, later took the notion and began to use it in various ways. "Parental empowerment" turned out to be a meme with legs—language that gave us a positive way to frame our side.

Since I believe we have a moral obligation to counter bad memes with good ones, I started using it myself every chance I got. I was tired of having the religious right claim that they were the ones who were pro-family, pro-children. I decided that the time had come to be very aggressive in meme warfare in the censorship battles.

That night I got a call from Philip, who was working late at *Time* on his story. I tried again to convince him that there were serious problems with the Rimm study, but we were now pretty late in the week. If Philip was writing it now, the chances were that cyberporn was going to be the cover story. I tried to give Philip as much balancing opinion and as punchy a quote as I could. "People are nervous about computers, they're nervous about their children, and they're nervous about sex," I said. "Put all three together, and you can drive people into a frenzy."

"That's good," said Philip. "Have you said that to anyone else?"

"No," I said.

"Mind if I use it?"

"Go right ahead."

As the interview wound down, Philip asked me what I thought would be the reaction to the cover story. I paused, then said, "It will be a disaster, Philip. No matter how much you try to balance the story, no matter how many qualifying quotes you put in, it's going to be used to justify all sorts of things, and it will inflame the public debate just as it was beginning to calm down a bit."

I think Philip was a little stunned at the heat of my reaction. "But, look, do what you have to do," I told him. "Just please talk to Donna—there are real problems with this thing."

We both hung up.

Thursday, June 22, 1995

Late in the day I called Donna Hoffman in Nashville and asked whether she had been contacted by Philip. She said she'd been interviewed by another *Time* writer, not Philip, and that this person seemed not to understand the points she was making about Rimm's methodology. She also told me that Rimm had admitted to her and her husband and coworker

Tom Novak that in his abstract, he'd overstated his claims about what adult BBS system operators do to market their wares. I asked if she'd kept the e-mail. She had. But she hadn't had a chance to raise that issue with the *Time* reporter, Hannah Bloch. Bloch, Donna said, "didn't seem to be interested" in hearing anything that might suggest the Rimm study was anything other than solid research. She'd stressed with the reporter that Rimm was (at least at the time he worked on the study) an undergraduate with no background in the kind of research he was purporting to have done and that law journals weren't peer reviewed. I told her I remembered telling Philip that myself. As she ended the phone call, she was pretty gloomy about the chances that her interview might have made any difference.

At about four P.M., I got a call from Steven Levy, *Newsweek*'s hotshot technology writer, whom I had known since he was a prominent columnist at *MacWorld*. He asked if I knew anything about the Rimm study of online pornography. I was a bit bitter about it. "Sure," I blurted. "*Time*'s making it the centerpiece of its cover story next week." I guess I must have figured that if every civil libertarian inside the Beltway knew about the Rimm study and the *Time* cover story, it made no sense not to tell Steven. But I remember feeling a pang of guilt. Even though it wasn't me, technically, who'd spilled the beans, I'd sure scattered them around a lot.

"You're kidding," he said. "Really?" He was a little jumpy on the phone all of a sudden. "Can I call you back in a few minutes? You may have kept us from making a terrible mistake."

It later turned out that Steven was writing his own cyberporn piece for *Newsweek,* and he'd been hearing about the Rimm study and had been trying to find a copy. Maybe I knew where to find one, he'd thought. After all, I worked in Washington, and the Georgetown University Law Center was in Washington. But of course I didn't have a copy. Nobody did.

Steven later called me back and told me how furious he was with the *Georgetown Law Journal,* which had stonewalled him when he'd asked for a copy of the Rimm article. I told him about the supposed "embargo" and how I had failed to get a copy. I also ran through the litany of problems I saw with the study and gave him Donna Hoffman's contact information. Steven ultimately didn't use anything from me, although he did quote Donna. It's notable, though, that in the single paragraph he gave to the Rimm study, he told readers more about its methodology than can be found in Philip's entire story. Steven's article about cyberporn, while lengthy enough to be a cover story, was merely billed on the cover of *Newsweek*'s July 3, 1995, issue. So while the cover story for *Time* was its hyping of the cyberporn study, the cover story of *Newsweek* for that week was an interview with Oklahoma City bombing suspect Timothy McVeigh.

Friday, June 23, 1995
Earlier in the afternoon, on a CNN talk show *Talk Back Live,* I had debated the Exon bill with Bruce Taylor, then the chief lawyer for the National Law Center for Children and Families. In introducing us, the host had noted that both Taylor and I were parents of small children. It gave me a way to try out my new meme in talking about free speech online: as a parent who was concerned about preserving it for our children. It seemed to catch Taylor flat-footed; he was low energy in his responses to my comments, and only at the end did he make one of his usual comments about how EFF, ACLU, and other civil libertarians are linked to "the pornography syndicate."

I called the *Georgetown Law Journal* and tried to get a copy of Rimm's study. They told me it would be available on Monday, the same day that the new issue of *Time* hit the streets. I didn't press the point. After all, if Steven Levy hadn't gotten a copy, what made me think I could get one?

I called Donna again. I told her I'd have a copy of the study on Monday, and I'd be happy to copy it and FedEx it to her. She told me she'd called Philip directly and expressed her concerns about her interview with Hannah Bloch. She said she'd be in New York on Monday and Tuesday of that week but asked me to send her the copy as soon as I had one. I agreed to do so.

By late afternoon I'd gotten a call from a producer for *Nightline*. They were looking for someone who knew about the *Time* story, and about the study, and who'd be willing and available on Monday evening to do the show.

Nightline? Ted Koppel? No way! (Yes way!) I'd love to do that show! I thought.

I said, with as much composure as I could summon, that I thought I'd be available for the show, but that I'd recommend someone else if they thought it advisable. (ABC had probably gotten my name from Philip, whom they had taped on Friday.) The producer asked me where and when I could be reached over the weekend and on Monday and said they'd get back to me.

Oh, and they told me one other thing: the other guest on the program that evening would likely be Ralph Reed, head of the Christian Coalition.

Saturday and Sunday, June 24 and 25, 1995

Saturday was a day of rest, which is to say I had come home the night before and collapsed with exhaustion. But I did get around to reading the WELL by Saturday evening. I discovered that Jim Thomas, a sociology professor at Northern Illinois University, had reposted the following message from Voters Telecom Watch's Rumor Central:

Time is expected to put out an issue this coming Monday that will contain a study of how much pornography is being transferred on the Internet. The catch is that no one even knows if the study's methods are valid, because no one is being allowed to read it due to an exclusive deal between *Time* and the institution that funded the study. Rumor Central is taking this opportunity to ask the editors of *Time* to let us see a copy of the study so we can see if the methodology is truly worthy of the high standards we hold *Time*'s science and technology staff to uphold.

Shortly afterward, Donna Hoffman had posted, "The study does not address how much pornography is being 'transferred on the Internet.'. . . The study is not credible."

My own feeling was that people needed to know what the problems with the study were as soon as possible. By Saturday evening, Philip had shown up and begun to defend the Rimm study. He also took a shot at those who'd voiced criticisms of the study already, including Donna. Specifically he argued that those who hadn't seen the study weren't in a position to criticize it yet skipped over the fact that several of us had tried to get a copy and been denied the opportunity. Whatever was happening, it wasn't normal scientific or journalistic practice.

I was peeved. The tone of Philip's responses was arrogant, as if it were impossible that *Time* could get the story wrong or that anyone was in a position to second-guess *Time*'s decision to cover the study and treat it as a serious enterprise. In response to Philip's defenses, however, I began to post information I'd gathered from correspondence I'd had with and about Rimm months earlier. I also showed how so much of what we knew about the study raised questions about *Time*'s willingness to feature it.

Still, I thought it was unfair that he and *Time* should be the target of attacks before anyone had seen what he'd written. So on Sunday morning, I wrote, "Let's hold off criticizing *Time* until we see what the story looks like."

It was the last charitable impulse I would feel toward *Time* for many months.

On Sunday evening, one WELL poster noted that the *Time* cover story was available on America Online. I logged in and read the *Time* story.

It was good for me to have read Philip's piece that way first. On America Online, you didn't see most of the illustrations that accompanied the story—you just got the text. And as I read through the text of Philip's story, I realized, with growing horror, that Philip had swallowed the Rimm story hook, line, and sinker. The cover story was little more than a puff piece on Rimm and the "Carnegie Mellon study," plus some scary conclusions about what the study tells us about online porn (It's pervasive! It's growing! It's cultivating our appetite for violent imagery!), topped off with a little earnest theorizing about the social impact of porn on the Net.

Almost as bad as what the story said was what it omitted: that Rimm himself had been an undergraduate electrical engineering major when he worked on the study, that nobody involved with the study seemed to have any background in social science or marketing research, that the law journal was not a peer-reviewed journal, or that anyone anywhere had doubts about Rimm's methodologies. Indeed, Rimm's methods themselves weren't mentioned in the article, so it was impossible even for a technically astute reader to draw an independent conclusion as to whether the research was any good.

I respected Philip's journalistic obligation to report what he took to be a real story. But in this case, so much of the basic underpinning of the story was so factually shaky, and so much of what we could find out about Rimm, the study, and the secrecy surrounding both was so troubling, that I simply couldn't shrug off this representation of the facts about the Internet and the availability of pornography there.

I later found out all sorts of things about Philip's research of the story: that he'd never actually met Rimm face-to-face, that he'd conducted the interviews with Rimm by e-mail, that Rimm, incredibly, had simply told Philip he wouldn't talk about his own background, and that Philip *simply accepted this,* even though Rimm's secrecy in itself raised questions and doubts for any other journalist I could think of.

Donna Hoffman, it turned out, had already begun, on the Saturday prior to publication of the story, to criticize *Time* for publicizing the study. Hoffman had corresponded with Rimm by e-mail a few months previously, after I'd forwarded a copy of Rimm's abstract to her for comment, and her doubts about the "Carnegie Mellon" study were only aggravated by Rimm's cagey answers to the methodological questions she and her husband and partner, Tom Novak, had asked him. She already had doubts about how he was characterizing his research.

Now that I'd seen what Philip and *Time* had produced, I knew that whatever was wrong with the Rimm study had been amplified by the magazine's sensationalistic treatment of it. But even then, that Sunday, although I was in touch with Donna and we had already begun to talk about framing some kind of response to the *Time* piece, I didn't try to post anything about the *Time* story. I wanted to sleep on it.

Monday, June 26, 1995

When I got to the EFF offices on K Street that morning, a number of messages were waiting for me. One was from the producer at *Nightline.* I called him back and discovered that, yes, they did want me to do a show with them, but the show they were planning would be pushed back until Tuesday. Would I be available at four P.M. the next day for a pretaping?

I asked one of my legal interns, Beth Noveck, to go with me to the taping on Tuesday. Since she'd been studying the *Pacifica* and *Sable* cases, which were central to understanding the theory behind the Communications Decency Act, I needed to have someone with whom I could discuss the issues as I prepared for the debate about the CDA, which I'd been told would be the focus of the *Nightline* installment.

I then called the *Georgetown Law Journal* to see if they'd follow through about giving me a copy of the study on the day the *Time* cover story came out. They did, and they had one sent over to my office. I immediately had EFF interns begin making photocopies of the Rimm packet I'd obtained from the *Georgetown Law Journal* staff. I needed a working copy, of course, but I also planned to send copies overnight to every academic I could think of who might be able to provide a substantive critique of the study. This included Donna Hoffman at Vanderbilt and Jim Thomas at Northern Illinois University, both of whom had already raised critical questions about the study based on its abstract and on the secrecy surrounding it.

Getting critical feedback on the study was a high priority. And I had to get that feedback *very quickly,* so that academics' responses to the study would be part of the same news cycle as the *Time* story itself. After all, it wasn't enough to know the study was flawed and that its flaws would emerge eventually as part of the give and take of academic scholarship. I couldn't wait. It might be months before anyone published a follow-up academic article dealing with the Rimm study. And it would be months before any respected journalistic criticism (the *Columbia Journalism Review,* say) dealt with the issues raised by *Time*'s handling of the story. I needed a response, and I needed it fast enough to provide a counterpoint to all the hoopla the *Time* cover story was generating.

The responses also had to be from academics. I flattered myself that I was capable of writing a reasonable critique, but anything I said would be discounted as biased. In contrast, academics like Hoffman and Thomas, regardless of their political sympathies, would have to be taken seriously. They could be relied on to articulate methodological and other questions that Philip and *Time* couldn't dismiss so easily. The important thing was to answer the study and the *Time* story *within the news cycle* and to make sure that other media had something more than hype when they did their follow-ups, which I knew were certain.

There was one other thing I could do to make sure that the study and *Time* were exposed: I could open up debate on the WELL, start with a deep, critical analysis of the study, and let other WELL users, including the many professional journalists who were longtime members of the system, decide for themselves whether the study deserved the kind of coverage that *Time* had given it and whether *Time*'s behavior was defensible.

It wasn't that I was trying to stir up a negative reaction to Philip's story; that reaction was more or less guaranteed by the story itself. But in the absence of a clear focus, most of the reaction might turn out to be angry blather, easily dismissible by Philip and anyone else as the ravings of a special interest group (Internet users) angry about damage done to its cause.

That didn't mean I wasn't going to express anger. I felt an overwhelming sense of betrayal at what Philip apparently had done. And it wasn't free speech I thought he'd betrayed so much as it was the ethics of journalism. I had always believed that righteous anger about the betrayal of those principles could be a good thing. Plus, an angry posting with pointed questions and criticisms was more likely to force a response from Philip than either anger or pointed questions would alone. Only if what I posted really stung, I thought, could I guarantee luring Philip into the open, where he could be questioned by his audience and his peers alike.

That Monday afternoon I went to work, posting my first salvo in the WELL's media conference. It read as follows:

media.1029.86: Avant Garde A Clue (mnemonic) Mon 26 Jun 95 14:39
Philip's story is an utter disaster, and it will damage the debate about this issue because we will have to spend lots of time correcting misunderstandings that are directly attributable to the story.

For example, when Philip tells us what the Carnegie Mellon researchers discovered, he begins his list with this:

"THERE'S AN AWFUL LOT OF PORN ONLINE. In an 18-month study, the team surveyed 917,410 sexually explicit pictures, descriptions, short stories and film clips. On those Usenet newsgroups where digitized images are stored, 83.5 percent of the pictures were pornographic."

Who but the most informed among us will not come away with the impression that the CMU study involved a survey of 917,410 items *on Usenet?* (Guess what—it didn't.)

And he concludes the list with this:

"IT IS NOT JUST NAKED WOMEN. Perhaps because hard-core sex pictures are so widely available elsewhere, the adult BBS market seems to be driven largely by a demand for images that can't be found in the average magazine rack: pedophilia (nude photos of children), hebephilia (youths) and what the researchers call paraphilia—a grab bag of 'deviant' material that includes images of bondage, sadomasochism, urination, defecation, and sex acts with a barnyard full of animals."

Problem is, this isn't the typical range of content you find in Usenet newsgroups, or on commercial services, or even on most BBSs. Instead, this is the range of content you find on the specialized subclass of commercial BBSs that focus on pornography.

Just to make things worse, Philip refers to the Internet in the next two grafs (and not at all to commercial porn BBSs).

This is an incredibly muddled abortion of a story, despite Philip's attempts to introduce balance. The *packaging* of the story—a cover with an innocent child at a keyboard, the paintings of men fucking a computer or being pulled into one—is deeply sensationalistic.

And the profound problems with the study's methodology go undiscussed. Sure, we have a guy pointing the possibility of a "gaper" phenomenon, which tells us something about how to interpret the results of a correctly conducted survey. But not a hint of how methodologically flawed the study is, or about how the people doing the study were rank amateurs, or about how the legal footnotes were spiced with citations from [articles by antiporn advocates].

The *Time* story aims at legitimizing the study as raising important issues. What it does instead is raise serious questions about whether the lure of an exclusive eclipsed *Time*'s professional judgment.

A research physician in New York City, Jon Glass, had already posted some criticisms of the story when he read it online. But he chimed in shortly after I posted: "Okay, now that I've seen the story in the additional context of the hard-copy packaging (cover art, etc.), I have to say that the overall effect is *much worse* than I previously stated. I have to agree with Mike's post to the iota. Also, Philip's nitpicking about balance is downright disingenuous once you actually view the magazine and see how much the child-entering-the-computer angle is hyped."

One of the great things about the WELL as an online community is the intellectual wealth there. It wasn't just computer enthusiasts, or hobbyists, or even journalists. Glass, an actual scientist who knew plenty about methodology and about the problems of separating fact from hype, turned out to have plenty to say about both the Rimm study and the *Time* story. (The Georgetown University Law Center, to its credit, later made the Rimm article, as well as the articles by all the commentators, accessible on its World Wide Web page.)

Aaron Dickey, who worked in New York for the Associated Press, wrote about the effect the *Time* story was already having:

Today at work, I was asked—three separate times—where to go on the Net to get porn: once by someone in my office, twice by two reporters upstairs whom I'd never met before . . . all three because they saw *Time*. At *best*, this means the cover and article are coming off as pure advertising: "You want cheap porn? Look no further!" At worst, this means the AP's about to jump on the cyberporn bandwagon with a nice series that will run in papers all over the country. And remember, the last two guys are professional reporters, not one of my goofy co-workers in the stocks department. If they don't get it, who will?

Shortly before leaving work that afternoon, I'd gotten a call from a journalist from an Iowa newspaper who asked me my reaction to the fact that Senator Charles Grassley had had the *Time* story (as well as Steven Levy's *Newsweek* story) read into the *Congressional Record*. Grassley also cited the Rimm study (which, thankfully, was not itself read into the *Congressional Record*) in support of his own "decency" legislation, which would have gone even further than Senator James Exon's Communications Decency Act in criminalizing nonobscene, constitutionally protected speech on the Net.[15]

It was easy to show how the *Time* article as a whole would convince any uninformed reader that all one has to do is log on to be confronted with what *Time* called "pervasive" and "surprisingly perverse" pornography. It made me especially uncomfortable that the word *pervasive* is a term of art in media regulation. The Supreme Court had said that the "pervasiveness" of radio broadcasting is one thing that makes federal control over broadcasting content constitutional.

On the way home, I grabbed a copy of the new *Newsweek* at a news-stand. The Levy article was there—a bit troubling on the issue of cyber-porn, but when you actually read the entire package, it was fairly well balanced. In fact, I suddenly realized as I read the magazine on the Metro home to Takoma Park that Steven had written a piece very much like the one I'd thought Philip would write.

Tuesday, June 27, 1995

Today was the day I was set to go on *Nightline*. I spent most of the morning at home, trying to make sure I was reasonably prepared with both the law and the facts to answer any questions I might be asked on the show. I took another long look at the Rimm study and was horrified once again. Whereas before I'd thought it was just barely possible that the problems with the study were due to an undergraduate's incompetence, an actual reading of the study seemed to dictate a different and more ominous conclusion: that the study had been *designed* to create the effect it was having. Lots of conclusions were asserted without any supporting data at all. Discussions of methodology were typically elided or even skipped over entirely. It would be difficult to show directly what was wrong with Rimm's conclusions because he'd obscured so much about what he'd done. As a result, identifying the problems with the study was like trying to corral a fog. Was it that Rimm was actively lying? Or was he perhaps merely the conduit for someone else's fraud?

A more troubling question was this: Why hadn't Philip seen what was there for all to see in the *Georgetown Law Journal* article? The only answer that made sense to me was that Philip hadn't actually read the article—that, at best, he'd skimmed the introduction and the conclusions and interviewed Rimm, who told him what the study said. (When I later asked him about this, Philip denied that he failed to read the entire article. I continue to find it difficult to believe his answer, however.) Fooling the law journal editors was a bit easier to understand. Not every law student has a background in statistics or social research. But the more I read, the more questions I had. Then I started working through my phone messages.

One of the first messages leaped out at me. It was from Elizabeth Corcoran of the *Washington Post,* and she wanted to know if I had any comment on the Rimm study or the *Time* story—she was doing a follow-up. I cursed myself for having come in late—her call had been a couple of hours ago, and by now she might have found another source for the comment she was looking for. In just a couple of hours, I wouldn't be available for her to interview, since I'd be off at the *Nightline* taping until five-thirty or six.

I remembered from my own minor league career of daily reporting that talking to a reporter *early in the day* is essential. A late afternoon interview is better than no interview at all—you may still be quoted—but if you want the reporter to have a chance to follow whatever leads you may have, you need to talk to him or her early in the day.

I panicked. This might be the opportunity to help turn this story around, and I'd blown it by not being at the office to pick up the phone. I took a couple of deep breaths and tried to calm down. I would call Corcoran back, but it was important that I have something memorable and useful to say to her. What should I say? The challenge was to communicate something about the fallaciousness of the Rimm study that was simultaneously *memorable* and *fundamentally true*. How could I make the problems inherent in the Rimm study understandable to a newspaper reader without misrepresenting or oversimplifying them? What I needed was a good meme.

In a moment it came to me: a major problem of the Rimm article was that Rimm (supposedly) had surveyed adult-oriented computer bulletin board systems, then claimed to be able to generalize about porn on the information superhighway. He'd skewed his sample, and he got skewed results. Since part of preaching about civil liberties for the Net means drawing parallels to traditional media, the thing to do was find a way to explain Rimm's blunder in terms of those media. I hit upon this phrase: "It's as if he'd surveyed adult bookstores in Times Square and then generalized about the content in Barnes and Noble nationwide."

Now I could call Corcoran. But, dammit, I got her voice mail. How to make sure that she called me back? Say something edgy and memorable, you idiot, I told myself—something that the Beltway bureaucrats she normally interviews would never say. "Hello, Elizabeth?" I said to her voice mail. "This is Mike Godwin at EFF, calling you back. I just want to say I'd be happy to give you a comment about that *goddamn abortion* of a study."[16] Not particularly subtle, but the best I could do on short notice. In any case, whether because of my comment or not, Corcoran called back within twenty minutes of my phone call, and I got to give her my Barnes and Noble sound bite and walk her through what I took to be the major problems with the study and the *Time* story. Amazingly, she'd read the study herself (not every newspaper reporter would have taken the time), so that part was easy. I also referred her to Hoffman, who was due back at her Vanderbilt office later that afternoon.

After the *Post* interview, I called Donna and told her that Corcoran might be calling and summed up what I knew about the study (she hadn't yet received the photocopy from me). "It's much worse than we thought," I told her. "It's worse than you can possibly imagine. It's as if someone had deliberately contrived something to generate a panic about online porn."

Then I sat down and tried to get calm for the *Nightline* taping, which was set for four o'clock. (Normally *Nightline* is live, but occasionally, when all the preparations for the show are already in place and the guests are available, it can be taped earlier in the day. That's what happened this time: the show had a taped lead-in about the Rimm study, featuring interviews with Philip and Rimm, among others, and the lead-in would be followed by a discussion among me, Ralph Reed, and Ted Koppel.)

I tried to plan what I wanted to say. I had been told that although the taped lead-in would deal with the Rimm study, the discussion component of the show would address the Internet censorship legislation (the Communications Decency Amendment) then before the Congress. So although I was prepared to discuss the Rimm study if I had to, my primary strategy was to reuse a tactic that had worked the previous week: I'd lead with my own commitment to children and family values and only then stress the First Amendment problems with the Communications Decency Amendment and similar legislation. I also resolved to volunteer little, if anything, about the problems with the Rimm study. Although I was increasingly worried that the study might be a deliberate fraud, I knew that I didn't yet have enough evidence to show it to be one. Corcoran, who'd quickly grasped the methodological questions I was raising (and might well have raised them herself even if I hadn't), could deal with them in tomorrow's *Post,* but it wasn't tomorrow yet, and I didn't have that story in hand. The last thing I wanted to do was get into some kind of argument about percentages. If I did, Reed could just say, "Who cares what the exact percentages are? What matters is that the porn is there at all! And kids can find it there!" Cut to a commercial.

Once my intern, Beth, and I arrived at ABC, we informed the desk of our presence and were soon met by a woman whose job it was to shepherd us to the show's "green room." As we went up the elevator, I "casually" mentioned to my intern that it looked as if Wednesday's *Post* would have a story detailing the problems with the Rimm study. Our escort looked alarmed. "Have you told Richard Harris about this?" she asked. (Harris was the ABC journalist who'd assembled the segment on the Rimm study that would be the lead-in for that night's discussion.) "Uh, no," I said. "I haven't talked to Harris."

"Well, would it be okay with you if I sent him in to talk to you while you're having your makeup done?"

"Sure," I said. Bingo! I thought. Maybe I could persuade ABC to look into the Rimm study themselves or at least not to hype it.

The makeup guy at ABC turned out to be a real artist—he made me look vastly more calm and more human than I was feeling. As I was being made up, Harris came into the makeup room carrying a legal pad. I tried to give him thumbnail sketches of the problems with the study and an account of what I'd told the *Post*. He realized that he had more questions than I could answer before the taping, so he asked me if it would be okay if he set up a conference call for me, him, Philip, and Rimm in the green room after the taping. (Remember that the show was being taped, and the discussion section wouldn't deal with the study directly, so if I managed to point out a problem with the study that ABC needed to address, they could fix the taped lead-in before it aired later that evening.) I eagerly agreed. Not only might I be able to get ABC to balance its coverage, but this might be my chance to question Rimm directly and see if I could find out what was really going on with the study.

As we were discussing the call, Koppel came in. At first I didn't recognize him. I'd been so preoccupied with my issues that I hadn't given any thought to the fact that I might meet the guy face-to-face. "Just today I learned something very interesting about the Internet," he said to me as he began to put on his own makeup. (I was very impressed that he was his own makeup man.) "Did you know the Internet was designed to survive a nuclear attack? Yet here's Congress, trying to censor the thing by passing a law."

I knew that what Koppel had "learned" was not technically correct, although it is part of the mythology of the Net. Certainly it is possible that the Internet, decentralized as it is, could survive such an attack, but that's not what it was designed for.[17]

But I didn't think it was the time or place to correct Koppel on what (I feared) he'd take to be a sort of nitpick. Hence my response: "And, you know, if it can survive a nuclear attack, it surely can survive a U.S. attorney." Koppel smiled: that was the theme he was planning to explore in the evening's show. I told him I'd follow his lead.

Conspicuous by his absence in the D.C. studio was Ralph Reed, who'd take the other side of the debate. Reed had arranged to be beamed in from a TV studio owned and operated by the Christian Coalition in Virginia. I was taken to the studio proper, where technicians attached a microphone and an earpiece to me, and a TV camera was positioned in front of me. Koppel would be in another room, positioned behind the desk now familiar to late-night-TV viewers. It was an odd feeling—the three of us in these separate rooms yet acting as if we were all physically in one discussion forum.

In that respect, I realized, it was very much like cyberspace.

Before the interview, I'd get a chance to see the next-to-final version of the taped lead-in segment that would, come airtime, precede the pretaped discussion segment featuring Reed and me.

What I saw wasn't exactly encouraging. The segment began in a way that couldn't have been better calculated to make anyone drowsing in front of the TV sit up with a start (which is to say, it functioned well as dramatic television):

Announcer: June 27th, 1995.

Marty Rimm: Necrophilia, for those who are interested in sex with the dead.

Ted Koppel: [voice-over] It's the kind of smut many of the porn stores won't even carry.

Marty Rimm: Pedophilia, bestiality, vaginal and rectal fisting, sadomasochism.

Ted Koppel: [voice-over] Now, it's the kind of material you and your kids can see with just the click of a button. . . . Tonight, cybersex: policing pornography on the Internet.

Announcer: This is ABC News *Nightline*. Reporting from Washington, Ted Koppel.

Great, I thought. *This* will really calm things down.

I paid close attention to the segment—not just to prep for our discussion, which would follow almost immediately afterward, but for two other reasons as well. First, I wanted to see what Marty Rimm looked and sounded like. Second, Harris had asked me back in the makeup room to take note of anything in the segment that was factually false, which I tried to do.

Although I'd hoped Harris and his team would produce something much less sensationalistic, the segment was consistently button-pushing throughout. Indeed, if you weren't paying attention, you might not even notice that a couple of the taped comments from one interviewee had nothing to do with "policing pornography on the Internet."

I almost laughed (maybe to keep from crying) at how *Nightline* was using *Joy of Cybersex* author Nancy Tamosaitis's comments, with their shocking revelation that you're likely to receive indecent proposals if you identify yourself as a fifteen-year-old girl and then pick a "chat" area labeled "Man Seeks Woman." Many folks in such chat rooms, it was widely known among chat room participants, would assume that a person using such a profile was an adult (possibly a male adult) playing a fantasy role—one deliberately attempting to be provocative.

Other aspects of the segment were also troubling, especially its handling of the issue of child pornography. At one point, for example, the segment confuses child pornography and children's access to pornography.[18] Most people find either phenomenon pretty disturbing, of course, but I knew from my first pass through the law journal article that the *actual data* Rimm supposedly had gathered scarcely touched on either of these issues any more than it had on child predation in chat rooms.

What the taped lead-in taught me, in short, was the degree of understanding on the part of the reporters who crafted it. I gave up hope of trying to persuade the ABC guys they had anything wrong.

Of course, they were right to see a child porn theme in the Rimm study. Although he had no data on child pornography or on children's access to porn, Rimm seemed to delight in writing about it, whether in his discussions about the laws regulating the Net, his speculations about the issues that his study supposedly raised for policymakers, his discussion of what he said were the marketing strategies of Robert Thomas (an individual BBS operator), or his litany of shocking descriptions used to market (non–child pornographic) images over the "information superhighway." It was still another aspect of the study that seemed crafted for its shock value and that suggested Rimm was pursuing some kind of agenda.

This was why I was disturbed, as I sat there watching the tape and trying to get focused, at this comment from Rimm:

Dave Marash: [voice-over] And the Carnegie study turned up even more disturbing data.

Marty Rimm: The demand for child pornography is way out of proportion to its availability or supply, so that those pornographers willing to risk violation of child pornography laws are reaping huge profits.

Finally, it came to me: the manner, delivery, and context of *each* of Rimm's comments seemed precisely calculated to maximize the alarm it would cause in *Nightline*'s audience. It was as if Rimm, while trying to keep a straight-faced, professional manner, was also trying to stress each sexual term.

If I'd been called upon to talk on national TV about explicit sexual imagery, whether violent or otherwise, I'd probably come across much the way Philip did in his segment:

Philip Elmer-Dewitt, Time magazine: He found that if he—if he—if he just described an act of oral sex, a photograph of oral sex, just straight oral sex, it wasn't a particularly popular picture. Not a lot of people chose to download it. But if, in his description, he included the word "choke" or "choking," it would double the number of hits.

Philip's self-presentation—some stutters, some repetition, and a nervous look—was something of a contrast to Rimm's delivery, I thought. True, there was something a little strained about Rimm's comments, yet the sheer ease with which the words rolled out of Rimm's mouth had me wondering whether he enjoyed saying them on national television.

But nothing I saw in Rimm's broadcast comments that afternoon amounted to solid evidence of anything—not even his helpful willingness to define *necrophilia* when his article does not even contain that word or any discussion at all about finding that kind of content on the Net.

Maybe the sensationalism was a result of the editing process. I knew from other times I'd been interviewed for TV that producers and editors often construct the illusion that a taped comment is the answer to the particular voice-over question coming from the correspondent. In reality, the voice we hear during the broadcast at that point is a spliced-in retake of the correspondent, often done much later in the production process. The justification for that practice, I knew, was that sometimes the producers want to make the question fit more closely to the answer the interviewee gave. It might be that everything weird about the substance of Rimm's comments could be attributed to the editing process.

I couldn't get a thing from Rimm's performance that proved anything one way or the other about his agenda, or even if he had one. The most I had was what I'd come to the studio with: a strong sense that the study had been skewed to have a particular effect and absolute certainty that, considered simply as social science research, the law journal article was deeply flawed in ways that should be obvious to anyone who'd ever had to read such literature, including Philip.

Which meant zip. Even if the problems with the Rimm study were so compelling that any subsequent scholarly review of it would kill it, that review could take months.

This is such a disaster, I thought as I waited for the voice in my earpiece to tell me that the interview was about to begin. Despite the *Post* story I expected to be published tomorrow, I had nothing in place big enough to counter the enormous impact the *Time* story had already had. Regardless of how I did on *Nightline* (where I was not asked about the Rimm study and didn't talk about it), and regardless of how good the *Post* story tomorrow was, I thought, I didn't know how far I could take it all beyond that. In the final minute before I'd be talking with Koppel, my only thought was that I was up the creek with no paddle in sight.

By contrast, the procensorship forces were getting every possible break. Deen Kaplan, then a vice president of the National Coalition for the Protection of Children and Families (formerly known as the National Coalition Against Pornography), appeared in the taped lead-in yet somehow escaped being identified with the antiporn group. Not that this association would have hurt Kaplan necessarily, but it seemed as if the social-conservative connection was being deliberately obscured, with ABC's cooperation:

Dave Marash: It's literally child's play?

Marty Rimm: Is it literally child's play? I think, within the next few years, within the next year or so, it will become child's play.

Dave Marash: [voice-over] How easy? Deen Kaplan showed us on the computer in his Virginia office.

H. Deen Kaplan, family welfare advocate: A child who is on the Internet, as we are now, would merely go and call up a little window, and if they wanted to search on the word "sex" in the Usenet newsgroups, and find some of those groups, at least, that have to deal with the topic of sex, they would put the word in and start searching. Then they could go through and the first thing that they would come up to is alt.binaries. pictures.group-sex, which is a group devoted specifically to distribution of photographs and images devoted to group sex.

That such a scenario was extremely unlikely bothered me less (as I watched Kaplan on the tape) than the fact that Kaplan's political association had been omitted. It was so unfair! Since the Constitution benefits families, I asked myself, don't I get to be a family welfare advocate too?

Still, I kept my composure and managed to stay on message when the interview segment of the show began. I had resolved to answer whatever question Koppel first asked me in a way that affirmed my own commitment to family values and the well-being of children. And I had to take the lead on this point. If I waited until my pro–First Amendment position was attacked, anything I said in response to that attack would sound as if it were desperate or defensive. Hence my almost comical non sequitur of a response to Koppel's first question to me:

Ted Koppel: Joining us now from Virginia Beach, Virginia, Ralph Reed. He is executive director of the Christian Coalition. And joining us from our Washington bureau, Mike Godwin, counsel for the Electronic Frontier Foundation. He advises electronic networks about their legal rights and responsibilities. Is there, first of all, Mr. Godwin, any disagreement about whether some of this material needs to be kept out of the hands of children?

Mike Godwin, Electronic Frontier Foundation: Well, you know, I'm a parent myself, and I'm concerned about my little girl who will grow up, be the first person in my family to grow up with the Internet, so I'm concerned about being able to make choices for my little girl about what kind of material is appropriate.

But non sequitur or no, my staking out of the pro-parent position early on seemed to work against Reed as it had against Taylor. Although he was no pushover, Reed never cast me in the role I feared I couldn't avoid: that of the antifamily liberal activist. Although I stumbled here and there, I felt at the end of the taping that I had held my own. This allowed me to focus on what I'd say to Marty Rimm and Philip when I had a chance to talk with them in the conference call, which ABC's Harris hoped would show him whether he needed to alter the taped lead-in before it aired and which I hoped would give me a handle on what was going on with the Rimm study.

I had already decided how I'd handle myself during the call. If given the chance to take the lead in questioning Rimm, I would ask him cross-examination questions designed to see whether he would admit the weaknesses in his research. If he did admit them, it would at minimum buttress some of the criticisms of the study that (as I was trying to convince ABC) were the most troubling. If he didn't, well, then I'd have a sense of how honest Rimm actually was. As it happened, though, the most explosive comment during the conference call came not from me or from Rimm but from Philip.

As we wound down but before we lost the connection, I heard this:

Philip: Marty, you there?

Rimm: Yes, I'm here.

Philip: (slight pause) Good job!

As I posted a summary of the *Nightline* experience along with Philip's final remark on the WELL for journalists and nonjournalists alike to read, I hoped they would also see in Philip's last comment what I saw in it: that he had become so invested in the success of the story on the Rimm study that he had actually *taken Marty's side* and abandoned the kind of skepticism that reporters are routinely expected to apply to all sides in a controversial story.

In fact, that was how it had been playing out in the WELL's media conference. (Even as I had been preparing to respond to the *Time* story using traditional mass media, I'd been taking the time to read the study and post about it to the WELL.) WELL members who followed the topic were appalled first of all by Philip's having identified himself with Marty and then by Philip's attempt to explain it away in a publicly posted message:

media.1029.215: Philip Elmer-DeWitt (ped) Tue 27 Jun 95 19:13
OK, I confess. I told Rimm he's done a good job. He had. It was a fascinating conversation.

Philip explained the *Time* story's flaws as a function of deadline constraints. "If we'd had more time—and more presence of mind—we would have called in an outside expert to review the study. But I had to go from editing the Estrogen cover to writing the Cyberporn cover with only a weekend in between to catch up on my sleep. Such is life at a newsmagazine these days." With regard to the story's packaging, Philip said, "I'm pissed at whoever wrote the caption that painted me as "shocked" by the stuff online. I'm also not crazy about the art inside. I kind of like the cover, on the other hand." This led to a posting by a user named <lizabeth>, whose outraged response was more eloquent than anything I'd posted:

media.1029.220: little modem on the prairie (lizabeth) Tue 27 Jun 95 19:33
Phil slipped in.
Phil, you've just said the first thing in your responses that really is annoying:
  ["]If we'd had more time—and more presence of mind—we would have called in an outside expert to review the study. But I had to go from editing the Estrogen cover to writing the Cyberporn cover with only a weekend in between to catch up on my sleep. Such is life at a newsmagazine these days."
  Let me see if I get this straight: the Rimm report is a story that just couldn't possibly wait for a week or a month or whatever, because it is newsworthy only this week, for one week only? I don't buy that. I don't buy it about the estrogen story, either—it was timely with recent research, but hardly the stuff of urgent publication. The Rimm report would have waited for the most important thing you could have done, and that is that outside expert review. This sort of review is so goddamn critical in something so volatile and important as this that I'm having trouble believing *Time* could bring itself to ethically do the article without it.
  I'm not minimizing the issue of being scooped by other publications, but even if you were, you could have then done the *real* story and made them look like idiots for rushing to press with a breathless tale of porn online that didn't even have its methodology scrutinized. Even if you were to have found that the study was flawless in every way, it would have been worth it.
  Time is extremely irresponsible in publishing this cover without this. It cannot be waved away by saying that these are the breaks the truth gets when people are in a hurry. You know, if a surgeon does that, and the results are not so hot, it's called malpractice. If a lawyer does it, it's called malpractice. If a journalist does it, it should be called fiction, at best. Rushing into something that doesn't get to really major and important aspects of a study like this and the real facts, which will probably result in a huge roadblock to the most sociological significant technology in recent history . . . well, it might be called obscene, if obscenity still meant something other than dirty pictures.
  Time really, really should regret this error. This cover story will be the single most important factor if the [Communications Decency Amendment, then before the Congress] gets passed after all.

From this point on, other participants in the WELL's media conference began to offer their own criticisms. Some of the most pointed comments came from people who'd seen nothing obviously wrong with the *Time* story when they first skimmed it, but who, once they realized how slipshod the crafting of that cover story had been, abandoned their earlier, more charitable presumption that Philip had gotten the story right. While the other participants began to play a more active role in challenging *Time*'s account of the study, I labored to get as much of the study itself in front of them as I possibly could—often by typing in a passage myself—so that they could see the questionable substance of the study and draw their own conclusions as to whether Philip and *Time* should have had second thoughts about endorsing it. Not a day went by over the next week or two when I was not scanning the *Georgetown Law Journal* article to find still more examples of the red flags Philip should have spotted himself. One of the most telling passages, it seemed to me, was the one I commented on in this posting:

media.1029.427: Avant Garde A Clue (mnemonic) Fri 30 Jun 95 14:00
Here's footnote 9 for the Rimm article:
"9. As a result of federal legal action against a few well-known adult BBS operators, including Robert and Carleen Thomas (Amateur Action) and Robert Copella (Pequena Panacha), some systems have removed their paraphilic, pedophilic, and hebephilic imagery from public display. This has created a thriving underground market for 'private collections' and anonymous ftp sites on the Internet, which cannot be studied systematically. Thus, it may be difficult for researchers to repeat this study, as much valuable data is no longer publicly available. See infra notes 89–95 and accompanying text."
Now, Philip, try answering this quiz:
Of the many unsupported assertions in this single footnote, which one would raise the *biggest* red flag for a reader/editor working for a peer-reviewed journal?
  If you can't answer this question correctly, you are not competent to evaluate this kind of research. If you can, you have some explaining to do.

A sociologist named Jim Thomas followed up on the same point and answered my question before Philip had a chance to:

media.1029.433: jim thomas (jthomas) Fri 30 Jun 95 15:32
((sorry for the length of these posts, but they can't readily be done in a single screen))
Beating me to a point I was going to raise later tonight, Mike slips in:
  This has created a thriving underground market for "private collections" and anonymous ftp sites on the Internet, which cannot be studied systematically.

As a practical matter, an ftp site can be studied in the same "practical manner" as adult BBSes. Rimm's presumption seems to be that identifying them would be difficult. If the market in fact is "thriving," identifying and gaining access should be trivial. Perhaps Rimm was confused by the term "*anonymous* ftp sites." Rimm's footnotes (such as this one) illustrate the importance of reading footnotes. Rimm makes an explicit claim as if it were a demonstrable fact. He is saying that highly visible porn busts have created an alternative market. This can be readily tested. Let's call it the "displacement theory of 'porn' distribution." The basic logic: As porn is actively suppressed in one area of cyberspace (BBSes), it emerges in other (likely less public) areas.

Independent variable: porn suppression on BBSes

Dependent variable: emergence of "underground" markets

If the hypothesis holds, we could expect to find covariance between our variables—in this case, as the magnitude of the IV increases, so, too, does the magnitude of the DV.

Now, we can argue about extraneous variables (e.g., the dynamics of any underground economy) as alternative explanations, none of which Rimm considers. But, there is another minor flaw here (other than the fact that no data are presented): Rimm violates one of the four fundamental premises of causal logic: A "cause" generally comes before its "effect." There has been a thriving "underground market" (effect) well before recent busts (cause). Logic aside, here's a clear case of a seemingly minor claim made without providing evidence or pointers. Such small claims combine to reinforce the central thesis of self-evident Net porn.

Let's take another example of such logic, which we can call the "deprivation thesis":

An unusual amount of data was freely available from commercial "adult" BBS primarily as a consequence of the evolution of the online industry. Large commercial BBS such as America Online, CompuServe, and Prodigy do not carry hardcore pornographic imagery, either for legal or policy reasons. As a consequence, several thousand comparatively small "adult" BBS have sprung up across the country (p. 1861).

Today's in-class exercise: Drawing from the first example, what's wrong with this picture?

"Thus, it may be difficult for researchers to repeat this study, as much valuable data is no longer publicly available. See infra notes 89–95 and accompanying text."

This is the best proactive dodge to hedge replication failure that I have ever seen. "What I tell you is true, but if you can't replicate it, hey . . . that ain't my problem."

Replication is a sine qua non of normal science. A credible scholar would identify ways to replicate rather than try to explain away a failure to replicate. In my eyes, this single tidbit alone disqualifies the "study" as legitimate. It also sounds warning bells about the quality of the data.

I'm also not sure which data Rimm feels are "no longer available." I also wish that somebody had taught him that "BBS" is singular.

The temptation to keep adding to the evidence that the Rimm story was a crock and that Philip should have seen it is nearly overwhelming, but perhaps I've done enough here already. And over time, I've come to believe that the particular evidence in this instance matters less than what we proved about the ability of a community like the WELL to correct the record when the traditional media get the story wrong.

This ability of online communities to see that the record gets corrected is something anyone can use. Sure, I had some friends I could call in for help (people like Donna and Jim), but even if you have different friends, the fact is that in the online world, you almost certainly know somebody who can cast some rays of light for you when you're seeking to correct a misrepresentation in the mainstream media. What mattered was less who I knew than what I knew.

Specifically, although I never allowed myself the luxury of supposing we would succeed in forcing *Time* to print a retraction (something the magazine had done only a very few times in its history), I still knew what steps to take to increase the likelihood that the magazine would do something to correct its blunder. In a way, I'd finally come up with an adequate encore to my 1990 posting on an Austin, Texas, bulletin board system about "Talking to Media."[19]

If my experience with the Steve Jackson Games case had served to illustrate the point that an individual citizen can bring a story to light, our experience on the WELL in responding to the *Time*-cyberporn scandal underscored the fact that a properly focused small group of individuals can use the Net to make even the most powerful institutions of the traditional mass media more accountable than they ever have been before. Here are the rules that seemed to work when we took on *Time* magazine:

1. Respond fast!

I knew the magazine would be on the stands for a week and that every day it was on the stands, its impact would increase. It was important that whatever response we came up with to the study—once we'd determined with a reasonable certainty how rotten it was—be launched *immediately*. The nine-thousand-word critique of the Rimm article by Donna and her husband turned out to be central to this effort, but it would not have been so had she and Tom not seen the need to respond quickly. Thanks to my legal interns, they had a photocopy of the study in hand by Tuesday of the week of the *Time* issue's publication; their formal responses to both the *Time* article and the Rimm study itself were complete by the weekend. And Donna and Tom had taken my insistence that we have a formal response one critical step further: they posted their responses to their own site on the World Wide Web, http://www2000.ogsm.vanderbilt. edu.[20] (The site is located at the Owen Graduate School of Management.)

2. Talk to the academics first, and give them the information they need.

In addition to the copies I had sent to Donna, copies of the Rimm article also went to Jim Thomas and, most significant, to Brian Reid, the DEC researcher whose long-standing publication of certain Usenet usage statistics had been cited (inappropriately, as it turned out) by Rimm. Reid's criticism, which came a week later, after I'd begged him in e-mail to take time to look at the Rimm study, was arguably the most damning criticism Rimm faced: it was worded more harshly and, coming from a person who was ostensibly the source of some of Rimm's more general data, was particularly telling in academic as well as in journalistic circles.[21]

3. Plan for the follow-up story.

Elizabeth Corcoran of the *Post* ultimately wrote a great story about the Rimm controversy, but the fact is that a single story in a daily newspaper, even a great newspaper like the *Washington Post,* can't balance the effect a story like *Time*'s article (which is distributed in the millions nationally and internationally, and which stays on the stand for at least a week) can have. When the *Post* story appeared, I allowed myself to feel good about it for twenty minutes or so, then began to worry about what I was going to do for a follow-up. Fortunately, the Rimm-*Time* scandal was so rich in bad judgment, media arrogance, colorful anecdote, and other details (or so it seemed to me) that it should be possible to persuade other journalists that there were important unexplored angles to the story—angles they could make their own. What I did next was approach the *New York Times*'s cyberspace writer Pete Lewis (by both telephone and e-mail) and tell him I thought the *Post* had neglected to tell the whole story about *Time*'s questionable arrangements with Rimm. (As always, and following the same principles that I outline in chapter 2, I was telling a reporter only what I had reason to believe was true.) I also told him that he need not rely solely on my intuitions. I invited him over to the WELL, where the public dissection of the *Time* story was in full swing. (By Wednesday the number of new messages was approaching one thousand, with no sign of any slowdown.) Pete later sent me a short e-mail message to tell me he'd read the *Time* topic and wanted to interview me formally about the story. The subject header of his e-mail, which came after he'd spent hours online catching up, was memorable: "Subject: Time. WELL. Spent."

Once the *Times* had done a story on the Rimm scandal, every other city newspaper in the country, plus the wire services, became interested in playing catch-up. There was a landslide of news stories, and it was all this attention that finally led to the disinterring of Marty Rimm's unusual past. Investigative reporters from the *Atlantic City Press* remembered that a guy named Rimm had figured in some casino-related pranks a few years back. Thus was Rimm's credibility finally sunk. He was disinvited from his guest star spot at Senator Grassley's upcoming cyberporn hearing.

Deen Kaplan of the National Coalition had also become a problematic substitute witness for the hearings once I'd learned and publicized his role as an editor of the *Georgetown Law Journal* and his likely involvement in crafting and placing the Rimm article there. Grassley's hearings became a sort of nonevent, which had a powerful result none of us anticipated at the time: that without Rimm and his study, crafted to be the central evidence for new legislation against the alleged problem of cyberporn, Congress was left with an awfully weak case when the government had to defend the CDA against constitutional challenges the following year.

4. Go to the other side's sources.

It was when I took the time to go to Rimm's sources—in context and with an eye for any clue as to his background and motivations—that I found quite a bit of evidence that led me to suspect he'd snowed the law professors who endorsed his study for the law journal. And it is in Rimm's footnotes that one can find much evidence that Rimm's help came from religious right antiporn activists, plus a lot of internal evidence that the study is deliberately manipulative. Thus, it turned out, Marty got his wish from me: I'd ended up reviewing his damned footnotes after all!

2002 Update: Brian Reid's Open Letter about the Rimm Article

When assembling the first edition of this book, I frequently felt that there was not enough evidence in this chapter to show the extent to which Rimm's study was patently, almost comically, a crock, and the sheer obviousness of the flaws in what Rimm said and published, which *Time* and others should have seen. The most succinct analysis of what was wrong with the Rimm article came from Brian Reid, a computer scientist who for years had researched trends among Usenet newsgroups. In June 2002, I obtained his permission to include here his "open letter" of 1995, drafted only a few days after I arranged to send him a copy of the Rimm article:

From: Brian Reid
Subject: Critique of the Rimm study
Date: Wed, 05 Jul 95 20:30:49 -0700
X-Mts: smtp

I have read a preprint of the Rimm study of pornography and I am so distressed by its lack [of] scientific credibility that I don't even know where to begin critiquing it. Normally when I am sent a publication for review, if I find a flaw in it I can identify it and say "here, in this paragraph, you are making some unwarranted assumptions." In this study I have trouble finding measurement techniques that are *not* flawed. The writer appears to me not to have a glimmer of an understanding even of basic statistical measurement technique, let alone of the application of that technique to something as elusive and ill-defined as USENET.

I have been measuring USENET readership and analyzing USENET content, and publishing studies of what I find since April 1986. I have spent years refining the measurement techniques and the data processing algorithms. Despite those 9 years of working on the problem, I still do not believe that it is possible to get measurements whose accuracy is within a factor of 10 of the truth. In other words, if I measure something that seems to be 79, the truth might be 790 or 7.9 or anywhere in between. Despite this inaccuracy, the measurements are interesting, because whatever unknowns it is that they are measuring, these unknowns are similar from one month to the next, so that the study of trends is meaningful. As long as you are aware of what it is that you are taking the ratio of, it is also meaningful to compare USENET measurements, because whatever the errors might be, they are often similar in two numbers from the same measurement set, and they are multiplicative, so they tend to cancel out in quotient. In other words, in the results that I publish, the two kinds of measurements that are meaningful enough to pay attention to for serious scholarship are the normalized month-to-month trends in the readership percentages of a given newsgroup, and the within-the-same-month ratio of the readership of one newsgroup to the readership of another. The reason that I publish the numbers is primarily to enable trend analysis; it is not reasonable to take a single-point measurement seriously. No matter what the level of accuracy you are seeking, it is imperative that you understand what it is that you are measuring. Whenever you cannot measure an entire population, you must find and measure a sample, and the error in your measurement will be magnified if your sample is not a representative sample. A small error in understanding the nature of the sample population will lead to an error like the famous "Dewey defeats Truman" headline in the 1948 US Presidential election. A large error in understanding the nature of the sample population can lead to results that are completely meaningless, such as measuring pregnancy rates in a population whose age and sex are unknown. Rimm has made three "beginner's errors" that, in my opinion, when taken together, render his numbers completely meaningless:

1. He has selected a very homogeneous population to measure. While he has chosen not to identify his population, he has included enough of his sample data to allow me to correlate his numbers with my own numbers for the same measurement period. His data correlate exactly with my numbers for Pittsburgh newsgroups in that measurement period; only his own university (Carnegie-Mellon) has widespread enough campus networking to make it possible for him to sample that large a population. It is therefore almost certain that he has measured his own university. I received my Ph.D. in Computer Science from Carnegie-Mellon University, and I am very aware that it is dominantly male and dominantly a technology school. The behavior of computer-using students at a high-tech urban engineering school might not be very similar to the behavior of other student populations, let alone non-student populations.

2. He has measured only one time period, January 1995. Having lived at Carnegie-Mellon University for a number of years, I know first-hand that student interests in January are extremely different from student interests in September or April. When measuring human behavior about which very little is known, it is important to take numerous measurements over time and to look for time series. Taking the last few years worth of my data and doing a trend analysis in the newsgroups that he has named as pornographic shows an average 3:1 seasonal trend change between low-readership months (November and April) and high-readership months (September and January). But the trends are different in different newsgroups. A single-point measurement is not nearly as meaningful as a series of measurements.

3. He makes the assumption that by seeing a data reference to an image or a file, it is possible to tell what the individual did with the file. We in the network measurement business are very careful to explain what it is that our measurements mean. Here is the standard explanation that I publish with my monthly measurements to talk about the number that Rimm calls "number of downloads."

To "read" a newsgroup means to have been presented with the opportunity to look at at least one message in it. Going through a newsgroup with the "n" key counts as reading it. For a news site, "user X reads group Y" means that user X's .newsrc file has marked at least one unexpired message in Y.

Rimm used my network measurement software tools to take his data, and he did not anywhere in his article state that he had made changes to them, so I must conclude that his numbers and my numbers are derived from the same software. But the number that he is using for "number of downloads" is the same number that I call "number of readers" by the above definition. It has nothing to do with the number of downloads. In fact, it is not possible for this measurement system to tell whether or not a file has been downloaded; it can tell whether or not a person has been presented with the opportunity to download a file but it cannot tell whether the user answered "yes" or "no."

In summary, I do not consider Rimm's analysis to have enough technical rigor to be worthy of publication in a scholarly journal.

Brian Reid, Ph.D.
Director, Network Systems Laboratory
Digital Equipment Corporation
Palo Alto, California
reid@pa.dec.com
http://www.research.digital.com/nsl/people/reid/bio.html

10

Courting the Future: The Communications Decency Act of 1996

It really struck me in your opening statement when you mentioned, Mr. Chairman, that it is the first ever hearing [about "cyberporn"], and you are absolutely right. And yet we had a major debate on the floor, passed legislation overwhelmingly on a subject involving the Internet, legislation that could dramatically change, some would say even wreak havoc on, the Internet. The Senate went in willy-nilly, passed legislation, and never once had a hearing, never once had a discussion other than an hour or so on the floor
—Senator Patrick Leahy (D, Vermont), on the Communications Decency Act

On a cold, snowy day early in January 1996, I tromped awkwardly through the midtown slush of New York City to meet Chris Hansen and Marjorie Heins of the American Civil Liberties Union for the first time. Another ACLU lawyer, Ann Beeson (a former judicial clerk, like me a native Texan), would also be there. I had met Ann in Washington, D.C., the previous year when she was working with another nonprofit group, Human Rights Watch.

Our plan for today was to meet for lunch and discuss the final preparations of our challenge to the constitutionality of the Communications Decency Act. The CDA, introduced in 1994 by Senator James Exon, had been ramrodded through both houses of Congress with no serious debate and no hearings at all in the summer and fall of 1995 partly as a result of the cyberporn panic stoked by *Time*'s cover story.[1]

The case we were planning would, we believed, become the first to go to the Supreme Court that directly addressed the First Amendment–free speech significance of the Internet. The Exon-sponsored law, as it was structured, would effectively ban from the public spaces of the Net a broad range of speech that would be perfectly legal if heard on the street corner or published in a book. The law addressed a misleadingly named category of speech called "indecent," which, contrary to claims made by the law's proponents, was not limited to pornography. There were cases in which comedy routines or talk radio shows or even poetry by the late poet Allen Ginsberg had been classified as "indecent"—a term that had never been defined by the Supreme Court but that nevertheless was used loosely by the Court to refer to content that the FCC could prevent broadcasters from disseminating on radio or TV when children were (presumably) most likely to be listening.

This strange, undefined category of speech called "indecent" had long been understood to be protected by the First Amendment, however, and the Supreme Court had consistently said it could not be banned altogether from a mass medium—unlike, say, obscenity or child pornography (which, being unprotected by the First Amendment, *can* be banned). Yet a ban of "indecent" speech in the public spaces of the Net was just what the Exon legislation seemed likely to accomplish.

Nor would that be the only impact of the law, which also seemed designed to take the federal government's role in regulating broadcasting— TV and radio—and expand it to cover the Internet. For me, this was even more troubling than the banning of "indecent" speech. In recent decades, the government's power to regulate content had been understood by the courts to be narrowly confined to the arena of broadcast programming— that is, the FCC can regulate NBC's content, but under our Constitution, it can't regulate content in the *New York Times* or in Paramount's movies . . . or in this book. But the pro-censorship forces behind the Exon legislation saw the Internet—and the public's anxiety about it—as an opportunity to establish, once and for all, the right of the federal government to regulate content in all new mass media, not just radio and TV. Such an outcome would spell disaster for freedom of speech in the next century and beyond, I believed, as did Chris, Marjorie, and Ann. This was why we (along with other ACLU lawyers and attorneys from the Electronic Privacy Information Center) were planning this challenge even before the Exon amendment had been signed into law. We knew what the censors were up to, and we believed they had to be stopped.

For several weeks Chris, Marjorie, Ann, and I had been discussing in e-mail the draft of our "complaint" (the document you first file when you bring a lawsuit). Other lawyers, notably Marc Rotenberg and David Sobel of the Electronic Privacy Information Center (EPIC), both of whom I'd known for years, had also participated. I had never actually met Chris or Marjorie face-to-face, however, and I was looking forward to lunch.

The very fact that I was meeting with the ACLU signified how much things had changed since I began doing cyber rights law back in 1990. When I started working for EFF, right out of law school, only a few lawyers were knowledgeable about the Net, so it was often the case that when trying to solve a free speech problem that had arisen in cyberspace, I had to work alone. But now dozens of lawyers around the country were well informed about these issues, thanks in part to a cyberlaw mailing list run by Professor Trotter Hardy of the College of William and Mary Law School. Most of us knew one another (or at least knew *of* one another) by now.

The ACLU had been largely absent from the debates about cyberliberties from 1990 to 1993, but the organization had been electrified into action by the Communications Decency Act when it surfaced in 1994. Even if they had arguably been slow to catch up, the sheer muscle and experience the ACLU brought to the cyber-rights fight meant that it had instantly become a central player.

This left me wondering what, if anything, I had to offer the team now gearing up to challenge the CDA in court. After five years of laboring for the EFF to establish the First Amendment framework for the Net, I knew the Net-specific issues pretty well, and I had a decent amount of Internet-related legal experience I could share with the other lawyers. Supposedly I was to use my particular knowledge and experience to complement the ACLU lawyers' more general First Amendment expertise, as well as the particular skills brought to the table by people like David Sobel. David, an expert at Freedom of Information Act (FOIA) litigation, had developed during his tenure at EPIC quite a track record at forcing strategic concessions from government lawyers. Like me, he was one of the non-ACLU lawyers on our legal team.

But the other lawyers' collective skills and experience were sufficiently daunting that I worried I might be little more than a fifth wheel. So although I was excited about meeting my ACLU co-counsel, I was also a little nervous. I had many thoughts about how to frame our case and about what its long-term significance might be, but maybe they weren't particularly new or original thoughts. What if I was just wasting the other lawyers' time? Chris, Marjorie, and Ann were quick to put me at ease, however, and by the time we negotiated our way down from the ACLU offices to a nearby eatery (which was tougher than you might think, since Marjorie had broken a leg recently and was wearing an imposing and awkward cast), I was chattering away about my views on the case. We noshed on burgers and talked through case strategy.

I expressed my conviction that we should have a case that "looked like America"—whose plaintiffs, in other words, represented the full range of speech interests that could be affected by the Communications Decency Act. The ACLU lawyers had already signed up a number of plaintiffs who engaged in controversial speech, but they had been reluctant to include Internet service providers and forum providers. There was an inclination to view corporate interests as standing in opposition to individual speech interests, but I believed that (in this case, at least) both sets of interests were the same. "What's revolutionary about the Net," I insisted, "is that it blurs the distinction between 'content producers' and 'content consumers.' Nowadays we're all doing both."

When I told the other lawyers that, in my view, this was more than a chance to establish the First Amendment for the Net—"It's also a chance to roll back *Pacifica,* to roll back *Sable!*"—Chris and Marjorie paused, then looked at each other without saying anything. Had they been having these same thoughts? Perhaps they saw the same problems with the *Pacifica* and *Sable* cases that I did. I knew from our e-mail discussions that they, like me, were critical of the legal reasoning in the *Pacifica* case (discussed in chapter 2 and elsewhere), which gave us the term *indecency* (without any precise definition), plus the principle that "indecent" content, while protected by the First Amendment, could be controlled to a large degree in government-regulated broadcast media. More ominous was *Sable* v. *FCC* (1989), which I had learned was being interpreted by the pro-censorship forces in a move to take the legislation and government regulation even further. Although the Court in its *Sable* decision struck down a law that banned "indecency" outright, it also seemed to hint that such material could be regulated by the government *regardless of the medium in question.*

Despite these troubling precedents, though, we thought the case we were building had some real potential to set a good precedent and not merely prevent the setting of a bad one. What *ACLU* v. *Reno* would give us a chance to do, we all could see, was put a stop to a long-standing historical pattern in this country of giving less First Amendment protection to any new medium. Although the Supreme Court itself had not done much expressly to expand the precedents of *Pacifica* and although Justice John Paul Stevens, who had authored the *Pacifica* opinion and was still on the Court, had attempted to limit the scope of that decision and the cases that followed and interpreted it, the lower federal courts had read *Pacifica* and its progeny (notably the *Sable* case) expansively. When it came to cases challenging the regulation of broadcasting content, the government usually won.

It was the federal judiciary's favoring of the government in the broadcasting cases that had encouraged the religious right pro-censorship forces to propose the Communications Decency Act. In a sense, their plan was to convince our legal system that the Net is more or less the same thing as the broadcasting medium and therefore an appropriate object of federal content regulation.

Given that traditional media organizations, from the *New York Times* to the *Boston Globe* to the *Houston Chronicle,* were increasingly using the Net to distribute their content, the new broom of the CDA might sweep even pillars of the traditional press cleanly into the realm of government censorship.

The Stealth Legislation

The Communications Decency Act (sometimes also known as the Exon amendment) was introduced by Senator Exon in August 1994. The bill, which in its first version would have put the Internet under the control of the Federal Communications Commission and would have outlawed so-called indecency on the Net altogether, followed on the heels of the successful prosecutions of Robert and Carleen Thomas, the owners and operators of the Amateur Action BBS. Their BBS, which specialized in the commercial distribution of pornographic images, keeps resurfacing in our story, in large part because the pro-censorship forces had seized on the Thomases as a symbol of the problem of pornography on the Internet.[2] That their BBS was not itself part of the Internet, or even connected to it, was of little interest to the panicmongers, who seemed to believe that the Amateur Action BBS situation stood as proof of some kind of cyberporn problem on the Net.

The September 12, 1994, issue of *Christianity Today* was one of the first publications to sound the cyberporn alarm and even to use the neologism *cyberporn*. And it was in this magazine that H. Deen Kaplan of the National Coalition for the Protection of Families and Children announced what the legislative strategy of the religious right would be: "We need to look at [computer networks] more in terms of a broadcast medium and some of the careful restrictions that go into that to protect children." Kaplan was at that time on the staff of *Georgetown Law Journal,* which would publish the fraudulent Rimm article that fueled *Time* magazine's cover story. In other words, the plan was to build a case for putting the Internet under the same governmental controls that already applied to TV and radio. Not so coincidentally, the kind of regulation that Kaplan called for was just the kind that the CDA was designed to provide.

By the time it had been passed by both houses of Congress and tinkered with in a legislative conference committee, the CDA looked a bit different from the way it had in the summer of 1994, when Kaplan was first being quoted about the "problem of cyberporn." But it was no less dangerous to freedom of speech on the Net. The most significant way it had changed had been in response to public criticisms from me and other Net lawyers that the bill relied on undefined terms like *indecency* and that it put Internet service providers in an untenable role as content policemen, a role that would chill all sorts of legal speech on the Net.

But the changes had been more cosmetic than real. As passed, the Communications Decency Act section of the Telecommunications Reform Act amended Title 47 of the U.S. Code by adding Section 223(a)(1)(B)(ii), which criminalized the knowing transmission by computer of obscene or indecent messages to any recipient under eighteen years of age. Another section, Section 223(d), banned the knowing sending or making available to a person under age eighteen of any content that, in context, depicts or describes, in terms patently offensive as measured by contemporary community standards, sexual or excretory activities or organs. At first glance (and legislators often glance only once at the bills they vote on—if at all), it may have seemed that there was little to object to here. The transmission of "obscene" material (to a minor or anyone else) was already a felony under state and federal law. Even if no one was quite sure what *indecent* meant, surely no one could object to the provisions that criminalized the display of "indecent" material or "patently offensive" material that "depicts or describes" any "sexual or excretory activities or organs."

(The "patently offensive" language came from the FCC's working definition of *indecent,* which appeared in the agency's broadcasting regulations. The new language in Section 223(d) had been substituted for the word *indecent,* which is what had appeared there in the first version of the CDA. This substitution occurred shortly after I had debated Bruce Taylor of the National Law Center for the Protection of Children and Families and stressed that the word *indecent,* standing alone, had no established definition set by the Supreme Court or by Congress. When I saw the "patently offensive" phrase for the first time, I worried that I had unwittingly helped the would-be censors craft a less vague and potentially more constitutional bill.)

Even if the language of the bill gave the impression that it was aimed at stopping someone from shoving pornography in the faces of children on the Internet, its real effect, and one fully intended by its crafters, was far more insidious. You see, both the word *indecent* and the *patently offensive* phrases were what lawyers call "terms of art," each a kind of token that has a special legal meaning or use. Although the words might give the impression that they referred to pornography, in fact they represented a vastly broader class of speech that could include safer sex information and even some sections of federal court opinions.

Another change to the bill was the addition of "affirmative defenses" legal protections for those who take "good faith . . . effective . . . actions to restrict access by minors to the prohibited communications" (Section 223(e)(5)(A)). This had been added to a defense for providers who restricted access by requiring certain kinds of proof of one's age, such as a verified credit card or an adult driver's license number (Section 223(e)(5)(B)). But neither defense was a sure thing. Did "effective" mean that one had to guarantee that no children could get access to "indecent" communications? And if you refused access to people without credit cards, would that mean you had a total defense against prosecution for indecency?

The language of the CDA had been fudged in such a way as to leave open the possibility that even if you set up your forum to take advantage of the legal defenses, *you might be prosecuted anyway.* All in all, the revised version of the law was just as much a minefield for users and providers as the original, more blatantly restrictive law had been. And no less than the original CDA, the law that finally was passed would put Internet service providers in the role of universal content policemen, reviewing and acting as editors for nearly every message posted by every user. This meant that what most users saw as a chief advantage of the Net—the ability to talk directly to anyone around the globe without any intervening editor deciding what one could say—would be destroyed. It was as if Congress had required the phone company to have its operators approve of the content of every phone call.

The nightmarish threat this legislation posed to the Net, and to the First Amendment in general, hung on the *Pacifica* opinion. Despite the efforts of its author, Justice Stevens, to narrow the opinion's applicability, *Pacifica* led to a sizable body of "indecency" opinions in the lower courts. In doing so, the case also gave the religious right an opportunity to extend the control the federal government already had over broadcasting to the Net and, potentially, to all new media. This was what scared me most: if the right had its way, the broad protections of the First Amendment would be confined mainly to face-to-face speech and to materials published on paper. In a world in which we increasingly communicated and received content, through computer networks and other electronic media, the First Amendment would be marginalized and maybe even made irrelevant.

Preparing for the Fight

At that lunch meeting with the ACLU in New York, I resolved again to help assemble a strong, broad, and immediate challenge to the censorship provisions of the Communications Decency Act. The ACLU's plan was to develop a challenge that could be implemented so quickly that within minutes of President Clinton's signing the CDA into law, we would be in federal court seeking to halt its enforcement. We were drawn into a mounting frenzy of preparation.

Our case didn't look like a typical ACLU case. Sure, we included many plaintiffs, like Stop Prisoner Rape! and the *Queer Resources Directory,* who engaged in controversial speech that nevertheless was protected under the First Amendment. But we also included publishers, service providers, and individuals and organizations whose speech, while often provocative, was clearly central to the American public dialogue. Here's the full list of plaintiffs in our case: American Civil Liberties Union; Human Rights Watch; Electronic Privacy Information Center; Electronic Frontier Foundation; Journalism Education Association; Computer Professionals for Social Responsibility; National Writers Union; Clarinet Communications Corporation; Institute for Global Communications; Stop Prisoner Rape!; AIDS Education Global Information System; Bibliobytes; *Queer Resources Directory;* Critical Path AIDS Project, Inc.; Wildcat Press, Inc.; Declan McCullagh d/b/a Justice on Campus; Brock Meeks d/b/a *Cyberwire Dispatch;* John Troyer d/b/a the Safer Sex Page; Jonathan Wallace d/b/a the Ethical Spectacle; and Planned Parenthood Federation of America, Inc.

I was pleased we were able to include so many people I'd worked with before, especially Brock Meeks, who had been an unwilling pioneer of the law of online libel (see chapter 4), and Declan McCullagh, who had helped me expose the Marty Rimm-*Time* scandal (see chapter 9). I was elated for another reason as well. One of my long-hoped-for dreams— to see EFF itself be a party in a leading First Amendment case—was about to come true in what might turn out to be *the* important case concerning freedom of speech online.

(Its importance was underscored when a second case, *American Library Association* v. *Department of Justice,* was filed in the same federal district court in Philadelphia where we'd filed our challenge. The list of plaintiffs for this second case, whose issues were fundamentally the same as those of the ACLU case, read like a Who's Who of New Media: the American Library Association; America Online, Inc.; American Booksellers Association, Inc.; American Booksellers Foundation for Free Expression;

American Society of Newspaper Editors; Apple Computer, Inc.; Association of American Publishers, Inc.; Association of Publishers, Editors and
Writers; Citizens Internet Empowerment Coalition; Commercial Internet
Exchange Association; CompuServe Incorporated; Families Against Internet Censorship; Freedom to Read Foundation, Inc.; Health Sciences
Libraries Consortium; Hotwired Ventures LLC; Interactive Digital Software Association; Interactive Services Association; Magazine Publishers
of America; Microsoft Corporation; the Microsoft Network, LLC; National Press Photographers Association; Netcom On-Line Communication Services, Inc.; Newspaper Association of America; Opnet, Inc.;
Prodigy Services Company; Society of Professional Journalists; Wired
Ventures, Ltd.)

I was fairly certain EFF had the necessary legal standing to sue on our
own behalf, since we were a membership organization, and since in the
course of answering legal questions about sexual content on the Net, I
was often called on to discuss matters that, to some people, at least, could
qualify as patently offensive or indecent. Our members, sympathizers,
and constituents often engaged in similar discussions on free speech–
related topics on the Internet or in public forums like the ones maintained
in our name on CompuServe and America Online. But to make absolutely
sure we could reasonably say we ourselves might be prosecuted under
the CDA, which is necessary if one is to have standing to sue in a court
challenge like this one, I had EFF's online activist, Stanton McCandlish,
post the full text of the Supreme Court's 1978 decision in *FCC* v. *Pacifica
Foundation* on our EFF Web page at http://www.eff.org (which, measured in sheer number of hits, was already one of the world's most popular Web sites). Posting the complete text of the *Pacifica* opinion on our
Web site, I reasoned would be an excellent test of the new law, since the
full text actually contained material the Court had found to be "indecent"—the transcript of a George Carlin comedy routine. So despite the
lack of a helpful definition of *indecent,* there would be no doubt that
EFF was publishing so-called indecent material that, as a Supreme Court
opinion, nonetheless had serious social and educational significance.

It was the Court's 1978 decision in the *Pacifica* case that had given the
term *indecency* its strange semilegitimacy as a legal term with clout but
no actual definition. Justice John Paul Stevens was able to command a

majority as to all parts of his opinion, except for the part that attempted to define *indecency*. Of the eight other justices, only two joined that section of his opinion. The remaining six justices, I strongly believe, were reluctant to create an "indecency" standard—that is, to define a new category of expression that is sometimes protected speech and sometimes not. Lacking those justices' support for his new standard, Justice Stevens attempted what any computer programmer anywhere would recognize as a "hack": he hammered away at what he wrote in the opinion until it fit the kind of support he *did* have from the other justices.

By insisting that his ruling was not a broad one—"It is appropriate, in conclusion, to emphasize the narrowness of our holding," he wrote as he wound up to his conclusion—Justice Stevens was able to get a majority of the justices to uphold the FCC's ruling that the George Carlin monologue was not fit to be broadcast, even in the absence of any established definition of what is indecent. In spite of his efforts, however, the Court's holding in the *Pacifica* case in 1978 turned out to be the very opposite of narrow.

In the ensuing years, the reasoning of Stevens's opinion had been expanded from a single case to a whole new communications medium— the Internet—in 1996. I wondered what he'd be thinking when he heard this case. That he'd be on the Court to hear it seemed likely; Congress had thoughtfully included a fast-track provision in the CDA to ensure that any appeal from a successful challenge of the law in the federal district courts would be reviewed relatively swiftly by the Supreme Court. Such an appeal would skip the intermediate federal appellate courts altogether and go straight to the Supremes. This meant that the whole case might be resolved within one or two years. (Most cases heard by the Supreme Court take far longer to get there.)

I had told the ACLU lawyers when I met with them in New York that I was interested in how Stevens would view our case—and not just because Justice Stevens might have to confront what a monster his *Pacifica* opinion had turned into, but also because of an important aspect of how the case was reported. The official published opinion includes, as an appendix, a verbatim transcript of comedian George Carlin's "Filthy Words" monologue. What this meant to me, in the absence of any solid general definition of *indecency,* was that here at least was one particular selection of material the Supreme Court had concluded was indecent. And that very same Court had then gone ahead and published the opinion in a volume that presumably any child of a certain age could find and read in a public library.

I believe that Justice Stevens, who I regard as a very thoughtful jurist, sought to have the monologue included for the purpose of illustrating what a nonindecent, non–"patently offensive" use of the very same language would look like. An example of the problem with legislating language or speech, though, is that most parents who become upset when their children come home from the library with new profanities added to their vocabulary will hardly be comforted to learn that the language has come from a Supreme Court opinion. To those parents, the words are still offensive. So, it seemed to me, the notion of "patently offensive" remained pretty slippery. In any case, it seemed clear that the CDA, read literally, could mean prison time for a lawyer like me who, even when speaking to lay audiences, likes to teach law out of the casebooks.

What most of us who'd been fighting the Net backlash were slow to realize was that the sheer breadth of the pro-censorship activists' victory in passing the CDA had set the stage for an incredibly broad, perhaps historic, First Amendment victory for us. Only later did we realize that their victory was something for us to be pleased about. Once we did realize it, we were even a bit cheerful! The Communications Decency Act seemed to us to be almost laughably unconstitutional, and as we pitched in to put our case together, there were moments when each of us would feel positively giddy. Here was a case we were confident, if not absolutely certain, we could win. In the CDA, which had so much momentum at the end of the congressional session that it met only token resistance on the way to President Clinton's desk, the censorship activists had won the battle compellingly, but that very victory made it more certain they'd lose the war.

Only much later did I realize how different the outcome of our challenge to the Communications Decency Act might have been if the Rimm-*Time* scandal had not been exposed. Rimm had been set to play a key role in making the factual case in Congress that there was a pornography problem on the Net that needed legislative fixing. Had Rimm's spurious findings been enshrined in Senator Grassley's congressional hearings—

had his study remained unrefuted and his Atlantic City shenanigans unexposed—our prospects for overturning the CDA would have been a lot grimmer, since a federal court will often give more weight to a congressional finding of a pressing social problem than it will give to what it perceives as more abstract constitutional arguments. In short, by nuking Rimm and his study, my cohorts and I, without realizing it at the time, had seriously injured the pro-CDA forces. Because we'd discredited the Rimm study, the censors had no claim to any particular factual findings to support their case against porn on the Net.

But that epiphany came only later, in the spring of 1997, when I had had some time to reflect on the series of events that led up to this court challenge of the CDA. In those hectic weeks at the end of 1995 and the beginning of 1996, I was too distracted by the details of preparing for that case to see the larger picture and understand how the Rimm scandal and the CDA fit together. In the short run, I was preoccupied with the issue of whom we'd choose to be our in-court witnesses for free speech on the Net. Ultimately, two of our witnesses were people I'd worked with before. Professor Donna Hoffman of Vanderbilt University, who'd demonstrated the statistical and other methodological problems with the Rimm study, was our expert on the kind of damage the CDA's restrictions could do to the Web. And my friend Howard Rheingold, whom I knew from the WELL, would be our expert on virtual communities. (Howard's contributions are described in greater detail in chapter 2.) The work on picking and preparing our witnesses distracted me from the disappointment I had been feeling since I'd begun to realize I'd never know the full story about the role Marty Rimm had played in bringing this social issue to the boiling point. Still, I'd been able to help uncover the connections between Rimm and the antiporn activists. I believed to a moral certainty that Rimm and the activists, working together, had in effect staged-managed the Great Cyberporn Panic of 1995, thus building the current climate for increased censorship of the Net. And I regarded the resounding passage of the CDA in the Congress (there were only a few dissenting votes) as a tribute to their success in fearmongering.

Although I continued to reflect on what Rimm and his various dupes and cohorts had tried to do, by the time we were mounting the challenge to the CDA, Marty was no longer at the center of my attention. Instead,

I spent almost all my waking hours, it seemed, thinking about our new case. There were larger issues at stake now.

Taking It to Court

After my meeting with the ACLU lawyers, matters progressed swiftly. On February 8, 1996, within minutes of the president's signing the Telecommunications Reform Act into law, Chris and Ann were in Philadelphia, filing the lawsuit that initially would be known as *ACLU* v. *Reno*. All that day, I was on the phone, talking to the press about the case, or rushing to a TV appearance to explain why we were filing it and what it was about. Later that night, I did the same thing in cyberspace, as an interviewee on a *Hotwired* computer forum. Again and again I explained to the press and the public our strategy: first we'd seek a temporary restraining order to prevent enforcement of the newly enacted Communications Decency Act provisions; then we'd seek a preliminary and next a permanent injunction against the CDA's enforcement, based on its unconstitutionality.

If 1995, the year of the cyberporn panic, was disheartening in what it revealed about the ways in which our legal and political systems can be subverted and deceived, 1996 and 1997 turned out to be years of redemption—or so it seemed to me. It was in this case that I had my first chance to see a court put to the test some of the fundamental constitutional arguments about free speech on the Net that I'd been developing and writing about for years. Even before I'd come to work for EFF—in fact, when I was still a law student—I'd begun to believe that it would be difficult to justify government regulation of Internet content under the First Amendment.

In the six years since I moved to Cambridge from Austin, Texas, to join the EFF as its in-house lawyer, the world's perception of cyberspace and Net-related policy problems had grown dramatically. When I began working on these issues, I wasn't sure I'd live to see the central First Amendment cases happen in this new field of law. After all, it had not been until more than a century after the birth of the Republic that the Court had begun to take the First Amendment seriously. Most of the important First Amendment questions hadn't even been raised until the twentieth century, so I thought it was at least possible that the First Amendment framework for cyberspace wouldn't be established until well into the twenty-first—maybe not until after I'd retired or even died.

Yet suddenly the very legal status of cyberspace itself—including whether I could continue to characterize it as made up of "public forums" or "homesteads" or "communities"—would be put to the test in a genuine constitutional battle. Most of the time I could participate in the battle only at a geographical distance, but I felt intimately involved with *ACLU* v. *Reno* at every phase. I was in regular contact with the lawyers doing the courtroom advocacy in Philadelphia, although I had to spend most of the actual trial, whose witnesses I'd helped pick and prepare, working out of my home office in Berkeley or EFF's new offices in San Francisco. But thanks to my editor at *Internet World*, Michael Neubarth, who paid for my plane ticket to the East Coast, I was able to be physically present at what seemed to me to be a turning point in the whole debate about the Net and a vindication of the arguments I had been working so many years to understand and to develop. This turning point occurred during the final argument phase of our trial in Philadelphia federal district court.

The final argument is the point at the end of a trial when each side must present its distillation of the basic issues of the case and have its arguments questioned by the trial court panel of judges. I like to watch court proceedings, as you might guess, but what I saw in the Philadelphia federal courthouse that day gave me the most hope I'd had up until then: a renewed belief that our inefficient yet highly adaptable judicial system would be able to respond properly to the alleged threats as well as to the real issues and facts of life in cyberspace.

I was sitting in the courtroom, typing quietly away at my notes, when suddenly I had to look up, stop typing, and just watch what was happening. It wasn't merely the pointedness of the questions Judge Stewart Dalzell was asking government attorney Tony Coppolino. Dalzell had already established himself that day as the most aggressive questioner of the three-judge panel reviewing the constitutionality of the Communications Decency Act.

No, it was the content of the questions. Holding a copy of the *Philadelphia Inquirer* in his hand and indicating an above-the-fold, page one photo of the battlefield execution of a soldier in some war-torn country,

Judge Dalzell questioned Coppolino about a hypothetical "Newspaper Decency Act." Suppose Congress is worried about the dangers to children posed by violent newspaper images, Dalzell said. And suppose that Congress, recognizing that it couldn't constitutionally ban such images altogether, chose instead to pass the "Newspaper Decency Act," which simply required newspapers that want to print such photographs on page one to print them below the fold? Would such a law be constitutional? It was that question, and the exchange that followed it, that convinced me, finally and completely, that the judges saw the constitutional problems with the CDA. At that moment, I was certain the CDA would be struck down by the trial court.

At the beginning of the proceeding, Chief Justice Dolores Sloviter instructed the attorneys that this oral argument was "for our benefit rather than for yours," and she warned them that "we will interrupt you with numerous questions." Each attorney would have to make his arguments and answer questions in a strictly limited period of time. Concluding her opening remarks, Judge Sloviter, flanked by Judge Dalzell and District Judge Ronald Buckwalter, announced, "We will hear counsel."

The lead attorneys for the two cases—our case and the companion case headed up by the American Library Association—had divided up in advance the burden of making the final legal and constitutional arguments. Basically, the lawsuit raised four primary First Amendment issues:

1. Whether the government has constitutional authority to regulate non-obscene content outside of broadcasting and dial-a-porn services.

2. Whether, even if the government has that authority, the terms of the CDA were vague or overbroad (grave First Amendment problems if so).

3. Whether, even if the government has the authority, and the terms aren't vague or overbroad, the CDA has provided for the "least restrictive means" of implementing the government's goal. (In other words, we were arguing that the CDA was not a measure that implemented the government's goals in the manner least damaging to freedom of speech.)

4. Whether a prohibition of commercial speech on the Net concerning abortion can be banned by Congress. (This was a somewhat separate point, and the government's attorneys essentially conceded this issue,

which was raised by an oddball amendment Congress had early on added to the federal obscenity statute.)

ACLU's Chris Hansen was up first, focusing on the overbreadth and vagueness challenges to the statute, after which the American Library Association's Bruce Ennis, a former ACLU attorney, focused on the least-restrictive-means argument. Both attorneys addressed the fundamental question of whether the federal government even has the authority to regulate nonobscene, First Amendment–protected speech.

Hansen opened his remarks by noting that there were "two subjects that are not in dispute in this case." The first, he said, is that "this is a criminal statute"; the second is that "this is a statute aimed at constitutionally protected speech." Hansen underscored a basic legal fact about the constitutional tests of both speech-restricting and criminal statutes: if either kind of statute is "vague" (you can't tell what is prohibited or regulated) or "overbroad" (it chills or prohibits lawful conduct or speech), it's unconstitutional. The terms of the CDA, Hansen said, are unclear as to what is prohibited (neither *indecent* nor *patently offensive* has ever been defined by Congress or the courts), so no one—from big conferencing systems like CompuServe, to newcomer Web publishers like Time Warner and Paramount, to individual Usenet and e-mail users like you and me—could be certain about what kinds of speech will or won't land them in hot water. What's more, the sheer scope of the legislation will cause lots of people to worry about what they post to Usenet or other public digital forums; it will chill their expression of even constitutionally protected content. What adds to the uncertainty, Hansen said, is that the "defenses" provided by the statute—that is, the things you have to do to avoid criminal liability—are defined in terms of whatever filtering or screening technologies happen to be available at any given moment. Subsection (e) of the CDA, he pointed out, conditions a defense on the defendant's use of "reasonable and effective measures under current technology." As a result, Hansen said, the defenses will change every time the technology changes. What worked last year won't necessarily work next year, which makes it hard to know what kind of planning is required.

Hansen then moved into the more basic constitutional question: "What this highlights—to me, anyway, is the nature of the medium we're talking about." In response to questioning from the bench, Hansen distinguished computer communications from TV and radio broadcasting, which the Supreme Court held to be more regulable than print or other, older media—partly because broadcasting frequencies are "scarce" and partly because, in the words of Justice Stevens, broadcasting is "pervasive" and "uniquely accessible to children, even those too young to read."

If the judges are going to insist that the Net is like any prior medium, he said, it's most like print. "There are a limited number of speakers in the context of television," Hansen argued, while the Net is arguably "the most democratic means of speech yet devised." Online communications, he said, potentially make "all of us as powerful as the CBS News." Since every individual is a potential publisher on the Internet, the CDA is "calling upon every single American to define 'indecency,'" a term on whose definition no majority of the Supreme Court itself has never been able to agree.

To impose such a burden on everyday citizens, on the pain of criminal penalties, said Hansen, is "particularly onerous." After all, he reminded the judges, "we're not talking about obscene speech." Nor, he added, is anyone defending child pornography, the other major category of illegal expression.[3] Instead, the challenge to the CDA is based on constitutionally protected speech—speech that may not violate community standards or that has serious social value. Such speech may not even appeal to what the Supreme Court has called "the prurient interest." Said Hansen, "It's hard to say how anyone would be turned on by the George Carlin monologue" that was at issue in *Federal Communications Commission* v. *Pacifica,* the 1978 Supreme Court case that established the government's right to regulate so-called indecency in broadcasting.

Hansen's presentation was frequently interrupted and even driven by questions from the bench, primarily from Judges Dalzell and Sloviter. And when Hansen's time was up, Bruce Ennis, speaking for the plaintiffs in the ALA lawsuit, got a similar grilling. "I'm going to speak primarily about the subsection (e) safe-harbor defenses," Ennis told the court. "Subsection (d), standing alone," he said, "would constitute a flat ban on speech that is constitutionally protected for adults." The infamous subsection (d) of the Communications Decency Act is the one that prohibits any "display in a manner available to a person under 18 years of age" of so-called patently offensive material. In effect, this part of the statute turns you into a felon if a seventeen-year-old college freshman obtains information from your Web site that would be perfectly legal if he obtained it from a bookstore. There would be no exceptions for parents or teachers. No discussion of whether the material is educational. If you knowingly publish perfectly legal material from your computer or Internet node, you can end up doing two years in federal prison.

Ennis stressed the fact that the CDA creates a criminal sanction for people engaging in certain kinds of constitutionally protected speech on the Net. Worse, he said, while in every other medium speakers have a sure and safe way of complying with the prohibition, there's no such guarantee under the Communications Decency Act.

Asked Judge Sloviter, To whom is the safe-harbor defense available? Ennis responded that while a credit card approval requirement might be available under the dial-a-porn law, which regulates only commercial speakers, there's no similar mechanism available for the noncommercial speakers who make up the majority of users of the Net.

Judge Dalzell jumped in. Even commercial speakers and publishers using those defenses "are, at most, [merely showing] evidence of compliance" with the statute, aren't they? That is, the judge was asking, these defenses don't amount to *guarantees* that the speaker or publisher won't be prosecuted and convicted anyway, do they? Ennis agreed. At most they're merely "substantial evidence," he said, citing a letter to that effect from one of the Department of Justice's assistant attorneys general. Dalzell then jumped in again with a question about the leading dial-a-porn case (*Sable Communications* v. *FCC*, in which the Supreme Court held in 1989 that a flat ban on "indecent" commercial phone calls was unconstitutional). Asked Dalzell: Didn't *Sable* say the existence of real defenses under the statute were what would make a regulation of indecency—as distinct from a ban—constitutional? The distinction the judge was making was an important one, since *Pacifica* and the other indecency cases turned on it. Specifically, the courts had held that restrictions on so-called indecent content can be constitutional in some contexts, although an absolute ban on that content would never be. We were arguing that the CDA, despite some fancy footwork in the legislative drafting that made the law appear to be somewhat less restrictive, amounted to a flat ban on this kind of constitutionally protected speech, at least in the public spaces of the Net. In short, the law would limit what adults could say in public on the Internet to whatever the courts determined was acceptable for minors, who might be seven years old or seventeen.

Ennis responded by noting what makes the Internet different from dial-a-porn services: "The vast majority of speakers on the Internet do not charge for access to their speech." Therefore, said Ennis, the statute provides a defense, if any, only to "that small subset of speakers" who can afford to use the credit card companies to screen out minors. In other words, said Dalzell, the people who could comply most easily are the commercial pornographers. Ennis agreed that this was so. "Credit card companies simply will not verify credit cards for noncommercial speakers," he said. Referring to testimony from the ALA's impressive array of technical witnesses, he added that "the evidence is quite clear that . . . there is no technological way to screen for age on the Internet."

It was later, when I was listening to the government present its final arguments, that I was overcome with a sense of the inevitability of our victory, at least here in the trial phase. This happened not too long after Department of Justice attorney Anthony Coppolino got up to give the government's side of the case. If the questioning seemed lively in the first part of the oral argument, it was so fierce, so skeptical, and so pointed during the government's argument that it fractured the government's presentation of the case. It wasn't that the judges' questions were any tougher for the government than they had been for the plaintiffs. Nor was it that the government attorneys were incompetent. The problem for the government was not any weakness in their advocacy; it was the weakness of their case itself. The government attorneys had to defend a statute that was of questionable constitutionality *and* incoherently drafted. And they were forced to rely heavily on statements about the statute made in the congressional conference committee report about it—a report that addressed the relevant legal and constitutional principles in inconsistent and misleading language.

All the judges asked the government attorneys tough questions, but it was Judge Dalzell who asked the toughest ones and whose questions seemed to pinpoint the crux of the case. Dalzell questioned Coppolino about the *Pacifica*–George Carlin case. "Tremendous weight," he said, was given in the *Pacifica* case to "the surprise element" inherent in radio programming. Was there anything like that degree of "surprise" on the Net, where users are making choices about what to see and read? Dalzell was relying on a distinction the courts had made: broadcast content has long been regarded by the judiciary as a bit more disconcerting and inherently surprising than older media like books and newspapers. I myself don't think this distinction is valid; I've been caught off-guard by something I've read in a book or a newspaper far more often than by anything on TV, which strikes me as deeply predictable. Feel free to disagree with me on this point, though—you'll be in good company, since half a century of federal court decisions in broadcasting cases rests on this very distinction.

But Coppolino argued that the Net was like the radio broadcasting in *Pacifica:* "Clearly you've got to compare [the Net] to broadcast," he said. It's "pervasive" because it can be received in the home. He noted that when it comes to radio and TV, the Supreme Court has established and consistently upheld the "less tolerant standard of broadcasting."

That's when Dalzell hit him with the artfully crafted hypothetical about the "Newspaper Decency Act." Would such a Newspaper Decency Act, which banned photographs of violence above the fold, be constitutional?

At first Coppolino misunderstood the question. He took it to be a general question about the meaning of "indecency." In reality, Dalzell was asking about general federal authority to regulate nonobscene content that might be harmful. The Supreme Court, despite attempts by the government and others to misread the relevant cases, has never approved of such general content control authority. Prudently, perhaps, Coppolino never answered this question directly.

But to me, sitting in the front row, it didn't matter what Coppolino's answer was. Dalzell's question and Sloviter's follow-up questions signaled that they fully understood what was at stake in the CDA cases: whether the Net would partake of the same freedoms that traditional media like newspapers have or be subjected to a strict regulatory regime of the sort that has turned most broadcasting into relatively bland and uninteresting fare.

When Coppolino did understand the question (to his credit, it didn't take him long), he said that the Net was more like broadcasting because it "comes into the home." Responded Dalzell: "The [*Philadelphia*] *Inquirer* comes into my home."

Exactly! I thought, watching in admiration as Judge Dalzell's questioning artfully dissected the government's arguments. Dalzell understood that this case wasn't about some special, marginal communications medium. Instead, it was about a far broader issue of whether the government, under our Constitution, has the power to control the content we receive *in general*. If the government could not claim to have the power to regulate "harmful" content in newspapers, then it couldn't claim to have the power to regulate that content on the Internet, which is far less "scarce" and far more democratic than newspapers.

In the rebuttal phase, Hansen and Ennis, sensing the possibility of a clear victory, strived to give the Court the strongest, broadest arguments for striking down the statute. Hansen said that even if filtering technology is constantly improving, "there are two things that are enormously troubling." First, he said, the nature of the speech being criminalized by the CDA is valuable speech, and the statute even applies to libraries—at three separate points, the statute refers to libraries and colleges. The second is that the requirement that providers and speakers label or "tag" indecent speech as such is "compelled speech," which is also barred by the Constitution. (Just as the First Amendment provides a general, although not absolute, freedom for each citizen to say what he or she pleases, it also has long been understood to bar the government, in general, from compelling us (if we're noncommercial speakers) to say something we disagree with. Perhaps the most famous case dealing with this aspect of the First Amendment is *West Virginia* v. *Barnette,* a 1940s Supreme Court case that ruled unconstitutional a public school's attempts to compel the children of Jehovah's Witnesses, who oppose oath taking, to recite the Pledge of Allegiance every morning.)

Ennis summarized his case with "three brief points":

1. Everyone agrees that regardless of what is available for the Web, there is no technology now, and none in the pipeline, that would screen Usenet, mailing lists, and chat rooms.

2. With regard to whether "tagging" content is a defense for providers, "I think it's important to recall that the government admitted that tagging is not a defense today." Government officials have already decided

(Ennis reminded the court) that content tagging or similar measures would amount to no more than "substantial evidence" that the potential defendant is complying with the law. That is, a service provider could never know for sure whether it was acting within the law.

3. Attaching a compelled label to your own speech is something the First Amendment bars government from doing. A court should never construe a statute that would create a new First Amendment problem, Ennis concluded. And Congress, showing it had no intention of doing so, specifically rejected compelled labeling of broadcast.

Then Ennis sat down, and the final argument was over.

I sat there, numb with the sense that we had surely won, that the judges had understood the issues at stake, that the government's defense of the CDA had been destroyed. Now, it's true that many lawyers and law professors will tell you that you can't predict the outcome of a case from an oral argument. But it was hard to sit in that windowless Philadelphia courtroom and not be morally certain that on one or more grounds, the singularly offensive and unconstitutional Communications Decency Act would be struck down.

It was a good day to be a lawyer *and* a good day to renew one's faith in the law.

If the Philadelphia trial court had been impressive during the final argument, it was even more so when it issued its opinion in the case a month later. Our judges seemed to be playing a sort of jurisprudential version of *Can You Top This?* Their decision, which they distributed on diskette as well as on paper, said more, did more, and aimed far higher than I had ever allowed myself to think was possible for any federal court. It was so remarkably structured and presented, in fact, that most people who read it the day it was published couldn't grasp its full significance at first.

Philadelphia Freedom, I Love You

I remember how stunned I was when I first read the decision, which, thanks to the trial court's decision to release it on diskette, I was able to receive and read within minutes of release. We had known on Tuesday, June 11, that the three-judge court in Philadelphia would be announcing its decision at nine A.M., eastern time, the following day.

That's why I was lucky to have decided a couple of months previously to put a couch in my office. Since I live in the San Francisco Bay Area, that meant I'd have to be up at six A.M. Wednesday, ready to grab the decision as soon as the other lawyers in the case were able to e-mail it to me over the Net. I also knew I'd have to be answering press calls soon after the decision was distributed. So the night before the decision was announced, I slept on my couch, with my laptop connected by modem to the Net on one side of me and my voice telephone (a second phone line) on the other.

I'm not used to getting up that early, so when I got the e-mailed decision (ten or twenty minutes after the diskette was released on the other side of the country) and began to read it, I had to wonder if I was still dreaming. It wasn't the fact that our side had won the case that floored me. The court had ruled three to none to grant an injunction against the enforcement of the Communications Decency Act. After all, I'd been confident, after watching the final argument, that we'd win at trial.

Rather, it was the sheer scope and force of the decision. Each judge had written a separate opinion, and each opinion differed to some extent in its reasoning, but among the three opinions, *every single one* of the constitutional arguments we had advanced had been proved to be effective with at least one judge, and all three judges had agreed unequivocally that the CDA transgressed the limits on governmental power laid out by the First Amendment of the United States Constitution. It was a slam dunk.

The more I read it and reread it that day and over the next few days, the more I was stunned by what a far-reaching, even visionary, decision it was. Federal courts almost never hold a federal statute to be unconstitutional (they often prefer to let federal appeals courts, or the Supreme Court, take the heat for that). But here we had a decision in which three lower-court federal judges (two district judges and one appellate judge), serving together as a trial court in a special "expedited review" process mandated by Congress, had not only found a law unconstitutional but had acted in a way guaranteed to have long-term consequences for the Net and for the First Amendment as a whole. It seemed likely that their decision would dictate even the Supreme Court's understanding of the Net. And Congress's expedited review process dictated that any appeal by the government of the Philadelphia trial court's constitutional conclusions would have to go directly from the Philadelphia trial court to the U.S. Supreme Court. The train had left the station, and we were on the fast track.

Findings of Fact in Philadelphia

The very structure of the trial court decision in *ACLU* v. *Reno* was highly unusual. The judges' legal conclusions are tightly segregated from the decision's "Findings of Fact" section (which all three judges agreed on unanimously). There are 123 separate and independent fact findings detailed in the section—findings that together amount to a comprehensive primer on the legally relevant facts about how the Net works and how it is used. Even when considered apart from the judges' legal reasoning, these facts in themselves seemed astonishingly likely to impose strong legal and practical limits on the Supreme Court's prerogative to reach constitutional conclusions different from those of the three-judge panel in Philadelphia. No wonder the court set them apart: the three judges wanted to leave no ambiguity at all as to their conclusions about the facts of the Net. By itself, the Findings of Fact section is a remarkable example of a lower court's ability to put significant constraints on what the higher courts, including the Supreme Court, can do.

In the federal court system, appellate courts normally must confine themselves to matters of *law*—that is, normally they must defer to the lower court's conclusions about the facts. (The idea is that appellate courts are not well suited to review the facts; after all, the appellate jurists weren't present for the trial.) This is true for the Supreme Court as well, in general, except that the high court has the prerogative to overturn a lower court's finding of a particular fact—a "constitutional fact," it's called—if the lower court can be shown to be mistaken about a fact finding on which the constitutional issues depend.

The Supreme Court has not yet had occasion to define the precise scope of its power to review "constitutional facts" in a challenge like this one. That is, it hasn't yet answered this long-standing question about its own power. But it was clear to me that regardless of how the Supreme Court might define its own prerogative for such factual review, the panel judges' lengthy, detailed, and comprehensive fact findings were deeply significant and a powerful tool for the anti-CDA forces. The overwhelming breadth of the panel's fact findings, which supported all of the constitutional theories on which we based the case, strongly suggested to me that a reversal at the Supreme Court level would be exceedingly difficult to justify and would require review and reversal of a huge number of factual conclusions. A majority of the Supreme Court justices would have to be willing to say, without benefit of having been present for the district court proceedings, that they know the *facts* better than all three lower-court judges.

The odds of this happening would be virtually nil, I believed, and I couldn't help but conclude that the judges in Philadelphia planned and structured their factual findings carefully in order to achieve that result.

Constitutional Conclusions

The strength of the legal and constitutional reasoning sections of the three separate opinions shouldn't be counted out, either. I heard a lot of lawyers wondering about the likely effect of the three separate legal opinions from the three Philadelphia judges. Wouldn't this make it hard to figure out the overall *constitutional* grounds of the decision?

In one sense, it did: the three judges disagreed among themselves on some constitutional issues and did not expressly agree with one another on all the others. But there clearly were major points on which at least two of the judges agreed: (1) that the CDA is unconstitutionally overbroad and (2) that the CDA had to be judged by the most demanding standard of constitutional review, the "strict scrutiny" standard, which puts a burden of proof on the government that is almost impossible for it to carry. And the decisions were tightly interwoven—Chief Justice Dolores Sloviter cited Judge Stewart Dalzell's broadly worded opinion, for example, and Judge Ronald J. Buckwalter's opinion cited Sloviter's.

Most interesting for me was the way in which the three opinions seemed to tie together two First Amendment theories that until recently, most constitutional analysts, including me, took to be mutually exclusive. These two theories and their relation to each other are discussed at length in an article by law professors Thomas Krattenmaker and Lucas Powe (my former professor) that appeared in the May 1995 *Yale Law Journal*:

"Converging First Amendment Principles for Converging First Amendment Media."

The first of these theories treats First Amendment jurisprudence as something like a new computer, just shipped from the factory with standard default settings in its hardware and software. In this theory, the "default setting" for *every medium* is that it must be treated more or less like the traditional press—and thus deserving of the highest level of First Amendment protection, which is referred to in a sort of constitutional lawyer shorthand as "strict scrutiny." Only in rare instances should the courts apply something other than strict scrutiny. Until the CDA had passed, radio and TV broadcasting and (arguably) cable TV regulation were the only broad areas in which (according to the Supreme Court) the default setting could be changed (to a lesser level of constitutional protection).

The second First Amendment theory is most famously articulated in a concurring opinion by the late Supreme Court justice Robert Jackson: "The moving picture screen, the radio, the newspaper, the handbill, the sound truck and the street corner orator have differing natures, values, abuses and dangers. Each . . . is a law unto itself" (*Kovacs* v. *Cooper*, 1949). This is not the dominant approach (the first theory, previously discussed, is clearly the more influential), and it has rarely been the central principle underlying any Supreme Court opinion, but it is still restated occasionally by some Supreme Court justices as if it were a more established rule of constitutional interpretation. Up to now, whenever a First Amendment lawyer heard any phrase like "different rules for different media" from a judge, it most likely meant that the court was about to uphold the law or regulation in question as constitutional—even though the same regulation might be obviously unconstitutional if applied to the traditional, ink-on-paper press.

The two First Amendment theories have long seemed inconsistent to constitutional theorists, but in the Philadelphia court's opinion in *ACLU* v. *Reno both are applied to support the same conclusion* for the first time anywhere, as far as I can recall: that a law is *un*constitutional. Judges Buckwalter and Sloviter argued for strict scrutiny in conservatively reasoned opinions based on current understandings of constitutional law. But had the Philadelphia court merely cited the strict scrutiny standard and then gone on to its conclusions, it would have left the door open for the Supreme Court to do in *ACLU* v. *Reno* (or a similar case) just what it had done in the broadcasting cases—that is, the Supremes could have opted to create a new, more content-limiting standard for the Net, all the while citing Justice Jackson's "each medium is a law unto itself" maxim.

Judge Dalzell attempted to close that door not by addressing and rejecting the Jackson maxim but by *embracing* it. In Section D of his separate opinion, titled "A Medium Specific Analysis," Dalzell refers to different media–different rules approach as "established First Amendment doctrine." (This is a rather stronger characterization of the principle than I would use, and Krattenmaker and Powe dismissively term a statement of this principle in a Supreme Court decision a "ritual incantation" that obscures the real theoretical underpinnings.) But Dalzell writes in his conclusions on *ACLU* v. *Reno,* "The extent to which a medium is different and the kinds of different rules it requires, has to be grounded in the empirical facts about that medium." Then he reviews the relevant items from the Findings of Fact section and shows how different the Net is from *both* the traditional press (where "strict scrutiny" applies) *and* broadcasting (where it doesn't). The Net is more democratic, more diverse, and more accessible to content producers than even the press, which has heretofore enjoyed the highest level of constitutional protection.

At the same time, Dalzell reasons (applying an argument I'd been advancing for six years), there's no "scarcity" rationale for regulation of Net content, as there is for regulation of the content of broadcasting. That is, the Net is not like the broadcasting frequencies, which the courts had declared to be a scarce public resource (and therefore more regulable under the Constitution), since not everyone who wanted a frequency of his own could have one. (Of course, not everyone can have his own daily newspaper either, but the courts had stopped short of applying this reasoning to any content printed on paper.) Instead, the Net, which allows every citizen—at least potentially—to have the power of a mass medium, is just the opposite of "scarce." It has the potential to make the First Amendment's freedom of the *press* just as much an individual right as we have long understood freedom of *speech* to be.

From these and other analytic arguments, Dalzell reaches the wholly logical, but nonetheless breathtakingly novel, conclusion that even if we assume that different media require different levels of protection, "the Net may deserve even more protection than the traditional press."

I felt especially vindicated to run across the following passage in Dalzell's opinion: "It is no exaggeration to conclude that the Internet has achieved, and continues to achieve, the most participatory marketplace of mass speech that this country—and indeed the world—has yet seen. The plaintiffs in these actions correctly describe the 'democratizing' effects of Internet communication: individual citizens of limited means can speak to a worldwide audience on issues of concern to them." I'd stated the same or similar sentiments myself many times over the years I had worked on Net freedom of speech issues.

Dalzell was best at underscoring the CDA's failure to recognize how different media cannot be subjected to blanket regulation of so-called indecent (but not obscene) speech: "A Newspaper Decency Act, passed because Congress discovered that young girls had read a front-page article in *The New York Times* on female genital mutilation in Africa, would be unconstitutional. . . . Nor would a Novel Decency Act, adopted after legislators had seen too many potboilers in convenience store book racks, pass constitutional muster. . . . In these forms of communication, regulations on the basis of decency simply would not survive First Amendment scrutiny."

In short, Dalzell had taken the very approach I had been fearing the Supreme Court might take if at some future time it attempted to reverse a lower court victory for us in *ACLU* v. *Reno*. Yet he'd shown in great detail how such an approach necessarily led to the *very same result* that the more traditional "default-setting" approach would lead to. In effect, he'd put the Supreme Court in a more difficult position should the Court choose to ignore the facts, dismiss Sloviter's and Buckwalter's more traditional arguments, and attempt to establish a separate set of rules for the Net. The Supremes wouldn't be able simply to utter the "ritual incantation" that different media need different rules, then uphold the constitutionality of the CDA. Dalzell's use of the same principle to get to a different result makes such a tactic much harder to justify. The Supreme Court would have to go into great detail to show how Dalzell was wrong, and that would be a daunting task, given that any other result from applying the "different media" approach to the massive Findings of Fact section would look pretty flimsy.

Taken as a whole, the decision in *ACLU* v. *Reno,* although nearly guaranteed at that point to go up for review by the Supreme Court (we were certain the government would appeal), gave me and other Net advocates far more than we had allowed ourselves to hope for. The decision made it very easy for the Supreme Court to affirm its basic conclusion—that the CDA is unconstitutional—and seemed to make it difficult for the Court to do anything else.

The Philadelphia court did one other nice thing for the Net (nicer even than distributing the decision in digital form). The Findings of Fact (http://www.access.digex.net/~epic/ada/cda_opinion.html) and the discussions of the law are clearly written for the future as well as the present. For the first time anywhere, a federal court had systematically and correctly described the Net, including what makes the Net special and valuable to a democracy. No matter what the outcome of this particular case, I thought as I read it for the first, the fifth, or the tenth time, the trial court decision will be read and reread for decades, educating judges, lawyers, and society at large about why the Net matters. Judge Dalzell and the other trial court judges in *ACLU* v. *Reno* had given us a remarkable gift. Next stop: the Supreme Court.

The Supremes Perform

When the time came for the oral argument in the Supreme Court, I was too busy with other commitments to attend in person. I was deeply disappointed by this, but the disappointment scarcely lasted past the day of the argument (March 19, 1997), thanks to a nervy little stunt on the part of my colleagues at the ACLU, who, after receiving a transcript of the oral argument from the Court's official service, posted it to the Internet within a day of the proceeding.

Thanks to the Internet, I got to "witness" the argument after all. And in some ways, the transcript was better than merely being there, because I could read it over and over again and figure out how the Court was thinking about the issues. Anyone reading the text can see Seth Waxman of the Solicitor General's Office stumble when questioned about whether parents could become felons as a result of showing their so-called indecent material to their seventeen-year-old sons or daughters.[4] And anyone can see how smoothly Bruce Ennis was able to answer Justice Scalia's questions, which were arguably the sharpest and most skeptical of all.

It was the oral argument, more than anything else, that began to convince the rest of the world that we were going to win, and perhaps win big. Before that March proceeding, I had been one of the few people willing to go on the record and predict a major victory. One of EFF's own board members, himself a lawyer, had even published an article predicting a close decision, basing his reasoning on the Court's decision the previous summer in a cable TV regulation case. But the argument, especially after it was published on the Internet, changed perceptions. Thanks to the Internet, this was one of the most closely followed cases in the history of the Court. My friend Lawrence O'Donnell, Jr., who worked then as a political commentator for MSNBC, asked me not long before the decision came down why it was that "only in the last couple of weeks has everyone been calling this decision as some kind of slam dunk." The reason, I told him, was that only after the argument took place did it become "safe" to predict a big win.

It wasn't until the last few days of the Court's term, late in June 1997, that we got our decision. In the final week of each term, the Court usually issues its remaining decisions in a flurry. These cases are often the biggest and most politically important ones the Court has to decide.

Those of us who had worked on *ACLU* v. *Reno* were certain that our case would be one of the final ones, and it was. I was secretly hoping that Justice Stevens would be the author of the opinion. In part this was because I admired Stevens (even though he'd authored the troubling opinion in the *Pacifica* case), because, alone among the justices, he routinely drafted his own opinions rather than letting his law clerks do the preliminary drafts. More important to me, though, was the fact that Stevens had said in a speech published in the *Yale Law Journal* a few years ago that the *Pacifica* case could have been decided the other way if the lawyers for the radio station had argued that the government hadn't proved that the broadcast George Carlin routine had done any harm. In our case, I knew, the government had shown no harm at all.

So every decision day during the two weeks of the term, I had one of my summer interns, Tess Koleczek, pick me up before seven A.M. at my

Berkeley home and drive into San Francisco to EFF's main offices. There we'd wait by the phone, guzzling hot coffee, until we had word from the East Coast whether the decision had come down. An associate at the ACLU was to e-mail me a copy of the decision as soon as it was released so I could read it and finalize our press release, then take press calls while I wrote my speech for a decision-day rally that EFF and *Wired* magazine were cosponsoring in San Francisco's South Park.

An Early Independence Day

On June 26, as I sat in the EFF office connecting my laptop to the office local area network, I heard from another of the summer interns that the Associated Press was reporting that the Court had struck down "part" of the Communications Decency Act in a nine-to-zero vote.

"That can't be right," I announced to the staff members in the office. "It must be misreported." I knew that it would be hard, legally, to strike down one of the challenged parts of the CDA and not strike down the other. What I inferred (which turned out to be correct) was that the AP reporter had confused the CDA with the larger Telecommunications Reform Act of which it was a part. I paced back and forth in the office and waited for more reports.

Then my assistant, Deborah Pierce, took a phone call from the ACLU's Emily Whitfield in New York. "It's nine to zero that it's unconstitutional," she told me, "but [our ACLU contact] said there's a dissent." (It turned out that Justice Sandra Day O'Connor, joined by Chief Justice Rehnquist, had disagreed somewhat with the majority opinion's reasoning, but not with its conclusion that the CDA was unconstitutional.)

"Who wrote the opinion for the Court?" I demanded, almost shouting.

"Hold on," said Deborah. "It's Justice Stevens."

"Yes!" I shouted. "Yes!"

"You know," I heard my colleague Stanton McCandlish tell one of the summer interns, "that's the first time I've ever seen Mike leap into the air." When I finally snagged a copy of the decision from my e-mail, I printed it out and then proceeded to read it. Unlike Dalzell's opinion in the lower court, which was almost lyrical in singing the praises of the Internet, Stevens's opinion was prosaic, solid, and plainly spoken. Yet it said very clearly what needed to be said. As I read through it, I thought I detected some traces of the work I had done over the years to distinguish the Internet from broadcasting. And I also saw signs of Howard Rheingold's efforts to promote the notion of the Net as a basis of community:

We agree with the District Court's conclusion that the CDA places an unacceptably heavy burden on protected speech, and that the defenses do not constitute the sort of "narrow tailoring" that will save an otherwise patently invalid unconstitutional provision. In *Sable,* 492 U.S., at 127, we remarked that the speech restriction at issue there amounted to "'burn[ing] the house to roast the pig.'" The CDA, casting a far darker shadow over free speech, threatens to torch a large segment of the Internet community.[5]

I even saw that my little tactic of posting the *Pacifica* decision had had an effect, as had ACLU's initial choice of plaintiffs: "Could a speaker confidently assume," wrote Justice Stevens, "that a serious discussion about birth control practices, homosexuality, the First Amendment issues raised by the Appendix to our *Pacifica* opinion, or the consequences of prison rape would not violate the CDA? This uncertainty undermines the likelihood that the CDA has been carefully tailored to the congressional goal of protecting minors from potentially harmful materials."

But what was most important was Stevens's final statement, which stressed the lack of evidence for the government's side of the case: "As a matter of constitutional tradition, in the absence of evidence to the contrary, we presume that governmental regulation of the content of speech is more likely to interfere with the free exchange of ideas than to encourage it. The interest in encouraging freedom of expression in a democratic society outweighs any theoretical but unproven benefit of censorship."

Whose Victory?

After finalizing the press release, I had only one thing left to do, and that was to finish writing my speech and give the speech at the South Park rally. Although normally I don't write out my remarks ahead of time when I do public speaking, I make an exception for rallies and celebrations. Those are events whose attendees (I believe) want to hear something that reminds them of why they should care, that makes them feel good about caring.

When I decide to prepare a speech this way, I try to remember, on the one hand, what my goals are (which may include getting the right kind of news coverage) and, on the other, what it is like to be out in the crowd, listening. Most of all, I try to remember to speak from my heart, because I think audiences can tell when you do that, and they can feel what you you feel.

Tapping away on my PowerBook just before the one P.M. rally, I finally found the words I wanted to say. The thing I wanted most to share with my audience was that this was not a victory of Us over Them. It was instead a victory for everybody, because freedom of speech won and because the Internet had won. I knew enough of the history of controversial Supreme Court decisions to recognize what happens when the nation doesn't immediately form a consensus behind it—as it had failed to do in *Brown* v. *Board of Education,* which had led to desegregation of the public schools, and *Roe* v. *Wade,* which had legalized abortion. What you get is decades of turmoil and strife and dissension.

I hoped I could generate one or two memes that crystallized a consensus that, just maybe, this decision was good for everybody.

Bruce Ennis, who'd argued the case before the Supreme Court, spoke at the South Park rally before me, and he explained in unrehearsed remarks that this was a very good decision, one that would have a lasting impact when it came to protecting freedom of speech on the Net.[6] Then I got up to speak—to read before this expectant, elated audience (mostly cyberjournalists and techies) the words I had just hammered out.

"I thought this was an occasion for some poetry," I said. "But I couldn't find a poet, so I had to write something myself." As I lifted the paper on which I'd printed out my speech, I could see my hand trembling. Nerves. I told myself that the crowd probably couldn't see how nervous I was, and, calmed a little by that thought, I began to read:

These days we often try to rid our pockets of pennies, but today I ask you to take a look at one of the pennies in your pocket.

On the one side of the penny: *E Pluribus Unum*—out of the many, the one. And out of all the discord and chaos of the Internet, we have always been able to hear the one voice of freedom, the voice that says, over and over, in the face of every attempt to impose tyranny and to spread fear of technology and of the future, that freedom of expression remains for each of us a fundamental right. The one voice that says that whether it's my freedom of speech or yours, when we are told that freedom is too dangerous to allow, we will always respond, "*No! Not now! Not ever!*"

Every time someone says they don't believe in freedom of speech, a little justice and progress dies somewhere. But today freedom of speech lives. Today, everyone who ever lived and fought for freedom of speech is alive in our hearts and rejoicing with us, from John Milton and Thomas Jefferson to the martyrs of Tiananmen Square. And the future is with us as well today—our children, our grandchildren, and everyone who will come after us is here with us today. We can't join hands with those who have gone before us, or those who will come after us, but we can join our hearts with them. Let us join our hearts together and all rejoice today in this fulfillment of the promise of the First Amendment, the promise of Article 19 of the Universal Declaration of Human Rights, the promise of the beloved and utterly necessary principle of freedom of expression. Summer is here, and the time is right for dancing in the streets.

Today is a day when we should call former Senator Exon and congratulate him on his victory, because it is a victory for him as well as for his opponents. In fact, it is a victory for all of us, regardless of where we have stood in the past on the issue of free speech on the Internet. It is a victory for all of us, regardless of the political labels we gave ourselves in the tired debates of yesterday. It is a victory for conservatives and for liberals—we must thank our liberals for believing in the power of our courts and of our Constitution to make things right. We must thank our conservatives for wanting to preserve our best and strongest traditions, and to carry them into the next century and beyond. We must thank each other for the trust we have given each other in subscribing to the fundamental principle of freedom of expression.

Over a year ago, John Perry Barlow wrote a declaration of independence for cyberspace. Now is the time to think about what kind of First Amendment we will shape for ourselves and for those who come after us. Will it be based on fear or on faith? Will it be based on tyranny or on trust?

Freedom of speech is the greatest tradition we share as Americans—this is the reason that, of all the amendments in the Bill of Rights, this is the one that the states ratified first.

Because the Internet has the potential of fulfilling the full promise of the First Amendment for every American, today should not be an end, but a beginning. I call upon each of you to let today be the first day of a new American Revolution—a Digital American Revolution—a revolution built not on blood and conflict, but on language and reason and our faith in each other.

Look at the other side of this penny. It says "In God We Trust." We represent the full range of religious beliefs here, I suspect, but, just for today, I ask that you all share one religious belief with me—and that is that in each of us there is a spark of God that, once we give it freedom of speech, can be trusted to pursue the truth. Let us resolve, despite all the fights about freedom of speech yet to come, that at some fundamental level we will continue to trust each other and to trust in the freedom of speech and freedom of the press for everyone. That we will continue to regard these freedoms as the greatest and most powerful guarantee of both justice and happiness for ourselves, and for our posterity. Long live the Net, long live the First Amendment, and long live freedom of speech!

A couple of days later, after I'd had a chance to rest, I logged on and read some mail from a fellow lawyer I knew from the Cyberia law mailing list. He said he had to confess that he got a bit emotional when he read my speech, which had been reproduced on the Net and on the Web. "Well, you know," I told him, "I was crying when I wrote it."

11

Free Speech and Communities: What the Lawyers Know

There is in most Americans some spark of idealism, which can be fanned into a flame. It takes sometimes a divining rod to find what it is; but when found, and that means often, when disclosed to the owners, the results are often most extraordinary.
—Louis Brandeis

I'm often asked why I give so much effort to teaching people about the law of the Net. Why have I given so much energy to the struggle to ensure that the Net benefits from the long-standing protections for freedom of expression that apply to almost all other media? Aren't there other issues that are more important?

"Why does the Internet matter?" they ask. "Will this fight mean anything in five years? In ten? The Internet may even be surpassed by some new medium that's faster and more reliable. You may have given all this time and energy to something that will shortly turn out to be marginal or obsolete."

The reason it matters, I tell them, is that the decisions we make about the Internet don't affect just the Internet. They are answers to basic questions about the relationship each citizen has to the government. They speak to the extent to which we trust one another with the full range of fundamental rights granted by the Constitution.

They are also answers to questions about whether it is possible to structure a society that gives more than lip-service to the ideals we've learned in our public school civics classes about tolerance and about liberty. That sentiment commonly attributed to Voltaire—"I disapprove of what you say, but I will defend to the death your right to say it"—is put to the test when the right to say it becomes the right to say it to an audience of thousands or millions.

Despite the common perception that the job of a lawyer is to be an advocate for his or her particular clients, I think lawyers also have an overarching obligation to the society they live and work in. We American lawyers have sworn to uphold the Constitution. We all are bound by that oath to use and interpret and shape the laws of our country so as to bring to fruition the principles articulated in the Constitution and the Bill of Rights.

For some people, this interpretation of a lawyer's obligations is pretty iffy. Many people see the task of interpreting the text of the laws and the Constitution as subjective. They think what lawyers do is manipulate the language of the law and the legal precedents in order to reach a certain conclusion. They think advocacy is anything *but* objective—and scoff at the ideal that law might be a matter of reaching outside our subjective wishes and impressions to apply objective principles. They are amused by the claim of lawyers like me that the law *requires* us to reach certain conclusions in certain cases, regardless of our personal wishes. They think the outcome of cases is a function primarily of who has the most power in society. They think we already live under the rule of men and not under any objective rule of law.

I have a certain respect for that view. It's true that law is no science like chemistry or physics. It's not even a discipline as logically rigorous as mathematics or computer programming. But it's still possible, much of the time, to make correct predictions about the kinds of results the law, when fully understood and properly applied, will bring about, especially when we're talking about an area of the law as grounded in fundamental principles as constitutional law.

What Lawyers Really Do

Imagine you're a pollster, and stand on a street corner in an American city. Stop a couple of passersby and ask them what they think lawyers learn in law school. Assuming they're not lawyers themselves (an increasingly problematic assumption about American society), you probably would get something like the following:

First Passerby: They memorize a lot of laws and cases. And rules about applying them.

Second Passerby (having heard the first's answer):   No, that's not right. They learn how to argue cases. Techniques for winning the jury over. How to persuade a judge to decide points of law in their favor.

In short, the two common views of what lawyers do are that they (1) apply a set of objective rules or (2) create persuasive interpretations of them for their client. These two notions seem inconsistent. The first suggests that law is something objective, to be applied by and relied on by lawyers, and the second suggests that the law is essentially subjective and malleable, to be shaped by the lawyer according to his or her purposes. But each of my hypothetical laymen is partially right. Legal reasoning does in fact entail something "objective" (the learning and application of rules), yet it also requires something persuasive and creative (the application of those rules to new situations or the analogizing of old and familiar types of cases to new and unforeseen ones). In other words, both types of legal thinking are required for anyone who practices law. So it follows that both kinds of legal thinking are precisely what lawyers in the digital era should be engaging in.

If you get good at doing both kinds of lawyerly thinking, you may even get reasonably comfortable (in some instances, at least) about making predictions as to the outcome of any given case. And given that lawyering is no science, it's usually quite gratifying when your predictions frequently turn out to be right. I know that's how I felt when my predictions about the Steve Jackson Games lawsuit, the LaMacchia copyright case, the Baker "threat" case, the Santa Rosa Junior College case, and the CDA challenge turned out to be on the money.

But there are times when you hope your predictions turn out to be wrong. I recall writing an article for *Internet World* in the early 1990s that predicted an increase in publicity and prosecutions concerning pornography in the online world. My sense that such a wave was on its way came in part from the law. I knew that many of the images available on adult BBSs would be legally obscene in at least some jurisdictions. But it also came in part from knowing how the law enforcement community works.

In the late 1980s and early 1990s, there was strong movement among state and federal law enforcement agencies to gear up for what was perceived to be an oncoming wave of computer crime—a wave of marauding computer hackers. Various law enforcement agencies increased their staff, training, and equipment budgets in anticipation of a hacker crime wave that never happened.

The reason there was no hacker crime wave was that despite the hacker hype of those years, there simply weren't that many people in the country who were both technically adept enough and malicious enough to do anyone serious harm. (Of the few who were clever enough, such as the legendary Phiber Optik in New York, most felt ethically bound to do no damage to the systems they explored, and most believed it was both morally wrong and deeply uncool to use their skills for personal gain.) But it is not the nature of government agencies to ramp down once they've ramped up; I anticipated that the new computer cops would find new justifications for their budgets. Since many (but by no means most) BBSs and other online forums publish sexually oriented content, it didn't seem to be much of a leap to predict that the computer cops would be going after alleged "computer pornographers" next.

It's not that American culture is wholly intolerant of pornography. Forty years ago, it might have been a cause of shame to have it be known that one had purchased or viewed sexually explicit materials. Nowadays, even those of us who disapprove of such materials are rarely troubled by the fact that someone, somewhere, is watching a pornographic video in the privacy of his or her home. Couples sometimes purchase and view pornography together, a cultural development that few of our grandparents could have predicted. Most American cities have bookstores containing materials that could theoretically be the basis of a successful obscenity prosecution in those jurisdictions, but for the most part urban law enforcement personnel and local district attorneys overlook such enterprises, since an adult bookstore bust isn't any guarantee of favorable news coverage and since there usually are more serious offenses to investigate.

In spite of all this, I knew even the most boring prosecution becomes infinitely more interesting to newspapers and TV stations when you can find a computer or sex angle to it, and the prosecutions I was predicting would have both. I even predicted that the issue of children's accidental exposure to porn, while not then in reality a serious problem in the BBS world, would be a major feature of the publicity surrounding these prosecutions. In the course of 1995, I was saddened to see that my essentially cynical prediction had come true. The only thing I hadn't foreseen was the opportunism of religious right antiporn groups and certain members of Congress in exploiting that potential for publicity.

For all that pornography turned out to be the major theme of news coverage and political discussion of the Net in 1995 and 1996, the fact is that porn is only the current manifestation of a larger fear about the fundamental social shifts that computers and technology are bringing about. As I write this in late 1997, I'm imagining the themes of 1998 and beyond. Fears about copyright and fears about encryption, I predict, are likely to surface as the trendy computer issues du jour. And there will be those who exploit those fears in order to enact ill-considered or antidemocratic laws that serve their own interests at the expense of the rights of the man in the street (or the man on the information highway).

How I wish these predictions will turn out to be wrong.[1]

Why the Net Matters: Pluralism and Community

I'd rather be wrong because I think computers and the Net are likely to give us far more than they can take away. I'm not just talking about greater industrial efficiency or greater consumer comforts. The Internet— or, to put it more precisely, the technology symbolized by the Internet— marks a permanent change in American and world culture not least because it has now become possible for an ordinary individual to reach an audience of any size.

This is why the central political and social struggle over the next few decades will be whether we can tolerate a technological framework that puts the full promise of freedom of the press (as well as a much greater power to ensure communications privacy) into the hands of every individual. The dominant threat will be whether governments and other powerful institutions, acting out of fear of both social instability and their own loss of control, institute repressive measures that limit or destroy the full democratic potential of this new type of medium. The changes wrought by the Net will require all of us to become media-savvy social philosophers. We must now prepare ourselves for that role as we come to terms with the challenges wrought by the radical pluralism this medium will create.

Empowering people to speak freely on the Net in all the ways that we have said they can speak freely in other media, and with all the privacy that we've allowed them in other media, is a necessary condition for all the benefits that the online world has to offer us.

Rational and Irrational Fears

Giving people that power is also what's got so many segments of society worried. For example, companies with interests in intellectual property sit back and look at all the potential the Net gives individuals to be copyright infringers, or to facilitate others' infringements of copyright, and they get nervous. Maybe it's time, they think, to ramp up new copyright-related laws in an anticipatory crackdown on Net infringement. Or maybe it's time to pass laws that would turn Internet service providers and online forums into copyright police.

In other arenas, you see fear of the Net play out differently. Governments become worried that the Net is being used to disseminate information, like so-called hate speech, they were once easily able to ban or block at the border.[2] Law enforcement personnel worry that the increasing use of encryption to secure our communications will make their jobs more difficult, or even impossible, since encryption technology neutralizes the ability to wiretap. Professional reporters worry that the lack of professionalism of amateur Net journalists will lead to a flood of inaccurate stories that drowns out the solid work of the pros. Law professors wonder whether society can stand a medium in which it's possible to libel someone anonymously and leave the person whose reputation has been damaged with (as some believe) no effective remedy.

While most people who are knowledgeable about the Net don't worry much that their children will be passively victimized by Net-based smut purveyors, it's a little more reasonable to worry, if you are in the habit of monitoring everything your child reads or views, that your child may come across some material you don't approve of or even seek it out.

I think of most of these fears as rational ones, although I disagree that the potential problems just listed are all significant. (Children can routinely access materials in bookstores and libraries, even school libraries, that parents disapprove of, but we've never interpreted this as a problem that requires a new federal law to address.) They are rational worries in the sense that if you think through the possible consequences of a new medium with the characteristics of the Net, you can generate scenarios in which each problem turns out to be a major one.

But it's important to remember that the legal system, grounded as it is in precedent and aiming as it does for stability, works best retrospectively, not prospectively. To put it another way, it's easier to learn from history than it is to learn from what we imagine about the future. Justice Holmes observed in his book *The Common Law* that "the life of the law has not been logic: it has been experience." By this he meant that the law is a tool that is built from the real problems we have already faced, not the imagined problems that in the worst-case scenarios of the future, we may face someday.

This often means that the best thing to do, when technology opens up a new frontier for freedom of expression, is to wait awhile and see how existing laws and institutions cope with the problems. If there's any collective lesson to be drawn from all the cases discussed in this book, it's this: almost always, the time-tested laws and legal principles already in place are more than adequate to address the new medium.

Among the principles we have in place that seem to work for us is the principle of freedom of expression, especially for those whose expression offends us, and a strong guarantee of privacy (even though the instruments of privacy, whether encryption or anonymity or the Fourth Amendment, may make it somewhat harder for police to investigate and prosecute crimes). Society hasn't crumbled yet, although we have long assumed that most citizens can be trusted with freedom and privacy. Indeed, that assumption is implicit in the kind of government we've chosen for ourselves. We trust individuals with freedom for the same reason we trust them with the right to vote or the right to contribute to the laws and policies of our country as they are made. We have chosen to believe that most people are rational and that if we give them all the facts, we can trust them to make the right decisions.

That is why I found the tactics of theocratic social conservatives deeply offensive. They were afraid that their convictions about pornography were unlikely to sway the majority of citizens in this country—so afraid, in fact, that they contrived a crisis (the threat to children posed by cyber-porn) and even went so far as to help craft and position a purportedly objective (but in fact fraudulent) study whose real, cynical purpose was to promote a panic-driven anti-indecency legislative agenda. The Communications Decency Act was passed with no hearings and with little debate, by lawmakers whose understanding of the medium was pretty sketchy. That's just the way the theocrats wanted it: full-scale legislative review of the issue would never have led to the kind of ill-considered and overbroad legislation we ended up with.

Anthony Lewis summed it up well in a *New York Times* column about the issue that appeared in late 1995:

The right way to protect children would be to give parents the electronic means to exclude unwanted material. But that did not satisfy the real force behind this sweeping new national censorship: the Christian Coalition, which was regularly consulted by Congressional drafters. The effect of the provision—no doubt the intended effect—will therefore be to reduce all users of [the public forums of] cyberspace to the level of children. That is exactly what Justice Felix Frankfurter found unconstitutional, writing for the Supreme Court in 1957, about a Michigan law that banned sales to anyone of material unsuitable for children. "Surely," he wrote, "this is to burn the house to roast the pig."

Justice Frankfurter had found an elegant way of expressing how an overbroad law does more damage than good. Three decades earlier, Justice Brandeis found an eloquent way of expressing why, precisely, we should worry about damaging freedom of speech: "It is the function of speech to free men from the bondage of irrational fears." The real story of the religious right's involvement in the scandalous cyberporn study and the stealth legislation we first called the Exon amendment and then the CDA is simple. It's that the theocratic right is driven by an irrational fear—a fear that the citizens and Congress can't be trusted to do the right thing if they're presented with unvarnished, unmanufactured facts. What makes that fear irrational? Just this: Although the people and Congress both screw things up now and then on particular issues, in general we seem to be doing okay. Every era has its problems, and ours has no shortage of them, but we're a pretty good people when it comes to pulling our fat out of the fire when we have to, provided we're told the truth.

That's why we should be troubled by the law enforcement community's campaign against encryption and other privacy technologies. FBI director Louis Freeh and others insisted on arguing for their policies in secret briefings whose contents can't be shared with the voters at large. Yet it is supposedly to protect democracy that Freeh and the other functionaries are promoting these policies. It is not simplistic to argue, I believe, that those who so willfully sidestep democratic forums to promote their agendas are no friends of democracy or of open societies. Or that they too are driven by irrational fears.

That's why the media's susceptibility to the anti-Net backlash, culminating in 1995 in the poorly researched *Time* cover story about cyberporn, is almost as offensive as the religious right's antidemocratic tactics. While we can understand and even sympathize with a regular Joe who gets snowed by a fast talker, it's hard to see why we should understand or forgive *Time* or the other journals that unthinkingly bought into the various panics about the Net to serve up a better story. They're the pros, as they keep reminding us. They should have known better.

Responsible Net Citizenship

Fortunately the Net is not only no threat to the well-being of the nation, it's also a tool for preserving and advancing that well-being. People in the online world have learned that they can spontaneously organize and correct the oversights or mistakes of traditional media institutions. That's what happened in the Steve Jackson Games case, and on a much larger scale it's what happened in the *Time*-cyberporn scandal.

But with the power of the Net comes the responsibility for us to embrace the values inherent in the Net. A medium that gives everyone a voice is one that cries out for us to reaffirm our commitment to pluralism. We must tolerate those who offend us precisely because a society that tolerates divergent views is also one that empowers individuals to correct falsity and facilitate understanding. To look at it a different way, a free speech medium is necessary if any of us is to have the power to act on the moral imperative to answer bad memes with good countermemes—to defeat bad speech by answering it with speech.

Not only must we embrace those values, we also must actively teach them as well. In a society whose true diversity of backgrounds and opinions the Net is beginning to reveal, we can no longer assume that we're culturally united by shared experiences. It has been argued that television, and radio before it, once constituted the shared experience that tied us together as a nation. I have my doubts whether Milton Berle or *I Love Lucy,* funny as they were, did much to promote national unity and harmony, but even if this argument is true, the fact is that we no longer live in the world in which the television we viewed was shaped by a few monolithic entities. *Seinfeld* or *The Simpsons* may be the best comedy on television, but in a world of fractured broadcast and cable markets, neither of these shows is anything like the shared experience that *Lucy* was, nor can it hope to be.

No, it won't be TV comedy or a president's fireside chats that bring us together in the twenty-first century. It will be our collective commitment to pluralistic values. This will be a new problem for us; we've never really had to cope with pluralism before. (The reason some newspaper and magazine writers like to wring their hands over "flaming" on the Net is that they've never before had to listen to so many other people who disagreed with them.)

The world of Net free speech is different because traditional mass media, with their centralized mechanisms of creation and production, tended to steer us all toward uniformity of opinions, or at least the illusion of uniformity. (And when TV became the dominant news medium, federal control over that medium had profound consequences. Broadcasters' unwillingness to express nonmainstream political opinions created an even stronger illusion that the range of American political belief was a lot narrower than in fact it is.) What happens to us when we no longer have the masters of the traditional media limiting the range of debate?

More to the point, what happens when all the power of a mass medium—to choose content or to create it—is put into the hands of every individual?[3]

For lawyers, the answer is that we shall have to become philosophers again. (It seems only fair to require philosophy from lawyers. Our J.D. degree signifies a doctorate in jurisprudence, which is another name for "philosophy of law.") As each new case or cyberlaw problem arises, we will increasingly have to return to the first principles articulated by the framers of the Constitution and the architects of our legal system and think through how those principles should apply in the new contexts that arise in the online world.

For citizens in general, the Net means that we all shall have to turn our backs on the tendency of modern individuals to become increasingly specialized in our work and thinking. In a world where we all have a vastly increased power to participate in the public discourse of our nation, we all need to become generalists. In the past, we have been content to delegate our choices about what to believe and what to say to the owners of the traditional mass media tools.

But the *Time*-cyberporn scandal and the Net backlash have underscored the necessity of the public's being able to distinguish nonsense from truth and to think reflectively about the issues facing us, both on the Net and off. We can't trust the government or the traditional media to make decisions about these technologies for us. We can't trust those who've been willing to play to our fears when we were ignorant. We have to learn to become our own best newspaper editors and TV schedulers, and we have a moral obligation to speak up when we think something false is being said in the national colloquy of the Net—whether that false thing is being said about the Internet or about larger issues that matter even more.

You may think that everyday Americans aren't smart enough to be full participants in the radical pluralism of the Net. I used to think that way myself. But I've begun to see signs of hope. I've even found them in the otherwise depressing debacle of the O. J. Simpson trial. It was then that countless Americans found themselves discussing "probable cause" and "warrantless search" and "exigent circumstances" and "reasonable doubt"—all of them once arcane legalisms. Your average citizen turns out to be a pretty smart person if you don't begin with the assumption that he or she's a dummy.

Back to the Future

Pluralism is central to the design of our Constitution and especially to the antimajoritarian guarantees of the Bill of Rights. It's no accident that the Constitution includes so many roadblocks to the will of the majority. Almost certainly, an Enlightenment intellectual such as James Madison (whom most regard as the architect of the Constitution and the Bill of Rights) had read Plato's *Republic*. In *The Republic,* Plato discusses what he believes will inevitably result in a pure, majoritarian democracy. He has Socrates explain that such governments lead to dictatorships, since majorities can easily be swayed by a crisis or a social problem to put all the power into the hands of those few who claim to be able to solve the problem.

The framers of the Constitution were acutely conscious of the risks associated with majoritarian governments, so they constructed the Constitution with what our civics class teachers called checks and balances. (When I was a kid, it took me a while to get past the impression that the Constitution had something to do with banking.) Madison initially opposed the notion of a Bill of Rights, which would outline those rights the new government could not tread upon, but eventually he embraced the idea. A majority of the states ultimately ratified the Bill of Rights— the first ten amendments to the Constitution. At the head of the Bill of Rights were the forty-five words of the First Amendment: "Congress shall make no law respecting an establishment of religion or prohibiting the free exercise thereof; or abridging the freedom of speech, or of the press; or the right of the people peaceably to assemble, and to petition the government for a redress of grievances."

It's safe to say that neither Madison nor any other of the framers anticipated a day when the First Amendment's freedom of the press would be a right that can be exercised by any citizen—a day in which everyone is potentially a publisher. Thus it's certain that the framers never anticipated a day when everyone would have the power to violate copyrights, to defame someone in a mass medium, and so forth.

But suppose we were to take a time machine back to 1787 and ask James Madison, the drafter of the First Amendment, whether he would change its wording in light of the possibility that everyone would own a printing press. I think he would laugh at any suggestion that everyone would *want* to publish material that reaches mass audiences. (So would I, even in the era of personal home pages and Web logs.) But if we asked whether the First Amendment's freedom of the press is meant to be a guarantee *only* to that small percentage of citizens who happened to be printers and publishers, Madison surely would say no. It's meant, I believe he'd say, to be a guarantee to everyone.

Our central task as citizens in this digital age is to come to terms with that guarantee—in effect, to say to the world that when we established freedom of the press, even in the face of a majoritarian fear of that freedom, and even when the Internet intensifies that fear, *we really meant it.* It's always a good time for us to renew that commitment to freedom of speech. And the phenomenal growth and advance of the technology represented by the Internet means that this problem of coming to terms with that freedom is not a problem we can pass on to our children or grandchildren. We have to begin solving it now.

Notes

Chapter 1

1. I used to think that the freedoms of speech, press, assembly, and petitioning the government were the only First Amendment freedoms relevant to cyberspace. Then I came across an online debate between lovers of Microsoft Windows and fans of the Apple Macintosh. That's when I first realized the Net's connection to free exercise of religion.

2. *Antimajoritarian* is an adjective for those aspects of the Constitution that are designed to protect individuals and minorities in situations in which the majority of citizens want to deprive the less popular or the unorthodox of their rights.

3. In press reports and articles after the terrorist attacks of September 11, 2001, I came across much discussion and speculation about the extent to which the terrorists relied on computers, encryption, and the Internet itself in preparing for the coordinated attacks. There was no similar focus on the extent to which the terrorists relied on other technological tools—from telephones to rental cars to ATMs—in order to carry out their conspiracy, although clearly such tools were used at least as much as, if not more than, computers, e-mail, and the like. Even now, four years after this book was first published, the "Internet angle" is perceived as making a story more compelling. This is not to say that terrorists and other lawbreakers don't use computers and the Internet. Of course, they do. Criminals will always use the same empowering tools that ordinary citizens can use. But it is unclear whether this new medium poses any special threat as compared to other technologies. And while there is much to criticize in the U.S. Congress's rush to pass unreviewed antiterrorist legislation, it is to the Congress's credit that the issue of terrorists' use of e-mail was given far less attention than, say, the issue of being able to trace phone calls from suspects who are in no fixed location.

4. Many people refer to all online forums, including BBSs, as "chat rooms." That usage is generally a misnomer. A chat room is an online forum in which two or more participants talk to each other "live"; that is, they're all online at once and participate in a conversation or trade one-liners. But BBSs, which date back to the late 1970s, are forums in which individual users show up and post messages

that other participants can read later—often much later. Generally, chat rooms are understood to be synchronous forums because participants are present in the forum at the same time; BBSs, conferencing systems, and Usenet are asynchronous, because you may be reading what someone says in a forum even when he or she is offline or otherwise not present. What's more, chat rooms are ephemeral: what users say there disappears forever unless someone makes an effort to save it. BBSs and other asynchronous forums are less ephemeral, and you can often read conversations and exchanges that took place months or years ago, and that took days, weeks, or months to take place. The use of *chat room* has thus become a kind of shibboleth: if a writer misuses the term, say by applying it to an asynchronous forum like the WELL or like AOL's discussion topics, knowledgeable readers will recognize that the writer likely is unfamiliar with the online medium.

5. Kinsley announced his retirement from the editorship of *Slate* in 2002.

Chapter 2

1. Howard Rheingold, *The Virtual Community* (Reading, Mass.: Addison-Wesley, 1993), p. 5.

2. *FCC v. Pacifica Foundation* 438 U.S. 726 (1978). For the full text of this case, see http://www.farislaw.com/uscaselaw.html.

3. *Cohen* v. *California* 403 U.S. 15 (1971). For the full text of this case, see http://www.farislaw.com/uscaselaw.html.

4. It has not been determined, so far as I know, whether Justice Harlan ever listened to Country Joe and the Fish. See http://www.countryjoe.com/edsullivan.htm.

5. The difference between unconstitutional "vagueness" and unconstitutional "overbreadth" has been the bane of law students for decades; there's a lot of overlap between the two terms. I can't guarantee that this will help everyone understand the difference, but here's how I put the distinction: The Supremes did state nearly two decades ago that "indecent" content need not include any element that is intended to be sexually arousing. Which is why comic material such as the monologues of Lenny Bruce and George Carlin, or even Allen Ginsberg's poem "Howl," can be regulated on TV and radio. Even though this material isn't pornographic, it can be said to be "indecent" or "patently offensive." Should such material be banned from the public spaces of the Net? If Janet Reno's answer to that question is "Yes," then the CDA is "unconstitutionally overbroad." And the current uncertainty about her answer to that question is what makes the terms "unconstitutionally vague."

6. Starr Roxanne Hiltz and Murray Turoff, *The Network Nation,* rev. ed. (Cambridge, Mass.: MIT Press, 1993), p. 335.

7. Ibid., p. xxix.

8. John S. Quarterman, *The Matrix: Computer Networks and Conferencing Systems Worldwide* (Bedford, Mass.: Digital Press, 1990).

9. Donna Hoffman, William Kalsbeek, and Thomas P. Novak, "Internet and Web Use in the United States: Baselines for Commercial Development," Communications of the ACM Special Issues on Empirical Studies of the Internet, July 10, 1996. This paper can be found on the World Wide Web at http://www2000. ogsm.vanderbilt.edu/baseline/internet.demos.july9.1996.html.

10. See discussions of other estimates in ibid.

11. I suppose an argument could be made that any sense of community, virtual or otherwise, is in some sense hallucinatory, since it does not exist outside the minds of the people who feel it. But the sharing of that sense is, of course, a real sharing, and not an imagined one.

12. Rheingold, *The Virtual Community,* p. 41.

13. In 2001 law professor Cass Sunstein published *Republic.Com* (Princeton University Press) in which he theorized that the customizability of our Internet and Web experience (we can ensure that we see and read only the things we like) is potentially bad for democracy. He posited that we'd have the impulse to create "The Daily Me," a tailored newspaper that gave us only the news we agreed with and filtered out the rest. (He also made the case that government action might be necessary to ensure that content on the Internet remains diverse—as if that had been a problem up to now.) Sunstein demonstrated the classic mistake of an academic who learns about the Internet from reading books about it rather than experiencing it directly. In the real world of the Internet, it's quite common for individuals to seek out holders of heterodox opinions in order to argue with them. Sunstein found this out himself when his publisher started an online forum seeking discussions of the issues he attempted to raise in *Republic.Com.* Many individuals, including me, showed up to take issue with the claims and arguments Sunstein made. Note that if Sunstein's thesis had been correct, we'd simply have avoided his book and his publisher's forum, since both contained opinions we disagree with.

14. See my discussion of the Steve Jackson Games case, p. xxx.

15. "MUD" is a "multiuser dungeon"—a kind of virtual environment based on role-playing games. "MOO" stands for MUD object-oriented.

16. Pronounced "ass-key," ASCII is the abbreviation for American Standard Code for Information Interchange, which is a worldwide standard for communicating text. *Text* and *ASCII* are often used interchangeably. "[The term ASCII] has two meanings. ASCII is a universal computer code for English letters and characters. Computers store all information as binary numbers. In ASCII, the letter 'A' is stored as 01000001, whether the computer is made by IBM, Apple, or Commodore. ASCII also refers to a method, or protocol, for copying files from one computer to another over a network, in which neither computer checks for any errors that might have been caused by static or other problems." From appendix A of EFF's *Guide to the Internet,* v. 3.18, Copyright 1993, 1994, 1995, 1996 Electronic Frontier Foundation. This guide is available free of charge from the EFF online archives at ftp.eff.org; gopher.eff.org; http://www.eff.org/; or elsewhere on the Net.

17. T3 is a standard transport for electronic data that moves data at approximately 45 megabits per second.

18. See "National Security in the Information Age," speech given at a private conference at the U.S. Air Force Academy, Colorado Springs, Colorado, on February 29, 1996, by the Honorable Jamie S. Gorelick, deputy attorney general of the United States. On the Web, you can find it at http://www.upside.com/online/columns/cybersense/9607.speech.html.

19. A sample issue of *Release 1.0,* a high-priced insider newsletter, can be viewed at http://www.well.com/user/spiff.

20. Derived from the term citizen, [Netizen refers] to a citizen of the Internet, or someone who uses networked resources. The term connotes civic responsibility and participation." From the *ILC Glossary of Internet Terms,* Internet Literacy Consultants, copyright 1994, 1995. The glossary can be found on the World Wide Web at http://www.matisse.net/files/glossary.html.

21. Keith Henson, "Memetics," *Whole Earth Review* 57 (1987): 50–55. Glenn Grant, a self-styled "memeticist," has set up the mother of all memetic home pages on the World Wide Web at http://pespmc1.vub.ac.be/MEMIN.html.

22. Stephen Hawking, *A Brief History of Time: A Reader's Companion* (New York: Bantam, 1992), p. 185.

23. Ibid., p. 85.

24. In its entirety, the Second Amendment to the U.S. Constitution reads as follows: "A well regulated Militia, being necessary to the security of a free State, the right of the people to keep and bear Arms, shall not be infringed." For the full text of the Bill of Rights, see http://www.aclu.org/library/thebill.html.

25. misc.legal is an online newsgroup. Newsgroups are identified by their format—toplevel.subject.type—where type is optional.

26. Hanson, "Mimetics," p. xxx.

27. Ibid., p. xx. The meme-about-memes: An AltaVista search for "Dawkins" AND "The Selfish Gene" AND "memes" got 150 matches.

Chapter 3

1. Not too long after Chapman's remarks, activists of all political stripes began in earnest to use the Internet to organize political action. An example is the organization of antiglobalization protests at meetings of the World Trade Organization and of the World Bank.

2. A year later, Senator Feinstein introduced a bill that would criminalize any dissemination of bomb-making information by a person who has reason to know that the information would be used to commit a felony, regardless of the medium. Such a law might well be constitutional; our government has the power to penalize speech when it's merely one element of a larger crime such as criminal conspiracy or "aiding and abetting." But Feinstein's bill (unpassed at this

writing) remains troubling for two reasons: (1) speech that is part of a larger criminal act or criminal plan is already punishable under current law, and (2) despite the applicability of the proposed law to all media, the senator is pitching it to the press and to the public as a regulation of dangerous information on the Internet.

3. The Supreme Court disagrees with me on this point. Witness its categorical dismissal of obscenity as being without "serious" value, by definition, which is odd since the value of speech may vary in its context. Even a vice cop who specializes in obscenity cases, for example, might be trained to recognize materials that are "obscene" in his jurisdiction—in that context, it might well be valuable for the law enforcement agent to have seen a lot of the material.

4. Many of the changes Lehman sought in the nation's copyright law were enacted in 1998 as part of the Digital Millennium Copyright Act, which among other things expressly prohibited the use or dissemination of tools or information that can be used to circumvent technological measures designed to prevent copying of, or control access to, copyrighted works. This prohibition is controversial because it operates even if the user or disseminator of such tools is not himself an infringer or facilitating infringement (unlawful copying) of copyrighted works—as, for example, when a teacher copies copyrighted material to use in a classroom. The DMCA was passed as implementing legislation to the WIPO Internet Treaties, crafted by the World Intellectual Property Organization and adopted in 1996. The treaties themselves were the outcome of extensive lobbying by U.S. copyright interests, which had failed to pass the White Paper recommendations as simple congressional legislation. By getting the WIPO treaties passed and then bringing the treaties back home to be approved by the Senate and implemented by Congress, the copyright lobbyists effectively "laundered" the changes in the law that had been so controversial the first time around. In 1998 Congress was faced with having to implement the treaty to bring the U.S. into harmony with an international framework that U.S. companies, and their advocate Bruce Lehman, had put in place.

Chapter 4

1. The Alta Vista site operated by Digital Equipment is still accessible at no charge. You can spend hours or (I imagine) even days tracing links from topic to topic. Any day now, I expect to see a Twelve-Step program for Alta Vista or Google addicts.

2. By 1994, the year the king decided to sue Brock, EFF had a four-year track record involvement in civil liberties cases, but the only civil lawsuit we'd taken on as a major project had been the Steve Jackson Games case. That case had been special; we'd drafted the civil complaint ourselves, thus framing the precise legal issues we wanted to address. But Brock's case had come out of the blue. It wasn't immediately obvious to me that his case would raise any legal or constitutional issues specific to civil liberties in cyberspace. At first, it looked like a run-of-

the-mill libel suit that merely happened to have some connection to computer networks.

3. The following solicitation was broadcast on the Net:

Date: Wed, 11 May 1994 13:38:30 -0400 (EDT)
From: Meeks Defense Fund<fund@idi.net>
Dear Net Citizen:
How do you put a price on free and open dialogue on the Net?

How much are you willing to spend to preserve the concept of robust and open debate that have become a part of the Internet's culture? $100? $50? $20?

What if the cost of helping to preserve an open and robust Net was no more than $1.29? That's right, less than the cost of a fast food hamburger. Freedom on the Internet for only $1.29. . . . Cheap at twice the price.

A joke? Hardly. The free and open speech, indeed the First Amendment rights of the Internet—rights we've all enjoyed for decades—are now being challenge in court.

CyberWire Dispatch, the well-respected online newswire written and developed for the Internet community by journalist Brock Meeks, is the subject of a libel suit. CyberWire Dispatch has been at the forefront of bringing the Net community timely and insightful articles

This suit was highlighted in a *Wall St. Journal* article (April 22, page B1). The subject of a Dispatch investigation is suing Meeks for simply doing what journalists in the traditional print medium have done since the founding of newspapers: Print the facts and let the public decide the outcome.

Brock and the CyberWire Dispatch are examples of the "bottom up" journalism that characterizes the Net, where anyone with a modem can compete with the traditional press. Of course, most of us don't come to the Net with a lawyer in tow, or the resources to defend a legal action taken against us in courts located hundreds of miles from our homes.

This libel action is one of the earliest cases of libel involving alleged defamatory statements published over a computer network. It raises the extremely important legal and policy issues. Its impact may well determine how and to what extent anyone feels free to express strong opinions on the Net, without being put at risk of legal action.

It is crucial that Brock have a strong defense and that the principles that come out of this case provide the maximum protection to the exercise of free and open speech as possible.

CyberWire Dispatch is unique because it's distributed solely in electronic form. A service for the Net community at large. And all CyberWire Dispatch articles are free. Meeks neither charges anyone for receiving them; he gets paid nothing to write them.

For all these efforts, he's being sued. And being sued by a company with a large financial backing. Meeks, on the other hand, has no such resources. His attorney, Bruce Sanford of Baker & Hostetler is arguably the finest First Amendment lawyer in the U.S.

And although he has agreed to represent Meeks at a reduced rate, the cost of defending against this unmerited suit will not be cheap.

We have formed this committee to lend our support in helping him raise money for his legal defense. And all we're asking you to send is $1.29. That's it. Why that price? The math is easy: $1 in an envelope with a 29 cent stamp applied.

Who can't afford $1.29 to help save the great freedoms we all enjoy here today?

Can you send more? Of course. Any contributions will be welcomed and accepted. Tax deductible donations also are possible by following the instructions below.

All money sent for Meeks' legal defense fund will go to that purpose. All the administrative services for administering the fund are being donated; 100% of your money goes to defer the legal costs of this case.

You are encouraged to repost this message. But please, we urge you to keep proper Net protocol in mind when reposting or cross posting this message.

Thanks for your time. On behalf of Brock and for future generations of electronic journalists, we appreciate your contributions and support.

Sincerely,

Samuel A. Simon
President, Issue Dynamics, Inc.
ssimon@idi.net

Mitch Kapor
Chair, Electronic Frontier Foundation
Kapor@eff.org

David Farber
The Alfred Fitler Moore Professor of Telecommunications Systems
University of Pennsylvania
farber@central.cis.upenn.edu

Philip Elmer-DeWitt
Senior Writer
TIME Magazine
ped@panix.com

Marc Rotenberg
Electronic Information Privacy Center
epic@cpsr.org

Nicholas Johnson
Former FCC Commissioner
103-5393@mcimail.com

Jerry Berman
Electronic Frontier Foundation
jberman@eff.org

Mike Godwin
Electronic Frontier Foundation
mnemonic@eff.org

For Tax Deductible Donations:
Make Checks out to "Point Foundation" and clearly annotate on the check: "For Legal Defense Fund."
Send those checks to:
Meeks Defense Fund
c/o Point Foundation
27 Gate Five Road
Sausalito, CA 94965
For those who don't care about the tax deductible status, send contributions to:
Meeks Defense Fund
c/o IDI
901 15th St. NW
Suite 230
Washington, DC 20005

4. Since a common remedy for defamation is "counterspeech," the Net provides an open vehicle for the defamed person to respond rather than go to court. And counterspeech is often the appropriate remedy. Recall that in 1992 NBC settled a libel suit filed by General Motors against NBC's *Dateline* for staging an exploding pickup truck by publicly apologizing to General Motors on television during prime time.

5. *Masson* v. *New York Magazine, Inc.*, 501 U.S. 496 (1991). Masson sued the *New Yorker* for attributing quotes to him that he did not make. Central to the case were the forty hours of taped interviews with the reporter.

6. For an excellent discussion of the practical aspects and disincentives of libel lawsuits in the post–*New York Times* era, see L. A. Powe's discussion of defamation in *The Fourth Estate and the Constitution* (University of California Press, 1992, reprint edition). Powe's discussion of libel is particularly compelling where the author offers documentation of how as a practical matter, libel law in the modern era has never been much of a remedy for regular folks, for three reasons. First, it's largely a game for the rich or the privileged. Writes Powe, "Libel is a high-status tort. Those who sue tend to be male, well educated, professional, financially well-off, middle-aged, married, and long-term residents of the community. The majority of those characteristics could be deduced by asking who is likely to be named in newspaper articles."

Second, libel cases take a long time to complete (four years is about average, says Powe).

Third, and most important, it's hard to win a libel case given the constitutional framework that the Supreme Court has erected around libel law to protect First Amendment interests, notably in two cases: *New York Times* v. *Sullivan* (1964) and *Gertz* v. *Robert Welch* (1974).

7. Little did I know that this phenomenon—old legal principles yielding new and unexpected results in cyberspace—was soon to manifest itself spectacularly in the 1996 legal challenge to the Communications Decency Act. Judge Stewart Dalzell's use of a time-honored "different rules for different media" principle for

content regulation was breathtaking in its unexpectedness. Once you read it, however, you discover that his closely reasoned arguments have acquired the feel of inevitability.

8. The full citation for this case, which was decided in the federal Southern District of New York, is *Cubby Inc.* v. *CompuServe,* 776 F. Supp. 135 (1991). *Summary judgment* is a procedural device that allows either party to receive a ruling as a matter of law. This means that there is no "genuine issue" (neither party questions) of "material fact" (one relevant to the case at hand), so a jury is not required. In U.S. jurisprudence, the jury determines issues of fact, and the judge determines issues of law.

9. Discussions of legal liability issues on the Net at that time were typically grounded in the assumption that these two very different models were the only choices a court would have. Even now, the common-carrier versus traditional-publisher argument frequently resurfaces as new participants join ongoing legal forums and discussions. Although the dichotomy is a false one, it quite helpfully exemplifies something important about memes: that every effective or lasting meme is couched in a catch-phrase or simple idea.

10. Technically speaking, the *Cubby* case was only a federal district court case and therefore is not a binding precedent on other jurisdictions. But since Leisure's decision was the first to deal squarely with these issues, it was instantly elevated to the status of what lawyers call "persuasive authority"—not a binding precedent but a powerful one nonetheless.

11. At the time of the *Cubby* case, Prodigy, which insisted on a prescreening process before users' messages could be posted, was the only major exception to this modes. Shortly after the *Cubby* case, however, Prodigy essentially abandoned the prescreening approach.

12. The status of the Rumorville moderator as an independent subcontractor versus an employee or agent has legal significance under the doctrine of vicarious liability. Essentially, due to the employer-employee or agency relationship (hiring, control, and so forth), employers become liable for the acts of their employees or agents but are not liable for the acts of independent contractors. However, Judge Leisure did not rely on that distinction in *Cubby.*

13. The only significant condition the settlement imposed on Brock was his agreement that if he planned to publish another story about the king, he would give His Royal Highness a couple of days' warning. For Brock, this was the equivalent of no condition at all. There was no chance he'd run a story about the king without attempting to interview him *at least* two days before the story ran. His research for the first story had taken place over an entire month. The term of that restriction has since concluded, and Brock is no longer obligated to give event that much notice, although of course he will continue to do so.

14. In 2001, Blumenthal dropped the lawsuit against Drudge. America Online had already been dismissed from the case in April 1998, based on the federal district judge's ruling that Section 230 of the Communications Decency Act barred AOL from being held liable for Drudge's content, which it did not origi-

nate or approve. Blumenthal nevertheless kept the case alive for two more years, until mounting legal expenses and the fact that he could make no headway against Drudge (whose own legal expenses were paid by a conservative defense fund) essentially forced him to throw in the towel. Somewhat ironically, the case, which many believe was an effort to hobble Drudge's publishing of political gossip that hurt Democrats, in practice seemed to hobble Blumenthal instead, while Drudge went on, even under the cloud of the lawsuit, to surface much of racier material in the Clinton-Lewinsky scandal.

15. As it happens, libel lawsuits in general make up only a tiny percentage of the actual litigation in this country. The reason they receive so much press when they do occur, perhaps, is that the mainstream press has a strong interest in legal matters that could affect the press. Go figure. For one version of the story see http://www.wish.org/wish/craig.html or http://www.eff.org/papers/eegtti/eeg_83.html#SEC84 or http:/syspacemall.com/cook/recipe/111962232.html.

Chapter 5

1. In many respects, Karraker's relationship to the content of his students' postings in the male-only forum was similar to that of America Online's relationship with Matt Drudge's newsletter, discussed at length in chapter 4.

2. For a more comprehensive discussion of libel law, see chapter 4.

3. See chapter 9 and following for a more comprehensive discussion of the Communications Decency Act.

4. In mid-1997 the government attempted to mount an appeal of the case's dismissal. That effort was ultimately unsuccessful.

Chapter 6

1. In one narrow context in 2002, the anonymity question has begun to receive legislative attention—the efforts to regulate so-called spam, the slang term for mass e-mail. Some proposed regulation would forbid those who mass-e-mail commercial solicitations from disguising the origin of the e-mail (thus preventing disgruntled recipients from complaining to, or reporting on, the abusive mass mailer). But the scope of such a restriction, which might reach into political speech as well as commercial-transaction speech remains controversial.

2. *NAACP* v. *Alabama ex rel. Patterson,* 357 U.S. 449 (1958). The full text of this case is available at http://www.find-law.com/scripts/getcase.pl?navby=case&court=US&vol=357&invol=449.

3. *Talley* v. *California,* 362 U.S. 60 (1960). The full text of this case is available at http://www.find-law.com/scripts/getcase.pl?court=US&vol=362&invol=60.

4. Much of this issue was resolved by Section 230 of the Communications Decency Amendment, passed as part of the omnibus Telecommunications Reform

Act of 1996. That section, which was unchallenged by civil libertarians in *Reno v. ACLU* (1997), bars service providers from liability for content that they do not originate.

5. This, in fact, was more or less the legislative solution. In the Digital Millennium Copyright Act, passed in 1998, service providers escape liability if they have a procedure in place so that copyright holders can notify the provider about allegedly infringing content, whereupon that content is immediately removed. (If the person posting that content decides to challenge the takedown, the material goes back up, and the two disputing parties can take the copyright issue to court, but the service provider need not be a party to the case.)

6. An algorithm is a step-by-step procedure, most commonly mathematical, but not always. The verbal directions you get from a gas station attendant during a cross-country drive are an excellent example of an algorithm: "First, get back on the feeder for Highway 390 going north. Look for the third exit after you cross the bridge; it will have a sign saying 'Plum Avenue.' Exit there, then make a right on Madison. Go three blocks, or to the first stoplight, whichever comes first, and make a right. One block over is Jefferson Street, and you should be able to see the inn from there."

7. Internet standards are known as RFCs (request for comments), and the relevant Internet security standards are RFC1825–1829, available at http://ds.internic.net/rfc.

8. With regard to the September 11, 2001, terrorists, it seems to be the case that few of them bothered to encrypt their communications, many of which were recovered by investigating FBI agents only days after the attacks on the World Trade Center and the Pentagon.

9. So most of us involved in the cryptography debates believe; it is never wise to pretend certainty about the National Security Agency's capabilities. On the other hand, it's also never wise to accept uncritically whatever the NSA says about its capabilities either.

10. Charney has since left government service. He now directs the security program at Microsoft.

11. To be fair to poor old Glaucon, it's worth mentioning again that he offers this characterization of human nature for the sake of argument only. It seems unlikely that we are meant to understand that Glaucon actually believed what he was saying about human nature in that passage.

12. CESA was never passed by Congress, but some provisions similar to those of CESA were part of the omnibus USA-PATRIOT Act, passed in haste and with little debate or hearings in the weeks after the terrorist attacks on September 11, 2001. Perhaps surprisingly, cryptography measures were not given much attention in the USA-PATRIOT Act, perhaps because it's now recognized that crypto plays a key role in preventing terrorists from attacking certain points of our digital infrastructure. The few attempts to reawaken the anti-crypto debate were essentially dismissed in public policy circles.

13. As of 2002, the *Bernstein* case continues to be litigated in the appellate courts, although Cohn has left the case to become EFF legal director.

Chapter 7

1. *United States* v. *Lemire,* 720 F.2d 1327 (D.C. Cir. 1983), cert. denied, 467 U.S. 1226 (1984).

2. In what might be interpreted as an effort to tweak those lawyers who, like me, insist on distinguishing copyright infringement and theft, the bill amending the Copyright Act was dubbed the "No Electronic Theft Act" by its sponsor, Congressman Bob Goodlatte. The No Electronic Theft Act was signed by President Clinton on December 16, 1997. The bill, which expressly penalized distributing unlicensed copies of software over the Internet even if there is no profit or profit motive, had been strongly backed by the software and content companies but opposed by scientists and academics. Fortunately, the title of a law does not dictate its meaning, and so the actual language of the No Electronic Theft Act deals with infringement, not theft.

3. In December 1998, the SPA announced that as of the beginning of 1999, it would be merging with the Information Industry Association. The new organization, SIIA (the Software and Information Industry Association), continues to be active on the anti-piracy front, but has also played other roles, including suggesting various antitrust remedies against Microsoft.

4. We may imagine that after the September 11, 2001, attacks on the United States, the word *terrorist* is going to be thrown around a bit less in copyright-related disputes. Most of us have a clearer perspective on what qualifies as terrorism now.

5. *Kewanee Oil Co.* v. *Bicron Corp.,* 416 U.S. 470 (1974).

6. The Supreme Court recently reaffirmed the principle that under the First Amendment, the press is able to publish material that it obtained without violating the law, and without soliciting a violation of the law, even if that material originated in an illegal act. See *Bartnicki* v. *Vopper,* 121 S. Ct. 1753 (2001), in which the Court held that an illegally intercepted telephone conversation could be played on the radio by a radio station that had not acted unlawfully in acquiring it. "The enforcement of [law prohibiting illegal wiretaps and punishing disclosure of the information thus obtained] in this case, however, implicates the core purposes of the First Amendment because it imposes sanctions on the publication of truthful information of public concern," wrote Justice Stevens for the Court, adding that in this case, "privacy concerns give way when balanced against the interest in publishing matters of public importance."

7. In 2002, Wendy Seltzer, a fellow at the Berkman Center for Internet and Society at Harvard Law School, founded the Chilling Effects Clearinghouse (http://www.chillingeffects.org), a project she designed to track legal threats to freedom of speech. The project catalogues cease-and-desist letters and their chilling effect

on online speech that, though lawful, raises the hackles of some intellectual property holders. Here's part of the mission statement at the project's Web site: "Chilling Effects aims to help you understand the protections that the First Amendment and intellectual property laws give to your online activities. We are excited about the new opportunities the Internet offers individuals to express their views, parody politicians, celebrate their favorite movie stars, or criticize businesses. But we've noticed that not everyone feels the same way. Anecdotal evidence suggests that some individuals and corporations are using intellectual property and other laws to silence other online users. Chilling Effects encourages respect for intellectual property law, while frowning on its misuse to 'chill' legitimate activity." The project is cosponsored by a number of leading law schools, including those at Stanford and the University of California at Berkeley, as well as by the EFF.

8. See the discussion of defamation in chapter 4 and the discussion of threats in chapter 5.

9. Because Litman's account of the history of changes in American copyright law is both thorough and readable, I'm relying heavily on her book here as source material. But law professors Pamela Samuelson, Peter Jaszi, Julie Cohen, and others have written extensively on these topics, and you can find many of their articles on the Internet. What's more, Litman's book itself is worth owning and reading. And rereading. Jessica Litman, *Digital Copyright*, Prometheus Books, 2001.

Chapter 8

1. Even as late as November 1995, *Time* was apparently still reeling from the cyberporn cover story scandal. The *New York Times* reported in a November 20 article the following: "[*Time* editor-in-chief Norman] Pearlstine . . . replaced James R. Gaines, a former managing editor of *People* and *Life,* as managing editor of *Time*. Mr. Gaines was named corporate editor of Time Inc, a senior editorial management position.

"People at the company say Mr. Gaines may have hastened his own departure last summer with a cover story on "cyberporn," based on a seriously flawed study of pornography on the Internet. The study had been conducted by an undergraduate student at Carnegie-Mellon University in Pittsburgh.

"Mr. Gaines later told friends that Mr. Pearlstine had called him up just before the issue went to press and asked him if he was satisfied with the methodology of the report. Mr. Gaines said he was."

For a collection of articles relating to the *Time* cyberporn-story scandal, including some articles by yours truly, see the Hotwired "JournoPorn" Web site: http://hotwired.lycos.com/special/pornscare/.

2. More than six years after the Hatch Amendment to the federal child pornography statute (The Child Pornography Prevention Act of 1996) was signed into law by President Clinton, the U.S. Supreme Court struck it down in *Ashcroft* v. *Free*

Speech Coalition, 535 U.S. ___ (2002). The majority opinion based its reasoning on essentially the same distinction between content and conduct prohibitions that I outlined in this chapter. As Justice Kennedy wrote instructively for the majority in *Free Speech Coalition,* "While we have not had occasion to consider the question, we may assume that the apparent age of persons engaged in sexual conduct is relevant to whether a depiction offends community standards. Pictures of young children engaged in certain acts might be obscene where similar depictions of adults, or perhaps even older adolescents, would not. The CPPA, however, is not directed at speech that is obscene; Congress has proscribed those materials through a separate statute. 18 U.S.C. 14601466. Like the law in *New York* v. *Ferber,* 458 U.S. 747 (1982), the CPPA seeks to reach beyond obscenity, and it makes no attempt to conform to the *Miller* standard. For instance, the statute would reach visual depictions, such as movies, even if they have redeeming social value."

3. See the 2002 Update at the end of this chapter for a recent development in this area of the law.

4. A law that restricts "indecent" content and a law that restricts content that is "harmful to minors" both regulate content that is otherwise legal and protected under the First Amendment, but that government and society may believe children should not be exposed to. Some theorists have conflated the two categories of "indecent" and "harmful to minors," but I think this is a conceptual mistake. *Indecency* is a term of art that comes from the special world of broadcast regulation, and it's not clearly related to other legal concepts; by contrast, "harmful to minors" is generally taken to be a derivative of American obscenity law, and it derives its meaning in relation to the legal definition of obscenity.

Chapter 9

1. This would be true even in 2002 in the era of broadband. In 1994, most people were using relatively slow telephone modems for telecommunications.

2. That interview with Elmer-DeWitt can be found at the *Hotwired* Web site in 2002; the URL is http://hotwired.lycos.com/special/pornscare/transcript.html.

3. Elmer-DeWitt supplemented his e-mail contact with Rimm with one or more telephone interviews; he never met Rimm in person during his research on either of the two *Time* stories.

4. Law students typically spend a significant chunk of their first year in law school learning "cite form," which is famously arcane and tedious, although it arguably serves a practical purpose in helping to ensure that other lawyers and legal scholars can properly trace legal references and citations.

5. Due to the release in 1997 of correspondence to and from Rimm adviser David Banks, it is now known that the editors' account of these events is false. Rimm stated in September 1994 that he had already been approached by an editor of the *Georgetown Law Journal* about publishing the study.

6. It seems likely that the purpose of the Grassley legislation was less to supplement the Exon legislation than to create a record of congressional fact finding that defenders of the anti-"indecency" legislation could rely on during the inevitable court challenges to come. Senator Exon's bill had been passed as the result of a parliamentary maneuver and had not been preceded by hearings. Senator Grassley's hearings took place, but without witnesses or evidence that spoke directly to the issue being addressed by the proposed legislation. As a result of this loss of momentum, the Grassley measure was never passed into law and was essentially abandoned.

7. Rimm had originally referred to this "overview" of his article as an "abstract." An abstract of a scientific article is a summary designed to aid researchers in quickly determining whether an article is relevant to their research queries. Unlike the executive summaries you may find in some mainstream or business-oriented magazines, an abstract is meant to detail the methods, data, and results used by the researcher who authored a given article. Perhaps because someone had told Marty that what he had been calling his "abstract" didn't qualify as one—it left out too many methodological details—he started referring to it as an "overview," and these paragraphs later became the introduction to his law journal article.

8. The commercial character of Times Square has changed a bit since this passage was first written in the mid-1990s.

9. Philip had also played a prominent role in starting up the legal defense fund for Brock Meeks (see chapter 4, and that chapter's note 3 in particular). Despite this, Brock and I both found ourselves in the uncomfortable position little more than a year later of having to criticize Elmer-DeWitt in the strongest terms for his handling of the Rimm story. The period was emotionally wrenching for each of us. Nor do I imagine it was any less so for Philip.

10. See chapter 5.

11. See, e.g., "Virtual Community Standards," *Reason,* November 1994, online at http://reason.com/9411/col.godwin.shtml.

12. See http://hotwired.lycos.com/special/pornscare/ for a collection of *Hotwired*'s links to articles relating to the Rimm-*Time* scandal.

13. This discussion was later excerpted, to devastating effect, in *Harper's*.

14. Declan, who began publishing online reports on the WELL and on the Web as the Rimm scandal unfolded, went on to work professionally as a reporter for *Wired*'s and *Time*'s online publications. As of 2002, he had moved to CNET.com.

15. Senator Grassley and his staff may have been unwilling to put the Rimm study itself into the *Congressional Record* simply because there is so much sexually graphic, explicit language in it (notably in the descriptions of images available online).

16. I knew Corcoran was unlikely to use that profane quote—the *Washington Post* was and is a family newspaper—but I also knew it would signal to her that I'd likely say something colorful or otherwise interesting.

17. The best factual account of the origins of the Internet—and one that puts to rest the myth about the Net's having been designed to survive a nuclear attack—is Katie Hafner and Matthew Lyon's book, *Where Wizards Stay Up Late: The Origins of the Internet* (New York: Touchstone Books, 1998).

18. See chapter 8 for a discussion of this sort of confusion and of how to avoid it.

19. For a discussion of that posting, and of the general strategy for Netizens and others who are dealing with news coverage in traditional media, see chapter 2.

20. They're still there in 2002. You can find them easily by typing "Rimm" into the Search box on the home page.

21. Hoffman and Novak have posted the Reid critique and others at their Web site. With Reid's permission, it is included in the 2002 Update at the end of this chapter.

Chapter 10

1. By the summer of 1995, the CDA was also frequently referred to as "the Communications Decency *Amendment*." Although it originally had been introduced as a free-standing bill, which didn't go anywhere on its on, in slightly different form it later was added as an amendment to the omnibus Telecommunications Reform Act of 1996. Because that major piece of legislation was more or less certain to pass, the CDA was effectively guaranteed passage too.

2. Marty Rimm derived a large part of the material he used to craft his phony study from the Amateur Action BBS's catalogue of image descriptions. See chapter 9.

3. The meanings of *obscenity* and *child pornography* are discussed at length in chapter 8.

4. The CDA made no exception for what parents might show their own children and did not distinguish between very young children and (say) high school seniors.

5. During a last-minute review of our case's brief on the day it was to be filed with the Supreme Court, I noticed that the only use of the word *community* in the draft brief was in reference to "community standards," part of the legal test for obscenity that I discuss in chapter 8 and elsewhere. But I had the conviction that the Supreme Court, which in many contexts had supported the idea of community values, would need to hear that something more than a new medium of communications was at stake. The justices needed to hear that communities were at stake as well. I called Ann Beeson and made a pitch for additional language to make that point, and she and the other lawyers quickly agreed. On the first page of the brief that was filed in the Supreme Court, we said the following: "The Internet has no parallel in the history of human communication. It provides millions of people around the globe with a low-cost method of conversing, publishing, and exchanging information on a vast array of subjects with a worldwide

and virtually limitless audience. It also provides a foundation for new forms of community—communities based not on any accident of geographic proximity, but on bonds of common interest, belief, culture or temperament."

6. Bruce died in the summer of 2000 after a long illness. He is very much missed.

Chapter 11

1. From a 2002 perspective, it's clear that I was wrong to think the encryption debate would necessarily turn out to be a long twilight struggle. As detailed in the additions to chapter 6, the encryption debate seems to have ended in a general victory for the pro-crypto advocates. At the same time, Americans and the West generally have embarked, subsequent to the September 11 attacks, on what is likely to be a long struggle against terrorism. It's far from impossible that the encryption debate could be reopened and that governments could call for new restrictions on our use of that technology. At the same time, there has been a new recognition that encryption technology has the potential to make our communications and infrastructure more secure against terrorist attacks, as well as against other kinds of attacks. Let's say that in 2002, the long-term prediction for the issue is that it's a toss-up.

2. A French court's ruling to hold Yahoo!, an Internet portal company, liable for pro-Nazi content that's legal in the United States but illegal in France could signal that questions of jurisdiction will strongly influence the future course of Internet law and policy. Already, copyright interests favor a proposed Hague Convention treaty that will make it easier for companies and individuals to be sued in foreign courts, because that makes it easier to stop foreign-based copyright infringers. American Internet service providers, and other American Net-based companies are less than enthusiastic about the prospect of being easily sued in every other nation's court, under laws that may not be consistent with American constitutional principles.

3. Not impossibly, what happens is that every individual runs his own Web log full of commentary and links. So-called blogs signify what, really, we always knew: that individual citizens commonly feel they have both the right and the ability to comment on a full range of public issues and other goings-on. They're right, of course.

Index